A PHOENIX IN THE ASHES

The City in the Twenty-First Century

The Robert F. Wagner, Sr. Institute of Urban Public Policy
The Graduate School and University Center of the City University
of New York

The Robert F. Wagner, Sr. Institute of Urban Public Policy supports the development of volumes on the City in the Twenty-First Century in order to stimulate dialogue between policymakers and the research community and to provide a broad perspective on issues facing the modern city. The Institute was established at the Graduate School and University Center of the City University of New York in 1987 under the leadership of Joseph S. Murphy, University Professor of Political Science and Chancellor of the City University of New York from 1982 to 1990; it is directed by Professor Asher Arian. The Wagner Institute uses the resources of the academic community to understand and address the pressing social problems facing New York City and other large urban areas. Its agenda includes the analysis of the social, legislative, and political legacy associated with Senator Robert F. Wagner, Sr., a key architect of the American welfare state during the New Deal.

A PHOENIX IN THE ASHES

THE RISE AND FALL
OF THE KOCH COALITION
IN NEW YORK CITY POLITICS

John Hull Mollenkopf

PRINCETON UNIVERSITY PRESS   PRINCETON, NEW JERSEY

Library of Congress Cataloging-in-Publication Data

Mollenkopf, John H., 1946–
A phoenix in the ashes: the rise and fall of the Koch
coalition in New York City politics / John Hull Mollenkopf.
p.   cm.
Includes bibliographical references (p.   ) and index.
ISBN 0-691-07854-8
ISBN 0-691-03673-X (pbk.)
1. New York (N.Y.)—Politics and government—1951–.
2. Koch, Ed, 1924–.   I. Title.
F128.55.M65   1992
320.9747′1—dc20   92-8029   CIP

First Princeton paperback printing, with new afterword, 1994

This book has been composed in Linotron Sabon

Princeton University Press books are printed
on acid-free paper and meet the guidelines for
permanence and durability of the Committee
on Production Guidelines for Book Longevity
of the Council on Library Resources

Printed in the United States of America

10   9   8   7   6   5   4   3

To Kathleen

Contents

Acknowledgments

THIS BOOK uses the case of New York City to extend and improve upon my previous study of the politics of urban development, *The Contested City* (Princeton, 1985). That study focused on how mayors could coalesce a wide variety of sometimes conflicting interests into a powerful political coalition based on policies that promoted downtown development. While such pro-growth coalitions remain a primary feature of urban politics, my earlier study tended to take electoral politics for granted and did not give sufficient weight to the public sector producer interests and popular constituencies with whom political leaders must interact. This study of politics in New York City during the mayoralty of Edward I. Koch aims to rectify those shortcomings and to develop a fuller and more adequate theory of urban power. It follows in the footsteps of the classic work of Theodore Lowi and Martin Shefter.

Like all such projects, this study could not have been completed without a great deal of help and support from others. A decade ago, Margo Warnecke helped to connect me with the extraordinary opportunities of New York City. Herbert Sturz, then chairman of the City Planning Commission, and Robert Davis, his counsel, offered me a challenging and edifying introduction to the practice of city politics and development policy as a division director at the Department of City Planning in 1980–81, for which they have my deep thanks and appreciation. Subsequently, the Ph.D. Program in Political Science at the City University of New York (CUNY) Graduate Center has provided an ideal intellectual and scholarly home. The PSC-CUNY faculty research program supported the initial stages of data collection for this study, while the Robert F. Wagner, Sr. Institute of Urban Public Policy provided time to analyze and report the results. The author also expresses appreciation to the University Seminars at Columbia University for assistance in preparing the manuscript for publication. Material drawn from this work was presented to the University Seminar on the Changing Metropolis.

It has been my pleasure to interact with the many fine scholars who study the political economy of New York City. The Setting Municipal Priorities (SMP) Project organized by Ray Horton and Chuck Brecher has provided a unique venue for analyzing public policy trends in the city. The research work commissioned for the SMP volumes has made an invaluable contribution to our understanding of the city's problems and fostered a scholarly community among whom Tom Bailey, Matthew Drennan, Mitchell Moss, Emanuel Tobier, and Roger Waldinger have been particularly influential to my thinking. As the endnotes to Chapter Six suggest, Ray Horton has contributed much to this book, especially by offering trenchant criticisms of its earliest versions.

Beginning in 1985, the Social Science Research Council, then under the leadership of Kenneth Prewitt, established an interdisciplinary research committee on New York City, for which David Szanton served as staff and Ira Katznelson as chairperson. It was my privilege to serve on this committee, which afforded close working relationships with many outstanding people who took part in its work, including Ira Katznelson, David Szanton, Tom Bender, Christine Boyer, Manuel Castells, Michael Conzen, Herbert Gutman, Kenneth Jackson, Ann Markusen, Elizabeth Roistacher, Martin Shefter, and Oliver Zunz. Editing two books for this committee provided rewarding dialogue with Tom Bailey, Steve Brint, Peter Buckley, Frank DeGiovanni, Cynthia Epstein, Norman and Susan Fainstein, Angelo Falcon, Ian Gordon, Bill Kornblum, Michael Harloe, Mitchell Moss, Saskia Sassen, Ed Soja, Mercer Sullivan, Ida Susser, William Taylor, Emanuel Tobier, and Roger Waldinger.

My colleagues at the Graduate Center have also been a great source of stimulation. The Wagner Institute gave me a chance to collaborate with Asher Arian, Art Goldberg, and Ed Rogowsky on a study of the 1989 mayoral elections which draws in part on this book. Marta Fisch of the CUNY Data Service provided superb assistance with data-base construction and analysis. Lorraine Minnite, also of the Data Service, helped to compile the electoral statistics. David Olson provided crucial assistance in compiling and analyzing the data in the afterword. Years of discussing urban policy and politics with colleagues Ron Berkman, Christa Altenstetter, Marshall Berman, Frank Bonilla, Cynthia Epstein, Marilyn Gittell, Steve Gorelick, Bill Kornblum, Frances Fox Piven, Stan Renshon, Matthew Schoengood, and Ken Sherrill have enriched my thinking. My students have also been my teachers, especially José Cruz, Jeff Gerson, Liz Strom, and Phil Thompson. For someone interested in urban politics and public policy, it would be hard to imagine better surroundings than the Graduate Center.

This book has also been influenced by my contacts with practical politics, beginning with my service in the Koch administration. My debt to Edward Koch is doubly great, since his first administration provided my first job in New York City and his last provided an ending point for this study. My on-going dialog with Barry Ensminger, Angelo Falcon, Ester Fuchs, Don Glickman, David and Dinni Gordon, David Gurin, Sandy Hornick, Hulbert James, David Jones, Francesca Kress, Mark Lapidus, Andy Logan, Peter Marcuse, Joan McCabe, Carol O'Cleireacain, Steve Polan, Ed Rogowsky, Jim Sleeper, Phil Thompson and the late Bob Wagner, and Mark Willis have greatly enhanced my ability to write this book. The 1989 Dinkins campaign afforded a chance to work with John Flateau, and Bill Lynch, while the Charter Revision Commission directed by Eric Lane and Frank Mauro and the Redistricting Commission directed by Alan Gartner enabled me to explore the relationships among geography, demography, representation, and power in New York City.

Asher Arian, Jim Chapin, Rick Foglesong, Martin Shefter, Clarence Stone, Frances Piven, and Oliver Zunz gave the draft of this book thoughtful scrutiny which substantially improved it, though the usual caveat applies. This book might not have come to be without the continuous encouragement of Gail Ullman, formerly of Princeton University Press. Nancy Moore was a superb copy editor, while Lisa Kleinholz compiled a fine index. Cynthia Reynolds has kept our family going and given me a deep appreciation for the West Indian community. Last but most, Kathleen Gerson has made the greatest contribution to this book. She brought me to New York City, gave me constant love and intellectual support, helped me think through my argument, and made countless compromises in her own work commitments to enable me to make good on mine. It is wonderful to be her companion and to be able to dedicate this book to her.

A PHOENIX IN THE ASHES

One

Introduction

> When the next generation of historians
> looks back on the 1970s and 1980s, they
> will agree that these decades represented a
> major turning point in American economic,
> social, and technological history and that
> New York City was at the leading edge of
> this transformation.
>   (Thierry Noyelle, Conservation of Human
>   Resources Project)[1]

> For cities, two questions face us: (1) Who
> makes up the governing coalition—who has
> come together to make governance possible?
> (2) How is the coming together accomplished?
>   (Clarence Stone, *Regime Politics*)[2]

FROM 1977 TO 1989, New York City experienced a tremendous economic boom that reversed its previous misfortunes and led to an unprecedented increase in its previously declining population. During this period, Edward I. Koch served as mayor of New York City, built a political coalition based on white, ethnic, middle-class voters, and pursued policies designed to promote private investment and jail larger numbers of criminals. Under his leadership, the trajectory of New York City's political development veered away from the racial succession and neighborhood-oriented rhetoric prevailing in other large cities. This study seeks to explain how and why the Koch coalition came to dominate city politics during this period, what priorities it imposed on budgetary and development policies, and why, after a decade of great success, it met electoral defeat in 1989.

More generally, this book explores the interplay between social structural change and the organization of urban political power. Between the economic nadir of the mid-1970s and the explosive prosperity of the 1980s, New York City experienced the culmination of a postindustrial revolution.[3] This transformation weakened old constituencies, institutions, and interests, while fostering new ones. This process created new, distinctly postindustrial planes of conflict that challenged established political actors across the board. The Koch administration was able to weave a new dominant coalition out of these elements while keeping its opponents disorganized.

In 1976, the New York City economy touched bottom, mired in economic and fiscal crisis. In the subsequent decade, however, it expanded rapidly. Between 1977 and 1989, total employment in New York City climbed almost 500,000 jobs, or 15 percent, and the constant dollar value of the gross city product rose even more rapidly. Even the 1982 national recession had little impact on New York City. But in October 1987, the "black Monday" crash of the stock market heralded a contraction and reorganization in the financial services that, by early 1990, ended the cycle of expansion both locally and nationally.

New York City came to epitomize the debt-driven, deal-oriented, economic frenzy of the Reagan era. Indeed, its prosperity derived partly from bad national habits for which we are now paying. New York arranged the financing for federal budget deficits, national trade deficits, and highly leveraged corporate mergers and buy-outs alike. It probably constituted the largest market for illegal drugs. But New York also benefited from basic changes in the structure of the national and global economies that will remain after the excesses have been liquidated: it pioneered new forms of financial transactions, profited from the increased internationalization or globalization of the leading economies, and benefited from foreign direct investment, while playing a central role in promoting these trends. These economic trends and their associated social and demographic changes had important political consequences, but they were also accelerated by a local administration devoted to promoting the postindustrial transformation and managing the conflicts that it generated.

The Koch Coalition in Perspective

Mayor Edward I. Koch was first elected in the fall of 1977 and twice reelected in 1981 and 1985. During the 1980s, he forged an electoral base centered among white, ethnic, middle-class voters, augmented by support from the more conservative, property-owning elements of the black population and from the poorer but more conservative Latino population. His electoral popularity and strong support from the financial and real estate development interests that benefited from his policies gave him the base from which to convert an electoral coalition into a solidly entrenched governing coalition. This white, pro-growth governing coalition held sway even though whites became a numerical minority during the decade and despite the city's tradition of political liberalism.

Mayor Koch capitalized on the tensions generated by rapid social transformation. He appealed to white ethnics who were apprehensive about losing their dominant position, but he also appealed to the growing black and Latino middle class which was also worried about the threats posed by poverty, welfare, and crime. For a decade, Mayor Koch's strategies proved highly successful; by the 1985 mayoral elections, he had consolidated power into a new dominant coalition and thoroughly neutralized his opponents, specifically the would-be insurgents who wanted to form a multiracial liberal electoral challenge.

To become dominant in urban politics, a coalition must not only win elections, especially mayoral elections, but must convert electoral successes into a governing coalition by building working relationships with major centers of public and private power whose cooperation is necessary for carrying out policy. (While intimately intertwined in practice, the two are analytically distinct.) To remain dominant, it must be able to manage the tensions that inevitably arise out of the differences of interest between its electoral base and its allies in governance.[4]

Until the late 1980s, the Koch coalition was highly successful at these tasks. But his was not the only way to create a winning electoral coalition or a dominant governing coalition in New York City politics. Indeed, most other large cities were governed by African-American mayors put into office by biracial electoral coalitions or by progressive white mayors elected on pro-neighborhood platforms. New York itself had elected the classic model of an urban liberal, John V. Lindsay, in 1965 and 1969. Biracial electoral coalitions elected African-American mayors in Chicago, Los Angeles, Philadelphia, Detroit, and Atlanta during the 1970s and 1980s; they in turn sought to incorporate blacks, and to a lesser degree Latinos, into the local structure of power.[5] Many other large cities with smaller minority populations, like Boston, Seattle, or Minneapolis, elected "postreform" mayors who, despite fiscal constraints, pursued neighborhood-oriented policies responsive to the racial and neighborhood mobilizations of the late 1960s and early 1970s.[6] One of the most interesting aspects of New York City politics in the Koch era was that his administration explicitly rejected these paths.[7]

Despite its history as the archetypical liberal Democratic city and the decline of the non-Latino white population into minority status, the fiscal crisis of the 1970s gave way neither to a biracial reform coalition nor to a neighborhood-oriented white progressive coalition. To the contrary, the city turned its back on Lindsay-style liberal reform in the 1973 elections. After 1977, Mayor Koch consolidated an increasingly conservative administration by combining formerly opposed tendencies, namely the relatively liberal Jewish population and the more conservative white Catholic population.

It is tempting to think that external events determined this outcome, but such a conclusion would be fundamentally in error. While New York in the 1980s illustrates the constraints and opportunities operating on Ed Koch and other big-city mayors, it also shows how his grasp of the terrain of postindustrial politics enabled him to out-compete his opponents and how the negative consequences of his political choices ultimately led to his undoing.

While Koch built his coalition from ingredients present in other cities and in New York's past, it represented something new. Its electoral base and policy orientation differed not only from the liberalism of John V. Lindsay's administration but also from the clubhouse politics of Abraham D. Beame, who was elected mayor in 1973. In contrast to Beame, Koch came from the reform Democratic tradition, which stressed professional competence and government "on the merits," support for social programs, and tolerance for nontraditional life-styles. (Indeed, he had supported Lindsay in 1969.) Unlike the Lindsay administration, however, Koch did not seek to incorporate blacks, Latinos, and white liberals into the political establishment by expanding the local welfare state. Indeed, he relished criticizing African-American and white liberal leaders and removed city funding from organizations associated with those he perceived as his enemies.

Like all good politicians, Mayor Koch presented an interesting and contradictory mix of rhetorical postures. As a candidate, he positioned himself against the public employee unions, the black and Latino beneficiaries of the War on Poverty, and those he argued would coddle criminals by failing to support the death penalty. As mayor, he promoted private investment, advocated budgetary reform, and, in first stage of his mayoralty, attacked the interests that had entrenched themselves in the public budget. These stands harked back to the fusion administrations of Seth Low or John Purroy Mitchel and enabled him to project the ideals of political reformers, albeit in a conservative, "good government" mode.[8]

At the same time, Mayor Koch avidly defended the middle class (especially the white middle class but also blacks and Latinos) against the perceived threats of urban transformation. In articulating the interests and fears of New York's economically well positioned but socially diminishing white ethnic middle class, he appealed to and may have exacerbated their anxieties over racial transition.[9] His growing alliance with the regular Democratic county party organizations rooted in these constituencies strengthened this connection and improved his ability to govern. At the same time, he attempted to go over the heads of black and Latino leaders, with whom he feuded, to reach the middle-class segments of these populations, which often felt just as much fear of crime and the lower class as their white counterparts. Hence Mayor Koch's appeal was based on class as well as race and ethnicity.

Despite Mayor Koch's origins as a liberal Democratic from Greenwich Village, his administration came to exhibit an undeniably conservative thrust. He recentered his electoral coalition away from white Manhattan liberals toward middle-class, non-Latino Catholics and Jews living outside Manhattan. He disdained Manhattan's established African-American leaders, Brooklyn's insurgent African-American leaders, and white liberals alike. Koch rejected their demands to influence his appointments and programs and condemned efforts by blacks and white liberals to forge an alliance in the early 1980s as a "cabal" against him; this rhetoric endeared him to his Jewish and white Catholic ethnic base in the outer boroughs. At the same time, he diligently sought support in the Latino community and hoped to appeal as well to the more middle-class, homeowning, and conservative elements of the black population. He reinforced his broad electoral appeal by adopting policies that favored the city's real estate developers and corporate and financial elite, who in turn lavishly financed his political campaigns.

Mayor Koch backed up this rhetoric in his policy priorities. From the fiscal crisis until 1983, his administration reduced social spending, held down public wages, and made capital investment a high priority. After 1983, city spending rose faster than inflation, but discretionary spending remained weighted toward protecting property and promoting real estate development. While directly redistributive activities, such as welfare expenditures, continued to decline, the Koch administration also raised spending on community-based, nonprofit social service providers.[10] In this way, he put the institutional result of the community activism of the late 1960s and early 1970s to conservative political ends in the 1980s.

Mayor Koch's success was due in considerable part to his being better than his opponents at capitalizing on the changes that the postindustrial revolution was working in the political terrain of New York and other large U.S. cities. The severe downswing of the city's business cycle between 1969 and 1977 and its subsequent rebound crystallized this transformation. Few large cities experienced the sharp decline in the production and distribution of goods that happened in New York City between 1969 and 1977; only New York witnessed as large a subsequent boom in service activities.

These changes in economic structure were accompanied by vast demographic changes in the city's residents and labor force. Continued decline of the white population, massive immigration from the Caribbean and Asia, growing female participation in the labor force, and changing family and household patterns interacted with industrial decline and the growth of an advanced service economy to create a new racial, ethnic, and gender division of labor.[11] Economic and demographic change eviscerated old industrial zones and white blue-collar neighborhoods, sent central business districts skyward, and created a new mosaic of expanding black and Latino settlements, new immigrant enclaves, and gentrifying white professional neighborhoods.

On the face of it, these new spatial patterns of race, ethnicity, and class would not seem favorable to the emergence of a conservative, white, dominant coalition. To the contrary, such shifts have historically produced significant challenges to the prevailing political order in New York City, especially when punctuated by economic crisis. The decay of the economic and demographic underpinnings of the previous political order combined with the growth of underrepresented groups to set the stage for these new groups to seek greater political power.[12]

This certainly happened in other cities: beginning with Carl Stokes's 1967 victory in Cleveland, blacks and Latinos formed insurgent biracial coalitions to win the mayoralties in Los Angeles (1973), Detroit (1973), San Antonio (1981), Chicago (1983), Philadelphia (1983), and Baltimore (1987), among the ten largest cities. Other cities with smaller shares of blacks and Latinos, like Boston or San Francisco, often elected neighborhood-oriented white liberals and populists. When present in sufficient numbers and mobilized, a new generation of white reformers and previously underrepresented blacks and Latinos formed various kinds of what Browning, Marshall, and Tabb called "new liberal dominant coalitions."[13]

But, until David N. Dinkins's election as the city's first African-American mayor in 1989, New York City veered away from minority empowerment and a renewed urban liberalism. Despite its liberal tradition and its relative lack of the blue-collar, ethnic Catholics who provided the base for Boston's Louise Day Hicks, Philadelphia's Frank Rizzo, or Chicago's Richard Daley, Mayor Koch was still able to build an electoral majority by defending white ethnic neighborhoods and disparaging those he referred to as "poverty pimps." He was able to do so while retaining much of his initial base of support among white liberals and attracting both a majority of the Latino vote and a minority of the black vote.

Mayor Koch built such an electoral amalgam by blurring old lines of political cleavage—such as that between white regulars and white reformers or between white Catholics and Jews—and by taking advantage of emerging conflicts—such as that between native-born blacks and Caribbean immigrants or between blacks and Latinos. In part, Mayor Koch's electoral strategy was based on long-standing racial cleavages, especially white concern about falling into a political minority. This enabled him to bridge important divisions among whites. Equally important and less noticed, however, was the class dimension to his electoral strategy, which enabled him to capitalize on emerging tensions among and between blacks and Latinos. He reinforced this electoral coalition with support from the leading sectors of New York's postindustrial economy, finance and real estate development and those commercially dependent upon them, such as corporate law, the mass media, and major retailers. Meanwhile, he kept interests that might challenge him, such as public employee unions and community-based organizations, disorganized and constrained by their reliance on favorable budgetary treatment.

This outcome poses a major challenge for theorists of urban political coalitions. How did Mayor Koch establish and maintain such a conservative, pro-growth political coalition even though similar patterns of racial change and economic transformation produced quite different results in other cities? How did he prevent the growing populations of blacks, Latinos, Asians, new immigrants, and white liberals, all of whom were manifestly not core parts of his coalition, from coalescing against him? What obstacles did these groups face in seeking to challenge the Koch coalition? What factors finally enabled them to do so in September 1989? More generally, what "urban trenches" patterned political participation and power so that some interests could systematically prevail over others?[14]

New York City's experience also presents a more general theoretical issue regarding the relationship of an urban polity to its economy. The impact of the severe economic recession of the mid-1970s on big-city finances and the migration of capital investment away from racially changing old industrial cities led many observers to conclude that mayors can do little about economic change except try to promote growth.[15] Specifically, scholars on the left and right alike argued that mayors neither could nor would use the powers of local government to address issues of racial and class inequality.[16] Peterson, the leading proponent of this view, offers New York City's experience during the fiscal crisis as a demonstration of how no city can challenge the limits of the marketplace.[17]

Any reasonable observer would agree that the economic and fiscal crisis of the mid-1970s severely constrained city government by placing it in political receivership and forcing it to reduce its payroll and rate of expenditure growth in return for the refinancing of its debt. It does not follow, however, that "economic imperatives" explain why Mayor Koch got elected in 1977 and why he subsequently followed policies designed not only to promote private investment but also to expand social spending.

New York City's economic boom in the 1977–87 decade rapidly boosted the city government's revenues even as local taxes declined as a proportion of the city's economic activity. This influx of cash enabled

New York City to regain its fiscal autonomy and capacity to govern. Between fiscal year (FY) 1978, the last of the Beame administration, and FY 1989, the last full fiscal year of the Koch administration, the city's expenditures grew from $13 billion to $25 billion, far outstripping inflation. The number of city employees increased, as did the scale and diversity of social service programs.[18]

Given the seemingly forceful intervention of capitalist elites only a few years earlier, how was this possible? What political and economic motives guided this renewed capacity for local government expansion? What logic lay behind policies that the dominant coalition adopted to boost investment in the city's built environment and expand its social services? Did Mayor Koch undertake these policies out of some sort of systemic imperative or consensus among all interests within the polity? Or did he do so for reasons stemming from within the political system, despite the political conflict that they might arouse?

Finally, the election of David Dinkins in November 1989 provides the opportunity to ask a third question: what tensions and conflicts weakened the conservative dominant coalition and enabled an insurgent coalition to challenge it?[19] What triggered what Theodore Lowi and others have called the "reform cycle" in the city's politics.[20] Why was a coalition that seemed all but invincible in 1985 decisively defeated only four years later by an opposition that had seemed so fragmented and disorganized? What does this turn of events tell us about the dynamics of urban power in an era of postindustrial transformation?

New York as a Theoretically Important Case Study

While such questions are relevant to all cities, New York City is a particularly fruitful place to pursue them. New York concentrates and reveals forces that may only be starting to reshape other cities. Its scale and intensity, amplified by its nodal position in the global economy, make New York an import source of economic, cultural, and political innovation. It has long served as a template for political development in other cities and the nation, from the classic forms of machine politics and the reform attack on it to the emergence of a politics of fiscal austerity.

In 1949, E. B. White called New York the "loftiest of cities," meaning not only that it was densely developed with tall buildings but that the city stood at the pinnacle of a system of cities, drawing to it people from all sorts of social backgrounds and places.[21] For a century and a half, it has been North America's largest city, headquarters for the greatest number of its large corporations, a global financial center, and home to the leading organs of culture and communications. Manhattan contains a quarter of a million square feet of prime office space, two and a half times more than the next largest U.S. competitor, Chicago, and substantially more than London, Paris, or Tokyo.[22] The port, airport, and communications networks of New York connect the United States to the outside world, particularly Europe. (In the 1980s, four-fifths of all global transborder data flows and 40 percent of all international air cargo shipments passed through New York City, while one-fourth of all international business phone calls from the United States originated in the city.[23])

This nodal position in the national and global network of cities has opened New York to trends arising outside the United States, whether Asian and Caribbean immigration, foreign direct investment, or avant-garde ideas in the arts. Its magnitude, concentration of activities, and powerful economic, cultural, and social links to other cities and regions put New York in a class by itself. It is a study in exquisite cultural, economic, and political contrasts. By combining and intensifying the institutions and external ties that have powered the postindustrial revolution, New York makes visible social trends and conflicts that may be hidden, latent, or safely segregated elsewhere.

As a result, New York has had a disproportionate influence on national political development, despite its dwindling fraction of the national vote. Among its innovations have been machine politics as practiced by William Marcy Tweed, Richard Croker, and Charles Murphy; the attack on machine politics launched by Progressive opponents like Theodore Roosevelt and Seth Low; the expansion of the local welfare state by Mayors Fiorello LaGuardia and John V. Lindsay; and the inauguration of the politics of fiscal austerity in the 1970s fiscal crisis.

New York epitomizes the political dilemmas of the postindustrial city. While it richly articulates the structural constraints and imperatives facing the local political system, it also demonstrates the sources of leverage that system can bring to bear. Deindustrialization decimated its goods-making and handling jobs and devastated wide swaths of decaying private property and public infrastructure. But New York's role as a global business center also produced a startling growth in jobs, wealth, and population between 1977 and 1989. While back-office operations and the aging white middle class streamed out of New York, leading-edge businesses and groups ranging from young professionals to new immigrants streamed in.

If, as some hold, economy and demography dictate political destiny, New York should illustrate how market competition and the threat of capital flight shape and constrain the political system. Alternatively, if the city's locational advantages give its politicians the potential to squeeze wealthy businesses and individuals, notwithstanding its growing class and racial inequalities, then New York should illustrate how business interests must engage in latent and overt attempts to shape policy and maintain mechanisms of preemptive power.

On the other hand, if the local political system has some real autonomy, if it builds capacity not only by accommodating private elites but by responding to grass-roots mobilization, New York ought to illustrate that as well. New York has historically served as the forcing house of urban liberalism.[24] Public administration and modern urban bureaucracy had their roots in New York's Bureau of Municipal Research, Republican-based fusion government, charter reforms that favored mayoral power, and the emergence of public entrepreneurs like Robert Moses. The liberal reform experiments of Fiorello LaGuardia and John Lindsay concretely illustrated how federal resources could be used to expand and professionalize the urban welfare state while simultaneously widening its legitimacy. The size and scope of its budget and its capacity to extract resources through taxation substantially exceed those of other jurisdictions.[25]

New York City has an exceptionally rich, even kaleidoscopic, array of political constituencies. In 1990 non-Latino whites made up 43.2 percent of the population (though 55 percent of its general electorate), blacks 25.2 percent, Latinos 24.4 percent, and Asians and others the remainder. These groups are in turn divided by differences of ethnicity and nativity. Among whites, cosmopolitan Manhattan professionals differ from outer-borough ethnics, and the latter divide along lines of religion and ancestry. Among blacks, West Indians differ from the native born, while Puerto Ricans, Dominicans, and Latin Americans are distinct groups among Latinos. Important class, generation, gender, and spatial differences also fragment these populations.

New York City incorporates these groups through equally complex mechanisms of political articulation and participation. E. B. White noted, "By rights New York should have destroyed itself long ago, from panic or fire or rioting or failure of some vital supply line in its circulatory system or from some deep labyrinthine short circuit."[26] Yet it has not, though at times it seems to have come close. From the Workingman's Party and Henry George to the American Labor Party, the Communist Party, and black militants, radical influences have played a part in the city's political history.[27] The city's political system has simultaneously deterred radical expressions of group interest while promoting less threatening forms of incorporation.

Among the entities that mediate how interests get expressed in city politics are five Democratic county party organizations, regular and re-form political clubs in the city's sixty assembly districts, two Roman Catholic archdioceses, various strands of Judaism and the black church, declining but still influential private trade unions, growing but embattled public sector unions, and a great variety of community-based organizations. How Mayor Koch consolidated a dominant political coalition from this array of mass constituencies and intermediary organizations reveals a great deal about how politics mediates systemic constraints.

New York City politics is fascinating not only because it binds many interests together in intimate conflict but because the stakes are so high. New York has long had the nation's largest, broadest, costliest, and most intrusive local public sector. State intervention is taken for granted in many realms where it is weak or absent elsewhere. Land-use regulation can create or deny the opportunity for tremendous private profit. In 1991 city government had a $29 billion budget, 230,000 employees (or 454,000, if one includes nonmayoral agencies like the Transit Authority and the City University), and a greater array of services than any other municipality. With less than 3 percent of the national population, New York has nearly half of the nation's public general hospitals, the only municipal university, one-third of all mass transit patrons, and one out of eleven public housing tenants. Two million residents are poor, and almost one million receive public assistance, over 7 percent of the national total. (By one estimate, it contains 17 percent of the underclass census tracts.) Interests that produce and consume social services are thus extremely powerful, taxpaying central business district and small property-owning constituencies to the contrary notwithstanding.

Explaining the Conservative Dominant Coalition in New York

Three simple, obvious, but wrong answers suggest themselves in response to the question of why New York constituted a political anomaly in the 1980s. One view holds that corporate intervention occasioned by the 1975 fiscal crisis destroyed liberal politics and installed a conservative, corporate regime. A second explains the Koch administration by noting that blacks make up only a quarter of the New York City population, whereas they made up larger proportions of cities where biracial coalitions defeated conservative white coalitions. A final view would suggest that the white political establishment has excluded blacks and Latinos from electoral participation. While each view contains some truth, none provides a compelling explanation for why a conservative white coalition came to dominate New York City politics.

The 1969–72 and 1973–75 recessions devastated New York City more than any other city, with the possible exception of Detroit. Spending had increased more rapidly than revenues during the Lindsay administration

and the first years of the Beame administration. The city financed this gap
with increasingly short-term borrowing. The severity of the city's economic downturn made it doubtful that it could service the growing debt,
leading the city's lenders to close down its credit.[28] The resulting fiscal
crisis prompted the state government to put the city into a political receivership overseen by state officials and corporate leaders, with input from
municipal employee union heads through the Emergency Financial Control Board and the Municipal Assistance Corporation.[29]

Some observers have argued that the bankers closed the credit window
so that corporate interests could take over the political process, drive
public employee unions and minorities out of power, and reduce social
spending.[30] A variant of this view interprets the public employee pension
funds' role in refinancing the city's debts as a form of collaboration with
corporate interests and an acceptance of labor's thoroughly subordinate
political position.[31] Alternatively, Paul Peterson has suggested that cities
have a "unitary" interest in promoting growth and minimizing redistribution and that the New York City fiscal crisis shows what happens to a city
that strays too far from these principles.[32] But can the fiscal crisis intervention, however real during the 1975–77 period, explain subsequent
conservative developments?

In the short run, the fiscal crisis certainly reduced real city spending and
fostered greater political attention to promoting private investment and
increasing the city's economic competitiveness. Between the 1969 peak of
the local business cycle and its 1976 trough, the city lost one-sixth of its
jobs and income; the city government payroll fell 20 percent, or 60,000
jobs, between 1975 and 1977. Public employee unions could prevent neither layoffs nor wage settlements that did not keep up with inflation.
Pushed by the "new federalism" of the Nixon and Ford administrations,
the city cut such programs as community action and subsidized housing.
In 1981, even Raymond Horton, a Columbia Business School professor
and president of the Citizens Budget Commission, could write that local
government had lost its autonomy to a group of nonelected senior corporate officials.[33]

This loss of state autonomy to the private sector proved to be transi-
tory, however. Between 1976 and 1981, the local economy recovered rapidly, public revenues climbed, and the state and federal governments provided increasing fiscal aid, effectively ending the fiscal crisis by 1981. As
the Koch administration balanced successive budgets, city government
regained its autonomy and moved out of a climate of austerity and retrenchment. By 1983, the Financial Control Board and Municipal Assistance Corporation had retreated to a vestigial role, rendering the crude
picture of business "capture" irrelevant. Even during the 1991–92 budget
crisis, they have remained largely in the background.

More importantly, the rapid growth of tax revenues generated by the economic boom enabled public expenditures to rise after 1983 at a pace reminiscent of the late 1960s. As a result, as Chapter Six will show, many of the fiscal patterns that characterized the late 1960s reasserted themselves. After subtracting debt service and pensions, the city's expense budget doubled from $10.3 billion to $21 billion between 1978 and 1989. Public employment grew by 43,760, or 22.5 percent, between 1983 and 1989, becoming the city's second fastest growing industry sector after investment banking. City employees' wages also rose faster than inflation. In contrast to most other large cities, where Reagan administration austerity measures reduced spending on contracts to nonprofit social service organizations, spending for "third party government" also increased substantially in New York City.[34]

Despite or perhaps because of having the Koch administration at the helm, most of the budgetary patterns that capitalists or intercity competition were supposed to have ended during the fiscal crisis reappeared by the latter 1980s. Neither business-oriented monitoring groups nor the market competition for investment in central cities appeared to constrain the size and composition of city budgets in this period. The political rhetoric of the mid-1980s centered far more on restoring services to pre-fiscal crisis levels than on constraining the tax burden on the private sector, though the Koch administration continued to make major new tax concessions for favored projects.

While fiscal crisis conditions and economic imperatives may have contributed Mayor Koch's electoral success in 1977 (when he ran as a prudent liberal) and 1981 (when he was reelected as a conservative reformer), they cannot explain why the conservative coalition flourished during the booming mid-1980s, when the specter of fiscal crisis had retreated to the shadows. Mayor Koch was able to consolidate his electoral and governing coalition during this period, even though the economic, fiscal, and institutional constraints on him were being relaxed or removed.

New York City lacks the emerging black electoral majority that fueled racial succession in Detroit, Atlanta, and Chicago. Blacks make up a quarter of the city's population; the native-born black population declined significantly between 1980 and 1990. The Latino population grew more rapidly in the 1980s, almost equalling the black population.[35] Does the lack of an impending black (or Latino) majority explain New York's conservatism?

Biracial liberal coalitions did in fact succeed in many cities with relatively small black communities during the 1970s and 1980s. In Los Angeles, blacks and liberal Jews coalesced to elect Tom Bradley mayor in 1973 and reelect him subsequently.[36] While Bradley's policies have been criticized as excessively favorable toward developers, they have been liberal compared to those of his conservative Republican predecessor, Sam Yorty. Similarly, Norman Rice was elected mayor of Seattle and Frederico Peña of Denver despite the small proportions of their respective minority populations.

In other cities with relatively small black populations, such as San Francisco, black votes have been essential to electing reform coalitions.[37] Even in Chicago, Harold Washington could not have been elected without white and Latino support.[38] While the absence of a single emerging racial majority may complicate the formation of a challenging coalition, it clearly has not prevented it, as David Dinkins's ultimate victory in November 1989 amply demonstrated. Even though neither blacks nor Latinos will soon be a majority in New York, this condition should not prevent the emergence of a cross-racial insurgent coalition like that put together by David Dinkins.

In amending the 1965 Voting Rights Act in 1970, Congress applied Section 5 (requiring the Justice Department to preclear electoral changes) to Manhattan, Brooklyn, and the Bronx because of their consistently low rate of minority electoral participation.[39] Congress imposed this requirement where, as in the South and the three New York boroughs, a literacy test had been used in the past, less than 50 percent of the voting-age population had registered for the 1964 presidential elections, and ballots were published only in English, although more than 5 percent of the population belonged to one or more foreign language groups.[40] Moreover, many claim that the county Democratic party organizations used their control over ballot access, registration procedures, and gerrymandering of council boundaries to reinforce the racial bias in voting and to minimize minority electoral victories.[41] According to this argument, race and class bias in the electoral system and the consequent low numbers of minority voters produced a lack of minority citywide elected officials and electoral success for the Koch coalition.[42]

In fact, blacks and to a lesser degree Latinos have long been incorporated in New York City politics, though typically as a subordinate part of the regular Democratic county party organizations. Blacks broke into the city's political establishment with Adam Powell's and Benjamin Davis's election to the city council in 1941 and 1943. The first Puerto Rican assemblyman was elected on the Republican and American Labor party lines in 1938. Blacks and Puerto Ricans both have made steady, if not always continuous, progress in political representation.

They reached one high point in the late 1960s, when Herman Badillo, a Puerto Rican reformer, represented the Bronx on the Board of Estimate and Percy Sutton, an African-American party regular, represented Manhattan, and minority votes helped elect Mayor Lindsay who in turn appointed many blacks and Latinos to his administration. Another high point, at least in voter turnout, occurred in the 1977 mayoral primary, when Sutton and Badillo ran alongside Edward Koch and Mario Cuomo. (While this race produced a large black and Latino turnout, it also heightened divisions between these groups.) The 1970s also produced a new generation of black leaders in Brooklyn who displaced black regular Democrats from the State Assembly and the House of Representatives and have sought to win seats from whites who represent majority black districts.

Though absent from the dominant coalition during the Koch years, blacks and Latinos have clearly not been excluded from political representation. To the contrary, they have made up an important part of the regular Democratic establishment in the Bronx, Queens, and Brooklyn and have also generated successful insurgent candidacies in Manhattan, Brooklyn, and Queens.[43] Indeed, once their relative youth and lack of citizenship are taken into account, blacks and Latinos vote at roughly the same rates as whites.[44]

When three Puerto Rican candidates ran for city council president in 1985, Latino assembly districts (ADs) achieved a higher turnout of registered voters than black or white Catholic ADs. The Jesse Jackson candidacies in 1984 and 1988 led to dramatic increases in minority registration and voting, to the point where black and Latino voters made up 40 percent of the 1988 Democratic primary electorate. With white liberal support, they enabled Jackson to out-poll his competitors in the city. Because they register overwhelmingly as Democrats, blacks are in fact now better represented among voters in the pivotal Democratic primary elections than within the population as a whole.

When a primary presents them with a strong African-American candidate, blacks have turned out at higher rates than whites. (Latinos register and turn out at lower rates, partly because the Democratic party has offered them far fewer attractive candidates for citywide or higher office.)

A simple argument of electoral exclusion and/or minority demobilization thus cannot account for the weakness of a challenging coalition and the strength of the conservative coalition. Neither corporate intervention during the fiscal crisis nor the relatively small size of the black population predetermined the rise of the Koch coalition. To the contrary, Mayor Koch and his allies had to construct an electoral and governing coalition devoted to these ends. In the absence of a conservative political leader with his skills, city government might have done far less to favor private investment or more to favor redistributive programs.

Mayor Koch constructed his coalition by uniting a diversity of supportive constituencies, while keeping his potential opponents divided. He accomplished this by: (1) mobilizing middle-class white fears of black and Latino encroachment, (2) capitalizing on the ethnic, nativity, and geographic cleavages emerging among underrepresented but potentially challenging groups, (3) using the "new patronage" inherent in "third party government" to build up a subordinate following among community-based organizations and selected black and Latino elected officials, (4) striking accommodations with the regular Democratic party organizations that held sway in many parts of New York City, and (5) constructing a pro-growth coalition of real estate development interests and other corporate elites. These political objectives deeply influenced his major policy priorities.

Mayor Koch's position on private development won him great support from the corporate business community, just as his devotion to the white middle class in a racially divided city drew support from white ethnics. But Mayor Koch recognized that these sources alone would have been too narrow a basis upon which to build an enduring electoral and governing majority.[45] He also needed support from many white liberals and at least a minority of blacks and Latinos. Mayor Koch thus had to blunt tensions between white regulars and white reformers and mobilize the historical white electoral majority without excessively alienating the growing but underrepresented black and Latino populations. (In this sense, his task was the mirror image of that of African-American aspirants to citywide power who had to mobilize blacks without polarizing whites against them.) For more than a decade, Mayor Koch's emphasis on promoting private investment, expanding the city budget (and its "new patronage"), and playing on the city's increasing racial and ethnic fragmentation enabled him to do so.

Various complexities of New York City's political culture facilitated this strategy. The decay of white liberalism removed a powerful force from the potential biracial coalition that, in cities like Los Angeles or Chicago, enabled liberals to come to power for the first time. Despite their distinctive ideology, Manhattan's white reformers are no longer insurgents; their destruction of the Manhattan Democratic "machine," Tammany Hall, had enabled them to become part of the political establishment. As such, they were averse to risking their political gains by joining diverse, often warring, underrepresented minority groups in a black-led challenge to the mayor. To the contrary, they provided Mayor Koch, a product of the Village Independent Democrats and the Manhattan reform movement, with his initial constituency, and he took pains to "feed" significant parts of it. (Many of his initial senior appointees had served in the

Lindsay administration.) Many in the white liberal establishment had little incentive to challenge him.

Outside Manhattan, however, the regular Democratic county party organizations not only continued to dominate local politics but gained influence during the 1980s. This claim runs counter to the vast literature on the decline of machine politics; to be sure, the regular county Democratic organizations and their constituent clubs remain weaker than at the turn of the century or even in the 1950s.[46] They command few patronage jobs and have less membership, while the lower middle class, white, ethnic social base on which they were built has declined.

At the same time, the regular organizations retain a great deal of control over ballot access, continue to influence judicial appointments and jobs in the court system, raise substantial campaign funds, and enjoy the allegiance of most legislators (who in turn influence the award of government contracts and jobs).[47] Indeed, in some respects the regular county party organizations have become stronger. They shifted the funding of political activities from total reliance on private campaign contributions onto the state and city budgets. (Legislative district offices and campaign committees displaced the political clubs as the key locus of full-time campaign workers, for example.) Regular clubs also developed considerable strength in black and Puerto Rican communities. While insurgents challenged regulars in some black districts, notably the Coalition for Community Empowerment's challenge to black regulars in Brooklyn, the regulars remain strong in many other black areas and predominate in Puerto Rican districts. In the 1980s, the reform impulse waned throughout the city.

While New York City's governmental structure is relatively centralized, its political culture is also highly fragmented. There is not a single citywide political system, but rather each of the five counties has a separate system with its own history and peculiarities. The relative importance of reform clubs varies across them, as does Republican influence. Each is characterized by a distinct pattern of ethnic factionalism between whites and minorities as well as between blacks and Puerto Ricans. These conditions frequently enabled white regular political leaders to play minority leaders against each other.

In the context of this fragmented political culture, nearly unanimous support from New York's economic elites gave crucial assistance to Mayor Koch in forging a conservative dominant coalition. Drawn by the mayor's electoral popularity and his pro-development policies, real estate developers, investment banks, and law firms bountifully financed his campaigns. In the 1985 mayoral primary in which 688,000 votes were cast, Mayor Koch was able to spend over $7 million, or $10 per vote.[48] This enabled him to concentrate enormous campaign resources on the relatively small number of potential swing voters. His closest competitor in that race was able to raise less than one-tenth the funds. Koch also received virtually unanimous editorial support. The unity of elite support for the Koch coalition was a major, albeit not by itself controlling, factor that shaped the path of political development in New York City. Where reform challenges were successful in other cities, they were predicated on some degree of division within the elite. Certainly, John V. Lindsay could not have won in 1965 and 1969 without elite support. Until the late 1980s, Mayor Koch could count on uniform support from major business interests.

With this base of elite support, Mayor Koch could exploit the competition and conflict that New York's great social diversity had bred between and within the city's racial groupings. For much of the 1950s and 1960s, the major line of intergroup cleavage was between whites on the one hand and blacks and Puerto Ricans on the other. (Age differences overlapped with racial differences: younger minority groups were pitted against an older white population; minority youths often became the dominant presence in public spaces.) After the change in immigration laws in 1965, the nature of racial succession began to change, but this cleavage continued to operate in the 1980s. While native-born blacks and Puerto Ricans still constituted the city's largest minority groups, after 1965 their numbers began to decline relatively, and probably absolutely, compared to rapidly growing West Indian, Dominican, and Asian immigrant populations.[49] The feminization of the labor force and the revolution in household formation also made gender an important source of cleavage among blacks and Latinos as well as whites; income inequality widened greatly among blacks. These postindustrial cleavages cut across traditional race distinctions, complicating the task of minority political mobilization.

Mayor Koch and his regular Democratic allies also blunted the "community revolution" that was a key source of political reform in other cities by turning contracts to community-based organizations into an important tool of political cooptation. Community groups have relied increasingly on government contracts to fund their organizations. In general, groups need political sponsorship to secure these contracts and certainly will not get them if they actively challenge the political establishment. This has deterred community organizations from supporting insurgents for citywide, or even local, office. (Public employee unions, another possible source of challenge, also failed to perform this role until the late 1980s.[50])

While mayors in other cities have used contracts to community-based service organizations to build political support, those community organizations have apparently retained more financial and political autonomy than in New York. Its system of "government by contract" is larger and appears more subject to political control. It has provided a new source of patronage, albeit one that does not stipulate the same level of electoral performance as the old patronage, that the Koch coalition used to blunt a potential source of challenge.[51] Indeed, this new patronage may have made "machine" politics stronger in New York City than in most other large, old, industrial cities.[52]

The Policy Consequences

While the underlying postindustrial cleavages and fragmented party organization in New York City enabled a conservative political coalition to become dominant, they also constrained its policies. Economic development policy actively promoted development in Manhattan's central business district as well as its offshoots in downtown Brooklyn and Long Island City, yet it had to mask this policy with largely symbolic efforts at "retaining manufacturing" and "neighborhood commercial revitalization." The city's housing and neighborhood-stabilization policies promoted private rehabilitation and gentrification, so by 1988 the Koch administration felt compelled to launch a large-scale compensatory program to rehabilitate the *in rem* housing stock taken by the city for nonpayment of taxes.

The Koch administration balanced its emphasis on promoting development by increasing the amount spent on "government by contract" and restoring services to pre-fiscal crisis levels. Over half the employees hired as a result of this budget expansion were blacks and Latinos, although they tended to be in the lower-paid categories. In some ways, the Koch administration's budget priorities were thus more "liberal" than the mayor's conservative rhetoric, emphasis on development, and social base might suggest. However inconsistent they were from the perspective of the mayor's corporate and white middle-class supporters, they were nevertheless highly rational ways for him to attempt to cement political dominance in an increasingly divided city.

Ultimately, the Koch administration's development policies had a greater impact on promoting growth and increasing inequality than its social policies did on abating the cleavages generated by the postindustrial transformation. His strategy of coalition building produced its own contradictions. His alliance with the regular Democratic county party organizations left him vulnerable to the corruption scandals, which also weakened the Bronx and Queens organizations that helped to keep substantial parts of the black and Latino vote in line. (Ironically, Ed Koch's feud with Brooklyn Borough President Howard Golden's faction of the Brooklyn Democratic organization may have saved it from this fate.) His racially polarizing rhetoric, in the context of growing income inequality and worsening racial relations, alienated black and Latino constituencies and provided a basis for their leaders' overcoming their differences. His emphasis on promoting development turned influential white liberal neighborhoods (like the Village and the Upper West Side) against him; these areas also reacted against his racial polarization. In the final analysis, strategies that sought to bind together a conservative dominant coalition created new conflicts that ultimately proved to be its undoing.

Two

How to Study Urban Political Power

The city cannot be regarded as merely
incidental to social theory but belongs
at its very core.
  (Anthony Giddens, *A Contemporary
  Critique of Historical Materialism*)[1]

As any reader of *The Prince* knows, politics is
less about monolithic control than about
maneuvering for and capitalizing on strategic
advantages. . . . Power in the sense of a capacity
to promote or protect interests is therefore not
just the ability to influence the outcome of
a particular decision but rather the capacity
to shape and take advantage of a set of
arrangements that will produce an ongoing
flow of favorable actions.
  (Clarence Stone, "Social Stratification,
  Nondecision-Making, and the Study
  of Community Power")[2]

WHAT IS the appropriate way to conceptualize the organization of political power in New York City during the Koch era? The dialogue between
the pluralist interpreters of urban power and their structuralist critics has
produced a rich variety of answers to this question.[3] In the early 1960s,
pluralist political scientists launched an attack on the previously accepted
view, established by sociologists, that socioeconomic elites dominated
urban politics. The success of this assault enabled pluralists to establish
their view as the norm in political science.

From the mid-1970s onward, however, a new generation of structur-
ally oriented critics challenged the pluralist point of view. While they
were able to undermine the prevailing wisdom, they did not manage to
supplant it with a new one, in part because of defects in their arguments
that pluralists were quick to point out. More recently, students of urban
politics have attempted to synthesize the strengths of both approaches.
With respect to framing the study of how the Koch administration

amassed and exercised political power, the debate between pluralists and their critics focuses our attention on four interrelated questions:

1. Is urban politics worth studying at all, or is the urban political realm is so subordinate to, dependent on, and constrained by its economic and social context that factors from this domain have little independent explanatory power?

2. If urban politics does have an independent impact, how should we conceptualize power relations among interests or actors?

3. In particular, what factors govern the construction of a dominant political coalition within a given set of structural constraints and opportunities?

4. In constructing such a coalition, how important is promoting private investment compared to other strategies, such as increasing social spending to incorporate potentially insurgent groups?

The Pluralist Conception of the Urban Political Order

The classic pluralist studies of a generation ago, like Banfield's *Political Influence*, Dahl's *Who Governs?*, or Sayre and Kaufman's *Governing New York City*, made important theoretical and methodological advances over the so-called elitists they attacked.[4] They did not deduce power relations from the interlocks between economic and political elites. Instead, they went into the field to examine the tangled complexity of interest alignments around actual policy decisions and disputes. Pluralist scholars showed that no model of direct control by a unified economic or status elite could easily explain what they saw.

While most pluralists did not dwell theoretically on the larger relationship between the state and the economy, they implicitly rejected the notion that some underlying structural logic subordinated local politics to the private economy. They saw politics as an autonomous realm that possessed real authority and commanded important resources. They explicitly rejected the notion that economic or social notables controlled the state in any instrumental sense. Since they argued that every "legitimate" group commanded some important resource (if only the capacity to resist) and no one group commanded sufficient resources to control all others, pluralists argued that the bargaining among a multiplicity of groups defined the urban power structure.

In this view, coalition building was central to the definition of power. Political leaders and private interests built coalitions around specific issues, the coalitions varied from issue to issue, and they tended to be short lived. By selecting a range of different policy decisions as case studies for research, pluralists seemed to imply that urban development and social service issues had an equal importance in organizing political competition.

In the face of examples where entrenched interest groups dominated their own particular, fragmented policy areas over time to the exclusion of the public interest, the pluralist approach developed a clearly critical strand of analysis.[5] But these scholars simply saw the dark side of the pluralist worldview without fundamentally challenging its basic assumptions or deflating the optimistic claims about system openness or responsiveness prevailing among other pluralists.

Sayre and Kaufman's encyclopedic *Governing New York City* offers a good example of this analytic mood. Their introductory chapters discussed the "stakes and prizes" of New York City politics, clearly implying that this realm had an importance quite independent of the larger economy. They advanced a classic pluralist conception of power relations, arguing that "no single ruling elite dominates the political and governmental system of New York City" and that city policymakers were "disunited, focused in most cases on specific areas of governmental action rather than on the full scope of it, rent by rivalries and internal competition, and compelled to rely on significant but limited instruments for registering their own values on the outcomes." As a result, "nobody runs New York; it runs by a process of negotiation and mutual accommodation."[6]

Specifically, they found that New York's political system was still a ladder of upward mobility for the economically disadvantaged, responsive to civil rights organizations and public employee unions, and more influenced by "service demanders" than by "revenue providers." Moreover, parties and party leaders held a peripheral position relative to a core of organized, professionalized bureaucracies. Capital was, if anything, at a disadvantage. Having devoted less than one page to urban renewal, Sayre and Kaufman clearly felt that the main substance of city politics was providing services and that the politics of private investment was secondary at best. Forming a majority electoral coalition was far less important in their eyes than the bargaining and mutual accommodation that took place among these more or less permanent interests. Sayre and Kaufman's only criticism of the system was that innovators had difficulty pressing for change against resistance from interests with a stake in the status quo. Yet they felt the system had regularly overcome this tendency toward stasis. "What other large American city," they concluded, "is as democratically and as well governed?"[7]

While the pluralist studies may have been convincing and accurate portraits of urban politics in the 1950s and early 1960s, the eruption of turmoil and political mobilization in the 1960s and the fiscal crisis of the 1970s soon revealed basic flaws in the pluralist analysis. Except for Robert Dahl's work, *Who Governs?*, these studies lacked a context in economic and political development. Despite obligatory opening chapters

covering economic, social, and political trends, pluralist studies such as
Sayre and Kaufman's did not treat the changing structure of urban economies or racial succession as problematic for the urban political order. It
would, they thought, simply absorb and adapt to these changes. While
Dahl provided a fine treatment of the transition from patrician dominance to what he argued were the dispersed inequalities of pluralist democracy in New Haven, he also failed to see that blacks might be led to
challenge the system, not just participate in it as a minor interest. Neither
Dahl nor his colleagues foresaw how economic transformation and racial
succession might fundamentally challenge the previously observed "normal" patterns.

Dahl did seek to address the relationship between social inequality and
political power. For most pluralists, however, the emphasis on analyzing
overt disputes diverted them from asking whether deep and persistent
economic and social inequalities might create an equivalent political inequality underneath the surface of contending interest groups. Sayre and
Kaufman brushed against this issue in their concern about established
beneficiaries' resistance to change, but they did not face it forthrightly,
much less resolve it.

Dahl explicitly denied that economic and social inequalities would
overlap and reinforce each other in the political arena. Other pluralist
scholars also did not recognize the possibility that nonelite elements of
the urban population would feel systematically excluded from power and
would react by pressing for greater representation and more vigorously
redistributive policies. As a result, the urban battles that erupted in the
latter 1960s in New York City and elsewhere made their relatively tran-
quil picture of urban politics as a kind of market equilibrium-reaching
mechanism seem anachronistic.

Structuralist Critiques

As the pluralist political equilibrium unraveled on the ground, it came
under increasing challenge from structuralist critics. The broad outlines
of their progress may be traced from Peter Bachrach and Morton Baratz'
classic essay on the "two faces of power" to Clarence Stone's work on
"systemic power" to John Manley's "class analysis of pluralism."[8]
Bachrach and Baratz attacked pluralists for focusing on the "first face" of
power, namely its exercise, while ignoring the second, namely the way
that the relationship between the state and the underlying socioeconomic
system shapes the political agenda. "Power may be, and often is," they
said, "exercised by confining the scope of decision-making to relatively
'safe' issues." But while making a case for analyzing how the values em-

bedded in institutional practices bias the rules of the game, they do not specify the mechanisms that promote some interests and issues while dampening others.[9]

Stone advanced this line of thought by shifting the locus of analysis from decisions ("market exchange") toward the mechanisms that create systemic or strategic advantages for some interests over others ("production"). The unequal distribution of private resources, he argues, creates a differential capacity among political actors to shape the flow of benefits from the basic rules of the game, the construction of particular agendas, and the making of specific decisions. Business, in particular, derives systemic power not only from its juridical status and economic resources but from its attractiveness as an ally for those who advance any policy change and from the shared subculture from which private and public officials both emerge.[10]

Despite the structuralist leaning in his concept of "systemic power," Stone did not break decisively with the pluralist interplay of interests around decisions. Manley's Marxist critique does make this break. He embraced the argument that the legal and structural primacy enjoyed by private ownership of capital requires the state to reinforce the systemic inequalities that result from the drive for private profit. He attacked pluralists, even the later work of Dahl and Lindblom that concedes that business enjoys a privileged position in pluralist competition, for lacking a theory of exploitation and, hence, an objective standard of a just or equal distribution. In Manley's view, the juridical protection of private property inevitably commits the state to control workers and promote capital.[11]

While neo-Marxist work similar to Manley's stressed the systematic subordination of the state and politics to capital accumulation and the private market, a parallel and quite nonradical strand of public choice analysis reached quite similar conclusions. Focusing on the notion that cities compete to attract well-off residents and private investment, this line of analysis stretches from Charles Tiebout's work on the quasi-market competition among local governments to Paul Peterson's "unitary theory" of urban politics.[12] Despite drastically different evaluations of the state-market relationship, this body of work is logically quite similar to some neo-Marxist critiques of pluralism.

Neo-Marxist Critiques

Structuralists have decisively transcended the pluralist vocabulary.[13] They provided the social and economic context missing from pluralism and highlighted the ways that private property, market competition, wealth and income inequality, the corporate system, and the stage of capitalist development pervasively shape the terrain on which political competition occurs. They underscored the need to analyze how basic patterns of the economic, political, or cultural rules of the game bias the capacity of different interests to realize their ends through politics and the state.

Most importantly, neo-Marxist structuralists were able to empirically investigate these mechanisms, refuting the pluralist retort that "nondecisions" either must be studied just like decisions or else are unobservable ideological constructs. They have shown cases in which the systemic and cumulative inequality of political capacity undergirded, and indeed was ideologically reinforced by, a superficial pluralism.[14] Structuralist studies may be flawed by economic determinism, but they are factually on target in observing and describing mechanisms that generate systemic, cumulative, political inequality, which has a more profound impact on outcomes than the coalition patterns studied by pluralists. Such critiques won relatively broad support among the younger generation of scholars, if not their elders. They may be subclassified into theories that stress the political logic of capital accumulation, social control, or the interplay of accumulation and legitimation. Each offers a different perspective on the central mechanisms that generate cumulative political inequality.

Theorists influenced by Marx's economic works have tended to argue that the mode of production stamps its pattern more or less directly on the organization of the state and on the dynamics of political competition. Marxists as different as David Harvey and David Gordon have both argued that the stage of capitalist development and the circuits of capital have determined urban spatial patterns, the bureaucratic state, and for Harvey even urban consciousness.[15] While this strand of Marxist thinking made a breakthrough in orienting analysts to the importance of the process of capital accumulation, it has generally lacked a well-developed theory of the state that either identifies the instrumental mechanisms that link state actions to the power of capital or grants the relative autonomy to the state.[16]

This literature does stress one mechanism, however: the state's dependence on private investment for public revenues. If the mobility of capital can discipline the state and constrain political competition, then competition among polities (whether cities or nations) to attract investment leads them to grant systematic benefits for capital, a dynamic that Alford and Friedland have called "power without participation."[17] As Harvey wrote,

> The successful urban region is one that evolves the right mix of life-styles and cultural, social, and political forms to fit with the dynamics of capital accumulation. . . . Urban regions racked by class struggle or ruled by class alliances

that take paths antagonistic to accumulation . . . at some point have to face the realities of competition for jobs, trade, money, investments, services, and so forth.[18]

Sooner or later, the state and political competition will be subordinated to the needs of capital.

Several analysts, including Friedland and Palmer as well as Molotch and Logan, abstracted this mechanism from the larger Marxian vocabulary and made it central to their analysis of urban power. Friedland and Palmer argued that, while businesses do directly influence policy-making, such intervention is logically secondary. "The growth of locales depends on the fortunes of their firms," according to Friedland and Palmer, thus "dominant and mobile [corporate] actors set the boundaries within which debate over public policy takes place."[19] As capital has become more mobile and less tied to specific locations, the need for business to intervene directly in politics has waned, while the structural subordination of local government to the general interests of business has waxed.

Molotch and Logan took a different tack on the same course. While conceding that the mobility of capital gives local government a powerful incentive to defer to capitalists, they argued that certain classes of business are not mobile: real estate developers, utilities, newspapers, and others with a fixed relationship to a place. Large sunk costs give these interests a powerful incentive to intervene in and dominate local politics in order to get local government to promote new investment. They saw this "growth machine" as a ubiquitous, inevitable, and at best weakly challenged feature of American cities.[20] For Molotch and Logan, New York City is a paramount case of the political influence of real estate development interests. They cited both the long career of Robert Moses as a builder of public works that favored private investors and the predominance of real estate interests among those who financed Mayor Koch's later political campaigns.

Neo-Marxist analysts of New York City found ample evidence that the city's fiscal crisis in the mid-1970s enabled corporate power to have direct and indirect impacts on public policy. William Tabb argued that

> throughout New York City's history there have been cycles of overexpansion of local government spending, accompanied by charges of corruption and mismanagement, followed by reform undertaken by elites and used as a vehicle for restructuring the city physically and reorienting budget priorities to favor a new pattern of accumulation. . . . Real elites only enter the day-to-day operations of governments in periods of crisis; they move to the background as soon as possible, after they have restructured the context of decision-making in ways they find congenial. . . . The urban fiscal crisis is a derived problem. Its cause is ultimately intertwined with the freedom of capital from democratic control.[21]

Others joined Tabb's view that corporate interests to some degree precipitated and then used the fiscal crisis to reorient politics and city policy-
making toward their interests.[22] Even Raymond Horton, not a proponent
of radical views, concluded at the time that corporate elites had taken
control of city government.[23]

While this strand of thinking argued that the multiplicity of competing local governments forces the state to reproduce and protect basic
features of the advanced capitalist economy, a second, equally important
school of neo-Marxist thinking stressed the way urban politics serves to
dampen and regulate the conflicts inevitably generated by capitalist urbanization.[24] Castells' work on "collective consumption" and urban social movements,[25] Piven and Cloward's studies of urban protest,[26] and
Katznelson's studies of the absorptive capacity of local bureaucracies and
the bias against class issues in urban politics[27] represent the best of this
work.

While these analysts differed over how the state coopts movements
that challenge urban governments, they share the idea that this process is
a central feature of urban politics in advanced capitalist societies.[28] Not
everyone, even on the left, has agreed with these contentions. Theret,
Mingione, and Gottdeiner have criticized the explanatory power of the
notion of collective consumption, while Ceccarelli has argued that urban
social movements did not turn out to be the force in West European urban
politics that Castells portrayed them to be.[29] Whatever the situation in
Europe, the civil rights movement, urban unrest, and community organization clearly had a profound impact on urban politics in the United
States after the 1960s, particularly in the rise of programs designed to
absorb and deflect these forces.

Piven and Cloward have stressed that "the occasions when protest is
possible among the poor, the forms that it must take, and the impact it
can have are all delimited by the social structure in ways which usually
diminish its extent and diminish its force."[30] When institutional crisis creates a space for defiance, established patterns of political competition
tend to shape the form it takes. When protest sometimes breaks those
boundaries, it is still shaped by the everyday-life situations of the protesters and the targets those situations afford. But in a highly unsettled national electoral environment, protest can still lead political leaders to
"break with an established pattern of government accommodation to private elites."[31] This response generally aims to isolate and undermine as
well as conciliate protest and to "reintegrate the movement into normal
political channels and to absorb its leaders into stable institutional
roles."[32] Government attempts to coopt dissidents on terms that do not
threaten the basic institutional arrangements of capitalism but leave

behind a residue of reform, thus providing the central means of social control.

Katznelson has developed several of these themes. He first approached the subject matter of *City Trenches* with the notion that government programs ostensibly aimed at reducing poverty and increasing citizen participation absorbed and deflected black protest in the Inwood/Washington Heights section of northern Manhattan. Upon reflection, however, he discovered a more deeply embedded set of barriers to and channels for protest: the physical separation of work and residence and the consequent dampening of class issues in the residence-based world of urban politics. Without fully abandoning his initial conception of governmental co-optation, he argued that the reproduction of class inequality is deeply embedded in and shaped by the spatial organization of residential communities.[33]

A third stream of neo-Marxism, stimulated by James O'Connor's and Claus Offe's contributions to the theory of the state, attempted to develop a multivariate approach to the structure of urban power that accorded equal place to the imperatives to promote accumulation and to achieve legitimacy.[34] In this approach, the two imperatives are crosscutting: the state must promote accumulation but cannot be seen to be doing so without risking its legitimacy. Efforts to bolster legitimacy through expanded social spending may hinder corporate profits if they are financed through progressive taxation. The structure and political orientation of the state become a battleground where these issues are fought out.

Friedland used this approach to study how the presence of corporate headquarters and organized labor influenced patterns of spending on urban renewal and antipoverty programs in sixty-seven cities during the 1960s. He found that the presence of either of these interests, particularly corporate headquarters, promoted spending in these areas but also contributed to fiscal strain and the intensity of urban rioting. His work suggests an implicit distinction between two types of cities: those where corporations and labor unions are prevalent, with a more liberal, Democratic political culture, and those where they are not, with a more conservative and repressive political culture.[35]

Friedland, Piven, and Alford used O'Connor's distinctions to construct a compelling theory of how accumulation-oriented and legitimacy-oriented functions become segregated into different local government bureaucracies. This segregation reduces the tension between the two functions: activities that promote growth are lodged in independent authorities lacking political accountability, while those related to social spending are subject to extensive public control.[36] They felt New York exemplified this pattern of segmentation. Piven and Friedland extended such thinking to intergovernmental relations and the fragmentation of municipal government. In this case, competition among local jurisdictions for private investment not only favors the interests of capitalists, as argued by Harvey, Molotch, and others, but reconciles the tensions local governments face between raising revenues and securing electoral majorities. "The politics of vote and revenue generation diverge," Piven and Friedland argued, "because they are acted out in different parts of the local state, with the result that voter politics and investor politics each tend to be insulated from the other."[37]

Although he eschewed the formal language of neo-Marxism, Shefter's analysis of New York City politics expanded this theme by suggesting that local governments face not two but four imperatives: they must not only raise revenues and construct electoral majorities; they must also preserve access to the municipal bond market and regulate conflict among citizens. The core of Shefter's analysis stressed how the New York City fiscal crisis stemmed from a basic conflict between attracting electoral support and extracting revenues from private investment: the Lindsay administration expanded spending to secure the former but could finance it only with debt, not increased taxation of local investment. Fiscal crisis was the inevitable result.[38]

Public Choice Critiques

Neo-Marxist thinking is not the only source of structural criticism of the pluralist paradigm, however. Microeconomics, in the form of public choice theory, has contributed its own critique. Tiebout's seminal work led to Forrester's simulation of urban systems and ultimately to Paul Peterson's sophisticated "unitary" theory of urban politics. This tradition, born of the economists' distrust of state allocation of resources, has sought a functional equivalent to the marketplace in the multiplicity of local governments. They would compete, Tiebout argued, for residents of different means and desires by providing different service packages at various tax costs. An equilibrium would thus be reached in the sorting of populations across urban and suburban jurisdictions within the metropolis. This equilibrium would represent an efficient production of public goods, matching the marginal prospective resident with the jurisdiction's need to add (or subtract) residents on its own margin to provide services at the most efficient scale.[39]

Such thinking has undergirded much of the orthodox literature on urban economics and local public finance. Urban housing, for example, has been analyzed as a function of how consumers trade off housing and commuting costs, given various levels of residential amenities. Forrester built the underlying assumptions into a model, influential for a time, that implied that whatever cities do to provide housing or social services for the poor will attract more of them, drive out the better off, and erode the tax base.[40]

This analysis reached its highest form in Paul Peterson's *City Limits*. Like neo-Marxists, Peterson analyzed how external economic conditions shape and constrain the urban political arena and concluded that "political variables no longer become relevant to the analysis."[41] Unlike neo-Marxists, however, he posited the importance of consumer as well as investor demand and imputed a unitary interest in economic growth to all constituent urban interests. "The interests of cities," he said, lie not in an optimum size for efficient service provision nor in some pluralist bargaining among constituencies, but in "policies [that] maintain or enhance the economic position, social prestige, or political power of the city, taken as a whole."[42]

Of these, he found economic position paramount and equated it with the health of export industries. The overwhelming importance of promoting exports means that "the issues screened out of local politics are not eliminated by local electoral devices, bureaucratic manipulations, or a one-sided press . . . [but because they] fall outside the limited sphere of local politics."[43] In fact, local politics is so limited in Peterson's view that it cannot even generate partisan competition or serious group challenges to prevailing policy. Observed intergroup struggles are only ethnic competition over jobs and contracts. Subsequently, Peterson concluded that, owing to economic decline and racial transition, "the industrial city has become an institutional anachronism."[44]

New York would seem to be a counterexample to this argument, since intense intergroup conflict and the liberal ambitions of the Lindsay administration led to sizable efforts at redistribution. Not so, wrote Peterson and his co-author Margaret Weir: while "New York City's near-default seems to suggest that local governments are fundamentally responsive to short-term political forces within their cities regardless of the long-term economic consequences of their policies," they argued that the growth of the New York City budget in the late 1960s "was a consequence of two factors for which local officials could hardly be blamed: (1) inflation, and (2) increased assistance from state and federal governments." As a result, they concluded, "not much should be made of the variation in the percent of the budget increase from one administration to the next."[45] The forces that pushed the budget upward were not the result of short-term conflict but rather of a long-term, built-in tendency to overspend. According to Peterson and Weir, this tendency lasted longer than it would have in poorer or less influential cities, but "the importance of economic interest became so painfully apparent that . . . the city's business elites, politicians, and voters have all ensured that such deviation no longer continues."[46]

While this market-based explanation of the limits on urban politics has a markedly different and more positive evaluation of the final equilibrium than do neo-Marxist formulations, it has a similar logical structure and reaches similar conclusions. Politics—at any rate urban politics—loses its autonomy and even its explanatory relevance. Intercity competition drives redistribution off the urban political agenda and puts the promotion of economic development in top position.

Structuralism Reconsidered

By providing the missing economic and social-structural context, these structuralist critiques achieved a considerable advance over pluralist analysis. Cities can no longer be taken as independent entities isolated from the larger economic and social forces that operate on them. Analysts can no longer ignore the impact of global and national economic restructuring on large central cities.[47] Since cities cannot retard these global economic trends (though New York and others may propagate them), nor remake their populations at will, they clearly navigate in a sea of externally generated constraints and imperatives.

The structuralist critiques also make it clear that urban politics can no longer be considered to be unrelated to the cumulative pattern of inequality in the economy and society. They have focused attention on how the state's dependence on private investment fosters political outcomes that systematically favor business interests. Structuralists have explored specific mechanisms that produce this result, such as the invidious competition among fragmented, autonomous urban governments for investment, the segregation of local government functions into quasi-private agencies that promote investment and politically exposed agencies that absorb and deflect protest, and the organization of the channels of political representation so as to articulate interests in some ways but not others. By stressing that advanced capitalism characteristically generates urban social movements and political conflicts, some structuralists have also implied that political action can alter some of the constraints capitalism imposes on democracy.

Despite these strengths, however, structuralist perspectives also have grave flaws. The assertion that the state "must" undertake activities that favor capital tends to be functionalist. Such a standpoint begs the question of how these "imperatives" are put in place and reproduced over time, which inevitably must be through the medium of politics. As a result, structuralists may not see that political actors can fail to fulfill or to maximize their supposed imperatives. Dominant urban political coalitions have certainly done things that cost them elections and the ability to exercise power; they have persisted in increasing the tax burden on private capital and imposing exactions on private developers even after the point that they diminish further investment. Others have chosen to increase budget deficits and risk their bond ratings.

Given the right conditions, nothing is inevitable about an administration's pursuit of electoral success, private investment, well-managed social tensions, or even good bond ratings. Nothing guarantees that city government will be willing or able to fulfill the functions structuralists have assigned to it. As Piven and Friedland observed in rejecting a "smoothly functioning determinism," a structural analysis cannot be adequate until it specifies "the political processes through which . . . systematic imperatives are translated into government policies."[48]

Structural critiques also tend not to be disconfirmable. For example, if structuralists argue that the use of legal injunctions by the conservative Republican administrations before the New Deal illustrates how the state supports capitalism, while the New Deal's recognition and promotion of trade unions also illustrate state support for capitalism, then they are explaining everything and nothing. Put another way, structural theories tend to have a hard time explaining the real and important variation over time and across places.[49] The basic features of capitalism are common across nations and evolve slowly, while the political outcomes that capitalism is supposed to drive are highly varied and change more quickly.

Finally, when structuralists appeal to an ultimate economic determinism, they aggravate these problems. Agency fades out of the analytic picture.[50] To be sure, the most attractive variants of neo-Marxism sought to avoid this trap by using the concepts of the "relative autonomy of the state" and "conflicting imperatives of accumulation and legitimation" to introduce a political dimension into an otherwise inadequate economic determinism. Yet in their discomfort with granting politics a co-equal causal role, even these variants ultimately retreat to the view that politics is subordinate to economics: autonomy is after all only relative. From Gottdeiner at one end of the spectrum to Peterson on the other, structuralist analysts have made no bones about calling politics analytically irrelevant in the face of the economy's ability to constrain and impel.

To summarize, for all their strengths, structuralists conceptualized the political system as ultimately subordinate to economic structure. They tended to reduce urban politics to the fulfillment of economic imperatives; even social control achieved through political means serves capitalist ends. The most promising threads of structuralist thinking examined how systemic imperatives might conflict with each other or generate system-threatening conflict, thus opening the way for political indeterminacy. Here, however, they risked moving outside and beyond a structuralist paradigm. Indeed, orthodox Marxism (or for that matter orthodox neoclassical economics) simply does not provide a good basis for building a theory of politics. To the extent that structuralist theorists held true to the logic of their argument, they underplayed the importance of politics. They did not appreciate that policies that promote private investment must be constructed in a political environment that may favor but by no means guarantees this outcome. Indeed, popular, social, and communal forces pressure the state and the political process just as strongly in different, and often opposed, directions.

This tendency to trivialize politics removes a way to explain why outcomes vary even though capitalism is constant. States may be constrained, but they are also sovereign. They exercise a monopoly on the legitimate use of force, establish the juridical basis for private property, and shape economic development in myriad ways. Economies are delicate. They depend on political order and have been deformed or smashed by political disorder. State actions may be conditioned by economic structure, but they cannot be reduced to it. Many substantially different capitalisms are possible, and politics determine which ones evolve. Just as the state is dependent on the economy, economic institutions depend on and are vulnerable to the state and its changing political circumstances.

Even as dedicated a Marxist as David Harvey has conceded that the political arrangements supporting capitalism are "complex," "open to a curious mix of private and class pressures, social traditions and conventions, and political processes," "not entirely imposed from above or given from outside," and constitute a "powerful shaping force."[51] As Schumpeter said, the state's influence on the economy and society usually "explains practically all the major features of events, in most periods it explains a great deal and there are but a few periods when it explains nothing."[52] If politics is conceded to have causal power, then any judgment that external economic structural causes are more important than internal political ones must be substantiated, not simply assumed.

Peterson to the contrary notwithstanding, an excellent case can be made that urban politics is a high-stakes game with winners and losers, even on matters of economic development. Close to one-quarter of the Gross National Product (GNP) passes through the public sector in the United States, much of it through urban governments. Local regulation strongly shapes land values. Variations in public spending priorities can become quite significant, as the post-fiscal crisis experience in New York shows. Moreover, private investments in cities are sufficiently fixed in the short term—and even in the long term when a city has a strong competitive advantage—that many investors can neither escape nor easily resort to the sledgehammer of a capital strike.

Even where capital mobility places real limits on politics, local governments still have considerable power to tax, regulate, and direct economic activity. Where cities enjoy an underlying competitive advantage, this political leverage is all the greater. While capital enjoys systemic advantages, neither capital as a system nor businesses organized as an interest group can dictate outcomes in spending, tax, and development policy. Contrary to Peterson's contention that questions of city development are essentially nonpolitical, they have been characterized by extensive conflict.[53] The spirited political challenges to the established urban political order since the late 1960s and the depth of the private sector reaction against them suggest that participants in urban politics certainly believe they can influence important outcomes.

"Polity-centered" thinking must thus augment the "economy-centered" theorizing of the structuralist critiques.[54] This does not require an equally one-sided political determinism. Rather, it requires us to extend the lines of structuralist thinking that stress conflict among imperatives or developmental tendencies until we go beyond the limits of economic determinism. We must recognize that "state power is *sui generis* not reducible to class power," as Block put it.[55] Or as Manuel Castells recently reflected, "experience was right and Marxist theory was wrong" about the central theoretical importance of urban social movements and the impossibility of reducing them to a class basis.[56]

But if we give politics an analytic weight equal to that of economic structure, how can we avoid returning to a voluntaristic pluralism? How can we develop a vocabulary for analyzing politics and state action that reconciles the political system's independent impact on social outcomes with its observed systemic bias in favor of capital? A satisfactory approach must operate at three interrelated levels: (1) how the local state's relationship to the economy and society conditions its capacity to act, (2) how the "rules of the game" of local politics shape the competition among interests and actors to construct a dominant political coalition able to exercise that capacity to act, and (3) how economic and social change and the organization of political competition shape the mobilization of these interests.

Toward a Theoretical Synthesis

We can begin to build such an approach by recognizing that city government and its political leaders interact with the resident population and constituency interests in its political and electoral operating environ-

ment and with market forces and business interests in its economic operating environment.[57] This approach emphasizes two primary interactions: first, between the leaders of city government and their political/
electoral base; and second, between the leaders of city government and
their economic environment. It also suggests that political entrepreneurs
who seek to direct the actions of city government must contend with three
distinct sets of interests: (1) public sector producer interests inside local
government, (2) popular or constituency interests (which are also public
sector consumer interests), especially as they are organized in the electoral system, and (3) private market interests, particularly corporations
with discretion over capital investment, as they are organized in the local
economy.

To be sure, these interests are highly complex in a city like New York
and cannot be captured by simple dichotomies like black versus white or
capitalist versus worker. (The following chapter explores these complexities.) The city's residential communities are highly heterogeneous. Terms
like "minority" hide far more than they reveal; even "black" or "Latino"
blur important distinctions regarding nativity and ethnicity. Business interests come in many sizes, industries, and competitive situations; even
corporate elites vary greatly. Still, a focus on the relationships among
state, citizenry, and marketplace provides an entry point for analyzing
what determines the shape of the urban political arena.

The concept of a "dominant political coalition" gives us a focal point
for this analysis. A dominant political coalition is a working alliance
among different interests that can win elections for executive office and
secure the cooperation it needs from other public and private power centers in order to govern. To have an opportunity to become dominant, it
must first win election to the chief executive office. To remain dominant,
it must use the powers of government to consolidate its electoral base,
win subsequent elections, and gain support from those other wielders of
public authority and private resources whose cooperation is necessary for
state action to go forward. Put another way, a dominant coalition must
organize working control over both its political and its private market
operating environments.

This formulation improves on the pluralist approach by directing
our attention toward how the relationship between politics and markets
biases outcomes in favor of private market interests, as structuralist
approaches have pointed out. The notion of a dominant political coalition would not sit well with pluralists, who have argued that coalitions
are unstable, form or re-form according to the issue, and may be stymied
by the capacity of any sizable group to resist. We posit instead that
coalitions can be stable, operate across issues, and create persistent win-

ners and losers. Challenging and supplanting such coalitions have generally been difficult, particularly for constituencies that lack resources or are particularly vulnerable to sanction. Effective challenges generally arise only at moments of crisis in periods of rapid social and economic change.

This formulation also improves on the structuralist approach by according the political/electoral arena an influence equal to that of economic forces. It also points us toward how strategies to control the direction of city government are shaped by (and in turn shape) the political environment and by the public sector producer interests that have a permanent stake in its operation. It posits a scope for political choice and innovation that is lacking in the structuralist perspective.

This approach points us toward the following central questions: how do political entrepreneurs seek to organize such coalitions, what enables them to succeed in the first instance, and how do they sustain success over time? In what ways can such coalitions be bound together? What interests do dominant coalitions include and exclude and why? How do the economic and political contexts affect these binding relationships? And what tensions or conflicts undermine dominant coalitions, opening the way for power realignment?

As structuralists have shown, one part of the answer to these questions lies in the relationship of politics to the structure of economic interests. Efforts to explore this relationship may be found in Stone's studies of Atlanta, Shefter's study of New York, and my own work on pro-growth coalitions in Boston and San Francisco.[58] Stone distinguished three levels at which to analyze the relationship between a dominant coalition and various urban interests. The least interesting is the pluralist domain of individual decisions or "command power" in which one actor induces or coerces others to follow his or her bidding. The two others are more relevant to this analysis.

Political actors wield "coalition power" when they join together to exercise the policy powers of the state to produce a steady flow of benefits to their allies, without the need for coercing or inducing specific actions. Stone showed how the Atlanta regime used public and private subcontracts to minority business enterprises to cement its political support, but he gave relatively little attention to other aspects of how the coalition tried to dominate its political operating environment.

Instead, he emphasized the "preemptive" or "systemic power" enjoyed by private interests whose command over private resources are so great as to make their support crucial to the dominant coalition.[59] Among the mechanisms of preemptive power in Atlanta, Stone identified the unity of a well-organized downtown business community, newspaper and television support for policies that favored downtown development, the reliance of politicians on campaign contributions from developers, business control over the equity and credit that government needed to carry out its plans, and the business community's ability to provide or deny access to upward mobility for the black middle class. These systemic powers made corporate interests ideal allies for politicians seeking to achieve and sustain political dominance.

While the arrival of a black majority in the electorate, militant new black leadership, and neighborhood mobilization eventually destabilized and modified the tradition of white dominance that prevailed in Atlanta until Maynard Jackson was elected mayor in 1973, Stone argued that they did not overturn the preemptive power of corporate interests. Jackson's successor, Andrew Young, chose to abandon the fragmented and undisciplined neighborhood movement in favor of pro-growth politics with a new face, consolidated by white business support for set-asides to minority entrepreneurs.[60]

It is theoretically instructive to contrast New York with Atlanta, however. In New York, business interests, while large and powerful, appear to be less cohesive and less well organized than in Atlanta, while the power of city government is greater, public sector producer interests stronger, and its political constituencies better organized. Shefter's analysis of New York City politics parallels that of Stone but offers some interesting departures.

Although Shefter used the notion of "accommodation among interests" rather than "regime" or "dominant coalition" and thus veers toward pluralism, he argued that political interests reached a stable pattern of accommodation with private interests in the 1950s. As in Atlanta, these broke down under the political mobilizations of the late 1960s and early 1970s, but the fiscal crisis of 1975 set the stage for reasserting a conservative pattern of accommodation. Like Stone, he argued that the elite interests who refinanced the city's debt, particularly the large banks, were the major participants forging policy accommodations. Unlike Stone, however, Shefter argued that other parties played a major role, including the public employee unions and the fiscal monitors that were buttressed by the "reform vanguard." (The last include good-government organizations whose funding and leadership may come from corporate headquarters but whose social base lies in the city's middle-class, opinion-shaping professionals.)

Shefter argued that business elites and public sector labor leaders constructed a new, postreform dominant coalition during the fiscal crisis by shifting city spending away from social welfare and reducing the burden of government on the economy while protecting public service producer interests, particularly the municipal unions. In his view, black leaders and the dependent poor were relegated to the sidelines.[61]

My own study of how political entrepreneurs constructed pro-growth coalitions in Boston, San Francisco, and other large cities in the late 1950s and 1960s also advanced reasons why politicians would want to forge alliances with private sector elites. Promoting private development was an obvious way to bring together such otherwise disparate elements as a Republican corporate elite, regular Democratic party organizations, and reform-oriented rising public sector and nonprofit professionals.

These perspectives on how dominant political coalitions shape development politics and budget policy to secure business support, while convincing, remain incomplete. The "preemptive power" of business interests only explains part of how political actors construct a coalition to direct city government in the exercise of its powers.[62] As Lincoln Steffens long ago observed, dominant coalitions needed to develop a grass-roots base of legitimacy as well as support from elite interests.[63] However much they may need corporate support, dominant coalitions must also have support from popular constituencies organized by such organizations as political parties, labor unions, and community organizations.[64]

Mayors can lead dominant political coalitions only when they win electoral majorities and keep potential sources of electoral challenge fragmented or demobilized. The mobilization of blacks and Latinos and the neighborhood organization that began in the mid-1960s and continue today have prompted many currently dominant political coalitions to adopt policies that do not follow from a devotion to private market interests or public sector producer interests.[65] For example, dominant coalitions must respond to mobilizations against the negative impacts of downtown growth and inadequate public services, or demands for government programs that provide upward mobility for excluded groups.

Rufus Browning, Dale Marshall, and David Tabb have argued, for example, that when insurgent liberal biracial coalitions came to power in a few of the northern California cities they studied, the coalitions shifted policies in favor of the formerly underrepresented groups that helped to elect them.[66] Albert Karnig and Susan Welch's and Peter Eisinger's studies of the impact of black mayors reach a similar conclusion.[67] My work on Boston and San Francisco showed that, while neighborhood protest and greater mayoral sensitivity toward neighborhood concerns did not halt the transformation of these two cities, they did produce numerous specific policy changes.[68] In a comparative context, studies by Michael Aiken and Guido Martinotti and Edmond Preteceille suggest that left-wing local governments in Europe produced more progressive policy outputs.[69] Castells concludes that "grassroots mobilization has been a crucial factor in the shaping of the city, as well as the decisive element in urban innovation against prevailing social interests."[70]

The analysis of how dominant urban political coalitions are constructed and operate in New York City must therefore be mindful of pressures from below and the requirements of constructing electoral majorities as well as "preemptive power" from above. While taking into account how promoting central business district development helped bind the Koch coalition together, this analysis should also pay close attention to how the culture, organization, and dynamics of political participation shaped the formation of the dominant coalition.

The organization of political institutions and processes are especially important in determining how political leaders form coalitions. Their strategies arise not just from a pluralist "parallelogram of forces" but in response to deeply embedded political practices that govern the articulation of political interests.[71] Questions raised in Martin Shefter's work—when and why do political parties have an incentive to mobilize some constituencies and demobilize others?—take on a central importance.[72] The literature on the decay of political parties, the nature of one-party politics in large cities, and the evolving role of municipal labor unions and community organizations is particularly relevant.[73] The dimensions of space, place, and community should have equal importance to the systemic power of corporate interests as building blocks of political dominance.

After some years of torpor in the study of urban politics, scholars have begun to analyze the political and electoral bases and policy consequences of dominant coalitions in different cities. Browning, Marshall, and Tabb assembled case studies that sought to apply their framework to large, important cities outside northern California.[74] Michael Preston and his associates examined the black succession to power in Chicago, Cleveland, Detroit, New Orleans, and Philadelphia.[75] Todd Swanstrom has investigated Cleveland and compared it to Boston, while Raphael Sonenshein, Richard Keiser, James Regalado, and Byron Jones et al. have undertaken promising comparative studies.[76] Clarence Stone and Heywood Sanders and Gregory Squires also assembled volumes that compare the politics of urban development across U.S. cities.[77]

In sum, the analysis of how Edward Koch and his allies constructed a new dominant political coalition in New York City must be framed in terms of three broad sets of factors. Building on the structuralists, it must understand how the local political system's interaction with private interests creates constraints and imperatives for the local state but also opportunities that astute political entrepreneurs can seize. Second, it must go beyond the structuralists by recognizing that how popular constituencies are organized in the city's political and electoral arena has an equally strong impact on the strategies pursued by coalition builders. Finally, a sound theory must be sensitive to how the organization of interests within the public sector, embodied in political practices as well as formal authority, also influenced their choices and actions. Let us turn to how the broad forces of the postindustrial revolution have been transforming these interests in recent decades.

Three

The Postindustrial Transformation of New York City

> New York is nothing like Paris; it is nothing
> like London; and it is not Spokane multiplied
> by sixty, or Detroit multiplied by four. . . . The
> city is like poetry: it compresses all life, all races
> and breeds, into a small island.
>   (E. B. White, *Here Is New York*)[1]

> New York has become the major synapse in the
> world's major information flows. During an
> average business day the VISA card user in
> Paris, the job applicant in San Francisco, the
> emergency-room physician in Stockholm,
> the stock market investor in Zurich, indeed the
> telephone user anywhere in the country will be
> switched in and out of dozens of data bases at
> the speed of light, right here in Manhattan.
>   (Kenneth Phillips, chairman, Corporate
>   Committee of Telecommunications Users)[2]

> The overriding employment issue of the
> 1980s is: which groups will, within the next
> decades, suffer the brunt of the industrial and
> occupational changes that are occurring in the
> city and the nation?
>   (Walter Stafford, *Closed Labor Markets*)[3]

THE PREVIOUS CHAPTER argued that the distribution of political power in New York City can best be analyzed in terms of how those who would build a dominant political coalition interact with constituency interests in an electoral and political environment, with economic interests in a market environment, and with the producer interests that make up the extended family of government. The next chapter will provide a detailed examination of how these interactions have been institutionalized in New York City politics. First, however, we must consider how the transformation of the city's economy, demography, and fiscal base has altered

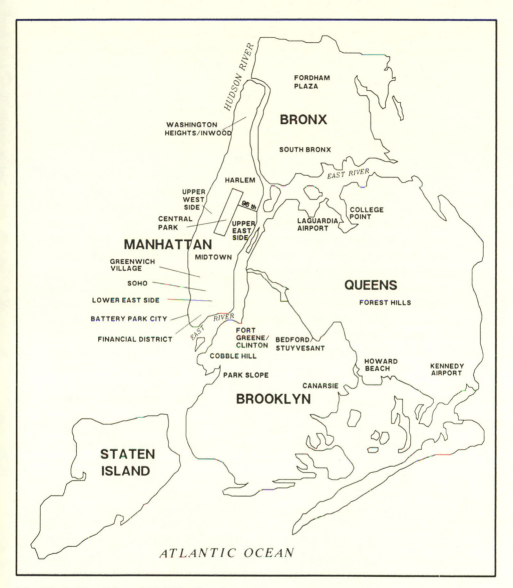

New York City, Selected Neighborhoods

these three domains, creating new pressures on the New York City political system.

Interactions between state, society, and economy have not unfolded in a stable environment. Between 1970 and 1990, the culmination of the postindustrial revolution subjected all three to rapid and thoroughgoing change. Some analysts reject the term "postindustrial" because manufacturing retains a large share of the national output and continues to be a key determinant of economic competitiveness, even though its share of employment has fallen steadily.[4] While these facts cannot be denied, the "postindustrial" concept nevertheless captures crucial aspects of the current transformation that other terms miss.

Narrowly construed, the concept highlights the massive and irreversible shift of employment away from the manufacture and distribution of goods toward services and the associated shift from blue-collar to white-collar work settings. In this sense, New York and other large central cities have become highly postindustrial. (In 1982, 14.7 percent of the residents of Los Angeles were employed as manufacturing production workers; in New York, the figure was only 10.6 percent.[5])

The postindustrial transformation is far richer and more complex than a simple shift in economic sectors and occupations, however. Like its predecessor, the industrial revolution, the postindustrial revolution has been driven by basic changes in global capitalism: rapid technological change, the globalization of economic competition, the increasing importance of finance relative to production, the globalization and centralization of financial markets, and the formation of a new international division of labor, with renewed migration from third world industrializing nations to the core cities of the first world.[6]

This increasing global integration has been centered in and fostered by a small number of world-city nodes. None has been more central in propagating change nor has felt its impact more strongly than New York.[7] Between the low point of the business cycle in 1976 and its peak in 1989, the forces of change were particularly rapid. New York City's sustained economic boom caused employment in the advanced corporate services, social services, and the public sector to mushroom and increased the city's gross product and median household earnings. At the same time, manufacturing continued to decline.

The composition of the city's population also changed rapidly. The old pattern in which blacks and Puerto Ricans replaced whites was steadily eclipsed by a new pattern in which black, Latino, and Asian "new immigrants" displaced the native born of all races. The movement of women into the labor force and the rise of nontraditional households reshaped the city's social base. These demographic changes intertwined with the restructuring of the city's economy to forge a new racial/ethnic/gender division of labor as well as new forms of inequality.[8]

This transformation erased many of the social and spatial features that distinguished the preceding era. While always important as a headquarters city, New York's single largest social stratum in the mid-1950s was blue-collar white ethnics. Turn-of-the-century immigrants and the children they bore before World War II constituted an industrial working class of considerable proportions. Today, few white blue-collar workers remain; many once categorized this way are now elderly.[9] New groups have replaced them, ranging from white professionals and managers to minority and female clerical workers, to immigrant service workers. Office workers in corporate, social service, and government settings vastly outnumber production workers.

While many women and blacks benefited from the departure of white males from the city's labor force, many were also excluded from its growth. The overall poverty rate and income inequality both increased noticeably during the 1980s. Poverty rose from 15 percent in 1975 (about 20 percent over the national average) to 23 percent in 1987 (almost twice the national average).[10] Low labor-force participation rates for blacks, Latinos, and women, the growth of female-headed households, and the decline of the real value of transfer payments contributed to the growth of poverty.[11] At the other end of the income distribution, the most rapidly growing and remunerative occupations in the advanced corporate services largely excluded blacks and Latinos.[12] These trends transformed New York from a relatively well off, white, blue-collar city into a more economically divided, multiracial, white-collar city.[13]

The contradictory forces of investment and abandonment in New York's postindustrial revolution also reshaped its built environment. Corporate office towers and zones of luxury residence and consumption arose amidst a decaying public infrastructure and declining neighborhoods, making New York a "phoenix in the ashes."[14] (Only after 1983 did the city begin to experience net gains in the size and quality of its housing stock.) Uses and places associated with the industrial city and the poor declined heavily, while investment surged into office construction, the institutional expansion of hospitals and universities, the conversion of former loft-manufacturing areas, the gentrification of late-nineteenth-century upper-class neighborhoods, and the growth of new immigrant neighborhoods.

Growth of West Indian, Latin, and Asian immigrant communities like Crown Heights, Jackson Heights, and Elmhurst, together with upward mobility for some native-born blacks, drove the boundaries of the old ghettos outward into former white working-class residential neighborhoods. Prompted by this minority invasion, white ethnics retreated to ethnic enclaves on the city's periphery.[15] The growing number of poor blacks and Latinos reinforced the collapse of the old ghetto cores of the South Bronx, Harlem, the Lower East Side, and Central Brooklyn. The city thus presented itself as a paradoxical mix of splendor and decay.

These radical economic, social, and spatial changes had potentially large political implications. First, they altered the economic, demographic, and governmental interests with which local political entrepreneurs interact. Economic restructuring strengthened one set of economic interests while severely undermining others. Commercial banks, investment banks, the diversified financial firms, corporate law firms, and real estate developers accrued vastly increased revenues and assets. Public sector producer interests—particularly public employees and nonprofit organizations that rely on public funds—also increased in size and resources. Deindustrialization, on the other hand, undermined manufacturing industries and the unions that represented their workers. Firms and employees in the rising service sectors displaced manufacturing in the competition for space, capital, labor, and political support.

On the demographic front, the postindustrial revolution altered constituencies upon which electoral alignments had rested. Jewish garment workers or Italian stevedores disappeared, while the managerial and professional strata of the growing sectors became more Jewish and Italian. The growth of the native-born black and Puerto Rican populations slowed, while the new immigrants became the driving force in the city's population. Since the old and new minority groups colonized distinct locations in the evolving division of labor and experienced different economic trajectories, they developed different and sometimes conflicting interests. The youth, lower-class position, lack of English, and noncitizen status of the immigrants tended to exclude them from the political arena. Broad demographic trends nonetheless significantly altered the composition of the electorate compared to the 1960s. In short, the post-industrial revolution altered the raw ingredients from which political entrepreneurs might seek to organize a dominant political coalition in New York City.

Second, these changes also exacerbated tensions along the characteristically postindustrial fault lines of race, nativity, ethnicity, gender, household form, and industry sector. The primary tension operates between numerically declining but still politically and economically dominant whites and the numerically increasing but economically and politically subordinate majority of blacks, Latinos, and Asians. The diversity and competition among these latter groups, however, generates secondary tensions within the emerging nonwhite majority. (For example, black protesters have conducted boycotts against Korean greengrocers.)

Third, the highly cyclical, bust-and-boom nature of the economy from the 1960s to the 1980s sped the pace of change, accentuated the level of conflict, and destabilized local government's revenue base. As Shefter has argued, this broke loose old patterns of political accommodation and opened the way to new ones.[16] From 1960 into the 1970s, local public expenditures rose faster than revenues. Until the early 1970s, city government financed this gap with substantial increases in federal aid and borrowing. Economic contraction, dwindling local revenues and inter-governmental transfers, and the closure of the capital market led to the mid-1970s fiscal crisis.

This crisis eroded the autonomy of city government, threw elected offi-cials and public employees on the defensive, and made public support for private investment politically attractive. These outcomes fostered a re-newed economic boom and, as city revenues and governmental authority recovered, a renewed struggle over the "stakes and prizes" of local power. The city budget doubled between 1977 and 1987, financed largely from increased local revenues. It once more became a powerful prize for those who built the new conservative dominant coalition and for those who sought to challenge it.

The postindustrial revolution thus exerted strong but contradictory in-fluences on the local political order. It transformed the economic and the social contexts in which New York City government operates. It erased some claimants for power while creating a variety of others; it altered the relative influence of these interests, what they wanted from government, and their strategies for getting power. The economic and fiscal collapse of the mid-1970s sped the pace of change and broke down old patterns of political accommodation; renewed economic growth after 1977 in-creased the potential rewards of power.

Restructuring the Economy

The forces that drive economic growth in New York City spring from its historic role as the leading port city and as the continent's premier corpo-rate headquarters complex.[17] They generated a legacy of market, bank-ing, and corporate service functions that sustain the city's position as one of the globe's three leading centers of business decision-making. The depth and breadth of the city's advanced corporate services have become its primary competitive advantage. These activities are concentrated in the Manhattan central business district, where two million people work in 600 million square feet of office space, surrounded by a 30-county region that contains another eight million jobs. In 1985, they produced a gross city product of $150 billion and a gross regional product of $425 billion.[18]

Internationalization and the Corporate Headquarters Complex

The industrial growth that was synonymous with urbanization between 1850 and 1950 may turn out to be an historical exception, while the comparative advantages enjoyed by port cities in the early nineteenth cen-tury have returned to drive urban growth in the second half of the twentieth century. New York has organized much of U.S. foreign trade since 1800. The Port of New York and New Jersey remains the largest gateway for U.S. merchandise imports, accounting for 20 percent of the ocean cargo and 40 percent of the international air cargo.[19] As international trade rose from 12 percent to 20 percent of GNP since 1970, and the trade balance worsened, New York prospered.[20] Though ocean cargo now moves through New Jersey, the brokers, lawyers, and financing remains in New York, while John F. Kennedy's Airport air cargo facilities have become massive. Imports and exports of goods and services (exclusive of factor payments) account for a third of the region's product and probably more of the city's.[21]

Since the founding of combines like U.S. Steel at the turn of the century, New York has also been the leading center for corporate headquarters in the United States. Drennan includes in this grouping the "chief administrative office and allied" employment of industrial corporations, corporate services such as management consulting, and ancillary services such as hotels and restaurants. Within this complex, however, the fate of industrial corporations has diverged from headquarters activities in other sectors. The number and employment of industrial corporations headquartered in New York have declined significantly in the last two decades; the number of *Fortune 500* industrial firms headquartered in Manhattan fell from 128 to 50 since 1965. The number of headquarters of the largest banks, life insurance firms, and diversified financial firms grew over the same period.[22]

In the mid-1960s, New York contained over a quarter of the *Fortune 500* industrial headquarters. Although they departed, they left behind an unparalleled array of advanced corporate services firms that serve clients on a regional, national, and global scale. The increasing economic role of investment banking and the capital markets had a powerful effect on New York City. With London and Tokyo, New York began to form a single global capital market, to which New York firms contributed a steady stream of new financial "products." The rapid growth of employment and earnings in investment banking had a strong multiplier effect on other sectors, such as legal services.[23] The international operations of U.S. firms, and the U.S. headquarters of foreign firms remain concentrated in New York. Drennan has shown that 24 of the 100 largest U.S. multinational firms are located in the city and another 16 in the suburbs. Half the New York City firms' revenues were from foreign operations, compared to a third nationally. While these New York City firms were then a quarter of the national total, they accounted for over a third of total foreign revenues.[24]

Commercial banking also played a major role. With deregulation, New York banks sought to diversify their financial services and build national and international branch networks. Large foreign banks, especially Japanese banks, now have far larger deposits than do the large U.S. banks, but New York's share of foreign deposits in U.S. banks[25] and U.S. offices of foreign banks[26] increased. Meanwhile, its share of U.S. banking assets held steady at one-third during the 1980s.[27] Returns to these assets were considerably higher than for the larger Japanese banks. Moreover, New York City firms held a quarter of the assets of the world's 130 largest institutional investors.[28]

New York's dominant position in advanced services reaches far beyond financial services. While a quarter of all securities firms with more than fifty employees were located in New York, more than a third of all large law firms and more than half of those with foreign offices were.[29] New York could also claim five of the "big six" accounting firms and nineteen of the world's thirty largest advertising agencies.[30] Drennan has found that New York accounts for 20 percent of national employment in "information intensive industries," with a higher concentration than any other city except Washington and Boston. By contrast, New York lags behind Cook County (Chicago) and Los Angeles County in absolute numbers of people employed in the central offices of business corporations, and the concentration of its workers in this activity does not rank in the top ten cities.[31]

The Telecommunications and Computer Revolution

The revolution in computers and telecommunications technology has reinforced New York's role as a global business services center. Global banks such as Citicorp, the securities firms operating on Wall Street, and large financial institutions such as American Express have provided a primary impetus for technical innovation. As Kenneth Phillips, a Citicorp vice president and chairman of the legislative affairs committee of the New York Corporate Telecommunication Users has observed,

> A literal revolution has taken place rendering the bits and bytes entering New York via a large satellite dish, or flowing under the streets of Manhattan at the speed of light, in a fiber optic cable, which are part of a multi-million dollar electronics funds transfer. . . . This comparatively small area of land had over twice the telecommunications switching capacity of the average foreign country, more computers than a country the size of Brazil, and more word processors than all the countries of Europe combined. Capital investment by business users in private telecommunications systems, communicating work processing stations, computer mainframes, minis, and micros is currently in the billions of dollars and is growing annually.[32]

The stock exchanges and the interbank funds transfer networks account for a large volume of intercity and transborder data flows, but the major financial institutions also generate immense traffic. In 1983, an American Express official noted that the firm processed 250,000 authorizations per day with an average response time of five seconds and "respond[ed] virtually instantaneously to 500,000 daily messages directing high-speed trade in securities commodities, bonds, treasury bills, and a host of other items."[33]

Processing this volume naturally requires increasingly sophisticated computer hardware and software. The "turrets" in Wall Street firms may tap up to 150 information-vendor services, provide access to a worldwide voice network, and cost $50,000 to install. They are wired into redundant fiber optic and satellite digital communications systems, on which the twenty largest New York brokerage firms spent $2.2 billion in 1987.[34] Noyelle has observed, "New York is usually regarded as the leading developer of new computerized technology in the financial services. . . . Financial innovation is increasingly based in part on the development of new computer-driven products and processes."[35]

These communications nodes depend heavily on local network capacity, which is greater in New York than anywhere else. New York Telephone has installed three fiber optic networks in and around Manhattan, while the city government, with Merrill Lynch, Western Union, and the Port Authority, has installed another ring connecting the four other boroughs to the city's "teleport" on Staten Island. New York is served by five intercity fiber optic networks and six satellite common carriers, along with private earth stations run by the television networks and other large firms. In 1981, New York accounted for almost one-fourth of the nation's overseas business calls and 15 percent of the residential calls, twice as many message units as originated in Los Angeles, the second leading origin.[36]

As massive as the growth of financial and corporate services has been, they constitute only one leg of the triad of service sectors. Government itself is the second sector. What some have called "the third sector" or "the independent sector" also made major contributions to the growth of the New York City economy during the 1980s. Nonprofit and public services helped make possible and enhanced the city's dominant position in the advanced corporate services.

Even though some of these institutions, such as foundations or museums, do not employ large numbers, their prestige and resources can still be extremely significant. A Regional Plan Association study showed that New York City foundations made 29 percent of the total dollar value of U.S. foundation grants in 1975, which in turn helped to support a broad array of city-based nonprofits.[37] Elite cultural institutions have helped New York keep its competitive edge as a global city; as geography becomes less determinant for economic location, cultural amenities become stronger.[38] The richness of the city's popular culture and its ethnic diversity reinforce this attraction.[39]

Office Construction Boom

Until the recession that began in 1990, the growth of these service sectors produced a huge demand for new office space in New York City. Construction-contract awards in New York City rose (in constant dollars) from $2.4 billion in 1979 to $4.8 billion in 1987; commercial contract awards alone grew from $1 billion in 1979 to $2.5 billion in 1987.[40] In the 1980s, fifty-six buildings added 24.2 million square feet of space in midtown (with an estimated 28 million more coming available between 1988 and 1994). Similar patterns held for downtown Manhattan, radically changing the city's skyline.[41] The ownership and development of these buildings was highly concentrated: according to Salomon Brothers, thirty-six "real estate families" owned 60 percent of the prime office space in Manhattan.[42] Construction employment doubled between 1977 and 1989, making it virtually the only blue-collar, goods-related activity that expanded within the New York City economy.

Industrial Decline

A surfeit of forces has diminished goods production and distribution in New York. Some are generic, like foreign competition with U.S. industries concentrated in New York, such as the garment industry. Others are specific to New York, such as rising space, energy, and labor costs, the retiring of the turn-of-the-century immigrant generation that dominated small business in New York, the decline of the port, the devastating effect of recession in the 1970s and the early 1990s, and the failure to capture growing high-technology industries.

Employment in printing and publishing, which is closely tied to the advanced services, was stable during the 1980s, though it too was hit by the 1990 recession. Broadly speaking, however, New York is no longer an industrial city. Table 3.1 shows that manufacturing employment was cut by two-thirds since 1950 to less than 10 percent of the city's employment.[43] Trucking, warehousing, and wholesale trade experienced the same fate. One study shows that total goods-related employment fell from 35.4 percent of the total in 1969 to 21.8 percent in 1985.[44]

The decline of small business parallels the departure of industrial headquarters. New York historically specialized in small or light-weight goods that had high value in relation to their transport costs, such as apparel,

furs, jewelry, as well as books, magazines, and newspapers.[45] The parts of
these industries that produce high-fashion items with small runs or that
require quick resupply and close supervision of production have been
slowest to leave the city. Other parts can rely on low-wage immigrant
labor.[46] Foreign competition, the retirement of a generation of immigrant
Jewish tailors, diamond cutters, and factory owners, and business-cycle
downturns destroyed much of the rest, however.

These long-term shifts in the New York City economy were accelerated
by the rapid fluctuations in the city's business cycle. The 1970s contraction devastated manufacturing while only slowing the growth of the services; the boom of the 1980s spurred the service sectors, without much
slowing the fall of manufacturing. Table 3.1 shows that the whip of
the business cycle reduced manufacturing from almost a third of city employment to less than one-tenth in four decades.[47] Conversely, finance
and private services almost doubled from a quarter to nearly half of city
employment.

The economic boom of the 1980s expanded all three components of
the service economy. Finance and other advanced corporate services
emerged as the most powerful motors driving economic activity in New

TABLE 3.1

Employment in Nonagricultural Establishments, New York City Annual
Averages, 1950–1989 (in thousands)

Industry	1950	Percent	1970	1977	1980	1989	Percent
Construction	123	3.5	110	64	77	121	3.4
Manufacturing	1,040	30.0	766	539	496	360	10.0
Nondurable	(810)	(23.3)	(525)	(376)	(351)	(265)	7.3
Apparel	(341)	(9.8)	(204)	(153)	(140)	(100)	2.8
Printing	(119)	(3.4)	(121)	(90)	(94)	(88)	2.4
Durable	(230)	(6.6)	(241)	(163)	(145)	(95)	2.6
Transport	232	6.7	203	157	150	134	3.7
Communica-tions	66	1.9	95	76	82	59	1.6
Utilities	34	1.0	26	26	25	23	0.6
Wholesale	322	9.3	302	248	246	228	6.3
Retail	433	12.5	434	372	368	402	11.1
Finance, insurance, and real estate	336	9.7	460	414	448	530	14.7
Services	507	14.6	785	783	894	1,147	31.8
Government	374	10.8	563	508	516	602	16.7
Total	3,469	100.0	3,745	3,188	3,302	3,607	100.0

Source: New York State Department of Labor. 1950 Transportation, Communications,
Utilities and wholesale and retail employment figures estimated. 1989 Communications
figure depressed by labor dispute. Columns may not add to total due to rounding.

York City and indeed the surrounding region. Financial services generated high earnings and had a large multiplier effect on related sectors, but Table 3.2 shows that it accounts for only 14.7 percent of total employ-

TABLE 3.2
Employment Trends, Nonagricultural Establishments, Rising Sectors in New York City, 1969, 1977, 1989 (in thousands)

Sector	1969	1977	1989	1977–1989 Annual	Percent of 1977–1989 gain in services
Goods production and distribution	1,961	1,307	994	−0.96%	n.a.
Services	1,837	1,881	2,675	3.25%	100.0
Financial services	466	414	531	2.36%	15.9
Banking	97	118	171		
Securities	99	70	137		
Corporate services	183	228	541	11.44%	42.6
Legal services	28	39	76		
Management consulting	35	22	33		
Accounting	23	21	31		
Engineering and architecture	21	16	21		
Building services		35	47		
Personnel services	27	54			
Communications, transport, and media	249	212	220	0.31%	1.1
Communications	86	76	66[a]		
Advertising	39	32	39		
Publishing	70	52	61		
Entertainment, culture, and tourism	185	162	230	3.49%	9.3
Restaurants, bars	123	106	131		
Hotels	34	24	34		
Legitimate theater	10	14	30		
Museums	4[b]	5	8		
Education and research	158	248	316	2.28%	9.3
Elementary and secondary	151	151	184		
Colleges	—	77	113		
Health and social services	198	240	350	3.82%	15.0
Hospitals	104	119	139		
Other health services	47	66	100		
Social services	47[b]	55	121		
Government (noneducational)	398	377	427	1.11%	6.8
Local	254	242	299		
State	38	51	56		
Federal	106	84	76		
Total	3,798	3,188	3,669	1.10%	n.a.

Source: New York State Department of Labor.
[a]Reflects reclassification due to break-up of AT&T and adjustment for a labor dispute in 1989.
[b]Estimate.

ment and contributed only 15.9 percent of the city's job growth during the 1977–89 boom. New York's uniquely broad array of nonfinancial corporate services experienced truly explosive growth, accounting for 42.6 percent of the jobs gained.

Nonprofit education, health, and social services and the public sector also made significant contributions to the city's economic fortunes, as Table 3.2 shows. Health and education alone constitute 18.4 percent of the city's employment base and produced 24.3 percent of its employment gains in the 1980s. Government services excluding education constitute 11.8 percent of employment and contributed another 6.8 percent of the gain. The public and nonprofit sectors thus accounted for almost a third of the overall expansion.

Racial Succession, the Racial Division of Labor, and the New Inequality

Like the city's economy, its population has also been "globalized" and "deindustrialized." Much of the white, ethnic working- and middle-class population moved away from the city during the 1970s and 1980s; those who remain are far more likely to be elderly than the rest of the population. In recent decades, the "new immigration" has become the driving force behind social change, redefining the nature of racial succession.[48] At the same time, women's roles, the nature of families and household formation, and the array of subcultures have been radically altered. Of all these forces, the impact of migration on New York City has been most distinct.

Waves of Migration

Four waves of migration have washed over New York City: the Irish and Germans after 1848, the Italians and middle European Jews from 1890 to 1920, Southern blacks and Puerto Ricans in the 1940–70 period, and the current "new immigration" from the Caribbean, Latin America, and Asia.[49] These waves intersected with different phases of the city's economic growth, creating a distinctive racial/ethnic division of labor. The groups arrived with different resources and employed varied strategies with respect to the economic context they found. Each wave thus produced a characteristic pattern of ethnic competition.

The first two immigrant waves built upon each other and produced a cumulative layering characterized by the ability of earlier groups to gain upward mobility by colonizing good economic niches and defending them against newcomers. In this respect, New York resembled other large, old, industrial cities of the northeast and midwest. But white flight and the economic decline of the mid-1970s complicated economic progress for the latter part of the third and the fourth waves.

The black and Puerto Rican immigrants after World War II and the post-1965 "new immigrants" confronted previously established immigrant generations and their assimilated children who occupied a range of industry/occupational niches. During the first part of this period, ethnic succession in the labor market took on a distinctly racial form. Blacks and Puerto Ricans faced a slowly declining but still well entrenched and resistant white population. In the 1970s, rapid white flight changed this situation in two ways. White flight created openings for minority entrants even in declining goods-related sectors because whites left faster than the industries declined.[50] Access to growing sectors with well-remunerated jobs, whether in commercial construction or investment banking, remained effectively closed to minorities.

The surge of immigration in the wake of immigration-law reform in 1965 also redefined the nature of racial succession. During the 1980s alone, the city experienced a net gain of roughly half a million immigrants, reversing the city's previous decades of population loss. Roughly one-third of this influx came from Caribbean blacks, one-quarter from Asians, and one-fifth from Latinos.[51] The native-born black and Puerto Rican populations began to decline in absolute as well as relative terms in 1980s, so that foreign-born blacks and Latinos were displacing native-born blacks and Puerto Ricans as well as whites. The 1980 census found that 18 percent of the adult black population was foreign born; by 1988, a CUNY survey found that the rate was over 30 percent. The Puerto Rican share of adult Latinos declined from 61 percent in 1980 to 54 percent in 1988.

Social Change in the 1970s and 1980s

The "subtle revolution" has also had an enormous impact on New York City. Women entered the labor force in massive numbers, the female labor force became almost as large as the male labor force, nontraditional households displaced the traditional family as the dominant household form, and birth rates fell below the replacement rate.[52] Though black, Puerto Rican, and some immigrant women have higher fertility rates than native whites, they are falling over time. And while labor-force participation for native-born black and Puerto Rican women has been lower than for native-born white women, immigrant black, Latin, and Asian women are likely as native white women to work or more so.

The basic changes in population, race, family patterns, and labor-force participation during the 1970s and 1980s are highlighted in Table 3.3. In both decades, New York became less white and more foreign born, its

TABLE 3.3
Changes in the New York City Population, 1970–90

	1970	1980	1990	1980–90 Percent Change
Total population	7,894,862	7,071,639	7,322,564	3.55
Non-Hispanic white population	4,972,509	3,668,945	3,163,125	−13.79
(percentage)	(63.0)	(51.9)	(43.2)	
Non-Hispanic black population	1,525,745	1,694,127	1,847,049	9.03
Native born		1,300,144	1,270,000[a]	−2.31[a]
Foreign born		393,983	577,000[a]	64.50[a]
Hispanic population	1,278,630	1,406,024	1,783,511	26.85
Puerto Rican	846,731	860,552	896,763	4.21
Non-Puerto Rican	476,913	545,472	886,748	62.57
Non-Hispanic Asian population	115,830	300,406	489,851	63.06
Foreign-born population	1,437,058	1,670,199	2,082,931	24.71
Total households	2,836,872	2,788,530	2,819,401	1.11
Family households	2,043,765	1,757,564	1,734,908	−1.29
Married couple families	1,603,387	1,203,387	1,098,418	−8.72
With children ‹ 18	774,496	535,581	510,813	−4.62
Female-headed households	353,692	462,933	507,459	9.62
With children ‹ 18	209,006	307,709	325,299	5.72
Nonfamily households	793,107	1,030,966	1,084,493	5.19
Average persons per household	2.74	2.49	2.54	2.00
Males in labor force	1,988,774	1,732,165	1,891,211	9.18
(percentage males › 16)	(74.1)	(69.5)	(71.1)	
Females in labor force	1,355,654	1,435,533	1,695,217	18.09
(percentage females › 16)	(42.2)	(47.1)	(53.7)	

Source: U.S. Census, 1970, 1980 Public Use Microdate Sample Files; 1990 STF1 and STF3.
[a]Estimated on the basis of 1988 CUNY Survey.

Latino and Asian populations grew rapidly, its households were less likely to be families, and families were less likely to have two parents. But while the city lost population heavily in the 1970s, the economic boom and immigrant surge of the 1980s increased the population by 3.6 percent (roughly 251,000). Moreover, the growth of immigrant families halted the fall of mean household size and slowed the growth of nonfamily and female-headed households. The population gain reversed three previous decades of decline; more remarkably, New York City gained population relative to its surrounding metropolitan, breaking the pattern of the previous six decades. The white population decline continued in the 1980s but far less rapidly than in the 1970s. During the 1980s, immigration brought the number of Latinos almost even with the number of blacks, while immigrants from China and elsewhere in Asia were the most rapidly growing group, though still small relative to the others.

The New Racial/Ethnic/Gender Division of Labor

Economic and demographic changes intersected with the rapid changes in the economy and labor market to produce a new pattern of how groups are distributed across the lattice of industries and occupations. The white, ethnic, blue-collar working class shrank to the point where it accounts for perhaps 5 percent of the city's adult population. As it aged and diminished, its male offspring entered managerial and professional occupations. Minorities, particularly Latinos, replaced retreating whites within the shrinking manufacturing labor force. The female white-collar working class expanded greatly. White women make up about half this group, while black and other minority women hold another quarter. (Men make up the rest.) This new pattern is associated with both growing poverty and worsening income inequality. Race, gender, nativity, and ethnicity all played a role in sorting groups across economic niches.

In broad terms, whites disproportionately hold managerial, professional, and clerical jobs in construction, transportation, finance, advanced corporate services, education, and government. Blacks tend to hold clerical and service jobs in health, social services, and government. Latinos are concentrated in service and operative jobs in manufacturing, restaurants, and health services. In each of these groups, male white-collar workers are more likely to be managers or professionals and females to be clerical workers, while male blue-collar workers are more likely to be craftsmen and women to be operatives.[53]

These broad patterns do vary across specific combinations of race, ethnicity or nativity, and gender, however. Among white males, for example, those of Jewish ancestries are strongly represented in the apparel industry, wholesale trade, the corporate services, while women of Jewish ancestries are concentrated in education.[54] Males of Italian ancestry are disproportionately in construction, transportation, and wholesale and retail trade; high proportions of Irish males may be found working in transportation, banking, the bar and restaurant business, and public service. Among blacks, native-born men are more likely to be in transportation, communication, and utilities and women in education, social services, and especially government. Jamaican males, on the other hand, are more likely to be in manufacturing (especially of durable goods), construction, and hospitals. Similarly, Dominican immigrants are more likely than Puerto Ricans to work in manufacturing (especially apparel) or restaurants and less likely to work in health services, social services, or government. Some groups achieved extremely high concentrations in a few industries: for example, in 1980, 44 percent of all Chinese males worked as waiters and cooks in restaurants, while 40 percent of all Dominican women and 64 percent of all Chinese women worked behind sewing machines in the garment industry. Even among whites, 21 percent of Jewish ancestry women worked in education, while 15 percent of the White Anglo-Saxon Protestant and Irish males worked in banking.[55]

This pattern of ethnic specialization reflects the imprint left by the initial immigrant generations, though to be sure with upward and outward mobility over time.[56] One can see Jews in the garment industry, Italian construction workers, and Irish firemen, though they are now more likely to own or manage their enterprises, or to be craftspersons rather than operatives. By looking at where groups have spread from the initial concentrations, one can also sense the trajectories that prior immigrant groups have followed. The Irish, for example, certainly did not begin with concentrations in investment banking and corporate law but used politics as a springboard to gain access to them. Italians achieved a similar but lesser mobility into these sectors. Jews gained access to investment banking but evidently not nearly so much entree into commercial banking. Their specialization in the public school system also led to a comparatively high representation in higher education.

Blacks and Latinos have achieved less mobility into the best remunerated and most rapidly growing sectors of the economy, and there are continued indications of discrimination against them.[57] But blacks and Latinos diverge considerably in their labor-market concentrations. Reflecting their higher degree of political mobilization, blacks are much more heavily represented in health, social services, and public employment. Latinos, on the other hand, remain lodged in the declining manufacturing sectors and have experienced downward mobility with them. Women also lag behind men in gaining professional and managerial positions, with white women positioned better than minority women, and black women better positioned than Latinas.[58]

This new racial, ethnic, and gender division of labor has created complicated new patterns of intergroup tension that cannot be summed up in a simple dichotomy like "management versus workers" or "whites versus blacks." White males of English, German, Irish, and Jewish ancestries still clearly dominate upper positions in the economy, but their representation is declining relative to the kaleidoscope of groups that are striving to take their place. These challenging groups are differentiated by race, ethnicity, and gender. No single interest unites them against the dominant group; to the contrary, myriad differences fragment them.

The New Inequality

Against this highly complex mosaic has been laid an increasingly stark income inequality. While many people entered the labor market, the growth of female-headed families kept large proportions of blacks and Latinos out of it. Despite the overall prosperity of the 1980s, labor-force participation rates declined among both men and women and poverty rose. These poor families tend disproportionately to be native-born blacks, Puerto Ricans, and Dominicans rather than immigrant West Indians or Latin Americans. The people sorted into declining industries or out of the labor force experienced real income losses. Since welfare payments lost ground to inflation, the poorest households experienced the greatest loss. At the other end of the income distribution, the surge of earnings in managerial, professional, and even clerical occupations, especially when associated with Wall Street, caused median real household incomes to rise during the 1980s. The share of total income received by the lowest 20 percent of households declined from 15.4 to 11.6 percent between 1975 and 1987, while that of the top 10 percent rose from 43.8 to 49.2 percent, substantially worse than the U.S. trend.[59]

Rapidly rising rents accentuated this problem. Even though the city's households increased by 160,000 between 1980 and 1988, the net decline in the city's housing stock did not stop until after 1983, and subsequent net expansion did not match the household growth. Since more households with more income were chasing an essentially fixed housing supply, it was certain that rents would rise, rent/income ratios worsen, and doubling up and homelessness increase.[60] Those at the bottom were at an increasing competitive disadvantage with all those above them. The result was the disproportionate growth in New York of what some have called "the underclass."[61]

The Fiscal Context

Like the rest of the New York City economy, the public sector experienced major and often unsettling changes during the 1970s and 1980s. Four broad periods can be distinguished for public finance in New York City.[62] Between 1961 and 1969, the city's budget doubled in real terms from $8.6 billion to $16.2 billion (in 1982 dollars).[63] This growth was financed primarily through local revenues and intergovernmental transfers drawn from the war-induced economic boom of the period and increased federal aid from the Kennedy and Johnson administrations. The share of local revenues fell from 57.8 percent to 49.0 percent, however. The share borrowed rose from 11.6 percent to 13.8 percent in the first years of the 1960s but then fell to 9.1 percent. Intergovernmental aid, particularly federal aid, thus rose faster than the budget as a whole or any of its other funding sources.

Between 1969 and 1975, the budget continued to grow at half the rate of the 1960s, but the previous sources of financing did not follow suit. In 1982 constant dollars, the budget peaked at $21.1 billion in 1975. Local revenues shrank again from 49.0 to 42.2 percent of the total as back-to-back recessions reduced local tax revenues. Intergovernmental aid also declined from 42 percent to 40.4 percent in 1973, recovering to 44 percent in 1975 as the city's fiscal straits worsened. (This reflects a major falloff in federal aid under the Nixon administration, partially countered by increases in state aid.) The Lindsay and Beame administrations borrowed to close the gap, increasing their share from 9.1 percent in 1969 to 13.6 percent in 1975. (Borrowing peaked at 15.1 percent in 1974.) The city rolled up increasingly large debts, amounting to more than $13 billion in current dollars 1975 (including $7 billion in short-term debt at a time when the total budget was only $12.4 billion). Its inability to pay this short-term debt led the banks to cut off credit, precipitating the fiscal crisis period from 1975 to 1983.

In this period, city spending decreased from $21.1 billion in constant 1982 dollars to $16.5 billion, a decline of 22.2 percent. Borrowing dropped rapidly to 7.6 percent of the total in 1983. Local revenues increased from 42.2 percent to 51.5 percent of the total, reflecting renewed expansion that took hold in the city's economy after 1977. Intergovernmental aid rose in the immediate wake of the fiscal crisis, reaching 47.1 percent in 1978, but then declined to 40.9 percent in 1983, below the level of late 1960s. Most of this represented state efforts to assist the city; despite help from the Carter administration in 1977 and 1978, federal aid declined from $2.5 billion in 1978 to $2.2 billion in 1983 in current dollars.[64]

The post-1977 economic expansion set the stage for the renewed growth of the city budget between 1983 to 1989. The growth of local revenues was so strong during this period that the city budget rose in constant 1982 dollars from $16.5 billion in 1983 to $20.7 billion in 1989, or 27.3 percent.[65] Borrowing also increased from 7.6 percent to 10.7 percent, reflecting the city's return to the capital market and its desire to rebuild its capital budget. Remarkably, intergovernmental aid declined even further, from 40.9 percent to 29.7 percent of the total.

The stock market crash of October 1987 effectively marked the end of the boom era in New York City, and indeed in the nation, and the onset of a new recession in 1990. Between the month of the crash and the beginning of 1990, total New York City employment rose by only 56,000 jobs. Public employment grew by 26,000 during this period, while the financial services declined by 6,000 jobs. Between the middle of 1989 and the end of 1991, total employment declined by 190,000, while public employment held steady. This disparity between the private economy and public personnel expenditures led to renewed and increasingly severe fiscal problems in 1990 and 1991.

Political Implications of the Postindustrial Revolution

These profound changes in the city's economy, society, and public sector had three major consequences for the interests with which political entrepreneurs must interact as they seek to construct a victorious political coalition. They altered the size, disposition, and potential influence of the interests in the economic and social environments in which politics operates. They also created distinctly postindustrial tensions and conflicts among these constituencies. Finally, the sharply cyclical nature of the business cycle destabilized old patterns of accommodation among interests and opened the way for attempts at defining a new dominant coalition that would help determine who would benefit from the economic boom of the 1980s.

Changing Constituencies

The postindustrial revolution has altered the constellation of interests in the two operating environments of politics, the market and the citizenry, as well as within the public sector itself. In the marketplace, the 1970s and 1980s sharpened the distinction between the rising sectors—finance, the other advanced corporate services, private, nonprofit social services, and government—and the declining sectors—manufacturing, wholesaling, and freight transport. It propelled the former upward and outward, while diminishing and displacing the latter.

The rising economic constituencies had a clear, if latent or partially expressed, agenda for city politics. The city's corporate leaders wanted city government to reduce its tax burden on the private economy, shrink its functions and employment base, reduce seemingly unchecked claims for social services, and increase services relevant to the private sector and the middle class. Real estate developers and their investment bankers and corporate lawyers wanted city government to promote private investment more aggressively through a capital program that would restore economically relevant infrastructure and through regulatory and tax incentives that would foster specific projects. In general, the rising sectors of the private economy sought a more positive and supportive business climate in which their interests occupied higher priority with elected officials.

These rising economic constituencies had many important connections with the city's political leaders: their tax payments provided the bulk of the city's revenues; their investment capital was required to bring public development initiatives to fruition; their senior executives or partners provided the bulk of campaign financing and postgovernment employment opportunities for departing senior officials; and they exercised extensive influence over institutions that shaped mass and elite public opinion. The explosive growth of their revenues and earnings during the 1980s greatly heightened these sources of influence. Not only were corporate leaders highly attractive allies, but politicians and bureaucrats could refuse to accommodate their interests only at some political risk.

Declining economic constituencies also sought assistance from city government but had none of these political resources. Their industries experienced dwindling employment; firms survived only by becoming more like the rising sectors. (For example, apparel firms emphasized design, marketing, and finance, moving production elsewhere.) As the labor force in these industries dwindled and became poorer, so did the trade unions that represented them and defended their industries. Some declining industries were still large enough to wage a real, if losing, fight against the rising economic interests with which they competed for capital, workers, space, and favorable treatment by public policy. This sometimes induced local government to make symbolic gestures in defense of these industries, if for no other reason than the historic identification of blue-collar unions and workers with the regular Democratic party. But the real political incentives ran in the opposite direction.

This situation is nearly reversed when it comes to how the political system relates to rising and declining elements of the resident population and potential electorate. Despite substantial changes in recent decades, white, ethnic, formerly working-class constituencies cast the majority of votes. Though in numerical decline, these constituencies disproportionately occupied the managerial and professional positions of the rising economic sectors. The Italians and Jews who thronged into the city at the turn of the century and their children struggled from the 1930s to the 1950s to become ascendant in the Democratic party. They succeeded by the 1960s, largely through the regular party organizations in the city's five boroughs. While Jews and Italians initially forced the regular Democratic organizations to accept and advance them by threatening to defect to other parties or to periodic reform candidates, the regular Democratic organizations ultimately used these constituencies to sustain their power. As we will see in greater detail in the next chapter, these organizations by no means excluded blacks and Latinos during the 1970s and 1980s. To the contrary, white Democratic regulars promoted minority leaders allied to them so as to shape minority electoral mobilization. But they had little reason to make them equal partners.

Jews and white Catholics had represented distinct and competing tendencies in the Democratic party electorate. Jews were more liberal; they provided the bulk of the vote on the American Labor Party ballot line in the 1930s and 1940s and on the Liberal Party line after the 1950s and were potentially available to reform insurgents. (Jewish voters helped elect both LaGuardia and Lindsay.) White Catholics, especially Italians, were more conservative; many voted for Republican presidential candidates and provided votes on the Conservative and Right to Life ballot lines. As Jews competed with white Catholics for top positions in the Democratic party, they often sought minority support, forging a pattern of Jewish-black cooperation that was the basis for New York's brand of urban liberalism.

The decline in the numbers of Jews and white Catholics relative to blacks and Latinos during the 1960s and 1970s, the increasing racial divisions between whites and blacks, and overt conflicts such as the Ocean Hill-Brownsville school decentralization dispute and the teachers strike of 1968 drove a wedge between Jews and their former allies and led them in the latter 1970s to make common cause with the white Catholics. City-wide races between Democratic candidates of Italian and Jewish descent could divide this new alliance, but otherwise it held strong.

However much New York's electoral arena was dominated by declining constituencies, it could not ignore the rising but underrepresented constituencies. The county Democratic party organizations in Brooklyn, the Bronx, and Queens supported the rise of native-born black and Puerto Rican allies who could control the mobilization of these populations, and they encouraged competition between these groups based on the objective spatial and economic differences between them. Having come earlier and in larger numbers, and having undertaken more extensive independent political mobilization, blacks achieved more upward mobility in the Democratic party and in the labor market than did Puerto Ricans. In this way, the Democratic regulars incorporated and subordinated these constituencies.

During the latter 1970s and the 1980s, this racial/ethnic fragmentation took a new turn as the native-born black and Puerto Rican populations went into numerical decline relative to foreign-born blacks and Latinos. The rapid growth of West Indian, Dominican, Chinese, and other immigrant populations made the strategy of divide and conquer even easier. This political weakness was reinforced by these new constituencies holding jobs largely outside the advanced corporate services. Some immigrant groups, for example, West Indians, worked in such rising sectors as hospitals and local government. But even among West Indians, the largest number of immigrants worked in the declining manufacturing sectors, where the numerical decline of white workers was even more rapid than their loss of jobs, creating openings for immigrant workers. Their weak position in the labor market reinforced their weak political position.

Out of this contradictory pattern of declining population groups dominating the better jobs in the rising economic sectors and the rising groups colonizing the declining economic sectors, two deviant groups stand out: the largely white stratum of professionals of the baby boom generation and the more typically minority labor force in government and nonprofit social services. Here, growing groups held jobs in growing sectors.

In 1980, the first group comprised roughly one-tenth of the city's total labor force; the subsequent decade of economic boom increased it substantially.[66] Perhaps two-thirds of this group is employed in private corporations and advocates the business agenda, but the other third is based in nonprofit sectors and has a more liberal and reformist outlook. Steven Brint has commented:

> It seems likely that in recent years, many liberal professionals have accommodated to the prerogatives of the dominant business sector, just as in the 1960s and 1970s many business people accommodated to the then-ascendent rhetoric of the "service society," the "knowledge class," social reform, and community control. Together with these accommodations, however, are also persistent tensions arising from conflict between two status cultures: the utilitarian and profit-centered concerns of people close to the financial and business worlds, and the intellectual, expressive, and culturally cosmopolitan concerns of people close to the liberal professional world of the universities, the arts, the nonprofits, and government social services.[67]

Shefter has argued that these groups, embodied in the "reform vanguard," have played an important role in politics because their resources and influence far outstrip their numbers. As such, they might constitute a pivotal constituency drawn in certain periods towards a liberal version of the reform ideal and in others toward a more conservative vision. As we shall see below, the trajectory of this group is an important factor in determining the fate of insurgent coalitions in New York City politics.

Government employment and the allied nonprofit social service sector also grew rapidly between 1977 and 1989, despite the impression of retrenchment conveyed by the postfiscal crisis atmosphere of New York City politics. While the fiscal crisis caused local government to reduce its employment by a net of 55,000 jobs between 1970 and 1977, city government employment grew rapidly after 1983. By the end of 1989, local government employed substantially more people (469,000) than either manufacturing (353,000) or banking and securities (306,000).[68]

In contrast to the retrenchment in government support for nonprofits that took place in other cities during the early 1980s, local government contributions to nonprofit budgets grew in New York.[69] By late 1989, the employment in these sectors (676,000) outstripped government, as well as manufacturing and banking. Government and the nonprofit social services had a much higher rate of employment for blacks and Latinos than growing parts of the private, for-profit economy. Most black and Latino managers and professionals may be found in these sectors, as can white women. For government and nonprofit social service workers, race and industry often reinforce liberal social and political attitudes. While their incomes are far lower than those in the upper professions, their numbers are far greater, amounting to almost one-third of the total employment. Like reform-oriented professionals, they too represent a pivotal constituency for insurgent coalitions.

New Forms of Class and Race Conflict

These trends produced increasingly sharp new patterns of inequality among New York City residents in terms of income, housing, and political influence. Growing inequality fostered homelessness, rising crime rates, the breakdown of public order and civility, and deteriorating race and intergroup relations, which worsened the quality of life for all New Yorkers, not just the immediate victims. These are but the most visible of a network of characteristically postindustrial tensions that permeate the political arena.

These conflicts cannot be boiled down into simple dichotomies. While the social, economic, and political (if not always physical) distance between white investment bankers and Latino welfare mothers grew enormously during the 1977–89 economic boom, class cannot be reduced to color, ethnicity, or gender. At the extremes, class does have a color, and racial discrimination continues to occur even in the lower echelons of New York society. But not all blacks or Latinos are poor. Despite racial and ethnic inequality, the economic boom created paths of upward mobility for most blacks, Latinos, and Asians. Native-born blacks, especially women, gained a considerable foothold not only in clerical work but in social service professions and government. Foreign-born blacks benefited from the expansion of the health sector and government. While Puerto Rican, Dominican, and Chinese women were shunted into the declining garment industry and men into the rising restaurant industry, many foreign-born Latinos and Asians have also established thriving immigrant enterprises. Even the top managerial and professional jobs formerly reserved for white male Protestants have been opened to Jewish and Catholic males, as well as to token female and black Stanford MBAs.

The central problem of racial inequality has thus taken on a qualitatively new and more complicated form. First, the basic dichotomy between whites on one side and native-born blacks and Puerto Ricans on the other has been fragmented by ethnicity/nationality and gender.[70] West Indian immigrants differ objectively from native-born blacks in economic and cultural terms and compete against them, just as Latinos do against blacks and Dominicans do against Puerto Ricans.

Significant differences divide each group. Gender can be one such difference. Black women, for example, are better positioned in New York's clerical labor force and are beginning to gain better entry to managerial and professional jobs than black men. More importantly, as the income inequality *among* black households has grown greater, the social and political distance between the black middle class and the black poor has widened. As a result, the relationship between the established black leadership stratum and a significant portion of its constituency has become far more problematic. Important as such divisions are, however, whether latent or overt, they take on political importance only to the extent that actors in the political system mobilize them.

Political Destabilization

Finally, the sharp fluctuation of the business cycle also had a major impact on New York City politics. As Martin Shefter has argued, this cycle rocked the political system and ruptured old patterns of political accommodation among interests. The downturn of the fiscal crisis put severe stress on public sector producer interests, particularly the regular Democratic organizations and the public employee unions. This disarray opened the way, after 1977, for new forces to organize a new dominant coalition.

The post-1977 boom dramatically increased both the conflicts facing the political system and the size of the resources available to the interests that succeeded in organizing the dominant coalition. The creation of new constituencies, the decay of old ones, the changing power relations among them, and the clashes between them exert deep but sometimes contradictory forces on New York City's political system. The political responses, however, were deeply shaped by the ways in which interactions between the political system and its electoral, governmental, and economic environments have been institutionalized. It is to these institutional patterns and practices that we now turn.

Four

The Rules of the Game in New York City Politics

> In extremely oversimplified terms, there appear
> to be at least two "power elites" in the City, a
> party-centered one and a "status" centered one.
>   (Theodore Lowi, *At the Pleasure of
>   the Mayor*)[1]

> The successful politician in New York City has
> to focus on two audiences: prime voters and
> campaign contributors.
>   (Norman Adler, political consultant)[2]

> Analysts . . . must stop mistaking ethnicity for
> politics; while ethnicity may be more
> important than class to voting, economics is
> more important to government policy
> than ethnicity.
>   (Jim Chapin, "Who Rules New York
>   Today?")[3]

PREVIOUSLY it has been argued that political actors seek to construct and maintain a dominant coalition by using city government's relationships with economic and political/electoral interests to win elections and secure the cooperation from public and private power-holders required to govern. Over the last several decades, social change has altered the nature of these governmental, social, and economic interests and created new conflicts and tensions among them. These interests and conflicts take on political meaning, however, only within a specific setting of political institutions and practices. These institutional patterns strongly mediate the broader social changes described above and shape political actors' strategies towards interests in the government, the electorate, and the economy.[4]

The critical step toward building a dominant political coalition is to win mayoral elections. This means fashioning electoral majorities out of the constituent elements of the city's electorate. But having won office, the mayor and his or her allies must also govern. To do so, they must achieve the active cooperation from those who occupy positions inside and outside of government that endow them either with discretion over public authority or command over the private resources that are critical to carrying out government actions. Inside of government, this means building working relationships with the public sector producer interests, such as other elected officials, agency managers, organized workers, and contractors. In this task, New York City's mayor derives a distinct advantage from a history of charter reforms that has centralized authority and decision-making initiative in his or her office. The mayor can also make use of the city's relatively strong power position in striking accommodations with private interests, many of which seek favorable treatment from city government.

Those who would fashion—or challenge—a dominant political coalition therefore predicate their strategies on how the building blocks of political power are arranged in New York City. Conceptually, three aspects are particularly important: first, how formal authority and informal influence are distributed within the local state; second, how the electorate has been shaped by the political party system; and third, how the quasi-public and private interests that control the private resources necessary for winning elections and implementing governmental decisions are organized. Political actors who seek to form a dominant coalition must interact with three sets of interests: public sector producer interests associated with government, constituency interests associated with the local political system, and business interests associated with the local economy.

It is hardly surprising that the institutional arrangements in these three domains do not have a neutral or democratizing impact on the competition for political power. Despite the city's liberal tradition and the preponderance of minority groups in its population, the organization of New York's political system favored the establishment of a conservative dominant coalition rather than a renewed, biracial, liberal coalition during the decade of economic boom after 1977.

Political Authority and Public Sector Producer Interests

The Organization of Formal Authority

By all accounts, New York's governmental and political institutions are stronger and more centralized and the associated public sector producer interests better organized and more entrenched than in most other cities. New York City's government is certainly larger, broader, and more expensive than that of any other city in the United States.[5] It has the largest city budget in absolute terms, exceeding those of all other governmental entities except the federal government and the states of California and New York. Except for Washington, D.C., it spends several times more per capita than any other city. It operates more services and exercises a broader range of regulatory powers, including, until it recently shifted to the state, extensive rent regulation.[6] Whatever limits capital mobility might place on the power of local government to tax, to regulate, and to redistribute, New York City government appears not only to have approached those limits but to have persistently moved them outward.

Formal authority over these governmental capacities is highly centralized. In contrast to Los Angeles or Chicago, county government does not exist as a distinct level. The mayor of New York directly oversees all city agencies and strongly influences key nonmayoral agencies like the Board of Education, the Housing Authority, and the Health and Hospitals Corporation.[7]

The governor also wields influence through the state budget, the Financial Control Board, the Urban Development Corporation, and his appointments to the Port Authority and Metropolitan Transportation Authority boards. Since the state contributes one-fifth of the city budget and regulates most city agencies, Albany is an important arena of city politics. The revenue boom of the 1980s lessened the city's reliance on Albany, however, and restored the mayor's relative power.

One person obviously cannot control the vast array of functions in New York City, nor has New York repealed the bureaucratic axiom that departments seek autonomy from executive control. Yet New York stands at the centralized end of the continuum of executive influence over city government operations. The mayor's authority is enhanced by a system of deputy mayors, the Office of Operations that serves the first deputy mayor, the Office of Management and Budget, and the financial information system installed after the fiscal crisis that gives it an unusually good grasp over agency expenditures.[8]

Each function of city government has strong producer interests associated with it; to varying degrees, these interests contend with the mayor to shape agency work practices and policy outputs. Sayre and Kaufman termed "the organized bureaucracies" major forces in their domains, deeply influencing service recipients and community-based service-delivery organizations. (In a few instances, the consumers of a given agency's services are also organized, but they are quite weak relative to producer interests.) To be effective, the mayor and his or her allies in the dominant coalition must reach an accommodation with these producer interests. Producer interests include city workers organized through municipal employee unions and a vast network of private, nonprofit service providers funded by city government. (For example, much of New York City's locally financed $5.2 billion housing development program flows through community-based development organizations.) Just as when Sayre and Kaufman completed their study in 1960, these interests closely guard the "stakes and prizes" associated with the $29 billion city budget.[9]

New York City's charter framework does provide other centers of power with which the mayor must also contend. Until 1989, the Board of Estimate provided the primary counterweight to the mayor's power. The 1902 Charter established this unique body to give the other boroughs more influence relative to Manhattan. As a legislative body, the board adopted the city budget and made other vital decisions concerning zoning and planning, the purchase and disposition of city property, and the granting of municipal franchises. As a "cabinet" of the city's most important executive officers, the board also approved all city contracts over $10,000. Since the 1940s, it largely eclipsed the city council.

Members of the Board of Estimate included the five borough presidents, each casting one vote, and the mayor, comptroller, and city council president, each of whom cast two votes. The three citywide officials could thus in theory outvote the more parochial borough presidents. Although the mayor could not vote on the budget, the board could only decrease his spending proposals, not add to them. (The council president has no power in the council but serves only as an ombudsman and in-house critic whose leverage derives only from possessing votes on the board.)

While the mayor traditionally won board votes with little opposition, reciprocity among the borough presidents gave them considerable influence over borough-specific matters.[10] Moreover, mayors granted concessions to the borough presidents to win their acquiescence in major decisions or for the award of large contracts. Since the borough presidents were usually also the county Democratic party leaders or were close to them, the board was a key point of access to patronage for the county Democratic party organizations.[11]

In 1989, pursuant to a U.S. Supreme Court determination that the Board of Estimate violated the principal of one person, one vote, because Staten Island had the same weight as much more populous Brooklyn, the voters adopted a charter revision that abolished the board. Subsequently, the legislative center of gravity shifted to the city council, which former council member Robert Wagner, Jr., once called "worse than a rubber stamp because it leaves no impression." Borough presidents and the city council president lost much of their legislative influence along the way.

Like the borough presidents, most city council members are closely associated with the "regular" county Democratic party organizations. As Sayre and Kaufman pointed out decades ago, regular party influence on who wins an office increases as the size of its constituency decreases.[12] Though six blacks and three Latinos sat among the council's thirty-five members during the latter 1980s, they did not constitute an insurgent group; five of the blacks and all the Latinos were closely associated with their respective county organizations. Their votes followed their county leaders' direction in the closely contested race that put the council's current leadership in place.[13]

The council has traditionally adopted rules that place considerable power in the hands of its majority leader (now called the speaker). The incumbent in 1991, Peter Vallone, achieved this position as the result of the last major political deal engineered by Bronx county leader Stanley Friedman and Queens county leader (and borough president) Donald Manes before their downfall in the political scandals of 1986.[14] Thus, though the power of the borough presidents has receded, the regular Democratic party county organizations continue to exercise influence through the city council even when a black Manhattanite elected with support from white reformers holds the mayoralty. As he did with the Board of Estimate, the mayor exercises the initiative in framing major decisions for the city council and commands many rewards and sanctions that can be used to secure its assent.

Four distinct producer interests can be associated with city government. These include the organized public employees (stratified by civil service classification, agency, and the union that represents them); the private organizations that deliver public services under contract to city government (stratified by such categories as agency, function, and size); the investment bankers who float the city's short-term notes and long-term bonds; and finally, the political party organizations and elected officials who constitute a permanent part of local government.

The Organized Civil Service

The City of New York employs a quarter of a million people and the nonmayoral agencies several hundred thousand more. All are represented by public employee unions and have a fee deducted from their paychecks whether or not they are members. This has made city unions—particularly District Council 37 of the American Federation of State, County, and Municipal Employees (AFSCME, an amalgam of locals that represent a wide variety of rank-and-file city workers), the United Federation of Teachers (UFT, city school teachers), and Teamsters Local 237 (housing authority workers)—private potent forces.

At the beginning of their development, public employee unions sought to wrest control of public employment away from party influence and sought to exert their own political independence. Over time, however, they have generally used their considerable political resources to influence elected officials and make them responsive to union objectives. As a result, they have come to support the political establishment, not to challenge it.[15] Public employee unions seek to play a major role in the campaigns of legislators who are in a position to hurt or advance their interests. Unions like District Council 37, AFCSME, Teamsters Local 237, the UFT, and Local 1199 of the hospital workers make substantial campaign contributions and provide such valuable campaign resources as volunteers, phone banks, public opinion polling, mailings, and bringing their members to the polls. In return, city workers expect and have received generally favorable treatment at the bargaining table. City unions even managed to trade staff reductions for security for senior employees and maintenance of wage levels during the fiscal crisis.[16]

During the 1970s and most of the 1980s, even though their membership was increasingly black and Latino, whites led these unions. These leaders were not inclined to support insurgent minority candidates, especially when the chances of the minority candidates were slim. The advent of minority leaders for District Council 37 and Local 1199 in the latter 1980s made these unions more open to supporting a minority challenger. In the 1980s, the primary goal of public employee unions was to win labor settlements that would exceed inflation and restore the losses of earning power city workers incurred during the fiscal crisis. They lobbied the state legislature and city council for these goals, improved their political action capabilities, and provided campaign assistance to key legislators and legislative leaders to improve their leverage. Over time, mayors, agency heads, and other elected officials came to rely on public unions for this support, particularly for help in increasing state aid to the city.

City Contractors

New York City government directly provides such core services as police and fire protection, schooling, sanitation, park maintenance, and road building. For other functions, especially social services, it relies heavily on third-party providers. The Health and Hospitals Corporation uses affiliations contracts with the city's teaching hospitals to staff the municipal hospitals. The Human Resources Administration funds private, nonprofit social service agencies to provide most client services (though it directly administers the Aid to Families with Dependent Children system). The Housing Preservation and Development Department uses private, nonprofit organizations to build housing. Private contractors build projects funded by the city's capital budget. As Chapter Six will show in greater detail, the city had spent about 25 percent of its annual budget, or over $6 billion, on purchasing goods and services from private contractors by the late 1980s, of which $2 billion was spent on a no-bid basis. Of the total, $3.2 billion bought capital construction and office equipment, $168 million purchased professional services, and $1.8 billion funded program operations.[17]

These funds were important to the large, varied, and rapidly growing nonprofit social services sector of New York City's economy, including such institutions as hospitals, social service agencies, and private universities. An Urban Institute study estimated that the region's nonprofits (of which 77 percent were located in the city) spent $16.5 billion and employed 351,000 people in 1982. In the aggregate, they receive roughly 40 percent of their financial support from various levels of government. Indeed, unlike the other jurisdictions studied by the Urban Institute, local government contributions to nonprofits in New York City grew rather than declined at the outset of the Reagan administration.[18]

Needless to say, these nonprofit service providers and the constituencies they serve have an agenda for how government should go about its business and which elected officials are most responsive to that agenda. While local elected officials have sought to use government funding of these organizations as a form of "new patronage," the groups in turn have made their policy interests known through performing advocacy work in the relevant issue networks, organizing workers and clients to press for more funding, and participating in political campaigns. Community organizations across New York City have become so reliant on city funds that they have heavily blurred the line between service consumers and service producers; frequently, they have become service providers, not organizers of collective actions.

Investment Bankers

In the late 1980s, New York City issued about $5 billion worth of long-term bonds annually to finance its capital program, as well as lesser amounts of seasonal notes that provide working capital for the city's expense budget. In addition, the city's water and sewer authority and other city-related agencies issued substantial amounts of their own debt. As a result, New York City constitutes a major fraction of the national market for municipal debt; New York City in turn is home to the nation's largest concentration of the investment banks that underwrite public debt.

Investment bankers who advise the city about selling its debt and the investment banks that underwrite it make substantial fees from this activity. Since these fees are based on volume, the city's investment bankers have a stake in an increasing capital budget, just as city employees and nonprofit service-delivery organizations have a stake in increasing the expense budget. To get a local issuing authority's business, investment bankers typically make large political contributions to the campaigns of politicians who are in a position to influence the award of business. In New York, investment bankers have been a primary source of campaign financing for the mayor and comptroller, who have the strongest influence on choosing the city's investment advisers and underwriters.

The Party Organizations

Though in theory one should distinguish between the government and the political party system, in practice New York City's political parties have become an integral part of government, highly dependent on it for their financing and other political resources. Although five parties have ballot lines (Democrat, Republican, Liberal, Conservative, and Right to Life), the predominance of Democratic party registration means New York has many characteristics of a one-party political system. (Seventy percent of the voters register as Democrats; among the remainder, those who decline to state a party preference outnumber Republicans.) Barring a split among Democrats, their nominees generally win elections. Only the Democrats have a citywide apparatus of assembly district clubs, assembly district (AD) leaders, and county party organizations.[19]

The city's sixty ADs are like wards; each elects a male and female district leader. In each county, the district leaders elect a county leader, or "boss."[20] The county organization recognizes and rewards clubs associated with district leaders who supported the county leader's election. Especially outside Manhattan, the organization exercises considerable control over access to such elected offices as judgeships, the state assembly, the state senate, the city council, the borough presidencies, and even the U.S. Congress. Elected officials in turn constitute the leadership cadre of the county party organizations.

The city's sixty ADs, with an average 1980 population of 118,000, were designed to have a predominant racial or ethnic composition. During the 1980s, thirteen ADs had a black majority, three had a Latino majority (two more were close to 50 percent), and blacks and Latinos together outnumbered whites in five other ADs, for a total of twenty-four minority ADs. The thirty-six majority-white ADs also generally contained a preponderant group, ranging from the cosmopolitan white liberal ADs of Manhattan to the more conservative and religiously observant Jewish and white Catholic (Italian or Irish) ADs of the outer boroughs (OB). (White ethnic groups were, however, far less segregated from each other than both were from blacks.) While all ADs contained some variation in racial and ethnic makeup, the relatively high degree of segregation, incumbents' desire to concentrate their ethnic base, and the regular organizations' desire to concentrate minority voters ensured that most ADs had a predominant racial/ethnic character. For subsequent analysis here, the ADs have been classified according to their dominant group.[21] Map 4.1 shows the geographic distribution of these racial and ethnic concentrations.

While the Democratic party prevails in New York City politics, its internal structure is highly fragmented and, for some constituencies, even disorganizing. Each borough has its own party rules, identity, political dynamics, and county leader. Joint action among the five county party leaders has been the exception, not the rule. And as V. O. Key noted in his study of southern politics, one-party systems promote factions. Key argued that the factions in a one-party system do a poor job of articulating political differences compared to what would happen in a multiparty system. As in the South of Key's time, the politics of factions in New York tends to be fluid, personality-oriented, and based on invidious racial, ethnic, or status distinctions; issues are often driven out.[22]

Most observers would agree that the grass-roots organizational base of New York's political parties has decayed.[23] Evidence to support this view may be found in the weakness of the regular Democratic political clubs compared to the 1920s or even the 1950s. They are fewer, have smaller and more elderly memberships, no longer provide the sole access to political careers, and play a smaller role in citywide political campaigns.[24] Even races for the state assembly or the city council, where regular clubs have the most influence, have become more centered on candidates and campaigns.

It cannot be denied that reform movements have been the motor of change in New York City's political system. The periodic challenges that defector insiders and outside reformers have intermittently mounted against the regular Democratic party organization or "the machine" constitute a central theme in the city's political development.[25] Commenting on this tendency, Sayre and Kaufman wrote that "the specter of a 'split' haunts the Democrats at every mayoral election."[26] Before the 1970s, this "specter" formed around the Republican party in fusion with the American Labor party or, later, the Liberal party. These periods of reform introduced a stronger civil service, a more centralized administration, and other elements of the good-government platform.

It does not follow, however, that regular party organizations no longer have a major influence on the city's political system or that white liberal reformers do. New York City partakes strongly of the Eastern urban political culture of "regular" partisanship.[27] To use Wolfinger's distinction, while New York lacks a political machine, it still practices machine politics.[28] While they have much less influence over who wins the mayoralty

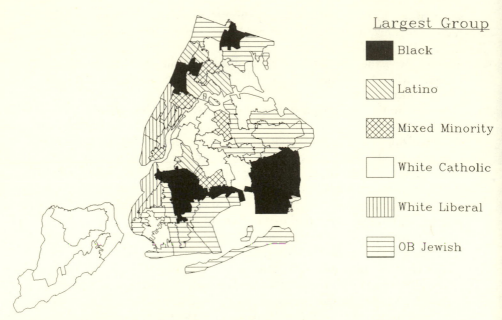

Largest Group

■ Black

▧ Latino

▨ Mixed Minority

☐ White Catholic

▥ White Liberal

▤ OB Jewish

Map 4.1. Ethnic Makeup of ADs

than they once did, candidates supported by the Bronx, Queens, Brooklyn, and Staten Island organizations typically win elections for lesser
offices and can absorb most of the few insurgents who win elections
against them.[29] Indeed, a new generation of leaders rebuilt these county
organizations during the 1980s. And as Theodore Lowi and Martin
Shefter have pointed out, the victorious white reform coalitions contained
so many disparate and conflicting elements that they quickly lost power
to the Democratic regulars.[30]

Reform clubs exist in roughly twenty-five ADs, but the first column in
Table 4.1 shows that they controlled only six ADs in 1988, and the second column shows that they elected one of the two district leaders in ten
others.[31] White reform strength has been centered in Greenwich Village,
Clinton, and the Upper West Side in Manhattan and Brooklyn Heights
and Park Slope in Brooklyn, where large numbers of cosmopolitan, white,
liberal voters live. (Map 4.2 shows the areas of reform and regular control.) Black reformers took hold only in the Bedford-Stuyvesant, Ft.
Greene, and Crown Heights areas of Brooklyn. As a result, reform clubs
have historically influenced the election of the county leader only in Manhattan.[32] From their base in Manhattan and with their ties to business, the
professions, and opinion-shaping institutions, white reformers have had
a major impact on competition for the mayoralty and other citywide

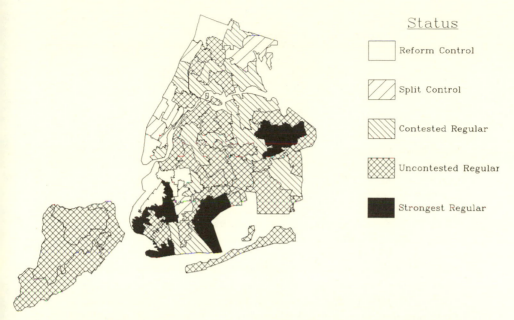

Status

Reform Control

Split Control

Contested Regular

Uncontested Regular

Strongest Regular

Map 4.2. Reform/Regular Control

offices since the 1960s, but their influence over lesser offices has been limited.

Regular clubs function in all but four of the city's ADs. As Table 4.1 indicates, they hold all the district leaderships in two-thirds of New York City's ADs. They control all the Latino ADs and most of the black ADs, but the strongest regular clubs are located in the Jewish and Catholic neighborhoods of the outer boroughs, such as Canarsie. Regulars thus select the county leader in the boroughs beside Manhattan.

Regular clubs have never been agents of political mobilization, whether one considers the 1920s, 1950s, or 1980s. Regular clubs do not seek to register new voters or turn them out in primaries. They rely instead on the "general nonparticipation of the public" to enable "a relatively small number of dependable followers" to control political outcomes.[33] Regular organizations also use New York State's highly complex election law to control access to elected office. Clubs and county organizations specialize in election law and petition filing. By challenging the petitions of insurgent candidates, they have knocked many of them off the ballot.[34] One expert estimated that New York generated half of all election-law cases in the country.[35] While well-financed insurgent candidates sometimes win lesser offices without club endorsement, clubs provide their candidates with enough resources to prevail over opponents

TABLE 4.1
Reform/Regular Control by AD Type (ca. 1988)

AD Type	Reform Control	Split Control	Contested Regular Control	Uncontested Regular Control	Strong Clubs	Total
Black	2	2	2	6	1	13
Minority	0	1	1	3	0	5
Latino	0	0	1	3	1	5
White Liberal	4	5	0	0	0	9
White Catholic	0	1	1	11	2	15
Outer-borough Jewish	0	1	3	4	5	13
Total	6	10	8	27	9	60

Source: Board of Elections and Expert Consensus.

who lack this support. The result is persistent, regular influence over lower-level elected offices.

The regular organizations have succeeded in "nationalizing" their campaign activities and patronage resources. Instead of seeking private contributions to fund campaigns as in the past, party campaign workers have moved directly onto the public budget, for example as legislative staff members.[36] Legislators' district offices have taken over many of the service functions once performed by clubs and district leaders. This has strengthened the power of elected officials relative to district and county leaders within the party organization and contributed to the erosion of the clubhouses.[37] But it has also reinforced the influence of the regular Democratic organizations.

While still controlling access to some public and private sector jobs, elected officials associated with regular organizations have also developed great influence over how city government contracts are awarded. The rise of state and city funding of community-based organizations to deliver social services has also created a "new patronage." Political sponsors (whether legislators or the mayor) determine the overall funding level for programs upon which community organizations rely and decide which groups will get the contracts. In some cases, the mayor takes the lead while legislators seek to influence his choices; in other cases, legislators appropriate funds directly as "member items." While neither the mayor nor legislators typically require recipient organizations to perform explicit political duties in order to get contracts, many leaders of recipient organizations belong to political clubs, and most let their clients know which politicians were supportive.[38]

The Electorate, Party Organization, and
Interest Representation

Those who would form a dominant coalition must first win elections for the mayoralty. To do so, they must work with the basic constituencies that make up the electorate as they have been shaped and organized over time by the institutional arrangements that characterize New York City's political system. The active electorate is a highly selective subset of the city's population, not a demographically representative sample. The constituencies into which it has been divided, and cleavages among them, have been fashioned not simply by demographic change but by the local political parties and the system of political competition.

Composition of the Electorate

Race and a complex of ethnicity and religion, not class, define the basic constituencies of the city's electorate.[39] As the previous chapter argued, the city's population was built up out of a succession of migratory streams. The earliest of these streams, those of Anglo-American, German, and especially Irish ancestry, came to dominate Democratic party politics during the middle and latter parts of the nineteenth century. Subsequent groups, including Italians and central European Jews at the turn of the century and blacks and Puerto Ricans after World War II, contested the earlier groups for entry into, and ultimately control over, the regular Democratic party county organizations and the offices to which they controlled access.

At first, these organizations tended not to recruit from rising demographic constituencies and not to promote them up through the ranks. When rising constituencies threatened to swell the vote for the Republicans or socialists, however, the Democratic regulars generally moved to install and promote friendly leaders from these groups, thereby incorporating them. In this process, the Democratic party organizations adapted to, benefited from, and tended to reinforce racial/ethnic as opposed to class-based political identities. The shorthand analysis of New York City politics is thus based on such categories as "Catholic" or "Italian," "Jewish," "Black," and "Puerto Rican."

In the early part of the post–World War II period, when minorities constituted a relatively small fraction of the electorate, the primary ethnic competition took place between white Catholics (the Irish and the Italians), associated with the regular organization, and Jewish candidates, more likely to be associated with reform campaigns. In this environment, Jewish candidates—and indeed reform Republicans like LaGuardia or Lindsay—could seek to consolidate a coalition of Jewish, black, and Puerto Rican voters to create an electoral majority. As time passed, however, the racial balance began to shift against whites and, beginning in the late 1960s, blacks and Puerto Ricans began to challenge their political subordination. This shifted the basic cleavage from ethnicity to race and led white Catholics and Jews to coalesce with each other in the late 1970s to retain an electoral majority.

While the demographic trends described in the previous chapter substantially altered the meaning of these categories and the composition of the city's electorate after 1970, they did not erase the white majority in the electorate. Whites declined from 63 percent of the city's total population in 1970 to 43 percent in 1990. Table 4.2 shows that they declined even further in the city's mayoral general electorate, from 79 percent in 1969 to 56 percent in 1989. Thus even though the excess of registration over population for whites shrank from 16 percentage points to 13 points, and despite the decline of the white population, they remained an absolute majority of the city's general electorate.

In this context, racially polarized voting would ensure the victory of a white candidate; even if a minority candidate could count on all black, Latino, and Asian votes (by no means guaranteed), he or she would have had to attract a significant fraction of white support to win. African-American and Puerto Rican candidates would, in other words, face major challenges in building electoral majorities for citywide offices, while racial polarization might work to the benefit of white candidates, especially if they could appeal to Puerto Rican voters.

This picture is complicated, however, by the great differences between the two most important electorates in New York City, the Democratic primary electorate and the general election electorate. Three million of

TABLE 4.2
The Makeup of the New York City Mayoral General Electorate, 1969 and 1989

	1969 Voters	1989 Voters
Non-Latino whites	79%	56%
Catholic	43%	24%
Jewish	30%	18%
Non-Latino blacks	15%	28%
Latinos	6%	13%
Others	—	3%
Total	100%	100%

Sources: 1969 Louis Harris Associates Exit Poll; 1989 New York Times/WCBS Exit Poll; Sampling error +/− 4 points.

New York's 5.6 million voting age residents were registered in 1991. Two-thirds of this number registered as Democrats. Those declining to state a party preference comprised the next largest group, 15 percent of the total, while Republicans enrolled only 14 percent. The tiny Liberal and Conservative parties attracted less than 1 percent each.

From a national perspective, the two million or more New York City voters who cast ballots in presidential general elections have considerable importance.[40] (Over 2.3 million voted in 1984 and 1.9 million in 1988, down from the 3 million votes cast in 1960.) They often determine how New York casts its large supply of votes in the electoral college. If Democrats can roll up large margins in the city, they can win the state. Republicans draw more general election votes in New York City than their registration would suggest; Ronald Reagan took almost 40 percent of the vote in 1984. But the mobilization of New York City's hard-core Democrats can still swing the state in one direction or the other. Those who cast ballots in general elections are whiter, older, and better off than registered voters as a whole.

A second, far smaller electorate is crucial to power in New York City, however: the seven hundred thousand or so voters who regularly cast ballots in Democratic primaries.[41] Democrats who seek to capture City Hall must win at least a 40 percent plurality of this electorate.[42] The primary electorate is only one-third the size of the presidential general electorate. (Only 688,000 voters, or 37 percent of the registered Democrats, participated in the 1985 mayoral primary in which Edward Koch overwhelmingly defeated his black and white liberal challengers; only 749,000 cast votes in the hotly contested 1982 gubernatorial primary that Koch lost to Mario Cuomo.) Because blacks and Latinos are more likely than whites to register as Democrats and because Democratic primaries tend to offer black or Latino candidates, the Democratic primary electorate contains more blacks and Latinos and fewer whites, compared to the general electorate.

From 1960 to the mid-1970s, the Democratic primary electorate was remarkably stable at about 750,000 voters. The hotly contested 1977 primary in which Mayor Koch emerged against other Jewish, Italian, black, and Puerto Rican candidates drew an exceptionally large 910,000 votes. By contrast, the 1981 and 1985 races in which he was reelected drew exceptionally small numbers: 578,000 in 1981 and a more typical but still low 688,000 in 1985. Except for 1977, turnout hovered around one-third of the registered voters.

At first glance, the tabulation of votes cast by ADs classified according to their racial makeup (presented in Table 4.3) bears out the received wisdom that minority groups do not vote. Predominantly minority ADs cast only a third of the votes in the 1984 presidential general election and

TABLE 4.3
Votes Cast and Turnout by AD Type (1984 Presidential General
and 1985 Mayoral Primary elections)

AD Type (Number)	11/84 Presidential		4/85 Mayoral Primary	
	Vote	Turnout	Vote	Turnout
Black (13)	420,569	70.0%	129,464	26.8%
Mixed minority (5)	153,106	68.8%	54,131	30.6%
Latino (5)	152,051	69.7%	55,353	31.6%
White Liberal (9)	474,175	82.2%	134,334	36.7%
White Catholic (15)	564,566	81.4%	135,122	31.4%
Outer-borough Jewish (13)	571,003	81.3%	180,150	37.4%
Total (60)	2,335,470	77.5%	688,553	32.6%

Source: NYC Board of Elections; turnout based on total and Democratic registration as
of May 1985.

only slightly more in the 1985 Democratic mayoral primary. Under these
conditions, an African-American candidate could win a citywide election
only with substantial white support. Even if she or he could attract every
minority vote, the candidate would still need a quarter of the white votes,
a level of white support that no other minority candidate beside Tom
Bradley of Los Angeles had ever won before 1989 in a first-time race
against a white opponent anywhere in the nation.

While one might assume that lower incomes, less education, and less
political efficacy account for the lower registration and turnout in minority ADs, Table 4.4 suggests that this is not so.[43] Once the AD population
is adjusted for the proportion that is of voting age (VPOP) and holds
citizenship (adjusted voting-age population [AVPOP]), it turns out that in
1985 black and Latino ADs actually had rates of registration comparable
to outer-borough Jewish and white Catholic ADs, despite their lower socioeconomic status! Indeed, black ADs, with 66.3 percent registered, had
a higher rate of eligible voters registered than did white Catholic ADs,
with only 57.7 percent registered. (Even Latino ADs, the poorest of all on
average, did better than white Catholic ADs on this score.)

These findings squarely counter the stereotype that minorities do not
register. Low minority registration in New York is a product of the relative youth and lack of citizenship among New York's black and Latino
residents, not a lack of political mobilization. In fact, the voter-registration campaigns conducted to promote Jesse Jackson's candidacy in the
1984 presidential primary produced substantial registration gains in
black and Latino ADs.[44]

While all ADs started out with nearly the same total 1980 population,
the minority ADs had about one-sixth fewer *eligible* residents. The sec-

TABLE 4.4
Population, Eligibility, and Registration, and Turnout by AD
Racial Composition in New York City

AD Type	Mean 1980 Population	Mean Voting-Age Population	Mean Citizen Rate	Adjusted 1980 VPOP	September 1985 Mean Total Registered	Registered AVPOP
Black	117,756	69.2%	85.6%	69,753	46,241	66.3%
Mixed minority	118,090	68.0%	86.6%	69,541	44,535	64.0%
Latino	117,566	66.4%	89.0%	69,477	43,611	62.8%
White liberal	118,627	84.9%	89.4%	90,039	62,928	69.9%
White Catholic	117,750	75.7%	89.0%	79,332	45,773	57.7%
Outer-borough Jewish	117,586	78.7%	91.3%	84,489	54,038	64.0%
Total	117,861	75.1%	88.6%	78,423	50,241	64.1%

Source: 1980 Census STF4(A) grouped by AD; New York City Board of Elections.

ond and third columns of Table 4.4 indicate that blacks and Latinos are both younger and less likely to be citizens than the white population. Roughly 85 percent of the population in the white liberal Manhattan ADs were old enough to vote in 1980, while only 69 percent of the black population and 66 percent of the Latino population had attained that age.

The minority ADs also contain many more foreign-born people who have not become citizens than the white ADs. While one of seven persons in the black ADs told the 1980 census that she or he was not a citizen, only one of ten did in the white ADs. In a 1988 CUNY survey, only 36 percent of foreign-born blacks and 38 percent of foreign-born Latinos of voting age who had lived in the United States five or more years reported they had become citizens.[45] While Puerto Ricans are citizens, more than half the city's Latinos are immigrants from such places as the Dominican Republic and Colombia, no more than a third of whom are probably citizens; the citizenship figure for Latino ADs may actually be much lower than given in Table 4.4, perhaps 75 percent.[46] This would mean that the Latino registration rate for eligible voters is even higher than Table 4.4 indicates. In any case, it is clear that youth and lack of citizenship substantially diminished the black and Latino vote, but that these populations are surprisingly well mobilized.

Registration does not always translate into votes, however. As we shall see, the presence or absence of charismatic black or Latino candidate has a strong impact on black or Latino political mobilization. The 1985 mayoral primary presented minority voters with an exceedingly weak black candidate, Assemblyman Herman "Denny" Farrell, who elicited little in-

terest even in black ADs; in fact, they produced the lowest average number of votes and lowest turnout rate in the city. (Latino AD turnout exceeded black and minority AD turnout because three Puerto Ricans ran
for city council president in 1985.) In 1988 and 1989, by contrast, the size
of the black vote and black turnout broke out of past patterns. Latino
turnout continued to lag far behind.

The nostrum that "minority groups don't vote" is thus a half truth.
New York City's black and Latino residents cast far fewer votes than do
its whites, but this happens because they are younger and less likely to be
citizens and because the ballot has tended not to offer them attractive
candidates. This lack of eligible numbers has been partly offset, however,
because blacks and Latinos were more likely than whites to register as
Democrats. Table 4.5 shows that this tendency means that blacks are
actually better represented among registered Democrats than in the voting-age population as a whole; Latinos are far less underrepresented
among Democrats than among registered voters as a whole.

While the increasing black and Latino share of Democratic primary
registration during the 1980s constituted a potential advantage in the
competition for City Hall, the Democratic party tended to demobilize
blacks and Latinos in the late 1970s and most of the 1980s. Barriers to
eligibility (youth and lack of citizenship), the influence of regular party
organizations in minority ADs, the disinclination of incumbents to mobilize new and possibly destabilizing voters, and the failure to offer attractive black or Latino citywide candidates all helped to stratify political
participation and representation. Whites constituted only 58 percent of
the city's voting-age population in 1980 and 48 percent in 1990, yet until
1989 whites held the mayoralty, 82 percent of the votes on the Board of

TABLE 4.5
The Demography of the New York City Electorate, 1990

| | Latino | Non-Latino | | | Total Number (in millions) |
		Black	White	Asian	
In population (18 and above)	22.0%	23.4%	47.9%	6.7%	5.64
Registered to vote	14.8%	27.1%	56.4%	1.7%	3.02
Registered Democrats	15.9%	36.3%	44.4%	1.4%	2.11

Source: 1990 Census for population and New York City Districting Commission counts
of Latino and Asian total and Democratic registration and estimates of white and black
voting-age population.

Estimate, 74 percent of the city council seats, and 67 percent of the congressional districts.[47]

The Decay of Liberal Reform and of Community Activism

The organization of the city's electorate is only a starting point for analyzing how political actors might seek to organize electoral majorities. Equally important are the ways in which the nature of political competition has influenced how different constituencies got represented. Particularly important trends over the last two decades include the decay of the white liberal reform impulse and the attendant alignment of white Catholics and Jews; emerging divisions within and between the black and Latino political leadership and within their constituencies; and the decay of community organizations into client-serving agencies.

The contemporary white liberal reform movement in New York had its origins in Adlai Stevenson's 1952 presidential campaign.[48] It gathered speed with the onset of the civil rights movement and the fight to defeat Carmine DeSapio's leadership of Tammany Hall, and crested in the antiwar movement and the elections of John V. Lindsay in 1965 and 1969. But by the late 1970s, the civil rights and antiwar "movement liberalism" of young white professionals and the traditional liberalism of older, unionized, blue-collar and lower middle class Jewish constituencies had both atrophied in New York.

To some extent, white liberalism was the victim of its own success. Beginning in 1952 with the inauguration of direct election of district leaders, reformers began to run for that office so as to dislodge the Democratic party establishment in Manhattan.[49] (Ed Koch got his start in politics by running against DeSapio in the latter's attempt to reclaim the Greenwich Village district leadership.) Mayor Robert F. Wagner, after his third-term victory as a newly-minted reformer in 1961, brought many white reformers into his last administration. Mayor John V. Lindsay also sought support from Democratic reformers and appointed many to key positions. Reformers thus became part of the governmental and political establishment.

The absorption of white reformers into the establishment coincided with a broader white reaction against the rise of black and Latino militancy and a consequent polarization of black-white relations in New York City. During the late 1960s, insurgent leaders from black and Latino neighborhoods picked up the direct attack on the party system that white liberals were in the course of abandoning. Given the increasing social base of blacks and Latinos who felt alienated from and poorly represented by the political establishment, these leaders mounted an "assault on the trenches," which included extensive community mobilization and the demand for community control of various institutions.[50] The Lindsay administration sought to blunt, absorb, and tame this assault through the expansion of community-based programs. As Katznelson observed of the period, "At issue was the attempt to take the radical impulse away from the politics of race by the creation of mechanisms of participation at the community level that had the capability to limit conflicts to a community orientation, to separate issues from each other, and to stress a politics of distribution—in short, to reduce race to ethnicity in the traditional community-bounded sense."[51]

In the wake of the racial conflicts of the Lindsay era, many liberal whites, especially Jews, joined then-congressman Edward Koch in moving towards the more defensive, conservative positions already held by those who provided the social base for the regular Democratic clubs. This shift eroded the social base for the liberal reform elite. Important milestones along this path included the police-community review board referendum in 1966, the dispute over community control of the Ocean Hill-Brownsville schools and the United Federation of Teachers strikes in September 1968, the small plurality of Lindsay's reelection in 1969, the racially differential impact of the 1975 fiscal crisis, and the competition between black and Latino candidates in the 1977 mayoral primary in the wake of the blackout looting that had taken place in minority neighborhoods earlier that year.

In 1966, when Mayor Lindsay sought to create a civilian police review board, the Patrolman's Benevolent Association mounted a ballot referendum to counter the proposal. Not only was civilianization of the review board defeated by 63 percent to 36 percent, but the majority of Jews outside Manhattan, especially those in the lower middle class, joined Catholics in the opposition. For the first time, a constituency that had been closely associated with liberalism and reform had swung to join the more conservative base that supported the regular Democratic organizations.[52] Shortly thereafter, the attempt by an experimental black community school board in Brooklyn to remove white teachers led the heavily Jewish, formerly liberal leadership of the United Federation of Teachers to call a strike against their actions; these events generated even more racial polarization and division among former allies.[53] Later, school integration in Canarsie generated picketing by people whom Jonathan Rieder has called "Jews and Italians of Brooklyn against liberalism."[54]

This shift in white liberal and Jewish sentiment registered in successive mayoral elections. In 1969, Lindsay won reelection with a bare 40 percent plurality on the Liberal line, but his two conservative opponents, an Italian-American Democrat, Mario Proccacino, and an Italian-American Republican, John Marchi, amassed almost 60 percent of the vote. As in the 1966 referendum, Jews split, and Lindsay won only 44 percent of their votes.[55] In 1973, the Democratic county leaders united behind Abraham Beame for mayor; he rolled over Herman Badillo in the Democratic primary and then over Republican John Marchi in the general election. White liberals and minority insurgents were obviously not capable of making common cause against him. Nor were they any more able to unite in the 1977 primary that ultimately led to the election of Edward I. Koch.

Simultaneously, the organizational bases around which a reform coalition could be assembled were falling away. New York City's Republican party lost its base in the governor's office and took a rightward turn, paralleling the ascent of Ronald Reagan in national politics. This ideological shift closed it to the discontented elements of the city electorate that in the past it had united into potent, if short-lived, fusion movements. The Liberal party weakened as its Jewish garment-worker social base disappeared, and the local Republican party also shifted in a conservative direction. By the late 1970s, therefore, white liberals had neither the political incentive nor the organizational framework needed to challenge the political establishment of which they had become a part.

Growing divisions among black and Latino elected leaders had a similar effect.[56] While the Democratic party's dominance enhanced the potential for minority electoral influence, splits among black and Latino leaders tended to negate this potential. Black insurgents not only prompted formerly liberal white constituencies to move towards the right, they also increased competition among black elected officials by challenging the black elected officials who had been absorbed into or were the product of regular political clubs.

In Harlem, regulars like J. Raymond Jones and his lineal descendants adopted some of the rhetoric of militant opposition while retaining influence over elected office. Jones defended Adam Clayton Powell in the late 1950s when DeSapio sought to oust Powell; when Robert Wagner sought to run for a third term in 1961 as a reformer against the county leaders who had previously supported him, Jones provided crucial organizational support.[57] Jones went on to be elected to the city council in 1963 and, despite initial resistance from white reformers and Mayor Wagner, became leader of Tammany Hall, the Manhattan regular Democratic county organization, in 1964. Though Jones retired in 1969, he mentored such figures as Congressman Charles Rangel, former assemblyman Percy Sutton, and mayor-to-be David N. Dinkins. Despite persistent factionalism, elected officials associated with regular clubs continue to hold sway in Harlem. With one or two exceptions, the regular organization has exercised a similar influence over black elected leadership in Queens.

In Brooklyn, a more independent black political leadership managed to challenge and displace machine-oriented black elected officials beginning in 1974 when Al Vann, who had presided over the Afro-American Teachers Association and had been assistant principal of Public School 271 during the Ocean Hill-Brownsville confrontations in 1968, was elected to represent Bedford-Stuyvesant in the state assembly. Candidates associated with the organization led by Vann, the Coalition for Community Empowerment (CCE), subsequently won adjacent assembly seats in Ft. Greene and Crown Heights, the state senate seat representing Bedford-Stuyvesant/Ft. Greene, and the 12th congressional district, covering Bed-Stuy, Crown Heights, and East Flatbush.[58] Congressman Major Owens, a former Brownsville librarian who had designed the area's community action program, had directed the poverty program in the Lindsay administration before becoming state senator. Assemblyman William Boyland had been an organizer for District 1199 of the hospital workers and was a member of the citywide Council Against Poverty (CAP) board in the 1970s. Assemblyman Roger Green was involved in Vann's Vannguard Improvement Association, a service organization, in the early 1970s; his father and brother had been active in the Brooklyn civil rights movement. Assemblyman Clarence Norman's father was a well-known pastor and civil rights activist in Crown Heights.[59]

The CCE's effort to represent all of black Brooklyn began to fall apart in the mid-1980's, however. When Brooklyn Democratic county leader Meade Esposito resigned in January 1984, Vann and his allies were unwilling to unite with regular black district leaders to support a black regular as the new county leader. Given competition between two factions of white regulars, they might have won.[60] In 1985, Vann ran a disastrous race for the borough presidency against white candidates from the two competing wings of the county regular organization, Borough President Howard Golden and State Senator Marty Markowitz. This split should have given Vann a good shot, but he finished a poor third. Candidates associated with the CCE also ran poorly against black regular incumbents in three city council races.

Over time, the instinct for self-preservation and the desire for legislative advancement led many insurgent minority elected officials to make peace with the regular Democratic organizations. Redistricting played a part as well: minority legislators preferred certain victory in districts where their constituencies were highly concentrated rather than having to mobilize their followers in a more competitive situation. This reinforced the low black and Latino turnout rates.[61]

Geography and political orientation thus divided New York's black political leadership during the 1970s and most of the 1980s. The Harlem regular establishment sought to preserve its influence against the new center of more nationalist, protest-oriented leaders in Brooklyn, who in turn contended with black regulars associated with the Brooklyn county organization. Over time, even the Brooklyn insurgents gradually became absorbed by the Democratic leadership of the state assembly, which in turn was an integral part of the Brooklyn regular organization.

The Puerto Rican political leadership appears to have been even more highly fragmented and more closely aligned with the regular Democratic county organizations than was true of blacks.[62] The overwhelming majority of Puerto Ricans feel that Puerto Rican elected officials are "more interested in their own careers than in serving the community."[63] Few Puerto Rican leaders have emerged with citywide followings, and borough-based leaders do not appear to cooperate with one another.

Just as importantly, differences of ancestry and nativity also divide both blacks and Latinos. Puerto Ricans are the single largest ancestry group among Latinos, but their numbers are declining relative to immigrant groups, especially Dominicans. Blacks of West Indian nativity or ancestry also distinguish themselves from the native born. These nativity groups occupy significantly different economic and occupational niches and have significantly different political outlooks. Finally, although most black and Latino ADs have elected men, women account for as much as two-thirds of the consistent Democratic voters in these areas.

The fragmentation within the leadership strata and mass bases of the two groups has been reinforced by competition between them. Black and Latino voters do not support candidates of the other background when they have the alternative of voting for their own candidate. When black elected officials sought a consensus minority candidate to challenge Mayor Koch in the 1985 mayoral primary, they refused to support Herman Badillo when no strong black candidate emerged and instead chose a weak black candidate, Denny Farrell.[64] The competition between blacks and Puerto Ricans in the Bronx has enabled a white minority to exercise continued power in the Bronx county organizations.

Finally, the 1970s and 1980s were marked by the progessive decay of the "community revolution" that had taken place in the 1960s.[65] Like white liberals, community activists and community organizations were absorbed into city government during the Lindsay administration and became progressively more reliant on city funding. As the Nixon and Ford administrations sought to prevent the poverty program from undertaking political action nationally, the Beame administration used what remained of New York City's poverty program for patronage purposes. As an increasing fraction of the surviving community organizations sought and gained funding from city government, their mission shifted from advocacy to service and their constituents became clients.[66] New York's community-based service organizations became highly fragmented by geography, client constituency, and programmatic focus. The few citywide coalitions that were established acted only as policy advocates, not as a base for independent electoral politics. Even they have fallen into disarray in the face of federal funding cuts.[67] The extra-party mechanisms that promoted "post-reform" politics in other cities thus failed to have the same effect in New York.

The Interaction of the State and Private Market Interests

Having won office, those who would form a dominant coalition must secure tacit consent, and preferably active support, from those who head institutions that command large supplies of discretionary resources. They need this support for many reasons: to finance election campaigns; to discourage business leaders from supporting challengers; to secure support in the media that shape elite and mass opinion; to achieve cooperation with the coalition's policy initiatives; and to realize the political benefits of these initiatives.

The political leaders who seek to construct a dominant coalition clearly favor private investments that yield increased tax revenues, provide political benefits, and enable them to carry out their policy initiatives. But by far the most immediate and intense connection between political entrepreneurs and private interests is the need for political support. Specifically, they need campaign contributions in order to win elections.

Campaign Finance

Campaigning for citywide office in New York is extremely expensive and has become more so over time. Though public campaign financing was adopted in late 1988, it is not yet clear that it will reverse this trend. In the primary and general elections of 1969 in which John Lindsay edged out his Democratic and Republican challengers, the three spent $3.3 million. In the hotly contested 1977 race, the seven Democrats spent $6.5 million the primary and general elections. In all, the Koch campaign spent $2.1 million, while Cuomo spent $1.8 million. In the 1981 Democratic primary in which Koch firmly established a conservative majority, he spent $1.6 million, while his opponent, Assemblyman Frank Barbaro, spent only $226,000.[68]

Against only slightly more formidable competition in 1985, Mayor Koch raised and spent a startling $7.2 million, or nearly $10 per voter. (Considering that he could target some of this spending only on swing voters, Koch could spend several times that amount attempting to reach his key audience.) Neither of the mayor's two opponents could raise more than a small fraction of this amount; only Carol Bellamy, the runner-up, came anywhere near raising the threshold amount of $1 million or so that campaign experts thought was the minimum required for a credible campaign.

This escalation in the cost of politics stems from the increasing importance of paid media, especially television, as well as the cost of the professional talent needed to mount the tactics of modern campaigning, such as direct mail, phone-bank solicitation, and targeted get-out-the-vote activities. In the first three weeks of August before the September 1985 primary, Mayor Koch's campaign spent $1,184,098, of which $838,000 represented purchases of television and radio advertising.[69] While television advertising is less relevant to lower offices, it is a cost-efficient way to enter voters' homes in citywide races. In an age when people throw junk mail away without opening it, when people will not open their doors to campaign canvassers, and when such canvassers in any case cannot be found, television advertising is practically mandatory.

For similar reasons, lesser offices have also become more expensive to seek. In the 1985 race for Manhattan borough president, David Dinkins raised and spent $1.1 million, while his opponent raised $455,000; the four-way Brooklyn race in which incumbent Howard Golden defeated two white challengers and the CCE's Al Vann, Golden spent $1.1 million, while Vann managed to raise only $168,000. The race for city council president proved even more expensive that year. Because it pitted a wealthy former investment banker and Deputy Mayor Kenneth Lipper against Andrew Stein, the heir to a legal publishing fortune who served as Manhattan borough president, the two leading candidates spent almost $4 million for an office that is generally conceded to have the least power of any of the citywide offices. Even in contested city council seats, candidates have spent in excess of $250,000.[70]

Raising the most money does not always guarantee that a candidate will win. Mario Cuomo raised somewhat more than Edward Koch for the 1977 mayoral primary, while Koch raised more than Cuomo in the 1982 race for governor; yet both lost these elections. Incumbent candidates do not always have to raise large amounts of money when their political position is judged to be unassailable. Nor can money make a contender out of a weak candidate, no matter how much he spends, as demonstrated by Ronald Lauder's failed $13 million effort to become the Republican mayoral nominee in 1989.

Money does flow to candidates who are already perceived to have a good chance in a race, particularly to incumbents. Incumbents generally seek to raise ample funds to deter challenges, ensure reelection, and create a fund from which they can aid allied candidates. For challengers, substantial early money is a crucial ingredient in creating this perception. Thus, while raising the most campaign funds does not always guarantee victory, raising substantial amounts is essential for victory, and the failure to do so is a virtual guarantee of defeat.

Private interests sensitive to government policy and public sector producer interests have taken the lead in providing political money. New York is a "land town" and a "money metropolis."[71] City government regulates the use of the former and is a major force in issuing short- and long-term local debt in the latter. Real estate developers who wish to build large projects, investment bankers who wish to participate in floating New York City's debt, and the lawyers who represent them have been the leading sources of campaign contributions. A host of smaller interests that are regulated by, sell to, or receive financial support from government, ranging from private sector labor unions, garbage carters, and taxi-medallion owners to private, nonprofit hospitals and the city's premiere cultural institutions, also make contributions. Additionally, individual wealthy people who seek access, wish to promote an agenda, or are merely public spirited also make campaign contributions, as do numerous small givers. But they account for a small proportion of the total.

An analysis of leading givers to the candidates in the 1982 Democratic gubernatorial race presents a representative picture. Among those who gave to Mayor Koch were the law firms of Shea & Gould ($15,000), Tufo & Zucotti ($21,000), Stein, Davidoff, Malito, Katz and Hutcher ($7,750), and Fisher & Fisher ($4,100); the public relations powerhouse Howard Rubenstein ($10,625); the investment bank Bear Stearns ($51,100); rental apartment owners (Neighborhood Preservation Political Action Committee, $17,500); the Uniformed Sanitationmen's Association ($5,000); and the Uniformed Firefighters ($5,150). Shea & Gould ($10,000), Bear Stearns ($73,000), and Rubenstein ($7,000) also gave to Mario Cuomo. (Bear Stearns was lead underwriter for the city's bonds.) The United Federation of Teachers gave heavily to Cuomo ($73,000) but nothing to Koch.[72] In the 1985 race for borough president, David Dinkins of Manhattan received 25.5 percent of his funds from businesses, 10.1 percent from labor, and 43.1 percent from individuals, while Brooklyn's Howard Golden received 49.7 percent from businesses, 9.5 percent from labor, and 28.4 percent from individuals.[73]

Thirty years ago, Sayre and Kaufman asserted that "logic would seem to dictate the conclusion that generous donors, given the nature of our economic system, must enjoy great returns on their investments. There is little empirical evidence to support or refute this proposition."[74] They could not say the same today. While it is difficult to pin down exchanges of specific favorable governmental decisions in return for specific contributions, there is an unmistakable pattern of incumbent politicians raising large amounts of money from interests that later receive favorable treatment.

A comprehensive report on campaign contributions to members of the Board of Estimate between 1981 and 1986 by State Senator Franz Leichter's office established that the mayor, the other board members, and the five Democratic county committees raised $30 million. Of the 200 largest contributors, 120 had business before the Board of Estimate or city agencies.[75] Another study by Leichter of contributions to Board of Estimate members in 1984 and 1985 showed that the 166 largest contributors gave $4.25 million of the total $8.5 million raised. Real estate interests accounted for $3 million of that amount, while $1.2 million came from financial institutions (of which $631,000 came from municipal bond underwriters). A substantial amount of this money was contributed while these interests had major items before the Board of Estimate.[76]

Contributions do not always bring forth a quid pro quo. For example, real estate developer Donald Trump was the single largest contributor during the early 1980s, but he and Mayor Koch fell into a highly public squabble. Contributions from a given interest nevertheless clearly enhance its chance of securing collectively favorable policies. A large contribution may not always produce the favorable zoning ruling that an individual developer seeks, but the real estate industry understood that its financial support strengthened a pro-development mayor. And even when contributors do not get all the favorable decisions they desire, they still get access.[77] In a city where many voices clamor to be heard, the ability to get through to senior officials and be heard by them is itself an extremely valuable commodity. Interests with business before or with the city thus view making campaign contributions as an ordinary and necessary cost of doing business—and achieving desired results.

The Political Benefits of Private Investment

The economic and fiscal crises of the mid-1970s dramatically impressed the long-term connection between private investment and public revenues upon the city's elected officials. The recessions of the early 1970s caused city revenues to fall far below the increases in public spending. Fiscal crisis and the collapse of political authority for the sitting government was the inevitable result.

The experience of the fiscal crisis changed the psychology of the city's political leaders, including those who normally favored increased outlays, regarding the need to foster private investment. It also created new institutions, such as the Municipal Assistance Corporation, the Financial Control Board, the Special Deputy State Comptroller, and the Setting Municipal Priorities Project, designed to monitor the relationships between economic trends, revenue receipts, and public expenditures.[78]

The roots of the political system's reliance on private investment go far deeper than its need to collect tax revenues, however. Real estate investments have many divisible benefits that are quite useful to individual elected officials and the agencies that promote them. They show city government can "make things happen." Large projects also generate subcontracts that can be awarded to allies of elected officials. Alternatively, elected officials may require developers to provide amenities to the adjacent communities in return for their support.[79] Finally, senior government administrators frequently go on to serve developers at far greater remuneration than they enjoyed while in public service.

Implementing Government Policy

That the political system benefits from real property investments is a particular case of a more general phenomenon: government relies on private interests to carry out public ends. This stems partly from the government agencies' ability to operate in an environment in which private interests can choose whether to cooperate. For example, the Department of Sanitation must get owners of private vehicles to move them so that it can clean the streets. Indeed, street cleanliness depends more on how litter-producers behave than on how the department manages its cleaning efforts. Public service providers must negotiate a complex maze of well-organized private interests, habits, and behavior patterns to do their business. This is magnified when, as is often the case, government relies on third-party providers to deliver services or seeks to induce private parties, like real estate investors, to carry out the projects that it defines.

The Social Construction of Political Power

The strategies of those who would construct a dominant political coalition in New York City are deeply shaped by the institutional patterns discussed in this chapter. Consider first the nature of New York City government. It constitutes a major prize not simply because it can distribute jobs, contracts, and regulatory favors to individual claimants but because it can redistribute these resources across broad classes of interests. It is a strong government that squeezes a substantial amount of revenue from the local economy. Its actions touch virtually every aspect as the city's economy and society. As Chapter Six will show in detail, it has considerable latitude in allocating these revenues across agencies, objects of expenditure, and classes of beneficiaries.

Equally importantly, the formal and practical authority over these capacities is highly centralized in the office of the mayor. This does not mean that the mayor can do whatever he or she wants; like any chief executive, the mayor must contend with potent interests inside government and in the political and market environments in which government operates. What it does mean, however, is that the mayoralty is the fulcrum point in city government and the chief object of any coalition that seeks to become dominant in city politics. The chief executive is more important, and countervailing centers of political power like the city council less important, than in most other cities. Since the end of the 1950s, successful candidates for the mayoralty came out of the Manhattan reform tradition; Abraham Beame was the only successful Democratic party regular.

Given the strength of city government and the importance of the mayoralty, it is not surprising that public sector producer interests are in the forefront of trying to influence the shape and direction of the mayor's political coalition. Nor is it surprising that those who seek to forge a dominant coalition would try to use the resources of public sector producer interests to reinforce their position.

Public sector employee unions have become increasingly important over the last two decades. They wish to increase wages, improve working conditions, and expand their membership, which entails growing city employment and expenditures generally financed by increasing taxes. They offer campaign contributions, workers, and technology and constitute a potent lobbying force in Albany for greater state aid to the city. Given their relatively narrow interests and their largely white and middle-class leadership (and in some, union membership), public employee unions were highly reluctant to challenge regular Democratic incumbents or support minority candidates for citywide office in the 1970s and 1980s. On the other hand, their strong political resources, their increasingly black and Latino membership, their liberal ideology, and their independence from the regular Democratic party organizations made them a potential base for political reform.

The regular Democratic party organizations and the lesser elected officials who make up its leadership lost their ability to determine who would hold the mayoralty after 1960, but they retained their hold on lower offices ranging from the borough presidencies to the city council, state assembly, and judgeships. From these peripheral positions, they extracted concessions from the mayoral center, including appointments to city jobs, influence over the award of contracts, and favorable decisions on matters that affected their jurisdictions. In return for these favors, they could offer some degree of control over the mayor's political environment and consent to the larger policy initiatives the mayor might propose.

Like the public employee unions, numerous and diverse community-based social service agencies constituted a potentially important independent base for political action. But their dependence on city funding and the ability of the mayor and Democratic party regulars to allocate those funds according to political as well as substantive criteria blunted this potential. These agencies could organize along functional lines to advocate increased funding for their program areas, but they proved unable to develop a community-based political agenda or to operate as an independent political force. Instead, they sought to exchange the good will of their clients and, at times, explicit political assistance to political patrons in return for their influence in winning public funding. The growing use of community-based organizations to deliver public services thus provided the mayor and elected officials with a new source of patronage.

The investment bankers who sought to float the city's debt were an even more pliant case of politicians' ability to put public sector producer interests to work. In return for the chance to be designated for this lucrative work, investment bankers were willing to make generous campaign contributions. From the politician's point of view, this was an ideal exchange.

Once in office, a mayor could therefore use the powers of government to strike political accommodations with the public employee unions, the regular Democratic party county organizations, community-based service-delivery organizations, and investment bankers. They would all exert an upward force on public expenditures, but a mayor who was capable of organizing accommodations with these groups could accrue an impressive array of political resources. The internal mechanics of government itself were thus a major influence on how mayors and their allies might go about fashioning a dominant political coalition.

First, however, he or she would have to win a majority of the electorate, and more specifically at least a 40 percent plurality of the Democratic mayoral primary electorate. For most of the period under review, white ethnic middle-class voters made up the majority of this electorate. But this majority was rapidly dwindling over this period, and in the process the racial and ethnic alignments shifted. The key to electoral victory, at least for a white candidate, was to bring relatively conservative white Catholics and Jews together while keeping white liberals, blacks, and Latinos demobilized and divided. The most important factors that favored such a strategy were the political decay of the white liberal tradition that had previously provided the initiative for reform; the continued and even renewed strength of Democratic party regulars, particularly in minority areas; the fragmentation of minority political leadership; and the competition between blacks and Latinos.

Having won office, those who would fashion a dominant coalition also needed to secure support from the broad range of private interests deeply affected by the tax and expenditure policies pursued by local government. Business interests in New York City are highly diverse, as the previous chapter argued. Yet, like city government, its most important components are relatively concentrated and well organized.

Apart from the investment bankers who wanted to sell the city's debt obligations, New York's business elite wanted government to hold down the tax burden on private profits and managerial salaries, increase public works investments that served the city's economy, promote real estate investment, and enhance public programs that made the city more attractive to the upper middle class. In return, the business elite would not only make the investments that would cause tax revenues to grow, but they would offer highly attractive and selective inducements, such as campaign contributions, support from the various institutions and media that shaped elite and mass opinion, and participation in the specific policy initiatives a mayor might wish to undertake, with all the political benefits that might be attached.

From these elements, a dominant political coalition can be woven. It will be shaped by the institutional arrangements that have been described, but it will not be determined by them. It is true that the shape of a successful political coalition will reflect the alignment of both popular constituencies in the electorate and private interests in the marketplace. At the same time, political coalitions can also influence and reshape these alignments, particularly once they gain office and are in a position to use the capacities of government for their political ends.

It is also the case that the "imperatives" that might arise from within government and from the relationship between politicians and their electorate on the one hand and their market environment on the other crosscut and conflict with each other. They are not static but rather have been altered by the forces of historical change. Political outcomes therefore cannot be predicted from structural features alone but reflect the choice and creativity of political actors. Let us now turn to how Edward I. Koch and his allies made their choices between 1977 and 1989 as they constructed a new conservative dominant coalition in New York City politics.

Five

Forging the Koch Coalition

Koch's politics are as inexorably tied to the
1970s as Lindsay's were to the 1960s.
  (Jim Chapin, "Who Rules New York
  Today?")[1]

More striking than the support that Ed Koch
the **liberal** has received from New York's
downtown business community is the alliance
that Ed Koch the **reformer** has cultivated with
the city's Democratic county machines.
  (Martin Shefter, *Political Crisis/Fiscal Crisis*)[2]

A CHILD of Jewish garment workers, Edward I. Koch entered the New York political scene as a volunteer in the 1956 Stevenson presidential campaign. He worked with the Village Independent Democrats (VID) to unseat county leader and Village district leader Carmine DeSapio leadership in 1959, became president of VID in 1962, and successfully ran for district leader in 1963, thwarting DeSapio's attempted comeback. Having been elected to the city council in 1966, he succeeded John V. Lindsay to the Village-East Side congressional seat in 1968, where he compiled a strongly liberal record. In these years he went to the South to support the civil rights movement, served as the *Village Voice*'s lawyer, opposed the Vietnam war, supported Lindsay's election, and campaigned for the civilian police review board.[3]

Koch began to think seriously about running for mayor in the early 1970s. At this point, he realized that he would have to diversify his support far beyond his liberal Manhattan base. In 1972, he backed neighborhood protesters who opposed the construction of subsidized (read minority) housing in upper middle class, white, Jewish Forest Hills, Queens.[4] Though he ultimately endorsed the compromise that Mario Cuomo fashioned in the dispute, this marked a turning point away from liberal orthodoxy. In 1973, he made a brief, unfunded, and abortive attempt to run for mayor, stressing a tough stand on crime and a desire to represent the white middle class. Comptroller Abraham Beame, a product of the Brooklyn regular Democratic organization, beat ex-policeman Mario Biaggi, then-congressman Herman Badillo, and liberal businessman Albert Blumenthal in the 1973 Democratic primary and went on to become New York City's first Jewish mayor and to restore Democratic clubhouse influence in city hall.

His achievement was quickly undone by rapidly deteriorating fiscal and social conditions in the city. The fiscal crisis of 1975 prompted the governor and the business community to put the city government into receivership, effectively removing Beame from a significant role in governance. As a prelude to the 1977 elections, widespread looting occurred in black neighborhoods during an electricity blackout in July 1977. The Securities and Exchange Commission also released a report that accused Mayor Beame of misleading investors about the city's financial condition before the collapse in 1975.[5]

Not surprisingly, these events caused Mayor Beame's standing with the public to plummet, which in turn elicited a large field of serious contenders for the mayoralty. Better financed and better organized, Edward Koch entered the race, though still as an underdog against such other candidates as Secretary of State Mario Cuomo, former borough president and Congressman Herman Badillo, and Congresswoman Bella Abzug. Surprisingly, Koch prevailed in the primary and general election and went on to build increasingly potent electoral majorities in his 1981 and 1985 reelection campaigns. In the process, he substantially redefined his electoral base and forged links with public sector producer interests and private sector elites so as to convert his electoral coalition into a governing coalition. His success at these tasks made him the dominant political figure in New York City politics for more than a decade and one of the most powerful mayors ever to have served. His first step, however, was to win the 1977 mayoral election.

Winning the Mayoralty and Gaining Access to Power

On September 8, 1977, over 900,000 Democratic primary voters narrowly enabled Congressman Koch to edge Mayor Beame from office and become the front-runner against Secretary of State Mario Cuomo. The initial primary, however, was extremely close and hotly contested. The sixth trailing candidate, Herman Badillo, was only 80,000 votes behind the first. Among the seven candidates were three Jews (Beame, Koch, and Abzug), an Italian-American (Cuomo), a Puerto Rican (Badillo), and the first major African-American and woman contenders (Manhattan Borough President Percy Sutton and Abzug).

This array of competitors and the perceived close contest among them drew large numbers of voters from every ethnic background to the polls. At 47.1 percent of registered Democrats, the turnout was the highest recorded for a mayoral primary in two decades. Moreover, the vote was highly racially polarized: the correlation between the white population of a precinct and the proportion of its vote that went to a white candidate was .903; the equivalent correlations for blacks in a precinct and black candidates was .940, and for Latinos .862.[6]

It surprised many that Ed Koch, with 20 percent of the vote, narrowly led the other challengers with a 10,000-vote margin over Mario Cuomo, the second-place candidate. In early polling, Bella Abzug had led the other candidates, only to fall behind as they became better known. As she lost the leadership, there was every reason to think that Mario Cuomo would assume it. Governor Hugh Carey had picked Cuomo four years earlier as secretary of state and strongly backed his candidacy. Known previously for his successful mediation of the Forest Hills subsidized housing dispute in Queens, Cuomo was endorsed by the *New York Times*, the Queens Democratic organization, and a number of public employee unions. He had also raised almost $1,000,000 in campaign funds, while Koch had only two-thirds that amount. Cuomo could also count on the Catholic vote, while three of his competitors would split the Jewish vote.

The Democratic primary campaign was not marked by sharp differences on most issues or policy priorities. The *New York Times*/CBS exit poll suggested that Koch's and Cuomo's supporters had broadly similar views. Regular Democrats leaned toward Cuomo, while reformers leaned slightly to Koch, despite his efforts to go beyond this base. (Conservatives favored Beame, while white liberals, who made up about 20 percent of the electorate, leaned toward Abzug; Koch and Cuomo divided the middle of the white population.)[7]

Though his primary campaign counted on support from his traditional Manhattan base, Koch sought to widen his appeal outside Manhattan and to distinguish himself from Cuomo and his other opponents by emphasizing his support for the death penalty (which Cuomo opposed), his determination to engage in hard bargaining with civil service workers, and his desire to crack down on welfare and those he referred to as "poverty pimps" in the community action program.[8]

Koch mounted an increasingly aggressive campaign through the summer. He almost prevented the liberal, reform New Democratic Coalition from endorsing Bella Abzug, thereby slowing her momentum and pulling ahead of her in overall support. In the last weeks of the campaign, he mounted a substantial media effort that enabled him to pick up a disproportionate share of undecided voters. "After eight years of charisma and four years of the clubhouse," his campaign slogan asked, "why not competence?"

His strongest support naturally came from the assembly districts (ADs) included in his congressional district, particularly Stuyvesant Town, Peter

Cooper Village, and the Upper East Side. (Koch's home base in the Village favored Abzug, as did the Upper West Side, but he still got more than a quarter of the votes in these ADs.) Having signaled that he was looking beyond his Manhattan base by stressing such themes as the death penalty, Koch also won pluralities in the moderate, upper middle class, Jewish neighborhoods of Queens and the Bronx. He also ran second in the more conservative, middle to lower middle class Jewish neighborhoods of Brooklyn, like Midwood and Canarsie, that provided Mayor Beame's core constituency. Where he did not run first in Jewish areas, he ran second. Since Jewish voters had become the single largest constituency within the Democratic primary electorate, this augured well for him in the runoff primary. Despite starting from the back of the pack, Congressman Koch thus got 180,248 votes against 170,560 for Cuomo and 163,610 for Beame. (Abzug took 150,719, while Sutton and Badillo together garnered 231,005, or 25 percent of the vote. The seventh candidate, Joel Harnett, won only a token number of votes.)

Since no candidate won the 40 percent plurality required to win the Democratic nomination, Koch had to face Cuomo in a runoff primary eleven days after the first primary. Both candidates sought to swing three "available" constituencies: the conservative Jews who had supported Beame, the liberals who backed Abzug, and the black and Latino supporters of Percy Sutton and Herman Badillo. A liberal strategy might win Abzug supporters and perhaps those of Sutton and Badillo, but a more conservative pitch would be required to gain support from the Democratic regulars who had supported Beame.

In the end, Koch sought to have it both ways by presenting himself as a "tough liberal" who could "make hard decisions and say 'No,' " while also seeking support both from regular Democratic organization leaders in the Bronx and Brooklyn and from Harlem's black political establishment. This strategy was designed to capture both more liberal and more conservative Jewish voters as well as blacks and Latinos. Since 34 percent of the primary voters had voted for Beame and Abzug, he could probably win the runoff by consolidating Jewish ethnic sentiment on his behalf; drawing a significant portion of those who had voted for Sutton and Badillo would cement victory. Cuomo, on the other hand, would have to expand beyond his white Catholic base of support into both minority voters and the Jewish middle class. (Only when racial succession was a salient element of an election, such as the 1966 police review board referendum, had the Catholic/Jewish alignment fallen into place in the past. A white Catholic/black alignment was highly improbable, though not impossible.)

Koch strenuously sought support from political leaders who represented and organized these constituencies. Bronx county party leader Pat Cunningham and his key operative and successor, Deputy Mayor Stanley

Friedman, backed Koch immediately after the primary. Friedman also helped convince Mayor Beame to endorse Koch. Herman Badillo, who had been a reform figure in the Bronx, also supported Koch. (Badillo was ultimately named a deputy mayor in the Koch administration.) Badillo and the Bronx regular organization encouraged Puerto Ricans in the South Bronx and elsewhere to back Koch. Queens county leader Donald Manes was supporting Cuomo, who had come up through Queens politics, but Manes allowed his Jewish district leaders to back Koch, since he had won their ADs in the first primary.[9]

Brooklyn was more problematic. Home to the largest number of Democrats, Koch had run third after Beame (a product of the Brooklyn regular organization) and Cuomo (who appealed to the borough's many Italian and white Catholic voters). County leader Meade Esposito was a machine boss in the mold that Koch made his career fighting. Yet on Sunday, September 11, Koch met in the basement of Esposito's mother's house in Canarsie to ask for his endorsement, something Cuomo declined to do. At the urging of Friedman and Canarsie district leader Anthony Genovesi, Esposito agreed to back Koch, but Koch required that the endorsement be kept secret.[10]

A few days later, Koch also met with members of the Manhattan black political establishment, led by Congressman Charles Rangel. Koch promised to name more minority officials than the two previous mayoralties combined and to give blacks jobs at the highest level of the administration. He also promised not to use the phrase "poverty pimp" any more and not to dismantle the poverty program. (State Senator Carl McCall and Congressman Major Owens, present at the meeting, had led the poverty program during the Lindsay administration.) On this basis, Rangel, the *Amsterdam News* (a black-oriented weekly), and all but a few Brooklyn black leaders endorsed Koch.[11] Koch also won support from Rupert Murdoch and the *New York Post* by providing the new owner a way to become influential in city politics. (Fifty of the *Post*'s sixty reporters later submitted a grievance petition to Murdoch complaining of "slanted news coverage" in favor of Koch.)

On the other end of the ideological spectrum, Abzug and most of her supporters favored Cuomo, although she did not endorse him until late in the game. Cuomo did win the endorsement of Victor Gotbaum of District Council 37, AFCSME, as well as the Transit Workers and the Firefighters. From his base in the Italian parts of Staten Island, Brooklyn, and Queens, Cuomo sought to expand support in middle-class, ethnic Jewish neighborhoods and as well as among blacks and Latinos. Governor Carey also weighed in with renewed support for Cuomo. Cuomo sought to bolster his position by running a controversial television ad trying to associate Koch with negative feelings about the legacy of former Mayor John V.

Lindsay. He also fought the perception that the campaign might have degenerated into a conflict between Catholics and Jews.

While Koch and Cuomo were both perceived as middle-of-the-road candidates and "fresh faces," Koch projected himself in a more conservative light and continued to attack liberal ideologues, black "poverty pimps," and municipal unions. Cuomo, from a culturally conservative background, sought support from liberals, labor, and minorities. While his support came from across the ideological spectrum, Koch was ultimately able to draw on his past to get the support he needed from Manhattan liberals, outer-borough Jews, blacks, and Puerto Ricans, thus recreating New York's traditional liberal coalition. He spent a total of $1.2 million in the two primaries against Cuomo's $1.8 million; both spent heavily on television and radio during the interprimary period.

Koch defeated Cuomo by 432,000 to 355,000 votes in the runoff. His coalition ranged from the white reform precincts of the Village and the Upper West Side to more conservative outer-borough Jewish neighborhoods like Canarsie, Sheepshead Bay, and Forest Hills. Koch also picked up a majority in black and Puerto Rican districts in Harlem, the South Bronx, and Brooklyn. Cuomo once more did best in white Catholic areas of the city. Table 5.1 shows that the ADs that had given a plurality of their votes to any Jewish candidate in the initial primary all shifted strongly toward Koch in the runoff. This shift was strongest in the liberal white ADs that had originally supported Abzug, while the Beame ADs shifted toward him at a lesser but still strong rate. Black and Latino ADs also shifted strongly toward Koch, even more so than the Jewish ADs.[12]

The falloff in votes cast between the first and second primaries is also instructive. It was much stronger in the ADs that had supported the lib-

TABLE 5.1
Shift From 1977 Primary to Runoff by AD Primary Winner

ADs Won by	Primary		Runoff		
	Vote	Koch %	Vote	Koch %	Vote Falloff %
Koch (10 ADs)	168,732	31.0	158,871	65.9	5.8
Beame (10 ADs)	197,632	23.9	185,995	63.9	5.9
Abzug (3 ADs)	67,230	23.8	47,193	66.3	29.8
Cuomo (19 ADs)	225,068	18.1	213,388	37.8	5.2
Sutton (14 ADs)	152,809	10.3	94,996	54.4	37.8
Badillo (9 ADs)	98,303	8.6	68,250	55.6	30.6
Total	909,774	19.8	768,693	55.3	15.5

Source: *New York Times*, September 10 and 20, 1977.

eral, black, and Puerto Rican candidates than in either the Jewish or the Italian-American areas. Among the Jewish areas, the falloff was least in Koch's core ADs, as might be expected.[13] The net effect of these shifts in preference and turnout gave Koch a sizable runoff majority built primarily on Jewish votes from his and Beame's ADs and secondarily on votes from the white liberals, blacks, and Latinos, who, though demobilized by the absence of favored candidates, still shifted strongly to Koch. Cuomo rallied white Catholics, but there simply were not enough of them to tilt the outcome in his favor.

Normally, the outcome of the Democratic primary would have insured Koch's victory in the general election. But he faced a November race not only against the Republican nominee, liberal Manhattan State Senator Roy Goodman, but also against Mario Cuomo on the Liberal party line. (The Conservatives nominated Barry Farber, who had lost the Republican primary to Goodman.) Despite Governor Carey and Victor Gotbaum's defection from the Cuomo camp to support the Democratic nominee, Cuomo was still running hard for the mayoralty. Since Koch's most supportive constituencies tended to be heavily Democratic, while Cuomo's were more likely to be Republicans or independents, Cuomo had reason to be hopeful, especially if he could peel away Koch's liberal and minority supporters in the period between the primaries and the general election.

Commenting on a "reversal of roles," Cuomo attacked Koch as "no longer a 'traditional' Democrat but a conservative who has made 'deals' with politicians."[14] Though Cuomo had initially been viewed as the candidate of the establishment and Koch the outsider, the Democratic nomination made Koch the candidate of the establishment. Endorsements Koch received from Governor Carey, Vice President Walter Mondale, Senator Patrick Moynihan, Bella Abzug, Percy Sutton, and even the New Democratic Coalition reinforced this perception. The *Times*, however, stuck with its endorsement of Cuomo.

Koch's margin in the general election proved to be surprisingly close, considering the size of his runoff victory. He received 712,976 votes, or 50.4 percent, compared to Cuomo's 587,257, or 41.4 percent. (The Republican and Conservative candidates garnered only 119,093 votes.) Koch's 30 percent margin in the late September polls shrank to less than 9 percent in the November election results. Koch's pollsters attributed this to the electorate's distrust of Koch's newly found establishment position.[15] But Cuomo was also able to capitalize on the better representation of his constituencies in the general electorate than in the Democratic primary electorate.

As Table 5.2 shows, Cuomo not only consolidated his support among white Catholics, but he mobilized far greater numbers of them to vote. Compared to the runoff primary, Koch retained his level of support in the

TABLE 5.2
Shift From 1977 Runoff to General by AD Primary Winner

ADs Won by	Runoff		General		Vote Increase %
	Vote	Koch %	Vote	Koch %	
Koch (10 ADs)	158,871	65.9	290,070	57.2	82.6
Beame (10 ADs)	185,995	63.9	291,211	58.1	56.6
Abzug (3 ADs)	47,193	66.3	87,750	65.7	85.9
Cuomo (19 ADs)	213,388	37.8	466,318	31.4	118.5
Sutton (14 ADs)	94,996	54.4	170,467	62.0	79.4
Badillo (9 ADs)	68,250	55.6	109,613	62.1	60.6
Total	768,693	55.3	1,415,429	50.4	84.1

Source: New York Times, September 20 and November 11, 1977.

white liberal ADs and increased it in black and Latino ADs. But the support for Koch declined in both his own core ADs and the "regular" Jewish ADs that had initially supported Beame; the increase of votes between the runoff and general election was also least among the Beame ADs, and highest in the Cuomo ADs.[16] This suggests that Koch's pollsters were dead wrong: Koch won because white liberals and blacks shifted toward him and turned out in substantial numbers; his margin was narrow because his white "regular" Jewish ADs shifted away from him and had lower turnouts, relative to most other groups.

Edward I. Koch thus became the 105th mayor of New York City by a relatively narrow margin. Aided by the institution of a runoff primary that forced divergent tendencies within the Democratic electorate to combine behind a single candidate, Koch was able to coalesce an alignment of reform-oriented whites; middle-class, outer-borough Jews; blacks; and Latinos. Koch's core ADs and those that had initially supported Abzug gave him about 224,000 votes; the black ADs gave him about 106,000, and the Puerto Rican ADs about 68,000. The Beame ADs gave him another 169,000 votes. Together, they outweighed the one sizable portion of the New York City electorate outside his coalition, white Catholics, but not by an overwhelming amount. Though white Catholics had once provided the central basis for machine Democratic politics, they had been defecting from the Democratic party since 1960.

Koch's 1977 electoral coalition was not cohesive. It was divided by issues of race, class, ethnicity, religion, life-style, and political culture. A major tension existed between the reformers and regulars. Koch had grown up among the reformers and sought and finally received their support in 1977. But the politics that Koch's liberal Manhattan professional social base articulated often clashed with that of the more conservative Jews from working-class and managerial backgrounds from Brooklyn, Queens, and the Bronx, who provided the social base for the regular Democratic organizations. Koch was able to bridge this division by stressing his Jewish ethnicity and by projecting values and policy stances that appealed to outer-borough whites. Though he took white liberals and the cosmopolitan Jews of Manhattan more or less for granted, they nonetheless rallied to his cause because they thought he was one of them.

Koch did not need the public endorsement of the regular Democratic county organizations to get their Jewish constituents to vote for him in the runoff and general elections. Moreover, as Table 5.2 shows, support from the regular organizations neither shifted their constituents toward him nor mobilized them to vote in the general election. At the same time, opposition from the county organizations would certainly have weakened his ability to govern, as it had Lindsay's during his first term; their support would strengthen Koch's ability to do business. Backing from the regulars would also save him from a regular challenger in subsequent elections and consolidate his electoral hold on the office.[17] In the long run, therefore, Mayor Koch determined to bring these organizations into his governing coalition.

Mayor Koch also faced racial divisions in his 1977 electoral coalition, as well as divisions between regulars and insurgents within the black and Latino leadership. A new generation of black and Puerto Rican activists had challenged the white dominance of the political system and the minority "gatekeepers" which they felt the white establishment had installed to control black and Puerto Rican political mobilization. Koch had seemed to identify with the earlier stage of this struggle by offering to help the southern civil rights movement.[18]

Most black and Latinos elected officials had made their way up through the regular Democratic organizations, however, and many had become accustomed to using Great Society programs as a new form of political patronage under franchise from those organizations.[19] As a white Manhattan reformer, Koch attacked this practice. As previous discussion has shown, black militancy had also polarized white opinion and caused Koch's core outer-borough Jewish supporters to move in the conservative direction in which white Catholics had preceded them. Yet outer-borough Jews and white Catholics were sure to find black and Latino regulars more compatible than militants would be.

Mayor Koch thus had to navigate the tensions between reformers and regular tendencies among blacks as well as whites. Koch had gone South, but he also sided with white Forest Hills opponents of subsidized housing that might bring blacks to their neighborhood. He had promised black elected officials like Charles Rangel not to use the term "poverty pimp" so that he would win crucial black support in the runoff and general elections, yet he continued to attack the Beame administration's use of the community action program for patronage purposes and moved to reorganize and take control of the program immediately upon election. He held the beliefs that had motivated Manhattan white reformers to oppose black regulars and support black insurgents in the past, but he keenly felt the Jewish anger at what he perceived to be widespread black anti-Semitism.[20]

Given these tensions within his coalition and the narrowness of his ultimate victory, Mayor Koch had to broaden, consolidate, and rationalize his base of electoral support. He had to win more votes than he lost in the process and prevent those he was causing to be dissatisfied from uniting against him. He also had to convert his electoral coalition into a governing coalition. Success at any one of these tasks would feed the others: the greater his perceived electoral invincibility, the more leverage he would have over the centers of private and governmental power; the stronger his governing position, the more key institutional actors would seek to do business with him and support him at election time.

Moving to the left offered Koch relatively little to gain. Cuomo had received some liberal support, but most of it had already gone to Koch. The greater part of Cuomo's base was conservative. Given that white liberal reformers had little history of cooperation with the regular black and Puerto Rican political leaders and given the weakness and fragmentation of the minority political leadership, it was unlikely that they would coalesce against Koch, especially if he could establish a solid governing coalition. So he had little to lose in moving away from them. Moving to the right, on the other hand, would appeal to white Catholics, the only large electoral bloc outside the 1977 Koch coalition. Since appeals to racial anxieties were the most obvious way to accomplish this shift, the challenge facing Mayor Koch was how to make such appeals without giving white liberals, blacks, and Latinos cause to coalesce. In seeking white Catholic support, Mayor Koch would also have to develop separate strategies for keeping liberal whites and minority political constituencies in his fold, or at least demobilized.

This overall strategy had an emotional as well as logical appeal to Mayor Koch. The racial tensions of the past decade had certainly moved the mayor's outer-borough, middle-class Jewish core constituency with which Koch identified against blacks and liberalism. Koch was convinced that Lindsay-style liberalism had been dangerously wrong. Given the fiscal crisis and the disinvestment of the 1970s, he also felt that government should encourage private investment. The mayor's actions were thus born of strong instincts, deepened over time by their obvious political effectiveness. His highly sensitive and acute political ear did not just hear what his core middle-class Jewish constituency was saying; for better and for worse, the mayor powerfully articulated its inner fears and hopes. In so shaping the political development of his people, he also shaped that of the whole city.

Forging a Conservative Coalition

Reshaping the Liberal Electoral Base

Having become mayor with the backing of such disparate political forces, Mayor Koch set out to redefine his electoral coalition and forge a new governing coalition. In the 1981 election, he brought in the white Catholics who had voted for Cuomo by mounting rhetorical attacks on ideological liberals, black defenders of the poverty programs, and municipal unions. In the domain of governance, Koch cemented alliances with the regular Democratic county party organizations and with the Manhattan corporate elite, especially the intertwined world of large real estate developers, investment bankers, and lawyers.[21] The former gave him the votes to dominate the Board of Estimate and a bulwark against electoral challenges; the latter consolidated support from the city's business elite and gave him the political resources it commanded.

Mayor Koch consummated these alliances by granting county leaders like Stanley Friedman of the Bronx and Donald Manes of Queens access to patronage, while fostering a positive climate in taxation, finance, and real estate regulation that brought the city's large corporations around to his cause. (Koch had started out with little support from Manhattan's corporate leaders, from whom he was separated by a large social distance.) In return, the county party leaders and the business elite strongly backed his reelection campaigns in 1981 and 1985 (as well as his abortive run for governor in 1982) and aided him in accumulating power within the city's political system. Though Koch would have won these elections without the county bosses, they certainly relieved him of a challenge they might have mounted had Koch locked them out. Moreover, their support gave him a considerable advantage over any other opponents.[22]

Mayor Koch apparently did not fear that he would alienate important components of his 1977 coalition, including "ideological liberals," the municipal unions, and the black political establishment, in making an implicit racial appeal to white Catholics. Koch reneged on some specific commitments to black leaders while carrying out others without consulting them. He named Basil Paterson, an ally of Charles Rangel and Percy Sutton, deputy mayor for labor relations, but Paterson did not last long in the administration. Koch failed to clear other black appointments with the Harlem establishment; he did not recruit appointees from their ranks, drawing them instead from foundations, law firms, and similar sources. He closed Sydenham Hospital in Harlem as an economy measure and later attempted to close Harlem's Metropolitan Hospital as well. He reorganized and retrenched the poverty program, producing a considerable outcry from black and Puerto Rican elected officials. "Every bit as important as these deeds," Shefter notes, "were Koch's words—when he was denounced in hyperbolic language by black political leaders, the mayor replied in kind."[23]

Mayor Koch first tested this strategy for building electoral dominance in the 1981 Democratic mayoral primary. In this election, dissident white liberals sought a candidate to oppose Koch; Assemblyman Frank J. Barbaro, a labor-oriented populist who represented a conservative, Italian-American district presented himself as their candidate. But Koch's potential opponents remained disunited. Black leaders neither put up their own candidate nor backed Barbaro. Public sector unions, which sought to make up for wage increases foregone during the fiscal crisis, were also not inclined to make a symbolic challenge to the mayor.

Mayor Koch, meanwhile, had so successfully redefined himself as a conservative that he won permission from the five Republican county leaders to receive the Republican nomination for mayor. His challenge in the Democratic primary thus came only from an Italian-American who, like Cuomo, might draw away the white Catholic votes that Koch had been courting. If Barbaro were able to do so, Koch's chief political tactician, John LoCicero, worried that Barbaro might combine them with the blacks and white liberals who had been disaffected by Koch's repositioning, potentially opening the way for a serious challenge.[24]

He need not have worried. The mayor raised a large campaign war chest from real estate developers, investment bankers, and lawyers, many of whom did business that was subject to city government regulation or approval. Assemblyman Barbaro could not raise the funds to pay for an extensive campaign; white liberals did not rally around the campaign, and blacks and Latinos had little desire or incentive to join it. Table 5.3 shows that the white Catholics who might have been Barbaro's natural base were neither strongly attracted to him nor disaffected from Koch. The result was general demobilization. Fewer voters cast ballots in the 1981 Democratic mayoral primary than in any since World War II, and they favored Mayor Edward I. Koch by a wider margin than in his race against Cuomo four years earlier.

Koch won sizable majorities in virtually every sector of the white population. He even barely won the ADs that had supported Abzug in 1977, despite his continual attacks on ideological white liberals. Most importantly, he received strong support from white Catholic ethnics, including

TABLE 5.3
Shift from 1977 Runoff to 1981 Primary by 1977 Primary Winner

	1977		1981		
ADs Won by	Runoff Vote	Koch %	Primary Vote	Koch %	Vote Falloff %
Koch (10 ADs)	158,871	65.9	105,750	70.9	33.4
Beame (10 ADs)	185,995	63.9	134,397	71.6	27.7
Abzug (3 ADs)	47,193	66.3	46,033	51.4	2.5
Cuomo (19 ADs)	213,388	37.8	139,456	62.5	34.6
Sutton (14 ADs)	94,996	54.4	94,175	37.0	0.8
Badillo (9 ADs)	68,250	55.6	57,641	46.6	15.5
Total	768,693	55.3	577,941	59.5	24.8

Source: New York Times, September 20, 1977 and September 24, 1981.

Italian-Americans, against a white Catholic opponent. The ADs that had voted for Mario Cuomo in 1977 shifted 25 percentage points toward Koch.[25] Koch beat Barbaro not only in Barbaro's home assembly district, but on his own block. He thus managed to unite two previously divergent segments of the white middle-class population; the relatively large falloff in their vote compared to 1977 may be read as contentment with Koch and an absence of fear of his opponent.

There were unmistakable indications, however, that Koch's rhetoric and policy actions had disaffected blacks, white liberals, and Latinos, among whom his share of the vote fell 17.4, 14.9, and 9.0 percentage points respectively. Moreover, unlike the white Catholic and Jewish constituencies, their total vote did not decline nearly so far, indicating a higher relative mobilization.[26] Nevertheless, Koch retained sufficient support from them, especially from white liberals, to give him a commanding overall margin. Since Republicans had already given Koch their nomination, he won the general election by an even more overwhelming majority, an historic 75 percent of the vote. Barbaro ran on the Liberal line in the general election as Cuomo had in 1977, but his poor showing ratified white support for Koch.

At this juncture an unhappy political interlude for Koch revealed just how fragile the Jewish-white Catholic alignment could be in a race when candidates who each had a strong ethnic appeal to one of these groups ran against each other. Fueled by the 1981 election results and urged on by the New York Post, Mayor Koch decided to run for governor upon Hugh Carey's retirement in 1982. Koch once more faced Mario Cuomo, whom Carey had chosen as his lieutenant governor after his loss to Koch. This time, the early polls and the early political money heavily favored Mayor

Koch. (Political donors in the real estate and investment banking industries understood that Koch would remain a pivotal figure in New York City whether or not he won the governorship.)

This race produced a famous news photograph of Mayor Koch flanked on the steps of City Hall by the four Democratic party county leaders or "bosses," Stanley Friedman of the Bronx, Donald Manes of Queens, Meade Esposito of Brooklyn, and Nick LaPorte of Staten Island, who all endorsed him early in the race. (The first three were subsequently found to have engaged in corrupt political practices.) A particularly important detail of this tableau was the shift of Manes and the Queens regular organization from Cuomo to Koch.

As in the 1977 general election, however, the Koch-Cuomo race proved to be closer than the pundits initially assumed. Assisted by a *Playboy* interview in which Koch disparaged suburban and rural life-styles, Cuomo won the race statewide and lost the city to Koch by a narrow 4,000-vote margin. Koch did beat Cuomo by two to one in the outerborough Jewish ADs of New York City, while Cuomo won heavily in Italian-American areas like Bensonhurst and Staten Island. Koch just barely matched Cuomo in liberal areas like the Upper West Side, even though they have relatively large Jewish populations; he also split the Latino ADs. The race narrowed because Koch lost black neighborhoods like Harlem and central Brooklyn by two to one. Despite Friedman's and Manes's support, Koch took the Bronx and Queens only by a thousand votes each. (Brooklyn provided Koch his largest margin, 14,000 votes; he lost Manhattan by 8,000 votes and Staten Island by 4,000.)

This race showed that white Catholic support for Koch was conditional and that an attractive and well-financed Catholic challenger could pull them away from the mayor's electoral base. This might be particularly vexing for Koch if they could be combined with white liberal, black, and Latino votes. Even against such an attractive competitor as Cuomo, and despite the disaffection of various elements of his 1977 and 1981 coalitions, Mayor Koch still assembled a small electoral majority within the city. As before, his most intense support could be found in the apartment houses occupied by lower middle class Jews in the outer reaches of Brooklyn and in the single-family homes occupied by upper middle class Jews in Queens.

The Seeds of Future Challenge

Coming on the heels of the smashing 1981 victory, Koch's 1982 loss did not seem to harm his popularity within the city. Koch retrospectively rationalized his loss by saying that those who voted for him in 1981 had pulled the lever for Cuomo in 1982 because they really wanted him to remain mayor of the city. As governor, Cuomo was no longer a threat to run against the mayor; white Catholics were unlikely to defect to a lesser white Catholic candidate and certainly not to a minority candidate. The defeat did redouble Koch's effort to appeal to Catholic voters, including Latinos.

Beginning in 1981, and quite clearly by 1983, city government emerged from its fiscal crisis mode. New York City's booming economy rode out the 1982 recession and generated rapidly rising city revenues thereafter, enabling Koch to raise city expenditures without increasing tax rates. The mayor could declare that the fiscal crisis was over, and he would now repair capital facilities and restore the city services to their pre-fiscal crisis levels. Budget increases enabled the mayor and his political allies to increase capital budget spending on contracts with private construction firms and expense budget spending on nonprofit service providers. He could also add employees to the city payroll and agree to wage settlements that exceeded the inflation rate, enabling city workers to recoup the losses they experienced in the fiscal crisis. His administration also vigorously promoted the office building boom occurring in Manhattan.

As the next chapter will show in detail, expanded fiscal capacity made it possible for Mayor Koch to reward constituencies whose support he sought and to extend his influence over those whose opposition he wanted to compromise. Not only real estate developers, but community-based organizations and municipal workers had an economic incentive to be responsive to the administration's political agenda. As a result, the mid-1980s marked a high point in Mayor Koch's governmental and electoral power. At the same time, however, seeds of a challenge to the mayor were being sown.

The mayor's increasingly combative stance against black leaders and white liberals progressively alienated their constituencies. Mayor Koch had already estranged the black political establishment during his first administration, but mass black alienation increased during his second administration. This shift coalesced around Jesse Jackson's candidacy for the Democratic presidential nomination in 1984. In anticipation of this race and in reaction to Harold Washington's 1983 mayoral victory in Chicago, some of New York City's African-American leaders, especially Al Vann and his Coalition for Community Empowerment (CCE) allies in Brooklyn, decided undertake a large-scale voter registration drive in order to have a similar impact on New York City politics.[27] Joined by advocacy organizations like HumanSERVE, these efforts greatly increased registration in black and Latino neighborhoods relative to much smaller gains in white areas. Table 5.4 shows that almost 465,000 new Democrats were registered between late 1982 and early 1985, well over half of them in black and Latino districts.[28] (Political leaders in Latino districts also succeeded in raising registration in anticipation of the 1985 race.)[29]

Even though a presidential year was approaching, the registration gain in white ADs was muted. In fact, registration in predominantly Jewish ADs, traditionally the largest and highest-turnout segment of the Democratic electorate, grew more slowly than in any other constituency, while registration grew almost three times as rapidly in white liberal ADs. As a result, the Democratic party registration base tilted toward the city's black and Latino populations and increased the relative representation of all the constituencies that had been least disposed toward Mayor Koch.

While many leaders of the Harlem establishment, such as Congressman Rangel, did not support Jesse Jackson's 1984 presidential primary campaign, preferring to ally themselves with Walter Mondale and the national Democratic political establishment, other black leaders enthusiastically supported Jackson in 1984. Assemblyman Al Vann and the CCE in Brooklyn were particularly active on behalf of Jackson; Vann served as Jackson's statewide campaign coordinator. Grass-roots opinion among blacks ran strongly in favor of Jackson.

In the April primary, despite significant black leadership support for Mondale and Jackson's catastrophic "Hymietown" comment, Jackson still attracted 34 percent of the three-quarters of a million Democrats who cast ballots, as Table 5.5 shows. Jackson took almost all the black votes, not quite half the Latino vote, and a small minority of the vote in white ADs. This encouraged black leaders to think that a black-Latino coalition that could draw labor and white liberal support for a less divisive candidate than Jackson might be able to mount a serious challenge to Mayor Koch in 1985. Yet these seeds of electoral challenge fell on barren ground in the 1985 mayoral elections.

TABLE 5.4
Democratic Registration 1982–1985 by AD Type

AD Type	November 1982	May 1985	Gain	Increase
Black	326,054	482,459	156,405	48.0
Mixed minority	116,513	176,829	60,316	51.8
Latino	116,818	175,414	58,596	50.2
White liberal	282,247	367,282	85,035	30.1
White Catholic	371,928	430,636	58,708	15.8
Outer-borough Jewish	436,288	482,041	45,753	10.5
Total	1,649,848	2,114,661	464,813	28.2

Source: New York City Board of Elections.

Challengers in Disarray

Beginning in July 1984, forty black leaders organized a Coalition for a Just New York (CJNY), chaired by Vann, to search for a consensus candidate to oppose Koch.[30] The group favored Basil Paterson, a widely respected former secretary of state and deputy mayor who practiced labor law and represented a number of influential city unions. In addition to the respect accorded him by a variety of constituencies, Paterson had demonstrated an ability to raise substantial campaign funds. But Paterson withdrew from consideration because he had a heart condition and would soon undergo bypass surgery.

Coalition members would not support an announced white candidate for mayor, Carol Bellamy. Bellamy had held elective office as a Brooklyn reformer and, as city council president between 1977 and 1985, had forged ties with and articulated the views of Manhattan reformers. While she could present herself as a reform critic of Koch, she bore the liability of having supported Koch's bid for governor because she would have succeeded him as acting mayor. Bellamy had also sought support from the Brooklyn regular Democratic organization. Her record on backing minority candidates was weak, and she was not inclined to support Vann's insurgent bid for the Brooklyn borough presidency. She was committed to the mayoral race regardless of whom the CJNY endorsed. The CJNY, therefore, did not find endorsing her particularly attractive.

Herman Badillo, former Bronx borough president, former congressman, and former Koch deputy mayor, offered another possibility, but he had badly lost his 1969, 1973, and 1977 mayoral bids. More importantly, in 1977, black leaders had wanted him to support Percy Sutton instead of running, which Badillo declined to do. He was regarded as erratic and weak on organization and did not have unanimous backing from Latino leaders. On the other hand, Al Vann and Reverend Calvin Butts, executive minister of the Abyssinian Baptist Church, supported him because he was the strongest minority candidate, and his candidacy would build stronger ties between blacks and Latinos, which Vann would find useful in his quest for the Brooklyn borough presidency.

Just when it seemed that the CJNY had no alternative but to back Badillo despite his flaws, CJNY member and Manhattan county leader Assemblyman Herman "Denny" Farrell offered himself to the group and won its endorsement. (In any event, a Badillo candidacy did not get off the ground.) Farrell's candidacy was virtually in name only. He raised little campaign money, had no organization, and could not articulate his positions or his rationale for making the race.

While the CJNY's choice may have been rational in that Farrell was more acceptable to its members' immediate constituencies than were the alternatives, it created a storm of criticism that reflected deep tensions within the black political leadership and between it and its potential allies. Black women criticized the CJNY for excluding them, even though a third of the black state legislators were female. Insurgents like Vann and Reverend Butts were upset that the Manhattan black political establishment had imposed a candidate who undermined their citywide coalition as well as the Vann candidacy in Brooklyn and Assemblyman José Serrano's run against Bronx Borough President Stanley Simon. (Butts resigned from the CJNY in protest.) The Farrell candidacy built no bridges to Latino leaders or public employee unions, neither of whom were party to the CJNY's deliberations or supported its choice. Some Latino elected officials actually showed up at Farrell's announcement to harass him.

At the same time, Mayor Koch took active steps to shore up his Latino and black support as well as his white Catholic support. In contrast to previous campaigns, the mayor put half his $8 million campaign war chest into field operations, primarily in minority neighborhoods. He invested heavily in advertising oriented to Spanish-speaking and black audiences. His campaign manager reported investing a quarter of the field operations budget in Harlem and Bedford-Stuyvesant and targeting 40 percent of his media toward black audiences and 30 percent toward Latino audiences.[31]

After the 1981 election, the mayor had appointed a Puerto Rican special assistant assigned to bring the Latino vote firmly into his fold. In August 1985, Koch held a news conference to describe what he had done and would do for Latinos in New York City, whom he described as the worst off and most deserving of government help.[32] His campaign chose South Bronx poverty program baron Ramon Velez to head a field operation in the South Bronx, despite Koch's attacks on him as a "poverty pimp" eight years earlier.[33] Mayor Koch endorsed and received endorsements from all three Puerto Rican city council members and two of the six black members; two others were also considered his allies.[34]

The Triumph of the Conservative Coalition

Mayor Koch routed his white liberal and black challengers in the 1985 Democratic primary and rebounded from his weak showing against Cuomo in 1982. He won 63.3 percent of the vote, holding his two opponents to a lower percentage than the Barbaro campaign had attracted four years earlier. Exit polls indicate that the mayor won 75 percent of the white vote, 70 percent of the Latino vote, and even 37 percent of the black vote. Among non-Hispanic whites, the mayor did even better among Italians and Irish Catholics (83 percent and 85 percent) than among Jews (75 percent).[35] These exit-poll figures are confirmed by the aggregate data by AD contained in Table 5.5.[36]

The 1985 primary consolidated the alignments that Koch had developed in the 1981 primary. Compared to his 1982 race against Cuomo, he increased his support in every component of the electorate. He did best in outer-borough Jewish ADs; according to exit polls, Jews amounted to 29 percent of the overall electorate. He did almost equally well in white Catholics ADs, bringing in line a group that constituted another 25 percent of the electorate, according to the exit polls. As Table 5.5 shows, turnout was highest in white Catholic and outer-borough Jewish ADs.

Mayor Koch also shifted the Latino electorate, which had more than doubled in size between 1982 and 1985, to his camp: his margin in the five majority-Latino ADs jumped from 40.4 percent to 62.4 percent. Because of the appearance of Latino candidates for citywide office for the first time since 1977, their turnout was also much higher than it had been. Since Latinos could swing towards blacks on the basis of class position and mutual political exclusion or towards white Catholics based on religion and relative conservatism, Koch's consolidation of support from Catholic constituencies made his electoral position practically hegemonic.

Koch also won considerable support in the constituencies that had most reason to defect, namely blacks and white liberals. He took ten of the thirteen majority black ADs and piled up substantial minorities in the three ADs that Farrell won. While the WABC-TV/*Daily News* exit poll showed Koch got 37 percent of the black vote, Farrell got only 41 percent,

TABLE 5.5
Democratic Primary Vote, Registration, and Turnout by AD Type

AD Type	November 1982 Koch %	April 1984 Jackson %	September 1985 Vote	Turnout %	Koch %	Farrell %	Latinos %[a]
Black	39.3	75.2	129,464	26.8	41.0	32.7	23.9
Mixed minority	44.0	51.1	54,131	30.6	58.2	19.8	39.5
Latino	50.4	40.4	55,353	31.6	62.4	17.8	43.3
White liberal	49.6	16.9	134,334	36.6	57.2	6.6	16.6
White Catholic	47.9	14.0	135,122	31.4	69.3	5.9	15.6
Outer-borough Jewish	62.3	11.8	180,150	37.4	77.6	5.6	12.0
Total	51.1	33.7	688,554	32.6	63.3	13.0	20.1

Source: New York City Board of Elections.
[a]Votes for three Latino candidates as percentage of total votes cast for city council president.

with 20 percent going to Bellamy. While the weakness of the Farrell candidacy explains much of this result, it may also indicate that Koch's rhetorical appeals to the black middle class had some effect. Koch did even better among white liberals. He won 44 percent of the votes of feminist supporters of the Equal Rights Amendment, while Carol Bellamy took only 45 percent of that vote. Koch systematically out-polled Bellamy among voters who took liberal positions on a variety of controversial positions.[37] Bellamy was clearly unable to spur turnout in the white liberal ADs, normally a high-turnout group.[38]

Across all groups, Farrell's candidacy attracted less than half the percentage of votes that Jackson had won a year and a half earlier. Farrell's weak candidacy depressed the turnout in black ADs. (The vote rose in Latino ADs due to the voter-registration effort and the candidacy of three Latinos for the city council presidency.) In the Latino ADs, Farrell got less than half the votes that Jackson had attracted; support in black ADs for the Latino city council candidates was even less.

In the midst of this debacle for the mayor's opponents, two outcomes did have a long-term impact that favored the mayor's potential challengers. First was the increase in black and Latino registration between 1982 and 1985. Even though minority registration subsequently declined and the registration campaign before the 1989 elections was not effective, the changes of the 1982–85 period still altered the terrain upon which future contests would be fought. Second, David N. Dinkins was elected Manhattan borough president. Dinkins "came up" through the Carver Democratic Club in Harlem, the regular black club run by the legendary J. Raymond Jones.[39] He had been elected an assemblyman and had been named a deputy mayor in the Beame administration in 1973 but could not take the position when a background check revealed that he had not filed income tax returns for the four previous years. Dinkins subsequently held patronage positions as head of the Board of Elections and city clerk in Manhattan, during which time he ran three times for borough president. He lost badly in 1977 but came extremely close to winning in 1981.

The Manhattan black political establishment may have accepted a weak citywide mayoral candidate in 1985 so as not to draw campaign contributions away from Dinkins's run for the borough presidency. Since Andrew Stein, to whom Dinkins had narrowly lost in 1981, was moving from the borough presidency to the city council presidency in 1985, Dinkins was ideally positioned to make the 1985 race. Though he had been Jackson's 1984 coordinator for Manhattan, Dinkins did not ask Jackson to campaign for him in 1985. Instead, he sought to appeal to white liberals, Jews, and Latinos as well as blacks. The 1985 NBC exit poll showed that Dinkins won 91 percent of the black vote, 79 percent of the Latino vote, and 50 percent of the white vote against a white liberal opponent.[40]

This breakdown held much more potential for a citywide candidacy than did Farrell's dismal performance.

Mayor Koch's third inauguration in January 1986 was soon overshadowed by another potential difficulty: the exposure and ultimate downfall of two of his most important supporters, Stanley Friedman of the Bronx and Donald Manes of Queens. A federal investigation of corruption in Chicago had led back to Manes, who had been taking bribes in return for awarding contracts to collection agencies that would pursue those who failed to pay their parking tickets. This web of corrupt activities would ultimately lead to a large number of indictments, convictions, and resignations of senior officials in the county party organizations and the Koch administration, thus severely weakening the mayor's organizational support and his standing in public opinion.

Dinkins aside, however, the 1985 elections defeated the other leaders of potentially challenging constituencies. José Serrano narrowly lost the Bronx borough presidency to Stanley Simon, amidst speculation that election irregularities had played a deciding role. Al Vann badly lost the Brooklyn borough president race, even though the white incumbent, Howard Golden, was also challenged by two other white candidates. Vann's candidates against two African-American regular Democratic city council members also lost by substantial margins. Vann took only 60 percent of the black vote, only 28 percent of the Latino vote, and a mere 6 percent of the white vote. This removed him as a threat to the Manhattan black establishment and markedly weakened his Coalition for Community Empowerment in Brooklyn. Sentiment within Brooklyn's large black community was clearly divided about Vann, just as it was on the race between Farrell and Koch.[41] This ambivalence rested on real social divisions within the black community between renters and homeowners, the native born and West Indians, and reformers versus regulars.

Not only was the black leadership in disarray, but so were relations between blacks and Latinos, between blacks and white reformers, and between these constituencies and the municipal labor unions. The promise that had seemed inherent in the 1984 Jackson campaign—that the right candidate could mobilize the black community as the single largest Democratic voting bloc and unite it with a broader coalition—had dissolved in the divisions and infighting of the 1985 mayoral campaign. Instead, it was Mayor Koch who had woven a "rainbow coalition" out of Jews, white Catholics, Latinos, and even a significant minority of the black vote.

The 1985 mayoral primary demonstrated the practical hegemony of the mayor's electoral coalition. It showed the effect that the challenge of a minority candidate and the none-too-subtle appeals to racial anxieties issuing from Mayor Koch could have on gelling the Jewish-white Catholic alignment. It showed that a conservative white candidate could make a strong and successful appeal to Latino voters and that the possibility of an alliance of blacks, Latinos, and white liberals was remote at best.

Forging a Governing Coalition: Party Regulars and the Corporate Elite

In the mid-1980s, Mayor Koch was able to translate this majority electoral coalition into a dominant governing coalition. The electorally unassailable occupant of the central office in New York City government, Mayor Koch was the pivotal participant in arriving at a decision on every important matter of discretionary governmental action. Anyone with "business" to move through city government had to have his approval. To a certain extent, therefore, the mayor's governing coalition was ready-made. He could forge alliances with any interest that wanted favorable treatment from government either by bringing other centers of governmental power into agreement or by threatening to withhold his consent.

Central to this power was the Koch administration's capacity to carry out its agenda with regard to taxing, spending, and urban development. This required ongoing support from the other centers of governmental power, particularly the members of the Board of Estimate. But through his electoral influence and his alliances with the county Democratic leaders and the borough presidents, he was generally able to dominate the board, though at the cost of various patronage concessions to them. He also sought support from the private organizations that wielded the resources necessary for carrying out public policy and that could reinforce his hand with other centers of public authority.

This led the Koch administration, despite its reform Democratic roots, to strike accommodations with party regulars and corporate elites in real estate development, finance, and corporate law. These interests desired policies that redounded to both their collective good and their individual benefit. While Mayor Koch sought to use his governing powers with respect to other interests, notably the growing network of government contracts to constrain the political activities of community-based organizations, his relations with the regular Democratic organizations and the real estate and finance industries were central to his regime.

Party Regulars

As the previous chapter noted, the Democratic party county organizations have been closely identified with the borough presidents and city council members. None of the former and few of the latter were insurgent or antiorganization figures in the years since 1977. While reformers more or less destroyed the Manhattan county party organization, the four other county organizations grew stronger during the 1980s despite racial tensions and the need to absorb the occasionally successful insurgent.[42]

Since the borough presidents cast five of the eleven votes on the Board of Estimate, and since the other citywide elected officials on it were the mayor's natural enemies, the mayor's search for governing power led directly to the borough presidents and the county party organizations. At election time, they could put the mayor on the ballot, keep his enemies off it, and help elect him. On the board, they could provide the mayor with the votes he needed to control it. With this commanding position, the mayor could usually induce the comptroller and city council president to join his position by making relatively minor concessions to their positions where they happened to diverge from his own.[43]

The electoral importance of Mayor Koch's ties with the regular Democratic organizations may be seen in Table 5.6. Except in the three Latino and seven mixed-minority ADs, the presence of strong regular Democratic political clubs consistently led to more support for Mayor Koch. Strong clubs were worth 10 percentage points over reform areas among black ADs. The presence of strong regular clubs made a similar differences in white liberal ADs and contributed 4 points in white Catholic ADs. Although basic racial differences determined the outcome in 1985, the impact of local political culture was real and could have been decisive in a closer election.

TABLE 5.6
1985 Primary Vote for Koch by AD Ethnicity and Club Strength

AD Type	Reform	Split or Contested Regular	Uncontested Regular
Black	37.0%	39.2%	47.2%
(13 ADs)	(2)	(7)	(4)
Latino	—	62.9%	61.2%
(5 ADs)		(2)	(3)
Mixed Minority	—	62.4%	54.7%
(5 ADs)		(2)	(3)
White Liberal	54.8%	65.8%	—
(9 ADs)	(6)	(3)	
White Catholic	—	70.0%	74.7%
(15 ADs)		(4)	(11)
Outer-borough Jewish	75.3%	77.9%	77.8%
(13 ADs)	(1)	(3)	(9)

Source: New York City Board of Elections and expert consensus.

In exchange for support in elections and votes at the Board of Estimate, the county organizations wanted what political machines have always wanted: jobs, contracts, and favorable land-use decisions in their domains. As the corruption scandals after 1986 revealed, Mayor Koch went a long way to respond to these desires. A contract to develop a hand-held computer was awarded to a virtually nonexistent company partly owned by Bronx county leader Stanley Friedman, while Queens county leader Donald Manes took kickbacks on parking ticket collections contracts let by Koch officials appointed at Manes's request. These deals attracted the most attention in the corruption scandals, but they were the island tip of a submarine mountain chain.[44]

The patronage-hiring operation run out of City Hall by Koch's key adviser on appointments and patronage, Joseph DeVincenzo, with the participation of key mayoral political aide John LoCicero, was particularly revealing. The cover for this operation was the "Mayor's Talent Bank," a computerized data base whose ostensible purpose was to promote the hiring of blacks, Latinos, and women. Mayoral agencies could not make discretionary or provisional appointments without considering resumes from the Talent Bank and clearing hires through "Joe D." In theory, the Talent Bank would ensure that the resumes of qualified minority individuals would be considered. The Talent Bank had been established in April 1983 in response to recurrent criticism from black and Puerto Rican political figures that the Koch administration was unresponsive on affirmative action and reflected the mayor's desire to establish a good record in this respect.

In practice, however, the Talent Bank became a computerized patronage-hiring system grafted onto an affirmative action program.[45] In addition to referrals made by DeVincenzo and LoCicero, the Talent Bank data file included names and resumes submitted by county party leaders and their trusted lieutenants for both senior policy positions and laborer positions in agencies like the Department of Environmental Protection (DEP) that did not require a civil service test. Political referrals were color-coded and assigned a "hot" or "super" priority; when departments reported openings to DeVincenzo, he would send over resumes of applicants suggested by political sponsors. For more senior positions, where qualifications mattered, agency administrators found that they would have to accept some City Hall referrals to get DeVincenzo's approval for hires that they wanted to make. Resistance to the referrals produced inaction on agency requests.[46]

Political referrals had long been linked with access to laborer's positions in departments like DEP, Transportation, and Parks. Koch had appointed Anthony Ameruso to head Transportation, for example, at the recommendation of Brooklyn county leader Meade Esposito over opposition of his own transition committee. Ameruso was forced to resign in 1986 because it became public that he did not live in the city and had failed to disclose his profits from an investment made with individuals whose companies he regulated. Laborers jobs and similar positions required no skills and had relatively low pay, but they were a good access point into the civil service and could lead to higher paid positions. Between 1983 and 1986, most placements to such positions were in fact Talent Bank political referrals from the Staten Island, Bronx, and Queens county organizations.[47] Most were white males, not the minority and women candidates whom the Talent Bank was designed to serve.

In the wake of the corruption scandals in early 1986, DeVincenzo ordered the Talent Bank to destroy records that would reveal that it had operated as a channel for political referrals. As part of this cover-up, he also ordered that all laborers' jobs would henceforth be filled the way the Talent Bank was supposed to operate. Subsequently, the fraction of minorities and women rose, but the patronage function also appears to have continued.

In late 1988, the former administrator of the Talent Bank turned over to the State Commission on Government Integrity a copy of the "black book" of political referrals she had inadvertently saved from destruction in 1986. The commission's investigation led DeVincenzo, one of the mayor's most powerful and confidential advisers, to resign. He was later convicted of lying about his cover-up. The mayor at first disputed that the Talent Bank was a patronage mill and then said, "I believe there's nothing wrong in terms of fungible jobs, no skills, ditch-diggers, to say to county leaders, district leaders, Donald Manes, Stanley Friedman, 'Sure! Why not? What's the difference?' "[48]

The Finance, Real Estate, and Law Elite

Parallel with his ties to the regular party organizations that dominated the peripheries of the city's political system and gave him control over the Board of Estimate, Mayor Koch also forged ties with the corporate elite, especially the parts based in real estate development and municipal finance. Here, too, there was a simple but compelling rationale for the exchange of support. The mayor could advance policies that collectively favored those who financed and developed commercial office building construction in the Manhattan central business district and grant specific discretionary actions that could substantially increase the bottom line of any given project. He and the comptroller could also select securities firms that underwrote the city debt that, after the city's return to the market in 1981, became a significant part of the national market for municipal securities. In return, developers, their bankers and lawyers, and the securities industry would invest in the city, build projects that had political benefits, make large campaign contributions, and lend corporate power and prestige to the mayor.

Campaign contributions provide one way of examining the relationship between the mayor and his key business supporters. The mayor came from a political culture that was distant from, when not at odds with, the culture of large corporations. When first elected, the mayor was unknown to New York's business leaders and not particularly comfortable with them. At the same time, however, Mayor Koch's highest priorities were to control spending, clean up the poverty program, and promote private development. This was consonant with the views propounded by such organizations as the New York City Partnership, an organization of top corporate executives organized by David Rockefeller in the wake of the fiscal crisis. As Mayor Koch made his policy intentions clear during his first administration, especially with respect to development and business taxation issues, business support grew.

By the 1982 gubernatorial campaign, the mayor's need for campaign funds had increased greatly over the already substantial requirements of the 1977 and 1981 campaigns. The 1985 mayoral campaign was even more expensive. The real estate and securities industries contributed heavily to all these races. Indeed, they provided the bulk of all political financing between 1981 and 1986, as studies by the office of State Senator Franz Leichter show. Leichter's staff collected individual candidates' reports of campaign contributions and collated them by the firms or entities with whom the giver was attached. They then analyzed the range of candidates and party organizations these givers supported.

In all, the mayor, the other members of the Board of Estimate, and the five Democratic county committees raised more than $30 million between 1981 and 1986. Mayor Koch raised $11.9 million, mostly for the 1985 mayoral race. Comptroller Harrison "Jay" Goldin received $3.2 million and City Council President Stein $4.3 million. The borough presidents raised $7.6 million, while their allied Democratic county organizations received another $3.1 million. (Perhaps reflecting its relative ability to peddle its influence, the Bronx organization raised the most money.)

The top 200 contributing entities gave one-third of the total amount of money; 60 percent had business matters before the Board of Estimate, and almost 80 percent contributed to more than one of the relevant officials. They thus appeared to be seeking access and influence, not supporting candidates whose qualities or philosophy they admired. The top 50 contributors gave almost a quarter of the total; of them, over 70 percent had business before the board. Of this group, 23 were real estate firms, 9 were securities firms, 6 were law firms, 2 were city contractors, 1 was a labor union (the International Longshoreman's Association), and the other 9 represented such diverse corporate interests as Leon Hess, owner of Hess Oil and the New York Giants football team, or David Margolis of Colt Industries.[49]

While much of this money reflects corporate gratitude for the collective benefits these industries derived from the favorable policies of the Koch administration, large contributors with significant matters requiring discretionary action from the Board of Estimate clearly also expected results.[50] From a broader political perspective, however, it makes little difference whether such contributions were given as a quid pro quo for favorable action or whether they were merely a political "tax" that would not necessarily determine the outcome. The result was that corporate interests gained differential and superior access to governmental decision-making on issues of concern to them and that the Koch administration adopted policies that generally favored their interests.

Conclusion

By the mid-1980s, Mayor Koch had assembled a new dominant political coalition capable of exercising an almost unparalleled degree of power in both the electoral arena and the governance of the city. These outcomes were interdependent: he wielded leverage in governance partly because his political position was so unassailable; his ability to forge alliances with the regular Democratic organizations and private elites gave Koch political resources that enabled him to contain any political force that might challenge him in mayoral elections.

Several factors contributed to the dominance of the Koch electoral coalition. First, Mayor Koch and his strategists managed to create a strong cross-ethnic alliance among whites. Previously, Jews and white Catholics had often gone in different political directions, with Jews providing the basis for the white liberal tradition in New York, while more conservative white Catholics had been defecting gradually but steadily to the Republicans (in the ballot box, if not always in their party registration). By attacking corrupt black politicians and advocating the death penalty, Mayor Koch tapped into, and helped to foster, white middle-class residents' fear of the problems that might come with racial succession in the city. Although the Jewish/white Catholic alliance could be sundered by an attractive white Catholic candidate, as in 1982, it served as a powerful motive force for Koch in the 1981, 1985, and even 1989 mayoral elections.

Second, Mayor Koch retained substantial support among blacks, white liberals, and especially Latinos during much of the 1980s, even as he was realigning the other segments of the electorate. The mayor's strong defense of middle-class interests, values, and aspirations was designed to reach over the heads of the black and Latino leaders he had antagonized and to speak directly to their middle-class constituents. Many of the mayor's themes, such as his attacks on special interests and his emphasis on effective management, continued to resonate with white liberals. Moreover, he brought a great many white liberals into his administration, especially in its early years. As a past master of the media and as a highly articulate person, Koch could speak directly to these audiences.

The great fragmentation among the leaders of potentially challenging constituencies and the extensive distrust and cynicism blacks and Latinos expressed about their leaders facilitated Mayor Koch's strategy. The organization of New York City's political culture encouraged this fragmentation. Black leaders, for example, were divided by borough, nativity, gender, and relationship to the regular Democratic organizations. The revival of the regular Democratic county political organizations during the 1980s also helped Mayor Koch to build his own version of the rainbow coalition. These organizations promoted their own black and Puerto Rican candidates, absorbed or coopted successful insurgents, and denied others access to the ballot. In this way, they exercised considerable influence over the scope and direction of minority political mobilization. Mayor Koch's alliance with black and Puerto Rican regulars reinforced his minority electoral support. Despite his initial attack on the use of poverty funds for political patronage, he eventually made use of this mechanism.[51]

Koch also took advantage of the deep and persisting divisions among white liberals, blacks, and Latinos. As Chapter Three argued, white liberalism in New York decayed under the combined weight of the national shift to the right, the defensive posture of its Jewish social base in New York, and its incorporation into the political establishment.[52] White liberal reformers had long been at odds with Manhattan's black political establishment, who constituted most of what was left of regular politics in the borough. Blacks and Puerto Ricans also had a long history of political competition.[53] During most of the 1980s, these elements lacked consensus on a political philosophy and had no organizational basis around which to unite even if they had a philosophy. Koch, on the other hand, was able to develop both a philosophy and an organizational base that drew on the themes of fiscal crisis, racial succession, rebuilding the Democratic party organizations, and that controlled the mobilization of either community-based service-delivery organizations and public employee unions.

Finally, Mayor Koch consolidated elite support for his campaigns and administration. At the most elemental level, he quickly raised huge campaign war chests from elites and deployed them effectively. Neither his 1981 nor his 1985 opponents could raise enough money to be taken seriously. Even Carol Bellamy, who under other circumstances might have made a strong candidate, could raise only a small fraction of what Koch had collected. United support from corporate elites also enabled Koch to govern and to deliver on his basic promise of promoting New York City's economic prosperity.

Using the tripartite conceptualization of political interests, Mayor Koch organized majority support from private market interests and electoral constituencies while gaining effective mastery of public sector producer interests. Among the former, key interests included the financial services industry, the real estate development industry, and the legal and other service firms connected to them. They got strongly supportive policies, as the next chapter will show, and gave him material support and legitimacy in return. (Favorable treatment from the editorial boards of the city's newspapers was particularly valuable.)

Among the electoral constituencies, Koch concentrated on the broad reach of middle-class white Catholics and Jews who, though a receding fraction of the resident population, remained a majority of its voters. Koch gave them symbolic support and reoriented city spending away from areas that they felt had characterized the Lindsay administration and contributed to the fiscal crisis. In return, he got their votes. For most of the 1980s, Mayor Koch used these two sets of coalitions to reinforce one another and to hold sway over other centers of power inside local government. Economic interests gave Koch plentiful resources to run campaigns and access to and support in the most important organs of the mass media, thus reinforcing his stand in the electorate. His perceived strengths in the electorate made him the political figure with whom all others had to deal. We now turn to the ways in which he used the resulting political power to change the priorities of public policy in New York City.

Six

The Exercise of Power—Who Got What and Why

Mayor Koch's ability to dominate politics and prevail in conflicts with expenditure-seeking constituencies is in part a consequence (and in part a cause) of the decay of institutions and organizations that might serve as political bases for potential opponents of the mayor.
(Martin Shefter, *Political Crisis/Fiscal Crisis*)[1]

Other industries and people occupying the buildings may come and go; the real estate fraternity is forever. That is why it makes special claims on local government through its lawyers, campaign gifts, and savants. . . . No matter what coalition elected him, any New York mayor must move in tandem with this remarkable establishment, whose members sift the sites for new industries, classes, and modes of consumption, shaping New Yorkers' housing options and preferences in a speculative process whose tides are swift and unsparing.
(Jim Sleeper, "Days of Developers")[2]

Analyzing the Impact of Government: An Overview

It is relatively easy to determine who gained and who lost economic ground during the 1977–89 economic boom in New York City. Chapter Four described how the intersection between economic restructuring and the city's changing population produced the new racial, ethnic, and gender division of labor characterized by significantly greater income inequality. It is much more difficult to determine how much the actions of local government shaped the trajectories of particular groups as they confronted this matrix of economic and social change. Indeed, some observers even reject the idea that local government can have much impact on such matters.

It is intrinsically difficult to undertake the mental experiment of asking how would things have been in the absence of government intervention.

While cities obviously vary according to the size and shape of city government intervention as well as socioeconomic outcomes, these dimensions are generally not well measured or even well understood at the city level; large cities also tend to have large governments.

This is particularly true for New York City, where city government has long been deeply intertwined with the city's private economy. In 1991, one out every six workers in New York City was on a government payroll, mostly local government payrolls; the city and state government heavily finance such large sectors as health, social services, and education. City government affects the terms and conditions for doing business in the city through the incidence of local taxes, the services it provides, its construction and maintenance of economically essential infrastructure, and the way it regulates the business environment. Even if we focused only on the city's $29 billion expense budget for fiscal year (FY) 1991, a prima facie case exists that New York City government has a significant impact on economic and social outcomes.

Even if one accepts this starting point, however, it remains difficult to say how much this impact reflects discretion, choice, and priority setting, that is to say political decisions, and how much government's actions are driven instead by bureaucratic momentum, contextual factors such as the state of the economy, and the intergovernmental grant system. No general conclusion about this question is likely to hold; instead, the scope of politics is likely to vary over time and across places. But just as a prima facie case exists for the impact of local government actions on economic and social outcomes in New York, it is reasonable to assume that policy trends sometimes reflect implicit or explicit political choices.

Phases in the Public Spending

Large economic and political forces highly constrained local governmental discretion during the New York City fiscal crisis and hence the scope of local political influence over governmental actions. In the post-1977 economic boom, however, government regained its capacity and autonomy. An analysis of changing city priorities must thus distinguish between different phases of governmental capacity and autonomy. The Koch administration was able to put its imprint on city budget priorities in part because city revenues and expenditures were growing in real terms and relative to the city's gross economic product.[3]

Chapter Three described Brecher and Horton's analysis of the phases in the city's recent fiscal history: the run-up of city spending between 1961 and 1969, the slowing expenditures between 1969 and 1975, the fiscal crisis contraction between 1975 and 1983, and the resumption of governmental growth between 1983 and the late 1980s.[4] This periodization is based on inflection points in the constant dollar size of city expenditures in relation to local value added. Since their analysis, the lagged impact of the October 1987 stock market crash and the national economic recession have made themselves felt in a downturn of employment and revenues in New York City and New York State during 1990 and 1991 and renewed severe fiscal distress.

Between 1961 and 1969, economic growth and rising intergovernmental aid enabled the city to double its spending in real terms from $8.5 billion to $16.2 billion in 1982 constant dollars. Spending also rose from 11.1 percent of local value added to 17.2 percent. Between 1969 and 1975, spending rose more slowly as local recessions cut local revenues and the Nixon administration cut back aid to cities. It still reached a peak of $21.1 billion (in constant 1982 dollars) or 25.9 percent of local value added in 1975. In that year, accumulated debt and falling revenues precipitated a fiscal crisis and extensive retrenchment in city spending. Although the economy and federal aid both began to recover after 1976, city spending declined to $16.5 billion (in constant 1982 dollars) in 1983 and fell to 17.9 percent of local value added. Subsequently, despite declining intergovernmental aid, the booming economy enabled real government spending increase once more, reaching $20.7 billion (in constant 1982 dollars) or 19.1 percent of local value added in 1989.[5]

The fiscal crisis era of the Koch administration between 1977 and 1983 must therefore be distinguished from the subsequent era of renewed growth. In both periods, budgetary priorities seemed more strongly influenced by political than economic factors, though in opposite ways. In the fiscal crisis period, real city expenditures declined in spite of renewed growth in the city's economy and new aid from the Carter administration. This may in part reflect the extremely high rates of inflation at the end of the 1970s, but it also reflected the Koch administration's desire to resolve the fiscal crisis.

In the early 1980s, however, conditions changed. The city government balanced its budget beginning in 1981 and returned to the long-term capital market; the city economy felt little impact from the 1982 national recession and experienced rapid growth thereafter. Despite a relative decline in intergovernmental aid, the Koch administration could declare the fiscal crisis over and set new spending priorities. Between 1983 and 1989, it increased real spending in the city budget by 26 percent.

Changing Functional Priorities

The most obvious place to look at the potential impact of city government on economic and social outcomes is where it raises and spends public resources: the system of taxes, transfers, and borrowing by which city revenues are raised, the size of the city budget and its relation to local value added, and its method of allocating funds across departmental functions and objects of expenditure (labor costs, contracts for goods and services, capital expenditures, and debt service).[6] In these respects, New York City's budget is as large and intricate as that of many nations; only the federal, California, and New York State budgets are larger in the United States.

A host of factors, in addition to the explicit choices of local elected officials, shape the allocation of budgetary resources across departments and functions. These factors include the rate at which economic growth generates new revenues, the size of transfers from higher levels of government, court mandates like the requirement that New York City provide shelter for the homeless, and unforeseen crises like the AIDS epidemic or drug-related street violence. The analysis of the Koch administration's impact on budget patterns must therefore be approached with caution.

The broad outlines of spending under the Koch administration are presented in Table 6.1. (The table excludes debt payments and pension payments and shows how remaining expenditures are distributed across

TABLE 6.1

New York City Expenditures by Major Function, Selected Fiscal Years (millions of current dollars, excluding debt service and pensions)

	1978		1983		1989	
	$	%	$	%	$	%
Redistribution	4,216	40.9	4,908	39.1	7,295	34.8
Health	915		771		1,337	
Social services	3,135		3,759		5,355	
Housing	166		378		603	
Development	789	7.7	918	7.3	1,858	8.9
Water/sewers	429		570		910	
Streets/bridges/TA	360		348		948	
Education	3,090	30.0	3,153	25.3	6,052	28.9
Board of Education	2,596		2,983		5,786	
Community colleges	494		170		266	
Property protection	1,579	15.3	1,705	13.6	3,174	15.1
Police/courts/jails	1,178		1,251		2,498	
Fire	401		454		676	
Other	633	6.1	1,850	14.7	2,589	12.3
Total	10,307		12,543		20,967	

Source: *Comprehensive Annual Report of the Comptroller*, Fiscal Years 1978, 1983, 1989. "Other" includes elected officials, overhead agencies, city planning, parks, libraries, and miscellaneous.

functions.) It reveals several clear trends. First, only spending on redistribution declined as a proportion of total spending in *both* the fiscal crisis and the recovery phases of the Koch era, from 40.9 percent in FY 1978 to 34.8 percent in FY 1989. Second, spending on the three other major functions lost budget share to overhead and miscellaneous agencies in the fiscal crisis period, although development functions were the least reduced.[7] In the postfiscal crisis period, however, these functions again gained share, while spending on infrastructure grew the most rapidly. Development-related operating expenditures doubled in current dollars between FY 1983 and FY 1989, rising from 7.3 percent to 8.9 percent of the total, exceeding the FY 1978 share. (When combined with the jump in capital spending by the city and the Metropolitan Transit Authority [MTA] during the same period, this represented a major commitment to the infrastructure.)

Spending on education also nearly doubled between 1983 and 1989, and its share rose from 25.3 to 28.9 percent, although it did not quite regain its 1978 share. (This gain went to the Board of Education and was offset by a decline in the share going to the CUNY community colleges.) Finally, the share of spending on the criminal justice system and fire protection also climbed from 13.6 percent of the total to 15.1 percent.

In sum, by the end of the cycle of fiscal crisis and recovery, it can be said that the Koch administration consistently cut the share of redistributive services, increased the budget share of overhead agencies and the executive staffs, and increased the budget share devoted to developmental activities. In the other areas, it first cut and then mostly restored the shares of education, criminal justice, and fire protection.[8]

Especially given that income and inequality and social pressures clearly worsened during the 1980s, these patterns suggest that the Koch administration made at least an implicit decision to slow the rise in social service spending, especially for public assistance, and to quicken the rise in spending on developmental activities and overall management. In the fiscal crisis period, the Koch administration also held down the growth of the core urban services, education, police, and fire protection; when the fiscal crisis was deemed to be over, it allowed these services to recover their share.

When all was said and done, social services suffered a loss relative to other functions, while developmental activities gained during the Koch administration. While the federal retreat from manpower, housing, and other social programs during the 1980s helped drive this trend, the Koch administration clearly allocated relatively few of its discretionary resources to countering it. The need for these services certainly did not decrease, since poverty and the rent burden on poor families rose substantially over this period.[9]

The Objects of City Spending: Labor, Transfer Payments, Capital, and Contracts

As Raymond Horton has cautioned us, however, we cannot simply equate budget inputs, departmental outputs, and service outcomes when examining broad patterns of expenditure by function.[10] Agencies deploy their resources in complex environments that are not under their control. Their success may depend not only on how efficiently management converts inputs into outputs (for example, dollars into sanitation workers and garbage trucks) but on how outputs interact with the public to produce outcomes (for example, how much garbage people create, how they dispose of it, whether their parked cars prevent street sweeping, and so on). Since consumers co-produce public services, public managers do not control a vital part of the production process. As a result, dollars allocated to the police department may well have little impact on the crime rate. A more complete analysis of the Koch administration's efforts to shape economic and social outcomes would have to consider the constraints embedded in the design of service-delivery systems and the way in which the Koch administration tried or failed to attack them.[11]

But if the service outcomes experienced by citizens bear a complex and indirect relationship to spending for a given service function, the interests that benefit as objects of public spending are relatively straightforward. Table 6.2 presents the major objects of expenditure in the New York City

TABLE 6.2
New York City Expenditures by Object, Selected Fiscal Years
(millions of 1983 dollars)

	1978		1983		1989	
	$	%	$	%	$	%
Expense Budget						
Personal Service	8,346	41.4	7,904	49.1	10,387	53.5
OTPS	4,961[a]	24.6	4,272	26.5	5,442	28.0
Medicaid	1,702	8.4	709	4.4	830	4.3
Public Assistance	1,957	9.7	1,461	9.1	1,366	7.0
Debt Service	3,214	15.9	1,756	10.9	1,397	7.2
Total Expense Budget[b]	19,929[a]		16,019		19,278	
Capital Budget	791		1,319		2,474	

Source: Comprehensive Annual Financial Report of the Comptroller, FY 1978, Part II, Statement 1; FY 1983, Part II-B, Schedule G8; FY 1989, Part II-B, Schedule G6; percentages may not add to 100 due to rounding.
[a]Adjusted to reflect shift of CUNY to State Budget.
[b]Reflects netting of interdepartmental transfers.

budget during the Koch administration.[12] Several major patterns stand out: first, between 1977 and 1983, the city budget contracted by almost one-fifth in real terms as the administration held current dollar budget increases to small percentages and as the high inflation of the period took its toll. The declining debt service only partially offset this reduction; spending on everything else still contracted by 14.7 percent. Then, between 1983 and 1989, real city spending expanded by one-fifth. Considering that debt service continued to fall, this expansion increased real spending on everything else to 7.0 percent more than its 1978 level.

Since local government is labor intensive, it is not surprising that Table 6.2 shows that public employees have been the major beneficiary of public spending. Horton found that labor costs amounted to 59.5 percent of the city budget in 1970 but fell during the fiscal crisis.[13] During the Koch years, real labor costs also fell between 1977 and 1983, but less quickly than did the budget as a whole. As a result, its share grew from 41.4 percent to 49.1 percent of the total. Between 1983 and 1989, real labor costs climbed more rapidly than the whole; its share thus rose to 53.5 percent.

Public employees are not the only powerful and well-organized objects of public spending. As previous chapters argued, city government has increasingly relied on grants and contracts to private, nonprofit groups to deliver public services. Table 6.2 shows that city contracts for goods and services (so-called OTPS or "other than personal services") accounted for a large and expanding share of the city budget. While nonprofit community-based service providers account for only roughly one-quarter of OTPS spending, or about 7 percent of the total, they have joined public employees as major beneficiaries of the public budget. Like total spending, spending on these entities fell between 1977 and 1983, but then rebounded to much higher levels by 1989.

Transfer payments, whether public assistance to poor individuals or Medicaid payments on their behalf to hospitals and doctors, also account for a significant part of the city budget, 11.3 percent in 1989. Unlike labor costs and OTPS, however, these activities fell in both absolute and relative terms during the fiscal crisis and the expansion periods of the Koch administration, mirroring the pattern already shown in Table 6.1. A major portion of this fall was driven by factors like eligibility and reimbursement rules that the city did not control. Yet the city government has consistently lobbied to reduce its financial exposure for these functions. To the extent that revenue growth in the 1980s gave the city government the option of increasing local discretionary spending on welfare functions, it does not seem to have done so.

Finally, debt service is also a major component of city spending, as Table 6.2 also shows. Falling interest rates and the city's improved credit rating sharply lowered the cost of this borrowing during the 1980s, thus substantially reducing its budget share from the peak attained during the fiscal crisis. But though the cost fell, the total amount of long-term borrowing rose rapidly. Since returning to the capital market in 1981, the city has steadily issued new debt. By the 1990 fiscal year, the New York City and the Municipal Assistance Corporation had $21.4 billion in debt outstanding, up from $13.8 billion in FY 1983 and $12.9 billion in FY 1978. Though this debt required only 7.2 percent of the budget in 1990, or $1.8 billion in current dollars, these payments still constitute a substantial transfer payment to investors who buy the city's notes and bonds. The public finance departments of securities firms that underwrite new debt issues also earned tens of millions of dollars in commissions each year.

Table 6.2 shows that declining spending on debt service did reduce expenditures from the capital spending program. The capital budget involves building facilities using money borrowed through long-term bonds. Real spending on capital projects tripled between 1978 and 1989 and exceeded $4 billion in FY 1990. (The Koch administration's concerted effort to increase the size of the capital program caused debt-service payments to rise in the Dinkins administration, forcing it to cut back the capital budget.) These capital expenditures constituted a major benefit to many important economic constituencies, including the contracting firms that built public works and the developers of central business district properties who relied on capital spending to improve access to the central business district.

The distribution of these capital expenditures across different functions is given in Table 6.3. It shows that capital spending patterns mirrored those of total expenditures. The Koch administration increased spending on economic development and roads (but not mass transit) faster than other functions. Since the state was also making large capital investments in bridges, highways, and the subway system during the 1980s, this represented a substantial investment in bringing the basic economic infrastructure back from its crumbling state. As with direct service expenditures on government overhead activities, the capital budget also allocated increased funding for city office buildings. It also made smaller, but still substantial, increases in the functions that are traditionally large components of capital spending, such as the water system, sanitation facilities, and schools.

What really stands out in Table 6.3, however, are two dramatic shifts in priority. One was mirrored in spending on direct services after 1983, namely the heavy emphasis on building up the jail system. The Koch administration's attack on crime was embodied not in expanding the police department but in locking up substantially larger numbers of criminals, many on Rikers Island, which may have become the largest penal colony

TABLE 6.3
Capital Expenditures by Function and Agency, FY 1980, FY 1989
(millions of FY 1989 constant dollars)

Function	FY 1980	FY 1989	Percent Change
Economic infrastructure			
Economic development	$26.4	$72.6	175.3
Department of Transportation	$140.8	$421.8	199.6
Transit Authority	$421.1	$472.1	12.1
General government			
Department of General Services	$30.5	$192.5	530.6
Department of Environmental			
Protection/Sanitation	$420.7	$831.6	97.7
Fire	$19.4	$22.9	18.2
Criminal justice			
Police	$14.2	$31.2	120.0
Corrections	$5.2	$169.1	3195.5
Redistribution			
Social services	$0.0	$66.5	n.a.
Housing	$32.4	$366.6	1032.9
Health	$31.5	$119.3	278.6
Education and amenities			
Education	$154.2	$214.1	38.9
Parks	$18.9	$137.3	625.5
Libraries	$6.3	$23.6	275.4
Total	$1,352.9	$3,141.6	132.2

Source: *Annual Comprehensive Financial Report of the Comptroller*, FY 1980, Part IIB, Schedule 9; FY 1989, Part II-B, Schedule CP2.

in the world.[14] The other is the city's recent commitment to spend city capital budget money on rehabilitating the large stock of residential buildings seized by the city for tax delinquency. Mayor Koch made this program the centerpiece of his third term, promising to spend $5.2 billion over a ten-year period.

Cui Bono?

We are now in a position to summarize who gained (and who lost) from changes in the patterns of direct governmental spending during the Koch administration. Between 1978 and the early 1980s, the administration sought to control spending, bring the budget into balance, and create a positive environment for private investment. By 1981, and certainly by 1983, it had succeeded in doing so. It reached these objectives by holding the growth of spending under the rate of inflation and decreasing its tax burden on the income being generated by the local economy. All primary functions were cut during this period except overhead management activities.

Since labor costs are the largest object of expenditure, controlling costs relied on reducing the number of public employees and, in many instances, the level of public services. (Organized labor and the Koch administration rejected the alternative strategy of reducing pay levels for individual workers so as to keep more of them and produce more services.) But the Koch administration treated city workers well compared to other objects of expenditure: it cut spending on OTPS, welfare transfer payments, and debt-service payments much more heavily. Put another way, the first half of the Koch administration favored what Sayre and Kaufman called "revenue providers" over what they called "service demanders."

But as the case of city workers suggests, "service demanders" were not all equal. The city employees who remained on the payroll were insulated from the worst effects of retrenchment, while community-based service-delivery organizations and users of city services felt more of its impact. Those who depended on public assistance fared the worst. These priorities also showed up in how the administration allocated shares of the budget across policy domains. In relative terms, the Koch administration reduced the budget shares going toward social services, property services, and education during the fiscal crisis period, while increasing the share going to executive and overhead functions. (After adjusting Table 6.1 for inflation, for example, annual spending on social services declined $1.4 billion, or 21.8 percent, between FY 1978 and FY 1983, accounting for half of the real decline in spending.)

As economic growth, higher revenues, and consecutive balanced budgets enabled the Koch administration to increase real spending after the early 1980s, aspects of this picture changed. Spending for all purposes except debt service grew by 25 percent between FY 1983 and FY 1989 after adjusting for inflation. Though the local economy also grew rapidly, city spending began to creep up as a share of local value added. The real increase in revenues and spending enabled the city to expand its employment, raise its employees' real rates of compensation, and dramatically increase its capital commitments, while paying a lower share of its budget for debt service.

In the recovery period, the Koch administration thus began to favor service demanders more than revenue providers. But as before, expenditure constituencies varied greatly in the degree to which they shared in the renewed growth of government. Real spending on those who provided and relied on redistributive social services rebounded, but at only half the rate of overall spending. Their share thus continued to fall relative to other functions. Within social services, spending on service providers, whether city employees or third-party providers, went up in real and relative terms, while transfer payments to individuals went down. As in the fiscal crisis era, the dependent poor suffered most, while the network of "third party" service providers grew.

In contrast to the decline in social services, the Koch administration put a disproportionate share of the real increase in spending into expanding development activities while also putting lesser shares into education and property services to restore them to pre-fiscal crisis levels. When combined with the increase in capital spending, the Koch administration's highest postfiscal crisis priority was clearly on developmental activities.

In both its fiscal crisis and recovery phases, the Koch administration therefore matched its conservative rhetoric with conservative budgetary practice. In some important respects, such as the loss of real and relative support for public assistance or subsidized housing construction, this practice reflected similar decisions made at other levels of government. But in many others, it reflected choices made by Mayor Edward I. Koch to advance his philosophy and strategy for governing.

Budget expenditures do not tell the full story, however. The Koch administration's commitment to increasing developmental spending, a small component of the expense budget and a larger share of the capital budget, hints at a broader dimension to its impact: using regulation to promote private investment in the physical environment that houses New York City's advanced corporate service sector. We now turn to this subject; subsequent sections will further explore the city budget's relationship with municipal employees and the growth of "third party government."

The Off-Budget Impact of Government: Promoting Private Investment

The Institutional Framework

New York City has a complex institutional framework for conducting its planning and economic development policies. City, regional, and state agencies are all important players; each is accountable to a different master. The components of this institutional framework have multiple and conflicting motives: some, like the City Planning Commission or the Department of Environmental Protection, exercise regulatory powers and are charged with balancing the interests of developers against the public good. Yet these agencies also actively sponsor certain developments. Other entities, such as the New York City Public Development Corporation (PDC, recently reorganized as the Economic Development Corporation or EDC) or the New York State Urban Development Corporation (UDC), unabashedly promote their chosen projects.

Private developers operate in a highly regulated environment. While land-use regulation and environmental review are undoubtedly the major regulatory arenas, developers must also negotiate landmarks preservation, building codes, and rent regulation, not to mention the informal yet pervasive Mafia influence in the building industry.[15] Many other facets of public policy, such as tax incentive programs, capital projects, and economic development programs, significantly influence investment decisions for specific projects, if not always in the aggregate.[16]

The highly complex regulatory and institutional environment reflects and mediates conflict over the reshaping of the city's built environment. The main conflict pits those who seek to exploit the city's space economy more intensely (real estate developers and investors) against those adversely affected by development (usually neighborhood residents and low-income renters). A collateral conflict pits rising sectors like finance against declining sectors like manufacturing.

Both conflicts erupted episodically during the rapid and extensive development of commercial office and prime residential space in New York City during the 1977–89 economic boom. Historically, they have provoked the expansion of the regulatory apparatus surrounding physical development. Whether it be developers against neighborhood residents or rising economic constituencies against declining ones, the forces favoring development have greater economic resources and usually greater political cohesion and influence as well. Yet residential neighborhoods and declining industries also represent important latent constituencies that can mobilize to exert influence.[17] Neighborhood mobilization against urban renewal in the 1960s, for example, led the 1975 Charter Revision Commission to give community boards an advisory position in the uniform land-use review procedure (ULURP).[18]

To the extent that a dominant coalition's development agenda would sharpen these conflicts and arouse overt opposition, it would rationally seek to obscure its major objectives within a more ambiguous array of policies. It would also attempt to control the extent to which mechanisms of public deliberation, such as the City Planning Commission or the environmental review process, offer points of leverage to its opponents. The Koch administration aggressively pursued both of these strategies.

With regard to planning, the administration never sought to articulate an overall planning philosophy but expedited specific projects instead. Professional planners and their allies attacked this lack of comprehensive planning. Paul Goldberger, the *New York Times* architectural critic, for example, commented that "much of what is regulated is minutiae, not large visions of what we want the city to be. . . . City government is offering not a vision of this proper role but an enormous amount of nit-picking and leaving the vision to others. . . . The city has essentially sat back and allowed developers to set the agenda."[19] The Koch administration sought to obscure its strong support for investment in the Manhattan central business district, high-rise luxury housing development, and conversion of loft factory buildings by also undertaking initiatives to encourage office building in downtown Brooklyn and the Queens waterfront, to downzone residential neighborhoods, and to regulate loft conversion outside SoHo and Tribeca, the areas of early conversion.[20]

As a result, the Koch administration hid a pointed latent agenda behind a more ambiguous manifest agenda. The manifest agenda sought to balance commitment to supporting central business district development with a variety of compensatory measures that responded in various ways to actual or potential critics of development. To offset hundreds of millions of dollars of support for the Times Square Redevelopment Project, the administration set aside $25 million dollars to be spent over five years on mitigating measures for the adjacent Clinton neighborhood, once known as Hell's Kitchen.[21] In addition to their focus on major Manhattan projects, the PDC and the Office of Economic Development manage a number of small industrial parks outside Manhattan and fund a neighborhood commercial revitalization program; together, both have a tiny impact on direct expenditures and the capital budget.

These counterbalancing measures have uniformly been more symbolic than substantive. The dollar amounts and administrative priority devoted to them have been minuscule compared to those lavished on enhancing the central business district. The latent, yet highly coherent strategy of the Koch administration was to promote private development and to minimize resistance from residential neighborhoods or displaced manufacturing industries. It accomplished this end by narrowing the parameters of public discourse on planning, by ensuring that regulatory and development officials were firmly supportive of growth, and by adopting symbolic mitigating measures where expedient.[22] The mayor rationalized his approach by praising the contribution developers and expanding business made to the city's growing economy. As he mused in a postelection interview in 1985, when he was at the top of his powers, "You know, there are some people, the ideologues, who believe it's a sin to make a buck, that somehow or other the government should own all the property. I am not one of those people. I believe that government sets the climate for jobs and profits in the private sector. That's what this administration is seeking to do, so you can get jobs for people."[23] Koch dismissed the argument that growth should contribute any broader benefits to the public interest.[24]

Development Projects

The specific projects championed by the Koch administration, beginning with the construction of the Jacob Javits Convention Center and the South Street Seaport in the early 1980s through the yet-to-be-built Times Square Redevelopment Project, Columbus Circle Project, and Hunters Point Redevelopment Project, show that the Koch administration sought above all to reinforce central business district functions. Even the projects it undertook in downtown Brooklyn and Long Island City, Queens, had the same thrust. Brooklyn projects included One Pierrepont Plaza for Morgan Stanley, Metrotech, Atlantic Terminal, Renaissance Plaza, and Livingston Plaza; in Queens, the Astoria Studio, the International Design Center, the 50-story Citicorp building, and the Port Authority's Hunters Point development. All were closely linked in space, function, and financing to the Manhattan central business district.

These projects were sponsored by one or more of the public development agencies, usually the city's Public Development Corporation, sometimes with the state UDC. PDC is a private, nonprofit corporation wholly funded by and responsible to the mayor's office. It is not subject to civil service nor are its contracts reviewed in the same manner as city contracts. It has served as the city's primary development organization. The UDC built the Convention Center and led the Times Square project so that the city could override local planning review to expedite project completion. The Port Authority of New York and New Jersey took the lead on the waterfront Hunters Point project in Long Island City. These agencies enabled developers to cut through the complex approval process and defended them against challenges from neighborhood residents, who were subject to negative impacts.

These projects also benefited from extensive public financial support, including special tax exemptions, zoning bonuses, city loans and grants, capital improvements to the sites, and in some cases leases from city agencies as tenants. It is difficult to calculate the total private investment and implicit public investment in all these projects, but the amounts are clearly large. A single city-sponsored project in Times Square, a John Portman-designed Marriott hotel, cost $300 million to build in the early

1980s, with the aid of a $42 million federal urban development action grant (UDAG).

The Times Square Development Project, a complex of office towers, retail space, theaters, and a merchandise mart, is emblematic of the Koch development policy. Estimates of its cost range upward of $2.5 billion. The city granted tax abatements worth $650 million over 20 years (with a net present value of $256 million in 1985), allowed the office building to exceed prior zoning by over 100 percent, and capped the developers' exposure to land-acquisition costs. Ultimately, these benefits represented an implicit city equity in the project of at least $400 million in 1985.[25]

In return for this stake, the city was to get new commercial buildings, a projected 24,000 jobs (though many would simply be shifted from other parts of the city), approximately $400 million in payments in lieu of taxation over 20 years, and nine refurbished theaters. At the same time, the project will loom massively over Times Square, displace the area's low-income-oriented uses, and undercut a weakened market for office space in other parts of midtown.[26] As such, the project has become a rallying point for critics of the Koch administration's development policies. A survey of the New York chapter of the American Institute of Architects found that 80 percent of its members considered the architecture uninspiring and thought the project should be reevaluated.[27] Though it is not yet under construction, many other buildings have pointed the way for it by benefiting from the Koch administration's management of the system of bonuses in the city's zoning ordinance.

Zoning

The 1961 zoning act granted "as of right" density bonuses in return for such "amenities" as the construction of plazas (which offset some of the impact of large buildings rising straight up from the sidewalk). During the 1960s, the City Planning Commission gained the discretionary power to grant additional zoning incentives by special permit. Since these bonuses could add as much as 20 percent to a building's marketable volume and greatly increase their profit, developers were willing to subject what otherwise could have been "as of right" projects to negotiation with the city planning chairman, who commanded the other commission members' votes.

During the Koch administration, the City Planning Commission granted numerous zoning bonuses and transfers of development rights in midtown Manhattan. They allowed such buildings as the Helmsley Palace to be built at a greater ratio of floor area to lot size (FAR) than would have been allowed as-of-right. As available sites in the East midtown area began to be built out and extreme density imposed clear congestion costs, the administration moved to downzone East midtown while simultaneously upzoning major parts of West midtown. The midtown rezoning, adopted by the Board of Estimate in May 1982, decreased FAR in East midtown from 18 to 15 and 16 on the avenues and 12 on midblocks and, for a six-year period, upzoned West midtown from FAR 15 to FAR 18 with opportunities to reach 21.6.[28] In some places, this would allow a building 44 percent bulkier—and more profitable—than previously allowed.

Subsequently, development in West midtown boomed, leading the department to call its policy a success.[29] Between 1980 and 1987, a study by Cushman and Wakefield, real estate consultants' found that 63 percent of the 24.2 million square feet of midtown office construction took place on the East Side and only 9 percent on the West Side. For 1988–94, however, 80 percent of the 28 million square feet under development will be on the West Side, a fact "directly attributable" to the zoning bonuses available to projects whose foundations were completed by May 1988.[30]

Working under the chairman of the City Planning Commission, the City Planning Department had, of course, also actively encouraged the construction of the 15.2 million square feet of office space in East midtown during the 1980s. Moreover, the westward shift in development was inevitable as East midtown filled up. Zoning incentives may have sped the shift and increased the ultimate volume of office space on the West Side, but they did not produce the basic change in direction. Finally, the surge of high-density development aroused growing opposition in the abutting communities, which were subjected to negative impacts on sunlight, crowding, transit facilities, and neighborhood displacement. For example, the upzoning set the stage for the fight over the Columbus Circle project.

A Natural Resources Defense Council study concluded that FAR limits had become a basis from which to accumulate zoning bonuses rather than a ceiling on development.[31] Similarly, the state comptroller's office determined that the value of zoning bonuses to private developers far outweighed the cost of the public amenities received as a quid pro quo. It reviewed ten special permits granted under the Housing Quality Program and five Special District permits granted between 1980 and 1987.[32] The former granted 340,000 square feet of bonus space worth $108 million in return for amenities costing developers only $5 million; the latter granted 309,000 square feet of bonus space worth $90 million in return for amenities costing developers a few million dollars. In the most egregious examples, developers contributed $5 per square foot of bonus space when the market value was $300. Moreover, the comptroller found that the City

Planning Department failed to ensure that the promised amenities actually were delivered.[33]

In 1981, the Planning Department also asked the Board of Estimate to legalize the conversion of manufacturing loft space in some areas of Manhattan, prevent it in others, and "grandfather" existing illegal conversions. The decline of manufacturing, the decay of the transit system, and the growing demand among professionals for housing in safe and newly stylish Manhattan neighborhoods like SoHo and Tribeca had set the stage for a major invasion of industrially zoned space.[34] Artists and others wanting large spaces at low prices and willing to put up with a lack of amenities began this invasion in the 1960s and 1970s. When the market was slack, no one objected to these illegal tenancies. (The commission permitted artists to reside in SoHo manufacturing buildings in 1971.) By the early 1980s, however, the boom had exhausted available space, and the pace of conversion had precipitated conflict among landlords, existing legal and illegal residential loft tenants, and manufacturers being displaced.

The City Planning Department approached this conflict by reaffirming the manufacturing uses of 46 million square feet of industrial space in the west midtown garment and lower Manhattan printing districts but legalized conversion in most other areas. It also required developers to preserve one square foot of manufacturing space for each foot they converted to residential use, preserving another 24 million square feet. Finally, it imposed a $4.50 per square foot relocation charge for the benefit of businesses being displaced. (At that time, the price of legally converted residential space was approaching $275 per square foot.) As noted, it also "grandfathered" existing illegal loft conversions, subject to applications to the department. Grandfathering and legalized conversion of manufacturing space were subsequently extended to such areas as Fulton landing in Brooklyn. In effect, this policy protected only the manufacturers that were already able to compete against alternative uses, while fostering legal conversion elsewhere, adding to the displacement pressures on lower value-added manufacturers, thereby contributing to the long-run decline of manufacturing employment in the city.[35]

The economic boom also placed great pressure on the city's housing market, increasing the rent burdens on lower-income households.[36] One aspect of this pressure was the construction of high-rise luxury housing, sometimes as midblock "sliver" buildings, in lower-density residential areas. As with commercial construction, these structures often benefited from zoning bonuses. The Housing Quality Program, enacted in 1976, allowed the commission to grant 20 percent zoning bonuses to apartment construction in the densest apartment districts in return for such neighborhood amenities as park improvements. This generated many Manhattan apartment buildings that were taller and denser than their immediate neighbors. The rise of Manhattan land values and the improvement of the subway system also enabled market-rate apartment development to spill over into less dense residential areas in the other boroughs. Most had experienced little or no construction in the previous decade, but they were zoned for greater densities than existing structures filled, making them appealing development sites. The resulting buildings generated intense debate regarding overdevelopment of residential neighborhoods not only in Manhattan but throughout the city.

In mid-1987, the commission reformed the Housing Quality Program, eliminating the objectionable discretionary bonuses while allowing buildings to cover more of the lot on an as-of-right basis in return for lower building heights. When it adopted this reform, the Board of Estimate, led by the Queens and Staten Island borough presidents, responded to neighborhood criticism by requiring the department to develop "contextual zoning" proposals that would further control building in low-rise residential neighborhoods outside Manhattan.[37] Subsequently, the department developed contextual zoning rules for such areas as Windsor Terrace in Brooklyn, and the commission has decreased the FAR in many low-density residential areas. It also adopted an inclusionary housing program, providing density bonuses in certain circumstances in return for the construction of low-income housing, though few units have been build under the program.

Tax Incentives

In the wake of the fiscal crisis, the city also developed a sizable program of tax incentives for new commercial developments. This program predated the Koch administration but was warmly embraced by it after 1977. The Industrial and Commercial Incentive Board (ICIB) granted discretionary tax exemptions to firms that would otherwise build or renovate space outside the city.[38] Ostensibly designed to support industrial development, the great bulk of the tax benefits actually went to midtown office buildings. AT&T received a $42 million abatement for its Phillip Johnson-designed "Chippendale" headquarters building. Between 1977 and mid-1981, 274 projects received exemptions of $446 million, costing the city roughly $50 million a year in foregone revenues; 28 office buildings in the Manhattan central business district accounted for 90 percent of this incentive.[39]

As the Manhattan construction boom gained steam and the actual need for these incentives became increasingly dubious, criticism of the ICIB mounted. The administration reformed the program in 1982 to change the terms of the exemptions, making them "as of right" in areas outside the Manhattan central business district, and eliminating them in Manhattan south of 59th Street and east of 6th Avenue. While this reform eliminated discretionary grants to East midtown projects that would obviously be built anyway, it increased the program's tax cost by making grants to projects outside this area automatic, not discretionary.

Studies by the office of Senator Franz Leichter found that 990 applications filed between 1982 and 1988 cost the city $420 million in unnecessary exemptions over their lifetime, while 880 applications filed between 1988 and 1990 will cost an additional $247 million in unnecessary tax expenditures. Of the total of $470 million of exemptions granted in the latter period, 30 percent of the value went to midtown Manhattan projects. Much of the rest went to doctor's offices, fast food franchises, and neighborhood commercial projects whose employment is a strict function of customers' disposable income. It could not therefore generate increased employment but only fattened business bottom lines.[40] According to the comptroller, the city's abatement programs cost about $45 million annually in foregone tax revenues in the late 1980s.[41]

Despite reforming the practice of giving discretionary tax abatements to commercial projects in the city's business district, the city continues to do so on a case-by-case basis. The Times Square project will receive $650 million in abatements. When NBC threatened to move from Rockefeller Center, the city granted its corporate parent, General Electric, $100 million in abatements. To encourage Chase Manhattan to build a new operations center in downtown Brooklyn, it granted another $235 million, amounting to $25,000 per job in the former case and $47,000 in the latter.[42]

The Missing Elements: Linkage to Housing and Labor Market Policy

In describing the prominent elements of the Koch administration's development policy, it is worth noting those that were absent. In return for its powerful support for central business district development, the city asked for virtually nothing in return for this massive subsidy. The administration specifically rejected the approach of cities like Boston and San Francisco that require developers to pay into housing trust funds in order to receive public approval.[43] Instead, Mayor Koch asked the Bar Association of the City of New York to support him in preventing community boards from bargaining with developers to get what he felt were "unrelated amenities," such as payments to community organizations.[44] He argued that his $5.2 billion housing program amounted to linkage, particularly since $400 million of it was to be financed through bonds issued by the Battery Park City Authority, a large state-city office building and luxury housing complex developed on land fill west of the World Trade Center. He felt that neighborhood efforts at developing their own linkages might become extortionate.

Increasingly intense conflicts around housing and development during the latter 1980s led Mayor Koch to mount a large, locally financed, subsidized housing program in his final term. His plan was to rehabilitate the city's stock of vacant and occupied *in rem* units, which had climbed to as much as 150,000, and to upgrade other buildings for a total of 252,000 rental units. About half these units would go for moderate- and middle-income occupancy, and half for low-income occupancy. (New production of low-income units was planned to amount to only 16,000; another 50,000 new moderate- and middle-income units would be built.)

As it got under way in 1988 and 1989, the mayor's program was subject to criticism, including its failure to give sufficient attention to production for low-income tenants and its concentration of formerly homeless families in rehabilitated *in rem* units in the South Bronx in response to political pressure to remove them from midtown welfare hotels.[45] More than half the units under construction were located in the South Bronx and the parts of Harlem and northern Manhattan located across the river from it, raising the question of whether the city was creating a new ghetto, much as the urban renewal and public housing programs of the 1950s did.[46] Construction costs proved to be higher than those originally projected, jeopardizing the plan's ultimate scope. Moreover, it did not respond to more than about two-thirds of the city's unmet housing needs.[47]

The city also refused to link its development policy to an employment program. In the early years of the Koch administration, Herbert Sturz, then a deputy mayor and latter Planning Commission chairman, proposed that developers be required to hire minority city residents. Mayor Koch sharply rejected this idea, saying he could not support anything approximating a quota system.[48] In contrast to Boston and Chicago, which set targets for hiring city residents, minorities, and women on its development projects, New York City virtually ignored the employment dimensions of the many large projects it supported, whether work on the construction or employment at the firms ultimately tenanting the projects.[49] Nor did it monitor the "job creation" commitments that firms made when receiving tax abatements, though it did caution AT&T not to shift its corporate operations to New Jersey after the break-up of the Bell system because of the abatement granted to its headquarters building.

Indeed, the city did not adopt an affirmative action policy for its own personnel.

Results

The Koch administration's support for office building and market-rate residential development in Manhattan and the Brooklyn and Long Island City satellites of the Manhattan central business district undoubtedly contributed to the magnitude of physical development in New York City during the 1977–89 economic boom. Though there is no way to measure precisely how large its impact was, the Koch administration gave real estate developers and investors a "positive business environment." This may explain why New York City could hold its share of regional office building construction during these years (despite much lower costs elsewhere in the region) and become more competitive in the national market for prime office space.[50]

The Koch administration also had some impact on the location of corporate office development. While midtown development would have shifted from the East to the West Side in any case, Koch administration policies probably hastened the shift and added moderately to the total volume constructed. The administration's concerted efforts probably also increased new office construction in downtown Brooklyn; the $143 million Pierrepont Plaza (tenanted by Morgan Stanley's back-office operation) was completed with $17 million in city funds, a zoning incentive, a 23-year tax abatement, a 37 percent reduction in electricity rates, and a 30 percent reduction in the commercial occupancy tax. By 1992, two other projects were largely completed: the $65 million Livingston Plaza office building (with a similar tax and energy package) and the $770 million Metrotech complex (for the securities industries back-office operation, Chase Manhattan's back-office operation, Brooklyn Union Gas, and Polytechnic University). The Metrotech complex involved $56 million in public funds as well as deep tax and electricity discounts. Two other major projects, the $530 million Atlantic Terminal complex of offices and housing and the $150 million Renaissance Plaza hotel/office structure, remain on the drawing boards but have been seeking prime tenants.[51] Without the deep public incentives and advocacy from City Hall, it is doubtful that development this extensive would have occurred in downtown Brooklyn. Similarly, administration support for development in Long Island City hastened the growth of central business district support services and office building in that area, one subway stop east of midtown, under the East River.

The net effect, though not the avowed purpose, of Koch's development policy was to promote the postindustrial transformation of the New York City economy. It benefited the advanced corporate services that tenanted the midtown and downtown office buildings, as well as private, nonprofit services such as hospitals and universities. This effect also occurred in the housing market as well, as new market-rate luxury housing and the rehabilitation of existing units upgraded the city's housing stock.

Political Implications

This policy also produced intended and unintended political results. The Koch administration's development policy certainly found favor with real estate developers, investors, and their lawyers. It elicited support from the city's business elites and the leading voices for the establishment, particularly the editorial board of the New York Times. While they might quibble with policies and argue for more streamlined development procedures, they knew they had a friend in office.

But the administration's policies also produced two kinds of unintended political results. The first, by reinforcing the market trends that were driving out manufacturing, these policies pitted the declining sectors of the economy, like the garment industry, against the rising sectors and the administration. Both the employers' associations and the unions of these industries argued strenuously for more protection and support.[52] The Koch administration responded with symbolic mitigating measures, but these had little effect on overall trends. Whenever the rising sectors came into conflict with declining sectors over a major development project, such as in Long Island City or the Brooklyn waterfront, the Koch administration sided with the former.[53]

More importantly, the Koch administration's backing for high-rise development triggered many conflicts between developers and neighborhood residents and their advocates. These conflicts erupted across the city in places ranging from outer-borough neighborhoods like Windsor Terrace to the upper-class neighborhoods of the East and West Sides.[54] Emblematic of these struggles were the mobilization of Upper West Side residents against Donald Trump's proposed development for the former Penn rail yards and the efforts of the Municipal Art Society and others to reduce the size of the Columbus Circle project.[55] The tightening of the housing market, the declining ability of those in the lower half of the income-distribution scale to afford housing, and the destruction of low-rent housing sharpened opposition to such developments.

The Koch administration responded to these critics by scaling down some projects, by downzoning residential neighborhoods, by introducing a program of "contextual zoning," and by making housing rehabilitation the major goal of its final term. Yet these measures only smoothed the rough edges from the negative impact of the administration's development policy. They did not change its basic thrust. Even the mayor's housing program, more ambitious than that of any other city, created numerous conflicts. Opponents include those who have criticized the massing of homeless families in the South Bronx without sufficient social services in what are feared may become "new ghettos," low-income housing advocates who have attacked the middle-class bias of the program, and the East Brooklyn Churches group, successful promoters of the Nehemiah Plan for privately owned, low-cost, single family homes, who were angry that the Koch administration would not grant new space upon which to build. Conflict also arose over the suitability of a number of housing projects, such as the Tibbetts Garden project in the Bronx and the Arverne project in Queens.

The On-Budget Impact: Public Employment and Third-Party Government

While the Koch administration used its capital budget and regulatory powers to promote private investment in the city's advanced services complex, it used its expense budget to expand public employment, better remunerate city employees, and increase city funding for private, nonprofit providers of public services. While off-budget actions benefited private market interests, on-budget actions disproportionately benefited public sector producer interests. Both of these dimensions of policy had an economic impact and rationale, but both were also strongly driven by political considerations.

Public Employment

To control spending during the fiscal crisis period between 1978 and 1983, the Koch administration reduced the number of city workers. Between FY 1983 and FY 1989, however, it once more increased the number of city workers substantially above the levels of 1978. It also increased their pay and fringe benefits. Table 6.4 shows the relative contribution that the growth of compensation and the number of employees made to changes in the city's total labor cost.[56]

Total labor costs, the number of employees, and labor cost per employee all fell between 1978 and 1983. The reduction of workers, and for the most part the level of services delivered, accounted for two-thirds of the spending decline, while reduced labor cost per employee accounted

TABLE 6.4
Labor Cost Changes by Component, Selected Fiscal Years
(total in millions of 1983 dollars)

	1978	1983	1989	Percent Change 1978–1989
Total personnel spending	$8,346	$7,905	$10,387	24.5
Employment				
Total	201,885	194,623	238,383	18.1
Share of labor cost change	—	67.0%	71.6%	
Personnel spending per employee				
Total	$41,341	$40,617	$43,577	5.4
Share of labor cost change	—	33.0%	28.4%	

Source: *Comprehensive Annual Financial Report of the Comptroller*, FY 1978, Part II, Statement 1; FY 1989, Part II-B, Schedule G6; Part III, "Number of City Employees," as of June 30 of the respective years.

for a third. This indicates that organized public workers were able to insure that declining manpower levels, not individual compensation rates, would account for most of the decline in personnel expenditures in the wake of the fiscal crisis, which required greater reductions in the number of employees (and probably reduced service outputs as well).[57]

In the upturn, the number of employees, real labor cost per employee, and real labor costs all rose substantially. Table 6.4 shows that the rising numbers of city workers accounted for 71.6 percent of the real growth of labor costs, but real levels of individual compensation also rose strongly in this period, accounting for more than a quarter of the rise in total labor costs. Comparing the fiscal crisis with a decade later, the restoration of public employment to pre-fiscal crisis levels accounted for most of the growth in labor costs, but increasing employees' real wages was also an important factor.

The net increase of 36,498 employees between 1978 and 1989 was not spread evenly across all functions. Table 6.5 shows that two of the four uniformed services, police and corrections, gained 9.2 percent and 21.1 percent of the gains respectively. As in total and capital spending, corrections stands out as a major policy objective of the Koch administration: the number of people working to keep more people behind bars almost tripled. Fire and sanitation grew by much smaller amounts.

Growth of manpower also varied across the nonuniformed bureaucracies. The city's school system was the single largest beneficiary, taking

TABLE 6.5
Personnel by Department (selected fiscal years)

Department	1978	1983	1989	Percent Change 1978–89	Percent of Total Personnel Increase
Police	30,040	29,030	33,414	11.2	9.2
Uniformed	24,830	23,291	26,303		
Civilian	5,210	5,739	7,111		
Correction	4,075	6,469	11,767	188.8	21.1
Uniformed	3,297	5,546	9,851		
Civilian	778	1,013	1,916		
Fire	11,919	13,241	13,321	11.8	3.8
Uniformed	10,931	12,157	12,075		
Civilian	988	1,084	1,248		
Sanitation	12,153	11,598	12,362	1.7	0.6
Uniformed	9,772	8,171	8,500		
Regular	2,381	3,427	3,862		
Environmental Protection	4,004	4,226	5,450	36.1	4.0
Board of Education	71,374	70,492	84,754	18.7	36.7
Pedagogical	64,248	64,315	75,980		
Other	7,126	6,179	8,774		
Community Colleges	5,522	3,551	3,828	−30.7	−4.6
Pedagogical	3,389	2,409	2,635		
Other	2,133	1,142	1,193		
Social Services	23,012	21,844	29,227	27.0	17.1
All Other	39,786	34,172	44,260	11.2	12.3
Total	201,885	194,623	238,383	18.1	

Source: *Comprehensive Annual Financial Report of the Comptroller*, Fiscal Years 1983 and 1989, Part III, "Selected Service Delivery Statistics"

more than a third of the total gain in employment, although the number of Board of Education employees remained the same relative to total city government employment. By contrast, the Koch administration severely cut the City University's community college system, for which it retained a financial responsibility when the state took over the financing of and authority over the CUNY senior colleges beginning in FY 1978. Reflecting its major capital commitment to the city's water and sewage systems (building the third water tunnel is a huge public works project), the Department of Environmental Protection also grew at twice the citywide average rate. The Department of Social Services also grew rapidly, despite the fall in welfare rolls and the declining real value of welfare payments.

The emphasis on increasing city employment in police, corrections, education, and social services had a nonrandom impact on who was hired.

Public employment has historically provided a major path of economic upward mobility to black women and men in New York City, as elsewhere. Even more than the city's overall labor force, the city government work force has become less white and more feminized. Blacks, and to a lesser extent Latinos, have been the major beneficiaries of this shift.[58]

The FY 1987 distribution of racial and gender groups across the occupations that make up the city's work force is given in Table 6.6. It too shows a clear racial and gender division of labor. Women, who make up a third of the city government labor force, are most likely to be clerical workers and least likely to hold protective, skilled crafts, and service and maintenance jobs. The strong representation of women among managers and professionals indicates that women can find more upward mobility in public service than in the private sector. Blacks, who make up a third of the city's work force, did almost as well as whites in the managerial and professional categories and noticeably better than Latinos. (Asians are only a small percent of the total, but they are heavily concentrated in the professional category.)

The uniformed protective services (especially fire and police) and the skilled crafts remained largely the preserve of white males in 1986. (Stafford and Dei report that the Fire Department was 89 percent white male and the Police Department 81 percent, while Correction was only 31 percent white male, but 51 percent black and 15 percent Latino.)[59] Reexamining Table 6.5 in light of Table 6.6, one can see that, except at the Board of Education, blacks were the primary beneficiary of growth of jobs in city government, since they are heavily represented in the agencies that grew most; Latinos were secondary beneficiaries.[60]

Because whites retained their disproportionate hold on relatively highly paid uniformed services and skilled crafts jobs, however, women, blacks, and Latinos made much less headway in earnings than in employment. Whites also retained their hold on policy-making jobs, including those at agencies like Social Services, where women, blacks, and Latinos were gaining clerical and professional jobs.[61] It is ironic that the Department of Correction probably contributed the largest number of relatively high wage jobs to blacks and Latinos, since those groups certainly made up the increased prison population.

In sum, the growth of public employment after the fiscal crisis benefited service producers relative to revenue providers (and possibly to service consumers). These service producers were concentrated in a few agencies, particularly police, the jails, the Board of Education, and social services. Since two departments that grew rapidly, correction and social services, also had large proportions of women, black, and Latino workers, these groups benefited. But the overall racial and gender division of labor within the municipal work force did not change much.

TABLE 6.6
Distribution of Gender and Racial Groups across Occupation Within the
Municipal Labor Force (percentage of year-end payroll, June 1987)

	Females	Whites	Blacks	Latinos	Asians	Total
Managers	14.2	9.7	8.6	4.9	7.3	9.0
Professionals	18.2	15.5	14.7	11.3	42.9	15.0
Technicians	7.5	8.8	9.0	7.6	14.8	9.0
Protective	12.0	38.2	18.8	32.4	10.2	31.0
Paraprofessionals	5.8	1.4	6.6	6.7	3.8	4.0
Clerical	40.2	6.5	30.4	21.7	15.4	16.0
Skilled craft	0.1	6.1	1.5	2.2	2.6	4.0
Service/maintenance	1.9	13.8	10.3	13.2	2.9	12.0
Percent of Total	32.2	55.4	33.1	10.0	1.7	100.0

Source: Summary of EEO-4 Report for FY 1987, New York City Department of Personnel. Does not include Board of Education, Transit Authority, Housing Authority, or Health
and Hospitals Corporation. Female category overlaps with racial groups. Totals do not add
to 100 due to rounding individual entries.

As Walter Stafford has shown, white males retained their hold on better paid city jobs, giving way only where courts and political mobilization
forced the Koch administration to give entry to minority workers. Even at
the end of his tenure, Mayor Koch continued to resist adopting an
affirmative action program for city employees and indeed had undermined the affirmative action monitoring effort by removing it from the
Commission on Human Rights and placing it instead under the Personnel
Department.[62]

Political Implications

The growth in public employment first and foremost favored what Sayre
and Kaufman called "the organized bureaucracies," namely the agencies
that expanded and the public employee unions that represented their
workers. Two agencies accounted for half the net gain in employment:
the Board of Education and the Department of Correction. The school
system already accounted for the largest portion of city employment, and
its gain kept it in line with overall gains in city employment. This priority
also reflected criticism of the school dropout rate and a consensus that
education mattered greatly in keeping the city competitive and providing
upward mobility for black and Latino youths. From the point of view of
organized interests, the pro-Koch United Federation of Teachers benefited most.[63]

Growth of the jail system constituted a genuine departure from past patterns. The Koch administration fulfilled its campaign promise to come down hard on criminals by building and staffing more jails and incarcerating more offenders. (Koch increased the size of the Police Department only at the same rate as overall city employment.) In so doing, it created a large, new supply of relatively well paid public service opportunities for black and Latino men and a huge penal colony of the same population. The white-led union representing correction officers has not taken a role in city politics, and it has been experiencing internal conflict along racial lines.

The remaining growth in city employment took place within the social services. The Department of Social Services, the Human Resources Administration, and smaller social service agencies like the Department of Employment all have heavily black and Latino staffing, though in the Koch years not in their senior management and policy staff. Their growth provided a major opportunity for upward mobility for lower level minority managers, professionals, and clerical staff. These workers are represented by District Council 37 of AFSCME, during the 1980s the most liberal and activist union in the city. (In 1987, its long-time president, Victor Gotbaum, was succeeded by Stanley Hill, an African-American.) DC 37 had considered opposing Mayor Koch in 1981 and 1985, but ended up not endorsing his opponents in either race because it thought they had little chance, and it did not want to worsen its bargaining position with a mayor known to have a vindictive disposition.

Third-Party Government

Spending on contracts to third parties that performed services for local government also grew during the 1980s. Some of these services helped city agencies do their jobs by designing buildings or conducting environmental impact studies. Others sold equipment and supplies to the city or build capital projects. But a large portion of OTPS spending goes to contracts to organizations that provide services to clients who reside in New York City. Table 6.7 shows that OTPS spending on service contracts rose by more than a quarter in constant 1989 dollars, between FY 1980 and FY 1989 and exceeded $2.6 billion.[64] Approximately 40 percent of the total in OTPS contracts is awarded without a sealed bid competition; the proportion is higher with the contracts for services detailed in Table 6.7. In short, New York City government spends more on private, nonprofit service providers than most other large cities spend on their total budget.

In contrast to the capital budget or personnel expenditures, spending on third-party government is heavily concentrated in the social services. The largest recipients in FY 1989 included private hospitals ($389 million in payments), other charitable institutions ($377 million), day-care providers ($221 million), foster-care providers ($189 million), and providers of home care to the elderly ($116 million). Some of these programs grew quite rapidly during the 1980s. For example, spending on agencies that provided assistance to homeless families went from nothing

TABLE 6.7
Contracting for Services by Function and Agency, FY 1980, FY 1989 (millions of FY 1989 dollars)

Function	FY 1980	FY 1989	Percent Change
Economic development			
Economic development	24.6	23.4	−1.2
Transportation	102.6	176.2	71.7
General government			
Department of General Services	364.7	337.5	−7.5
Department of Environmental			
Protection/Sanitation	169.7	256.6	51.2
Criminal justice			
Police	58.7	81.2	38.3
Corrections	47.5	49.9	5.0
Juvenile justice	4.3	41.4	862.8
Social services			
Human resources	329.9[a]	103.0	−68.8
Social services[b]	135.6	243.2	79.4
Aging	35.2	73.5	108.8
Youth Board	21.0	29.2	39.0
Housing	306.8	350.9	14.4
Health	62.4	97.0	55.4
Mental Health	171.9	232.4	35.2
Employment	—	81.0	—
Education and amenities			
Board of Education[c]	152.6	349.0	128.7
Parks	26.0	30.8	18.5
Cultural institutions	46.1	82.8	79.6
Total	2,059.6	2,639.0	28.1

Source: Annual Comprehensive Financial Report of the Comptroller, FY 1980, Part IIB, Schedule 7; FY 1989, Part II-B, Schedule G5.

[a]Excludes CETA appropriations.

[b]Excludes welfare, home relief, and medical assistance payments to or on behalf of individuals.

[c]Excludes pupil transport, buildings, power, and reimbursable programs.

in 1980 to $131 million in 1989. This spending undoubtedly provided services, but it also nourished a network of community-based nonprofit organizations.[65]

Organizations ranging from New York City's most prestigious cultural institutions and hospitals to small, neighborhood-based service agencies rely heavily on this funding. As Urban Institute studies showed, New York's nonprofit organizations got more of their budget from local government than did those in other cities, and this support rose in the face of federal cutbacks while it fell elsewhere.[66] Even small OTPS programs can have a large impact. For example, the Housing Preservation and Development Department's program to fund technical assistance to community-based housing developers ($32.6 million-a-year in FY 1989) enabled a number of the city's housing advocacy organizations to function. Large and influential organizations such as the city's leading teaching hospitals are equally dependent on city support.[67]

The data are not yet available to conduct a thorough examination of how city contracts are distributed across different kinds of organizations and constituencies. Contracts from the Parking Violations Bureau to private collection agencies to pursue scofflaws played a central role in the municipal scandal that unfolded in 1986. As a result of such problems, the city council mandated the development of a central contract database, and the Charter Revision Commission devised extensive changes in contracting procedures.[68] Neither of these initiatives had much effect by the end of the Koch era.

Political Implications

The vast majority of contracts appear to have been awarded with some regard for their substantive merit. Most cannot be classified as pure political patronage, though some politically connected organizations doubtless received contracts with little regard to their performance. Organizations that did merit support, however, had to have political sponsorship to get contracts. In the past, this has involved support from the mayor and contract-granting agencies both to get funding into the budget for the overall program and to be chosen as a vendor. In many instances, it has also required getting support from borough presidents and council members, who use this leverage to extract support for other organizations or programs that have not found sufficient favor with the mayor. The award of contracts is also highly political in a negative sense: no organization that directly criticized or politically challenged the mayor could expect funding. In both these senses, political considerations always played some role in the award of contracts by the Board of Estimate.

The pattern of using funding to community-based organizations not only to provide services but to achieve political cooptation dates at least to the War on Poverty in the latter 1960s.[69] The Lindsay administration used the poverty program to build electoral support; according to its former director, Congressman Major Owens, the Beame administration then corrupted the program:

> In 1975 Abe Beame wanted to destroy the Community Action Program. But corruption had not yet weakened the agencies to the point of helplessness and when Beame was confronted with a mass traffic tie-up in the streets plus a roadblock to his fiscal legislation, the crafty old clubhouse wizard retreated. Since he could not destroy it he assigned the program a definite political purpose. It became a plaything, a gift he gave loyal machine politicians like Raymond Velez and Sam Wright. Beame and the Council Against Poverty looked the other way while the favored political protegees ran community corporations as if they were their own private plantations.[70]

Mayor Koch, upon his election, attacked this situation. His administration felt that the local antipoverty agency, the Council Against Poverty (CAP), "lacked fiscal accountability and programmatic credibility" and had become "a closed system" where "programming had become stagnant and the chief benefit offered to poor communities were the limited employment opportunities available within the Program itself."[71]

In July 1977, the U.S. Community Service Administration suspended CAP funding because twenty-four of its twenty-six community corporations did not comply with federal guidelines concerning conflict of interest and board elections and had financial irregularities. In January 1978, the Koch administration declared CAP defunct, centralized financial control in the Community Development Administration (CDA), and abolished the community corporations. It established thirty-three neighborhood development areas, generally coterminous with community board boundaries, each with an area policy board (APB). While much of the APB membership would be elected under the new policy, a third would be local public officials. A new citywide Community Action Board to advise CDA was also established, with stronger representation from public officials and private social welfare groups.

These actions evoked a tremendous protest from New York's black leadership. They argued that the community corporations should be reformed rather than terminated. Owens decried the "heartlessness" with which "lower level workers who were guilty of nothing except long time service to their community were fired with only a few days' notice. . . . This butchering of human beings is what the Ford Foundation whiz kids have hidden between the lines of their excellent grammar and phony thoroughness." Terminating the corporations was a "symbolic ritual to make sure the natives understand that 'Bowana' is supreme."[72] The Koch reorganization went ahead despite these criticisms.

Over time, it appeared that Koch made his own political uses of the poverty program. He named an ally, Harlem City Council member Fred Samuel, to chair the citywide community action board. CDA funding decisions for Central Harlem were dominated not by Samuel, however, but by Casper Jasper, a two-time convicted felon formerly associated with Sam Wright and Senator Vander Beatty. (Beatty was convicted of vote fraud in a race won by Major Owens for the U.S. Congress.) CDA funding priorities also became enmeshed in local politics in many other neighborhoods where local officials had influence on the area policy boards. A number of those criticized for bossism and patronage regained their influence under Koch. An investigation by Annette Fuentes in *City Limits* found that Ramon Velez, a regular Democrat poverty baron of the worst sort, had reasserted control over South Bronx area policy boards and a CDA-funded health center. In the Lower East Side, an alliance between Roberto Napoleon, chair of the Puerto Rican Council, and the United Jewish Council, which represents tenants in the 4,500 unit Grand Street Cooperatives, dominated CDA funding and excluded reformers from support. Queens Democratic regulars also extracted funds for a favored organization. "On the face of it," Fuentes concluded, "the CDA seems doomed to repeat its unhappy history of favoritism, corruption, and political abuse."[73] Similar charges were made about the influence of Assemblyman Angelo Del Toro over poverty programs in East Harlem.

To be sure, many city-funded groups neither overtly supported nor opposed the mayor but simply navigated the political currents to acquire support for funding their valid services. Some politically well connected organizations also had strong substantive merits. But the correlation between a group (or its patron's) support for Mayor Koch and its receipt of funding through the CDA and certain of the other social service contract programs does suggest that third-party government is politicized in New York City and performs patronage functions. This resulted not from conscious design but because a decentralized funding process became enveloped in, and dominated by, the larger process of influence brokerage in New York City. But Mayor Koch was able to use this process to his advantage and prevent the networks of city-funded, community-based organizations from becoming an independent base for political mobilization.[74]

Even when organizations received contracts "on the merits" and individual politicians did not control the allocation decision, recipient groups needed political sponsorship to maintain program funding. They thus avoid associating with those who might challenge political incumbents. At most they lobby to increase program funding or change program de-

sign. They do not cross functional or geographic boundaries to support
political insurgents. Mayor Koch did not seek to use city contracts to
weld constituencies together but was content to use them to divide and
conquer the ethnic geopolitical checkerboard.

Conclusion: Uniting Supporters while Dividing Opponents

From the perspective of consolidating a governing coalition, it can be said
that the Koch administration used its fiscal policy, its capital budget,
and its off-budget regulatory powers to forge an alliance with private
market interests by promoting investment in corporate office construction. It used its ability to increase city employment, wages, and funding
for OTPS contracts to contain and coopt two important public sector
producer interests, public employee unions and community based service
organizations. By promoting real estate developments desired by elected
officials tied to the regular Democratic county organizations and giving them influence over the hiring of personnel and award of contracts,
the Koch administration forged alliances with these organizations as
well.

On the surface, the New York City case would appear to illustrate
Peterson's contention that cities have a unitary interest in promoting
private investment and curtailing redistributive spending. In fact,
however, New York City runs counter to his model in three respects.
First, the politics of development in New York City ultimately proved to
be highly divisive.[75] Not only did the postindustrial transformation generate broad racial and class tensions, but specific development projects created acute local conflicts. Second, while New York City spent a declining
share of its budget on transfer payments to the poor, it rapidly increased
spending on those who provided services to the poor (whether as public
employees or as contractors). Between 1983 and 1989, the city budget
grew as rapidly in absolute terms and relative to private value added as it
did in the late 1960s. The lessons that Peterson and structuralist scholars
on the left thought that the private marketplace had taught the New York
City political system in the fiscal crisis were certainly short lived.[76]
Finally, city officials pursued the interests of private developers not because business leaders forced them to, or because city officials wanted
property tax revenues to grow, but because this course of action generated necessary political resources. In sum, political considerations had a
far greater impact on the actions of the Koch coalition than any supposed
contextual imperative to promote private investment or avoid redistributive spending.

In the short term, the components of Mayor Koch's strategy for achieving electoral and governing majorities were mutually reinforcing. The vigorous promotion of private investment brought unified support from business interests, especially developers and their allies, who contributed large amounts to the mayor's campaigns and solidified elite public opinion behind him. Not until his third term did these policies begin to create opposition, as the negative consequences of the building boom for the quality of neighborhood life and the housing market became increasingly evident. Mayor Koch then adopted symbolic measures designed to mitigate these trends. Though opposition grew to be widespread, it remained sporadic and fragmented across the city's many neighborhoods. His ambitious ten-year, $5.2 billion housing initiative provided many of these erstwhile opponents an incentive to work with him.

Similarly, his budgetary policies did not create conflicts with his business constituents in the first half of his administration. He reduced the number and real wages of city employees, real welfare costs, and OTPS spending, thus reducing expenditures as a percentage of local value added, while increasing real spending on capital projects. These shifts delivered on the mayor's initial promise to be a fiscally prudent reformer. This helped his standing with business elites and did not hurt him with middle-class whites, who tended to identify the poor and minorities as the major beneficiaries of city services. (The middle class did, of course, grumble about the decay of the infrastructure, which the capital program sought to address, and the decline of basic services like police and sanitation.)

In the second half of his administration, however, Mayor Koch and his allies significantly increased real spending on city workers and contracts to third-party service providers. (Spending on direct aid to the poor continued to decline in real terms.) In theory, this would seem to have benefited the mayor's potential opponents, city workers and community-based service organizations that employed many minority workers and served black and Latino constituencies, and troubled his business constituency, which was averse to growing government spending and an increasing tax burden.

In practice, these trends helped to coopt potentially challenging political constituencies. The unions that represented city workers had varying racial compositions, leadership, political traditions, and strategies. In the mid-1980s, only District Council 1199 of the private hospital workers was led by a black, and this transition was attended by great political turmoil that was not resolved until the election of Dennis Rivera in 1988.[77] Most of the other major city unions were led by Jewish males facing the dilemmas of racial and generational succession within their organizations. Some, like the United Federation of Teachers, had battled against challenges from black nationalists who were seeking community control. Others, like Teamsters Local 237 President Barry Feinstein, tried to reorient their organizations to support minority politicians. But all desperately wanted to restore the wages and working conditions that had prevailed before the fiscal crisis. This in turn would strengthen union treasuries. None of these unions had the ability or the incentive to mobilize labor opposition to Mayor Koch, however much they might dislike him.

The growth of third-party government reinforced the functional, geographic, and political fragmentation in the city's policy system, regulated by the ability of Mayor Koch and his allies to veto funds to any group that might overtly challenge them. In other cities, community organizations and nonprofit service-delivery groups became a relatively autonomous base for independent political action, but in New York they were subordinated to the political establishment. The regular Democrat organizations used some sources of city and state funding as a form of patronage; in the process, they actually experienced a revitalization during the 1980s. At other times, the mayor rewarded allies, such as Reverend Floyd Flake in Queens, who were not part of the regular Democratic organization but who would steadfastly support the mayor in the black community.[78] Even where contracts were not awarded for political reasons, they precluded the organizations best positioned to organize opposing constituencies from doing so.

As with Koch's promotion of private investment, the potentially conflictual aspects of his budgetary strategies did not become overt until late in his administration. In the late 1980s, city spending once more began to climb as a percentage of local value added. As long as the growth of city spending seemed to enhance Mayor Koch's ability to project a positive environment for private investment, business elites had been largely content and the fiscal monitors remained in a passive mode.[79] In 1989 and 1990, however, overall city employment continued to rise while the private economy and city tax revenues began to fall, triggering increasingly acute fiscal problems. By that time, however, it was a problem for Mayor Koch's successor.

These strategies for building a governing coalition were consonant with the mayor's electoral coalition. The retrenchment phase of Mayor Koch's policies did not hurt his core constituencies of middle-class Jews and white Catholics, who felt themselves more burdened by city taxes than benefiting from city expenditures. (Mayor Koch took a number of steps to see that owners of one-to-three family housing would have the least property tax burden.) They liked Koch's emphasis on cutting welfare, putting more criminals in prison, and holding down spending. Even the aspiring middle-class segments of the black and Latino population could identify with these goals. His policies did alienate blacks and white liberals, but they were not core parts of the mayor's electoral base.

The upswing in spending during the recovery phase increased the tax burden on the mayor's core electoral constituencies, but building jails and bolstering school spending while continuing to reduce welfare expenditures still appealed to them. (The Board of Education, which received a large increase in personnel, was also the agency most closely associated with Jewish upward mobility through public employment.) Blacks and Latinos, who had borne the brunt of retrenchment, gained new employment opportunities, although they had much less chance to rise to senior positions within their agencies.

In both the retrenchment and recovery phases, the off-budget effort to promote investment in the rising sectors of the Manhattan economy and its satellites in downtown Brooklyn and Long Island City, Queens, as well as the city's gentrifying neighborhoods, won the mayor broad and powerful support from the business elite and from the rising young professional stratum feeding off the city's economic boom. Most blacks also benefited greatly from the economic boom, although overall income inequality worsened, as did the relative position of Latinos. Only toward the end of the boom did the housing affordability crisis, increasing racial tension, and widening income inequality begin to cut into the mayor's support from his key constituencies.

Mayor Koch's policies thus consolidated both his electoral coalition and his governing coalition. They united his most powerful supporters, the business elite and the regular Democratic party organizations, while dividing and coopting his most likely opponents, the public sector labor unions and community-based organizations that represented liberal, minority, and poor constituencies. These conditions were not set in stone, however. Over time, the conflicts implicit in his strategy for building a dominant coalition became increasingly overt. Feelings of invincibility led Mayor Koch to commit errors and ignore warning signals that, had he heeded them, might have enabled him to win a fourth term. Instead, the massively victorious candidate of 1985 was soundly defeated in 1989 by a challenging candidate and coalition that had been in great disarray only four years earlier.

Seven

The Fall of the Koch Coalition

I find the black community very anti-
Semitic. I don't care what the American
Jewish Congress or B'nai B'rith will issue by
way of polls showing that the black community
is not. . . . My experience with blacks is that
they're basically anti-Semitic. Now, I want to
be fair about it. I think whites are basically
anti-black [but] the difference is: it is
recognized as morally reprehensible.
    (Edward I. Koch, 1975)[1]

Business, labor, and even (or especially) the
media all now support incumbents. . . . Now
the city has a single unified leadership resulting
from a process that incorporates in the same
administration both civic reform and
"regular" corruption.
    (Jim Chapin, "Who Rules New York
    Today?" 1987)[2]

For the first time in anyone's memory, all the
defendants are Jewish and all the lawyers
are Italian.
    (Sidney Zion, commenting on U.S. Attorney
    Rudolph Giuliani's prosecution of Bronx
    Democratic leader Stanley Friedman, 1987)[3]

IN THE WAKE of his triumph in the 1985 mayoral primary and general elections, Mayor Edward I. Koch's grip on electoral and governing power in New York City was not only unchallenged but seemed unlikely to be contested seriously in the near future. Koch had badly trounced challengers who represented the two constituencies most likely to give him trouble: blacks and white liberals. Despite the excitement that the 1984 Jesse Jackson campaign generated in the city's black neighborhoods, Koch had actually slightly improved his level of black support in 1985 compared to his September 1982 gubernatorial primary against Mario Cuomo. He had achieved even greater gains among Latinos and white liberals: Latino ADs went from 50.4 percent to 62.4 percent in his favor, while white liberal ADs went from 50.6 to 59.2 percent.

While vanquishing African-American and white liberal opponents on their home turf, he had also consolidated his electoral base in the outer-borough white Catholic and Jewish ADs. Given the absence of a white Catholic challenger from the race, his support in white Catholic ADs went from 47.9 to 69.3 percent, while his support also surged in Jewish ADs from 62.3 to 77.6 percent. His electoral position therefore seemed unassailable at the end of 1985. His badly divided potential opponents were unable to put forward candidates who appealed strongly to their own constituencies, much less to other constituencies. Meanwhile, Mayor Koch mobilized Jewish and white Catholic voters while also drawing substantial support from constituencies that might have been expected to vote against him.

Mayor Koch's governing coalition also seemed unassailable. In the midst of a long and broad economic boom, the city's real estate developers, investment bankers, and other leading businessmen strongly supported him and his policies. They had poured unprecedented levels of funding into his 1985 campaign. Mayor Koch also enjoyed close relationships with the four Democratic county party organizations outside Manhattan, especially in the Bronx and Queens. (In Brooklyn, Koch had been feuding with Borough President and county leader Howard Golden, but he received strong support from a competing faction of the regular organization aligned with Assembly Speaker Stanley Fink and Canarsie district leader Anthony Genovesi. After 1985, the overt conflict between these two factions began to subside.) Municipal unions, a potential base for organizing against him, had little choice but to support him. District Council 37 of the city employees and local 1199 of the private hospital workers were in the midst of leadership successions. Given the mayor's power to exact retribution against them and their desire for wage settlements that made up for the losses suffered during the fiscal crisis, they had every reason not to challenge the mayor.

These conditions provided good reason to think that the mayor would realize his goal to be elected to an unprecedented fourth term.[4] This seemed a valid conclusion despite the gradual but steady emergence beginning in January 1986 of a major municipal scandal.[5] At first, this scandal seemed to take down only the county leaders and borough presidents of the Bronx and Queens, close Koch allies. Gradually, however, it proceeded to enmesh many members of the Koch administration and inner circle. But Mayor Koch himself was never directly implicated, and for a time polls indicated that voters continued to regard him as personally honest and not to blame for the corruption.

By the fall of 1989, however, Mayor Koch was clearly in serious trouble, and he lost the September Democratic primary to a black challenger, Manhattan Borough President David N. Dinkins, by almost 10 percentage points. What had seemed impossible in late 1985 had in fact transpired by late 1989. A city where blacks made up only a quarter of the population and at most one-third of the Democratic primary electorate had unseated a popular Jewish incumbent in favor of a black candidate.

In retrospect, a number of forces clearly worked against Mayor Koch. After 1985, the mayor further alienated blacks and Latino electoral constituencies and eroded his support not only among white liberals (his initial base) but also among outer-borough white Catholics and Jews. Reasons for these shifts included the mayor's increasingly vitriolic and unrestrained attacks on Jesse Jackson, the scandals, and the perception among white middle-class residents that the mayor's rhetoric was dividing the city while his development policies were having an adverse impact on their neighborhoods.

These shifts in opinion would not have been enough to threaten the mayor's electoral position if potentially challenging constituencies had not also been able to overcome their divisions and coalesce around a viable candidate. The nature of David Dinkins's victory in the 1985 Manhattan borough presidency race suggested that he might be such a candidate, but Jesse Jackson's solid New York City plurality in the 1988 Democratic presidential primary convinced Dinkins's potential backers that he could win a race against Mayor Koch. The change in sentiment about the mayor's role in race relations was also reinforced by a series of highly publicized incidents in which whites assaulted blacks and Latinos, together with an equally highly publicized black assault on a white female Central Park jogger. Not only did the reaction to these events increase Latinos' willingness to identify with blacks relative to whites, but they caused great concern among whites, particularly white liberals, about worsening race relations.

These trends in sentiment among voters paralleled developments among forces that sustained Koch's governing coalition. Federal prosecutions hit the Bronx and Queens regular Democratic organizations hard, indicting and convicting major party and electoral office holders. The loss of strong leaders like Stanley Friedman and Donald Manes opened up a racially and ethnically based competition for political succession within the Bronx and Queens organizations. The 1988 Jackson candidacy drew much greater support from established black and Latino politicians than had his 1984 campaign, creating a basis on which regular black leaders could join with outsiders and insurgents, in the same way as many black regulars had joined with insurgents to support Mayor Harold Washington in Chicago in 1983. This realignment gave regular black and Latino district leaders and elected officials the political space to begin to oppose the mayor, something that the county organizations would previously have restrained them from doing.

As the mayor's standing in the polls fell and his party organizational base went into flux, major business leaders quietly began to consider alternatives. Former Metropolitan Transit Authority (MTA) chairman Richard Ravitch and Comptroller Harrison "Jay" Goldin emerged as candidates whom elements of the corporate elite were willing to support against Koch. Ravitch, a former successful builder, had put the New York State Urban Development Corporation back on its feet during the 1975 fiscal crisis; as MTA chairman, he led the drive to recapitalize the mass transit system. Subsequently he bought and restructured the Bowery Savings Bank and sold it at a substantial profit. Ravitch embodied professional competence and the corporate civic spirit. As four-term city comptroller, Jay Goldin had also established a reputation for competence, political skill, and the ability to raise funds from the city's investment bankers. Like Ravitch, he was able to attract substantial financial support for a challenge to the mayor.

Koch's weakness also drew a formidable Republican candidate into the race, former U.S. attorney for the Southern District of New York, Rudolph W. Giuliani. Giuliani had begun his career prosecuting corrupt New York police in the late 1960s, had been an assistant U.S. attorney general in the Reagan administration, and had conducted highly publicized prosecutions of Mafia dons, Wall Street insiders, and corrupt Democratic politicians. Though he had no previous electoral experience, he exerted a potent appeal to the many voters concerned with crime and drugs. As an Italian-American, he exerted an especially strong appeal to white Catholic Democrats, who had indicated in Koch's 1982 race against Cuomo that they would defect from the Koch coalition if given an attractive candidate. Mayor Koch thus had to watch his flanks to the right as well as to the left.

Most crucially, many of the organizational forces opposed to the mayor were able to coalesce the growing ambivalence of their constituencies about the mayor. Two key unions, District Council 37, AFSCME, and Local 1199 of the private hospital workers, completed the racial successions in their leadership. DC 37 replaced Victor Gotbaum upon his retirement with a black successor he had groomed, Stanley Hill. After years of a debilitating leadership fight, 1199 emerged with a strong Latino leader, Dennis Rivera. Both Hill and Rivera and their political operations gave strong support to the 1988 Jackson campaign. Although DC 37 did not formally endorse Jackson, Hill co-chaired his city campaign, and many of its staff members worked strongly on Jackson's behalf. Other municipal unions with large minority memberships, including the white-led Teamsters Local 237 (housing authority workers) and the Transport Workers' Union (subway and bus personnel), endorsed Jackson, while 1199 provided office space and organizational support for the campaign.

The 1988 Jackson campaign gave black and Latino elected leaders (both independents and those allied with the regular organizations) and the municipal employee unions a chance to work together and win a plurality of the city's Democratic primary vote. While a minority mayoral candidate would need much broader support than this base alone, given that the Democratic primary electorate was still majority white, it was a major step. Jackson's and Dinkins's ability to raise substantial campaign funds in 1988 and 1989 also marked a turning point from the 1985 Farrell candidacy and the 1984 Jackson campaign.

In contrast to 1985, therefore, the elements for an effective challenge to Mayor Koch were in place. These included declining levels of support for the mayor not only among blacks, Latinos, and white liberals but also among his core white middle-class supporters; a growing convergence of support for an alternative among blacks, Latinos, and white liberals; an organizational basis for financing and running a campaign; and an attractive and effective candidate able to appeal not only to disaffected constituencies, as Jesse Jackson had, but to white voters who formed part of Mayor Koch's electoral base.

Scandal and the 1988 Jackson Campaign: Erosion of Support for Koch

Between 1985 and 1989, support for Koch eroded broadly among the city's residents and likely voters in the Democratic mayoral primary. This erosion had two components: the corruption scandal caused all racial and ethnic segments of the electorate to shift away from Koch, while Koch's attacks on Jesse Jackson and Koch's role in worsening the climate of race relations made this shift even stronger among blacks and Latinos. By contrasting support for Mayor Koch in the 1985 and 1989 primaries, Table 7.1 shows the final impact of these trends across the city's sixty ADs, classified according to their predominant racial and ethnic makeup; Map 7.1 shows their geographic distribution.

The unfolding of the city's corruption scandal, combined with growing public disenchantment with the mayor's style, weakened Mayor Koch's standing across the board. From its beginning with his allies in the Bronx and Queens, the web of scandal caught many who were quite close to the mayor in 1986 and 1987. Among those exposed for questionable financial transactions and abuse of official power were such close Koch associates as Consumer Affairs Commissioner Bess Myerson, whose presence in Koch's 1977 campaign defended him against rumors that he was not a heterosexual; Health and Hospitals Corporation chairman Victor Botnick, who many said was like a son to Koch; and Joe DeVincenzo, Koch's most sensitive operative on appointments and patronage. Koch was also

TABLE 7.1
Decay in Koch Support, 1985 and 1989 Democratic Primaries (total and percentage breakdown by assembly district type)

AD Type	1985			1989			Difference	
	Votes	Koch %	Turn-out %	Votes	Koch %	Turn-out %	Koch %	Turn-out %
Black	129,464	41.0	26.8	267,247	10.3	56.7	−30.7	29.9
Mixed minority	54,131	58.2	30.9	83,835	26.8	48.3	−31.4	17.4
Latino	55,353	62.4	31.2	80,438	31.8	47.0	−30.6	15.8
White liberal	134,334	57.2	36.6	201,733	44.0	52.6	−13.2	16.0
White Catholic	135,122	69.3	31.4	192,590	62.2	46.7	−7.1	15.3
Outer-borough Jewish	180,150	77.6	38.4	251,645	67.2	56.4	−10.4	18.0
Total	688,554	63.3	32.6	1,077,488	42.0	52.4	−21.3	19.8

Source: New York City Board of Elections.

forced to dismiss the commissioners of Transportation and the Office of Financial Services. These revelations caused Koch's approval rating to fall 10 percentage points by early 1987, with a majority agreeing that "it was time to give a new person a chance" at being mayor of New York.[6]

Interracial strife began to mount in New York City during this same period. Late one Saturday night in December 1986, a crowd of white youths attacked three black men whose car broke down in Howard Beach, Queens, and chased one to his death on a busy highway. While New York had experienced similar assaults in the past, such as Bernhard Goetz's shootings of four youths who threatened him on the subway, many New Yorkers found the Howard Beach case particularly offensive.[7] Black activists successfully demanded the naming of an independent prosecutor in the case and led a series of demonstrations that culminated in a massive subway disruption on the eve of verdicts in the case. Similar actions on behalf of Tawana Brawley, a young black woman who was eventually determined to have falsely claimed to have been abducted and raped by whites, further polarized race relations in the city.[8] The massive press coverage of these events created a wave of public sentiment that race relations were deteriorating badly in New York City.[9]

It was in this context that Jesse Jackson campaigned in New York's Democratic presidential primary in the spring of 1988. Earlier primaries had narrowed the Democratic field to Massachusetts Governor Michael Dukakis, with Jesse Jackson as his only substantial symbolic challenger. Since New York offered Jackson an opportunity to do well in a northern state, he mounted a strong effort in New York City with a substantially

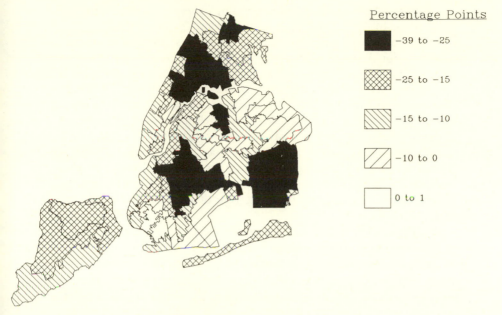

Percentage Points

- −39 to −25
- −25 to −15
- −15 to −10
- −10 to 0
- 0 to 1

Map 7.1. Falloff in Koch Vote, 1985–1989

larger and better funded apparatus than he had in 1984.[10] He now had nearly universal support from the many local black elected officials who had supported Mondale. The county leaders of the Bronx and Queens, in particular, could not keep their black assemblymen and district leaders in line for Dukakis. With additional support from black ministers, Jackson forces mounted full and sometimes multiple slates of delegates in every congressional district, operating more effectively on this score than the Dukakis organization. By 1988, Jesse Jackson had come to embody the self-esteem of African-Americans more than any other single person. The *New York Times* reported that black neighborhoods in New York welcomed Jackson as "a celebrity, not just another candidate."[11]

Mayor Koch had a strong negative reaction to Jackson's effort, saying that Jews "would have to be crazy" to vote for Jackson. Koch justified this criticism by citing Jackson's embrace of Palestine Liberation Organization leader Yasir Arafat, his endorsement of a Palestinian homeland, his acceptance of support from the Muslim activist Louis Farrakhan, and the furor created four years earlier by Jackson's reference to New York as "Hymietown." When combined with the left-oriented substance of Jackson's campaign, these stands evoked an emotionally charged attack from Mayor Koch.

This attack in turn provoked bitter controversy among African-American leaders. In April 9, 1988, the *Amsterdam News* launched an ongoing series of front-page editorials calling for Koch's resignation. It quoted reform rabbi Alexander Schindler to the effect that Koch's comments were "extremely unfortunate," and it exhorted Koch to remember that "he is the Mayor of the city; not just of New York Jewry." Manhattan Borough President David Dinkins expressed "distress" and "disappointment," saying Koch's remarks were "not helpful to our efforts to create an atmosphere whereby [racial] tensions can be eased. . . . Loose language such as that used by the Mayor to describe Jackson does not contribute positively to this cause."[12] Opinion about Jackson among New Yorkers was strongly polarized: less than 5 percent of blacks felt unfavorable toward Jackson, but only 10 percent of Jews felt favorable toward him.[13]

Koch exacerbated this polarization by refusing to apologize to Jackson or his supporters and by supporting U.S. Senator Albert Gore over Michael Dukakis on the grounds that Gore was more conservative and pro-Israel. Having consistently trailed Dukakis in the northern primaries, Gore sought to keep his candidacy alive by appealing to New York's Jewish vote, which had been 24 percent of the state total in 1984. (Gore needed 20 percent of New York's delegates to continue receiving federal funding.) Koch sought to aid Gore's effort to continue his campaign and to undermine Jewish support for Dukakis.

In the event, the Jackson campaign triumphed in New York City, although Dukakis took the state by a fair margin. Gore went down to utter defeat. The CBS/*New York Times* exit poll found that Jackson received only 17 percent of the votes cast by whites and only 9 percent cast by Jewish residents of New York City.[14] But Gore too had won only 9.1 percent of the citywide vote and only one-sixth of the votes in outerborough Jewish ADs, where Dukakis received his strongest support. Koch's core constituency had rejected the mayor's advice about whom to support. Compared to 1984, Jackson gained support across all types of ADs. Map 7.2 shows the breadth of Jackson's gains over Farrell's support in 1985 across black and Latino neighborhoods. In contrast to the 1985 mayoral primary or the 1984 presidential primary, the black candidate won this contest and Koch was the loser.

Jackson's victory in the city and his good showing in the state contained a number of lessons for Mayor Koch's opponents. First and foremost, a black candidate won a plurality of the Democratic primary vote sufficiently large to avoid a run-off had it occurred in a mayoral primary. Political experts regarded this as a minimum necessary condition for a black victory in 1989, reasoning that a black candidate would probably lose a one-on-one black/white runoff but might win a plurality in a di-

TABLE 7.2
1984 and 1988 Democratic Presidential Primaries in New York City
(by assembly district type)

AD Type	1984			1988				
	Votes	Jackson %	Turn-out %	Votes	Jackson %	Dukakis %	Gore %	Turn-out %
Black	192,464	75.2	50.5	227,879	88.2	9.5	1.8	48.3
Mixed minority	60,256	51.1	43.8	69,069	71.4	23.6	5.0	39.8
Latino	54,857	40.4	41.0	67,740	63.5	31.8	4.7	39.4
White liberal	148,271	16.9	51.5	173,879	29.0	59.3	12.9	55.6
White Catholic	137,419	14.0	35.2	165,777	21.9	63.8	12.5	45.3
Outer-borough Jewish	190,428	11.8	44.5	222,689	17.7	66.3	16.0	49.7
Total	783,270	33.7	44.6	927,060	45.3	44.8	9.1	45.0

Source: New York City Board of Elections.

vided field of whites. What is more, another African-American candidate who was equally attractive to blacks but less polarizing to white voters might do even better. Secondly, Jackson's candidacy drew nearly unanimous support and high turnouts in black ADs. Denny Farrell had failed miserably at the task of mobilizing his own core supporters in his 1985 mayoral race.

Equally significantly, Jackson also induced a significant shift toward his candidacy among Latinos (23.1 percentage points) and white liberals (12.1 percentage points) compared to his 1984 race, as Table 7.2 shows. Though the Latino vote was small, perhaps 10 percent of the total, it had not favored Jackson in 1984, had strongly backed Koch in 1985, and was strongly wooed by Dukakis, who spoke Spanish. Yet Latinos in New York City clearly broke for Jackson in 1988. White liberal ADs gave Jackson only 29 percent of their votes, not dramatically higher than white Catholic ADs, but their shift suggested that a more attractive candidate could shift them even further.

Finally, the minority surge for Jackson did not produce a large white countermobilization. Compared to 1984, turnout rose in the outer-borough Jewish and white Catholic ADs most opposed to Jackson, but turnout in the white Catholic ADs remained well below the citywide average. Moreover, both these constituencies shifted slightly in Jackson's direction. Only in the outer-borough Jewish ADs did some countermobilization appear to take place. The 1988 Democratic presidential primary in New York thus indicated that challenging forces were on the rise and Mayor Koch's electoral influence was on the wane.

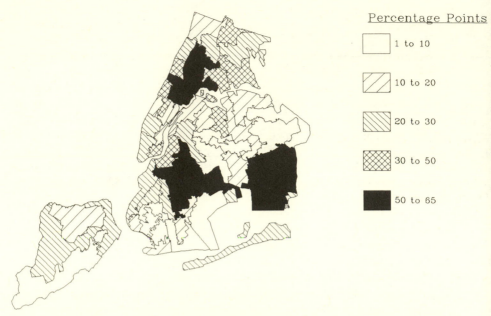

Map 7.2. Jackson 1988 Gain over Farrell 1985

By the summer of 1988, all the conditions that had favored Koch in 1985 had been substantially reversed. Koch had alienated the minority of black voters and the majority of Latinos who had helped him achieve a towering majority in 1985. A comparison of *New York Newsday* polls taken in November 1987, before Koch's criticism of Jesse Jackson, and December 1988 found that the percentage of blacks thinking that Koch should run again had fallen from 40 percent to 22 percent.[15] The mayor's positive job rating among Latinos also fell from 65 percent to 56 percent.

Polls also confirmed that the mayor had lost ground among his core constituencies. An early 1989 *Daily News* poll found every voting group less supportive of the mayor than they had been a year earlier.[16] Indeed, 63 percent said they definitely or probably would not vote for Koch. The *New York Times* reported that favorable opinions of Koch among white Catholics had fallen from 73 percent to 43 percent between 1985 and 1988.[17] Given Rudolph Giuliani's appeal to this group, many if not most were likely to bolt Koch if Koch made it into the general election. Some white Catholic registered Democrats might engage in strategic behavior, voting for an opponent to Koch in the primary (even Dinkins) and then Giuliani in the general election. Even among the mayor's core constituency, Jews, 39 percent said they definitely or probably would not vote for him. Taken together, these defections substantially reduced Mayor Koch's approval rating; a sequence of *New York Times* polls showed that his disapproval rating jumped from 20 to 30 percent after the scandals first became known in early 1986, jumped again to 40 percent after the 1988 presidential primary, and exceeded 50 percent in June 1989.[18]

In 1988, most blacks and Latinos and some white liberals gave Jackson, a charismatic black candidate, a near-majority of New York City's Democratic primary votes despite (or perhaps because of) Mayor Koch's vitriolic attacks on their choice. The Jackson cause put on hold the previous decade of electoral competition between blacks and Latinos. The pattern of interracial assaults, worsening race relations, the end of the economic boom in the October 1987 stock market crash, and palpable evidence of growing economic inequality in the city provided an issue basis for these constituency trends. In his 1985 borough presidency race, David Dinkins had shown himself far more able than Jackson to rally white voters to his cause. In 1989, he promised to achieve the same outcome on a citywide basis.

Mayor Koch violated three cardinal rules of electoral politics in 1988. He needlessly alienated constituencies that might otherwise have supported him; he failed to keep his disparate enemies from uniting against him; and he backed a poor-third loser. His opponents sought to close in on his weakness from two directions. The various wings of the African-American leadership, Latino elected officials, and public employee unions sought to organize a coalition to challenge him from within the Democratic party primary electorate. Meanwhile, Rudolph Giuliani believed he could construct a more traditional version of reform, from his Republican base, fusing Republicans with disaffected Democrats.

The natural candidate to whom the first group could turn was Manhattan Borough President David N. Dinkins, longtime member of the New York County Democratic party establishment and co-chair of the New York City Jesse Jackson campaign in 1988. Dinkins had had his share of setbacks. He had been forced to give up an appointment as deputy mayor in the Beame administration in 1973 because of his failure to pay income taxes; he also lost two elections for the borough presidency before winning in 1985. Yet he also had many strengths. Dinkins had a solidly "regular" political lineage, having come out of Raymond Jones' Carver Democratic club and "come up" through a series of patronage appointments. He had actively supported the cause of Israel and had stood outside Madison Square Garden to condemn the rhetoric of Louis Farrakhan when he spoke there. As borough president, he projected progressive rhetoric and actively sought support from white liberal Manhattan reformers. He had the momentum of the insurgent Jackson victory going for him. Soon, the 1989 mayoral contest became defined as Koch versus Dinkins.

The 1989 Elections and the Defeat of the Koch Coalition

Though Dinkins was the most logical person for New York's Democratic political leaders, especially the public sector trade unions, to embrace as an alternative to Koch, Dinkins was reluctant to declare his candidacy until they fully committed themselves to his cause. Discussion of a possible Dinkins candidacy began immediately after Jackson's victory in April 1988. Dinkins challenged the unions and other potential sources of campaign support who were critical of Koch to show that they would actually raise the massive campaign funds that would be required. Dinkins wanted to insure that his supporters would not return to Koch's camp after Dinkins announced his candidacy. He sought support not only from his core backers but from party leaders anxious to dump a failing Koch and latch on to a new winner. A new campaign-finance reform law limited the amount that Koch could raise and provided for public matching funds, but Dinkins would still have to raise $3.6 million to have the maximum amount of funds allowed. This amount was six times larger than Koch's two opponents had raised in 1985.

Dinkins's strategy worked. A wide range of political players who had previously backed Koch attended a Dinkins fund-raising event at the Tavern on the Green restaurant on February 1, 1989, which raised $100,000. Dinkins made his intentions clear at this event; his formal announcement in turn severely undermined the Ravitch campaign, which had hoped to bear the liberal reform mantle, as well as the Goldin campaign. Ravitch and Goldin nevertheless were able to raise substantial campaign funds, and both hoped to displace Koch to become the second candidate against Dinkins in a Democratic run-off primary.

In the Republican primary, Giuliani faced opposition derived from his poor relationship with Republican U.S. Senator Alphonse D'Amato. D'Amato convinced Ronald S. Lauder, heir to a cosmetics fortune and former Reagan administration ambassador to Austria, to run a campaign that ultimately spent over $13 million trying to convince New York's small but conservative cadre of registered Republican voters that Giuliani was a "closet liberal."[19]

The Primary Campaigns

By the spring of 1989, the campaign battle lines had been well formed.[20] On the Democratic side, neither Goldin nor Ravitch could convince voters they were a compelling alternative to Mayor Koch, making the race a two-person contest between the front-runner, Dinkins, and Mayor Koch.

On the Republican side, few beside Lauder himself considered him much more than an instrument of torment against Giuliani, but it was unclear how much damage he could do.

Successful campaigns require good timing and momentum as well as candidate assets, money, and organization. In the Democratic primary, Dinkins was not only reasonably well financed, but black churches, black elected officials, and the public employee unions gave him strong organizational support.[21] As the front-runner in the polls, Dinkins, like Koch, benefited from wide exposure in the "free media." Since Koch, Goldin, and Ravitch would all need Dinkins's voters to defeat Giuliani if they made it into the general election, they refrained from attacking Dinkins directly. Koch was especially careful because he was already perceived as polarizing race relations.

The 1989 campaign finance reform also helped Dinkins and put Koch at a disadvantage. While acceptance of the law's provisions and receipt of public matching funds were voluntary, all the Democrats felt compelled to participate in the new rules. Since the new law limited primary campaign expenditures to $3.6 million and donations from any contributor to $3,000, it prevented Koch from pursuing his 1985 strategy of raising and spending massive amounts of cash from large developers, lawyers, and investment banks. Dinkins had a comparative advantage in organizational resources not subject to the limit, including volunteers and union manpower.

Substantively, the Democratic campaign focused on the candidates' qualifications rather than on issues. During the first debate, Comptroller Goldin said of Dinkins, "Let's face it. If I hadn't paid my taxes, I wouldn't be running for mayor. I wouldn't be comptroller."[22] Koch had also referred to this issue at the outset of the campaign, and it constituted Dinkins's largest liability. By contrast, Goldin accused Koch of being "mean, petty, and nasty," and Dinkins called Koch "Alibi Ed."[23] Koch in turn cited his experience and said he had already accomplished more than the others said they would do. By sticking to these themes, Koch was able to come to within seven points of Dinkins in a *New York Post* tracking poll by the end of July.[24] In the Republican primary, Giuliani spent most of his time attacking Koch as racially divisive, while Lauder vainly spent his millions on television ads attacking Giuliani.[25]

There can be little doubt that a pervasive concern about race relations lurked beneath the overt debate about candidate qualifications. The Howard Beach trials had focused attention on white attacks on blacks. In early 1989, black teenagers out "wilding" in Central Park had brutally attacked a young woman investment banker, an event *New York Magazine* called a "psychic turning point for the city."[26] Then, on August 23, a crowd of white youths in the Bensonhurst section of Brooklyn cornered

16-year-old Yusuf Hawkins and three other black youths who had come to look at a used car, and a white youth shot and killed Hawkins. This senseless murder seemed to change the dynamics of the primary race and once more focused attention on the city's racial tension. Three weeks later, on Tuesday, September 12, 1989, this problem was on the minds of many who voted in the Democratic primary.

The Primary Vote

Dinkins won the primary by constructing a coalition of black, Latino, and white voters who gave him 50.8 percent of the vote against 42 percent for Ed Koch, thus ending the Koch era. Dinkins had initially hoped for at least 40 percent of the vote to avert a runoff but ultimately did much better. Exit polls showed that 94.2 percent of black primary voters supported Dinkins, as did 57.5 percent of Latinos.[27] The key to Dinkins's success, however, was that he won a third of the votes cast by white Democrats, more white support than a first-time black candidate for mayor had achieved in any city except for Tom Bradley's first victory in Los Angeles. Despite facing three Jewish competitors, Dinkins won 24.6 percent of the votes cast by Jewish Democrats, as well as 47.9 percent of the white Protestant vote and 62.7 percent of those whites who said they had no religion. The various groups that leaned toward Dinkins, nonreligious whites, blacks, and Latinos, comprised about 60 percent of the electorate.

Among Jews, blacks, and especially Latinos, Dinkins got more support from union members and teachers than those who were not. Jewish city employees were more likely to support Koch than other Jews, but Dinkins got more support among white Catholic, Protestant, black, and Latino city employees compared to their general populations.[28] Public union support thus seems to have helped Dinkins among rank-and-file voters as well as with campaign resources. In addition, Dinkins got more support from women than men across all groups, which took on added significance because of the preponderance of women among registered Democrats.

In aggregate terms, Table 7.3 shows the Dinkins vote across the different types of ADs and compares it to Farrell's performance against Koch in 1985 and Jackson's performance in the 1988 presidential primary. The implications are clear: support for Dinkins in black and Latino ADs was not quite as strong as for Jackson, but Dinkins largely reproduced Jackson's alignment of these groups and attracted substantially larger turnouts from them. Latinos had overwhelmingly favored Koch in 1985, but they shifted strongly towards Dinkins in 1989. Black Democrats turned out in even greater numbers to elect the city's first African-American

TABLE 7.3
Dinkins 1989 Performance Relative to Farrell 1985 and Jackson 1988

	1985			1988			1989		
	Votes	Farrell %	Turn-out %	Votes	Jackson %	Turn-out %	Votes	Dinkins %	Turn-out %
Black	129,464	32.7	26.8	227,879	88.2	48.3	267,247	84.8	56.7
Mixed minority	54,131	19.8	30.6	69,069	71.4	39.8	83,835	65.1	48.3
Latino	55,353	17.8	31.6	67,740	63.5	39.4	80,438	60.4	47.0
White liberal	134,334	6.6	36.6	173,879	29.0	55.6	201,733	46.5	52.6
White Catholic	135,122	5.9	31.4	165,777	21.9	45.3	192,590	29.7	46.7
Outer-borough Jewish	180,150	5.6	37.4	222,689	17.7	49.7	251,645	25.9	56.4
Total	688,554	13.0	32.6	927,060	45.3	45.0	1,077,488	50.8	52.4

Source: New York City Board of Elections.

mayor than they had in 1988 to vote for the first African-American presidential candidate.

Dinkins also did massively better than Jackson among all segments of the white electorate, as the table and Map 7.3 show. (In 1985 Farrell had gotten virtually no votes in white ADs.) Dinkins increased his share by half over Jackson's not only in the liberal white ADs but also in the outer-borough Jewish ADs. He increased his share by a third in the white Catholic ADs. In addition to mobilizing his core constituencies, Dinkins was thus able to swing important segments of white electorate in his direction.

Koch's failures reinforced Dinkins's achievements. As Table 7.1 showed, Koch lost ground across the board. Most fatal to the basic thrust of his political strategy after 1982 was the defection of white Catholics. When combined with the exceptionally low turnout in white Catholic ADs (the lowest of any group and further below the citywide average than in 1988 or 1985), the shift of this group away from him compared to 1985 delivered a major blow to Koch. A careful study of the vote in one representative white Catholic AD, the 31st in Richmond Hill, Queens, suggests that as many as 17 percent of its voters might have been "strategic," that is, they voted for Dinkins in order to get rid of Koch to clear the way for Giuliani, even if it meant voting for a black in the primary.[29] Though for different reasons, white Catholics had, like blacks and Latinos, rejected the mayor.

Outer-borough Jewish ADs remained the strongest base of support for Mayor Koch, but even there, his share dropped 10 percentage points from the previous mayoral primary. Moreover, turnout in these ADs was only 4 points above the citywide average in contrast to 1985, when it had been

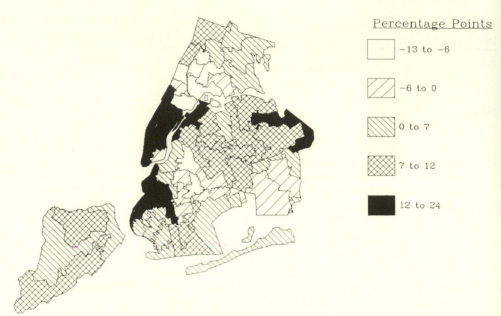

Percentage Points

☐ −13 to −6

▨ −6 to 0

▨ 0 to 7

▨ 7 to 12

■ 12 to 24

Map 7.3. Dinkins 1989 Gain over Jackson 1988

5.8 points above. Koch suffered an even larger decline in vote share in the white liberal ADs—which had relatively high turnouts—from whence Koch had originally sprung and in which many Jews also lived. In the context of his loss of 30.6 percentage points of support in Latino ADs and 30.7 percentage points in black ADs, this disaffection proved fatal to his chances for an unprecedented fourth term.

The General Election

Having made history by winning the Democratic mayoral nomination and renewing the power of the liberal reform coalition in New York City politics, Dinkins faced the landslide winner of the Republican primary, Rudolph W. Giuliani. Given the four-to-one ratio of registered Democrats to Republicans, the Democratic mayoral nominees have lost general elections only when a split between regular and reform Democrats caused large numbers of white reformers to defect to the Republican-fusion candidate, for example, in the election of John Lindsay. Given the lack of a split and strong support from Mayor Koch, Governor Cuomo, and the white county party leaders, David Dinkins should have easily won the

November 1989 general election. And indeed, Dinkins lead Giuliani by 24 points in an early October opinion poll. But never before had the Democratic nominee been black.

Race, and more specifically racially based mistrust, provided a new basis for whites who traditionally voted for the Democratic nominee to defect from their party.[30] The general electorate also presented Dinkins with an intrinsically more difficult political landscape than did the primary. White liberals, blacks, and Latinos (and by definition more strongly partisan voters) figured less heavily in the general electorate than in the Democratic primary electorate. In the general electorate, Republicans, independents, and whites were more numerous (indeed, whites constituted about 56 percent of the general electorate). It was entirely unclear where Mayor Koch's core of outer-borough Jewish support would go in the general election. These conditions opened the way for Rudolph Giuliani to seek to reconstruct the Koch coalition of white Catholics and Jews along somewhat more conservative lines than Mayor Koch had pursued.

The two-month general election campaign was hard fought to the point of brutality. To avoid explicit references to race, Giuliani mounted a vigorous attack on Dinkins's ties to the "corrupt" Democratic establishment, his financial shortcomings, and his "softness" on crime. Dinkins attempted to rebut these charges and stressed his ability to bring the city together, Giuliani's lack of managerial experience, and his unanimous support from the city's Democratic leaders. Dinkins campaigned heavily in Jewish neighborhoods, seeking to win over Koch voters by stressing his commitment to Israel and his stand on issues of concern to these areas. But as the campaign wore on, Dinkins's support was clearly eroding and Giuliani's rising.

On election day, the Dinkins forces again mounted a massive, well-targeted, get-out-the-vote effort. That Dinkins had a strong field operation and Giuliani did not may well have been a factor in Dinkins's extremely narrow victory. When the votes had finally been counted, Dinkins had beaten Giuliani by 47,000 votes out of 1.9 million cast; if 24,000 people, or slightly more than 1 percent of the total, had changed their minds, Rudolph Giuliani, not David Dinkins, would have made political history in New York in 1989.

The aggregate results and their differences from the primary are given in Table 7.4. Whereas the primary had a relatively high turnout but not as high as in the hotly contested race of 1977, the general election turnout was well above any other in recent decades. The results showed more racial and ethnic polarization than did the primary. Black and Latino ADs gave Dinkins larger percentages, while white Catholic ADs went more strongly against him. Particularly noteworthy was the strong Latino shift toward Dinkins, who gained 13.2 percentage points of the vote in

TABLE 7.4
1989 Mayoral Primary and General Elections in New York City
(by assembly district type)

AD Type	Primary				General			
	Votes	Dinkins %	Koch %	Turn-out %	Votes	Dinkins %	Giuliani %	Turn-out %
Black	267,247	84.8	10.3	56.7	348,820	89.0	10.4	65.9
Mixed minority	83,835	65.1	26.8	48.3	125,590	76.7	22.4	56.8
Latino	80,438	60.4	31.8	47.0	123,070	73.6	25.4	56.9
White liberal	201,733	46.5	44.0	52.6	356,685	50.7	47.8	59.4
White Catholic	192,590	29.7	62.2	46.7	455,597	25.8	71.9	65.8
Outer-borough Jewish	251,645	25.9	67.2	56.4	452,928	29.3	68.6	67.5
Total	1,077,488	50.8	42.0	52.4	1,898,690	50.4	48.0	63.6

Source: New York City Board of Elections.

these ADs. Map 7.4 shows that the defection of white voters in normally Democratic areas was greatest in outer-borough Jewish ADs and least in the white liberal ADs. More liberals defected on the West Side than downtown, however.

Trends in turnout were also significant. While turnout in black ADs remained above the city average, as it had in the primary, the margin of difference was not as great. In contrast to the primary, turnout in the white Catholic ADs shot up relative to the citywide average. Turnout in Latino ADs sagged compared to their relative position in the primary, while turnout in white liberal ADs also remained comparatively low. Patterns of mobilization in the general election thus favored Dinkins less and his opponent more than in the primary.

In the primary, Dinkins achieved nearly unanimous support and unprecedentedly high turnout from the single largest bloc of Democrats, black voters, to get not quite two-thirds of his total votes. Mobilized but ambivalent Latino voters gave him about a third of his remaining votes, or one-ninth of his total. This meant he still needed to raise one-quarter of his votes from whites to reach 50.8 percent of the total. His near-majority support in white liberal ADs, combined with lesser support in outer-borough Jewish and white Catholic ADs (including those who supported him merely to get rid of Koch) was sufficient to give him a comfortable margin over Mayor Koch.

In the general election, however, high turnout and even more solid support from blacks was sufficient to give candidate Dinkins just over half the votes he needed to be elected. The surge in Latino support for Dinkins

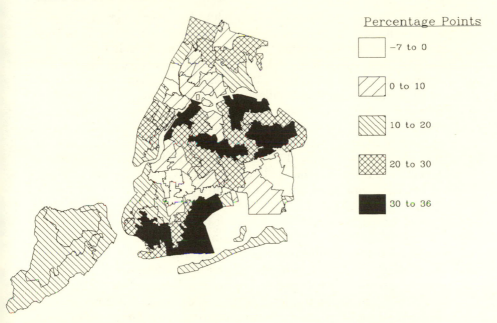

Percentage Points

☐ −7 to 0

▨ 0 to 10

▧ 10 to 20

▨ 20 to 30

■ 30 to 36

Map 7.4. Democratic Defection

contributed a third of the remaining votes he needed, but their contribution was attenuated by their relatively low turnout. Compared to the primary, Dinkins therefore needed an even larger minority of the white vote.[31]

White liberal ADs, which gave half their votes to Dinkins, provided over half of the white votes Dinkins needed. Despite massive defection from traditionally Democratic outer-borough Jewish neighborhoods and despite Giuliani's strong appeal to less solidly Democratic white Catholic areas, large enough minorities of voters in these areas backed Dinkins to give him the final election. Dinkins's general election victory was thus built on many pillars.

The solidarity of black voters and the shift of Latinos toward Dinkins were necessary but not sufficient for his election. Had whites as well as blacks been racially polarized, he clearly would have lost to Giuliani. Instead, Dinkins's ability to draw significant minorities of the vote from *all* the major white ethnic groups, including Italian-Americans, enabled him to win against an attractive Republican candidate. In short, the outcome of the 1989 general election turned on the ways in which it was *not* racially polarized. Dinkins's ability to draw on such cleavages as Democrats versus Republicans, Jews versus Catholics, liberals versus conservatives, and women versus men mattered.

The willingness of some Jews and white Catholics to stand by their party's nominee despite the deep racial cleavages within New York City differentiates New York from other older industrial cities. In Chicago, for example, almost all white Catholics defected from their party's black nominee in 1983. If New York's Italian- and Irish-American Democrats had behaved like their Irish, Italian, and Polish counterparts in Chicago, Dinkins would have lost. New York is not as racially polarized as Chicago, perhaps because its black population is smaller and its Jewish population larger. New York's leading African-American politician had to project a much more biracial rhetoric than might arise in Chicago, while his perceived threat to white political hegemony, indeed white survival, was correspondingly much smaller than in Chicago.[32]

Such a perceived racial threat was still widespread in the white Catholic neighborhoods of New York City, but racially based mistrust was far from universal. Where it was low, Dinkins had a fighting chance to win over white voters. The degree to which New York's left-liberal, multiracial, labor-based, Democratic political heritage has fostered interracial trust constitutes a precious political resource, albeit one that the blows of racial conflict have put at grave risk.[33] It remains embedded not only in white liberal precincts and labor union headquarters but in the tattered fabric of regular Democratic party organizational and political cultures of conservative white ethnic neighborhoods.

The cosmopolitan white young professionals dwelling in places like Manhattan's Upper West Side and Brooklyn's Park Slope were a major factor in the 1989 mayoral elections. Spurred by the postindustrial transformation, this group grew substantially between 1977 and 1989, perhaps even doubling. While this group is politically and ideologically diverse, it shares a life-style and neighborhood ecology. It was in these neighborhoods that development pressures, concern over racial polarization, and the activism of white reform political clubs remained greatest. These reform clubs faced little competition in mobilizing the political concerns of their neighborhoods into support for Dinkins in the general election.

Nevertheless, the margin by which an insurgent liberal reform Democratic coalition beat out Rudolph Giuliani's attempt to rebuild the Koch coalition was perilously close. Giuliani's strategy mirrored that of Dinkins. He could count on strong support from white Catholics, fewer of whom were Democrats and more of whom did not trust Dinkins to be fair to whites. In theory, Giuliani could write off the black vote and focus instead on courting outer-borough Jews and Latinos, especially those who had voted for Mayor Koch. In practice, the Giuliani campaign's largest strategic blunder—and one that could well have cost him the election—was to equate Latinos with blacks, writing off their votes as well.

New York's Latino voters differed from their black counterparts in a number of relevant ways. They were twice as likely as blacks to be Republicans, although a majority of each group were Democrats. They were more likely than any other segment of the electorate to call themselves conservatives. Moreover, while 56 percent of blacks believed that Giuliani would favor whites over blacks, only a third of Latinos thought so. Less than a fourth of the black respondents had a favorable opinion of Giuliani, but half the Latinos did. Latinos were twice as likely as blacks to have voted for Koch in the Democratic primary, and they were open to persuasion: 27 percent of the Latinos said that they decided their vote within two weeks of the election, compared with 15 percent of the blacks.[34]

Events pushed Latinos toward a black candidate despite these differences. As the poorest of groups in New York City, Latinos felt they should work together with blacks despite their political frictions. Latinos identified with the blacks who had been subjected to the series of white assaults on minority youths. And Jesse Jackson had stirred excitement in the Latino as well as the black communities. Yet many Latinos supported Mayor Koch and were, like his Jewish supporters, open to an appeal from Giuliani. His failure to address both these constituencies was costly.

Giuliani largely succeeded in his quest for the Koch voters. Two-thirds of those who told the CBS/*New York Times* exit poll that they voted for Koch in the primary also voted for Giuliani in the general election, including almost three-quarters of the white Catholics, two-thirds of white Protestants, and more than 60 percent of the Jews. (These three white groups made up 45 percent of the electorate.) Concern that Dinkins would favor blacks over whites rather than treat each group fairly and Giuliani's stand on the issues played important roles in this defection. Almost every white who did not trust Dinkins to be fair voted for Giuliani. Among white voters who did think Dinkins would be fair (roughly half of the whites) 60 percent voted for Giuliani. The many white voters who wanted a tough policy on crime and who were weary of corruption also found Giuliani's background as a prosecutor appealing. White voters who were concerned about reducing racial tensions and homelessness tended to vote for Dinkins but their numbers were much smaller.[35]

The persistence of Democratic party identification worked for Dinkins among whites, as did the trust many white Democrats and independents placed in Dinkins and concern for reducing racial divisions and homelessness. In the final analysis, the desire among a sufficiently large minority of whites to have Dinkins address the legacy of social polarization during the Koch years, when joined to black mobilization and the Latino shift towards Dinkins, provided the resurgent liberal coalition with barely enough votes to best Giuliani's effort to rebuild the Koch coalition.

Internal Contradictions of the Koch Coalition

Mayor Koch's strategy for building electoral dominance as a step to achieving a strong position with respect to both public sector producer interests and private market interests seemed virtually unassailable in 1985, yet it lay in ruins in 1989. Obviously, factors that had previously promoted his ascendancy evolved in ways that undermined his position. The success of the political strategies pursued by the Koch coalition created countertrends that proved beyond the mayor's capacity to manage.

Most obviously, electoral constituencies from which Mayor Koch had previously drawn substantial support began increasingly to desert his cause. While this defection spanned the electoral spectrum, it was accentuated among blacks and Latinos, for whom it was closely related to increased political mobilization. Blacks had been among the mayor's strongest supporters in 1977, and a substantial minority of black voters continued to back him during most of the 1980s, as did a majority of Latinos. This was consistent with Mayor Koch's origins in the liberal reform wing of the Democratic Party and the alliances that liberal Jews had forged with blacks and Latinos during their political ascent in the 1950s and early 1960s. It was also consistent with political fragmentation within the black political leadership, competition between blacks and Latinos, and the influence of regular Democratic organizations in most minority neighborhoods.

Mayor Koch sought to sustain his link to his minority supporters with appeals to their middle-class values and aspirations, their fear of crime, their ethnic differences, and their attachment to regular politicians. His larger strategy, however, was to forge a Jewish-white Catholic alignment based on white, middle-class anxiety about racial succession in the workplace, the neighborhoods, and the corridors of power. As he became more successful at the latter task, he became less so at the former. His antagonism toward Jesse Jackson, whom virtually all blacks regarded highly, became visceral. This was only the most public of a series of attacks, bordering on insults, that Koch launched at other black leaders. This in turn progressively alienated the mayor's black supporters and made it increasingly untenable even for black elected officials associated with the regular Democratic party county organizations to endorse his reelection.

Mayor Edward I. Koch represented the apogee of Jewish political influence in New York City. Unlike the city's first Jewish mayor, Abraham Beame, he was neither a clubhouse politician nor judged to be a failure. He liked to think of himself as having saved the city after the fiscal crisis and saw himself as an impassioned defender of the interests of New

York's Jews as he read them. He led a Board of Estimate where Jews cast 9 of 11 votes during the 1980s. He was steeped in the values of a great political tradition, but he also shared the deep anxiety that his core constituency felt with respect to its trajectory relative to other groups in New York City. Mayor Koch not only reflected the anger this group felt about threats to its position but projected and reinforced it. This led him to alienate a constituency that had been vital to his rise to power and subsequent electoral successes.

Mayor Koch's strong identification with the white middle class also served to swing Puerto Ricans and other Latinos away from him and toward black candidates in 1988 and 1989. Given the growing economic polarization in the city's population, the concentration of Latinos at the bottom of the social structure, and the rising tensions between whites and blacks, it is perhaps not surprising that Latinos ultimately felt closer to David Dinkins than to Edward Koch. While the mayor had taken political advantage of the competition between blacks and Latinos, the steady erosion of the position of Latinos reduced his ability to do so. The middle-class dimension of the coalition he sought to forge between Jews and white Catholics hampered his ability to make forthright appeals to Latinos.

Taken as an aggregate, black, mixed minority, and Latino ADs shifted from voting 49.9 percent in favor of Edward Koch to voting only 17.5 percent for him between 1985 and 1989. As residents of black and Latino neighborhoods shifted away from him and towards black candidates, their rate of turnout also increased relative to white ADs. While voters in all the minority ADs cast 34.7 percent of the ballots in the 1985 primary, they cast 40.0 percent in the 1989 primary. The black vote alone doubled between these two primary elections. Mayor Koch's downfall thus lay not only in the ways he alienated previously supportive minority constituencies but in how his black challengers succeeded in mobilizing their constituency and uniting it with constituencies from which it was previously divided. Mayor Koch thus violated the cardinal political rule of never allowing one's various opponents to get together.

The latent negative aspects of Mayor Koch's strategy for building a dominant political coalition also cost him support among whites between 1985 and 1989. To consolidate the Jewish-white Catholic alliance, to increase his control over the electorate, and to gain support from other power centers in government, Mayor Koch formed close relationships with leaders of the regular Democratic county party organizations. These relationships turned out to have a far higher cost than the mayor had anticipated after the corruption scandal unfolded. The shift was largest in white liberal ADs, whose leaders Mayor Koch had already subjected to great scorn, but it also took place in the less cosmopolitan outer-borough

Jewish and white Catholic ADs. Indeed, the willingness of some white Catholic voters to support Dinkins as the best way to maximize the chance for electing an Italian-American Republican candidate shows the conditional nature of Mayor Koch's white Catholic-Jewish alliance.

As Mayor Koch lost his hold over most black and Latino and many white liberal, Catholic, and Jewish voters, he also lost it over the public sector producer interests that were central to organizing the electorate: the political party organizations and the public sector unions. The corruption scandals threw the Bronx and Queens organizations into at least momentary disarray, while the Brooklyn organization continued to be internally divided. Black and Latino politicians took advantage of these conditions to improve their position in these organizations. In this process, black and Latino regular district leaders found it advantageous to support David Dinkins rather than Edward Koch. While the mayor's success in preventing community-based service organizations from emerging as an independent political force by subordinating them to elected officials did not hurt his political position, neither did it help him. Meanwhile, in the wake of racial succession in the leadership of several key unions and of heightened antagonism among black and Latino city workers toward the mayor, a number of public employee unions took the bold step of supporting insurgent candidates. The 1988 Jesse Jackson campaign became a proving ground for David Dinkins's 1989 election.

In sum, Mayor Koch's strategies for building a dominant electoral coalition among popular constituencies and public sector producer interests gave rise to contradictory results. In the short run, they enhanced his power, but in the long term they provoked counteractions that led to a successful challenge against him. Mayor Koch's relationships with private market interests neither contributed directly to his loss in 1989 nor saved him from the political damage he had inflicted upon himself. Having entered city government as an outsider to Manhattan's corporate elite, Mayor Koch managed to enjoy broad corporate support at the end of his administration. While some prudent corporate leaders covered their bets by making campaign contributions to the mayor's Democratic challengers in 1989, the city's business elite continued to like the mayor's policies and support his administration. Neither editorial commentary nor corporate campaign contributions could save the mayor from the loss of popular support, however.

The mayor's ties to the city's business elite, especially its financial community, did most probably have an indirect negative impact on the mayor's political position. The boom of the Reagan-Koch years had increased social polarization in the city, while the 1987 stock market crash ended the economic growth that might have justified that polarization. Many people felt the mayor was too close to real estate developers and thought developers wielded too much power. As building density pressured residential neighborhoods and the tight housing market increased the rent burden during the 1980s, his opponents succeeded to some degree in identifying the mayor with these problems. Despite making a large-scale, city-funded, moderate rent housing program a major feature of his third term, Mayor Koch was not able to dispel this perception.

Like his search for a Jewish-white Catholic alliance and his ties to machine Democrats, the mayor's association with investment banks and real estate developments worked against him as well as for him. These firms had generously endowed his campaigns, but their status was badly tarnished by the crash. When combined with his opponents' ability to overcome the barriers that had so thoroughly divided and weakened them since the late 1960s, the weakening of his main political and economic allies was sufficient to undermine Mayor Koch's long-dominant power, opening the way for Mayor David N. Dinkins to try to construct his own dominant coalition. This new coalition would certainly have a different electoral base and face difficult challenges, but it would also have to work with many of the same elements that Mayor Koch had mastered for so long.

Eight

The Koch Era in Perspective

All elements of the fragmented Democratic
opposition coalesced into a temporarily
effective weapon. *Fusion* is a most accurate
label for the past reform movements in New
York, if it is understood that the resultant alloy
was most unstable. . . . The settlements within
the alliance of one period of party control
contribute to the creation of new alliances
for another period.
   (Theodore Lowi, *At the Pleasure of
the Mayor*)[1]

The city's once-vibrant, predominantly white
ethnic and proletarian political culture . . . lie[s]
dead or dying. . . . In its place must come a new
political culture responsive to the burgeoning,
unfocused vitality of . . . the . . . black, Latin,
and Asian cosmopolis emerging from a
hundred immigrant streams deluging the city
at levels unprecedented since the 1920s.
   (Jim Sleeper, "Boodling, Bigotry, and
Cosmopolitanism")[2]

[T]he patterns of politics and fiscal policy
prevailing in New York and other major cities
embody an accommodation between those
who control credit and capital, on the one side,
and the ideal that government should be subject
to popular control, on the other. In American
cities . . . this accommodation is weighted
toward the concerns of the creditors—and
against the democratic impulse.
   (Martin Shefter, *Political Crisis/Fiscal Crisis*)[3]

BETWEEN 1977 AND 1986, Edward I. Koch and his allies forged an increasingly powerful coalition in New York City politics. On the electoral
side, he added middle-class Jewish and white Catholic residents of such
outer-borough neighborhoods as Canarsie, Midwood, the South Shore of
Staten Island, and Bensonhurst to his original base among Manhattan's

white liberals. His administration appealed to white ethnic constituencies through attacks on black leaders and vivid defenses of middle-class values and interests, policies that reduced welfare spending and put many more people behind bars, and alliances with the regular political clubs that were the main political forces in white ethnic neighborhoods. At the same time, it brought many ex-Lindsay administration white reformers into government and won support from good-government groups by arguing that its policy decisions were made "on the merits."

This strategy of electoral coalition building tended to marginalize black leaders, especially those who publicly criticized the mayor. Over time, it alienated an increasing proportion of black voters as well. Mayor Koch evidently accepted this as a necessary cost of his overall strategy, and he sought to limit the resulting electoral damage through his alliances with black regular Democrats, who supported him tacitly if not always overtly. Mayor Koch also used his control over contracts to community-based service-delivery organizations to reinforce his ties to minority politicians and to deter community-based service organizations from becoming the political launching pad for any of his opponents.

The Koch administration made strong efforts to appeal to Latino voters, most of whom are Catholic and identify racially as whites, and one-third of whom identify themselves as conservatives. It used city contracts to secure allegiance from Puerto Rican regulars like Ramon Velez of the South Bronx. For the best part of a decade, this effort was highly successful with Latino voters as well as with Latino elected officials. But growing economic inequality and worsening intergroup relations, fostered by the Koch administration's rhetoric and policies, ultimately caused Latinos voters to shift away from the mayor.[4]

Mayor Koch used his electoral dominance to strike varying kinds of bargains with public sector producer interests. The regular Democratic party organizations were particularly important to his overall strategy. He gave them limited influence over the margins of policy, particularly low-level hiring and political appointments, the award of contracts, and influence over local land-use issues. They gave him electoral protection and support within key decision-making bodies, such as the Board of Estimate.

Public employee unions were more problematic for Mayor Koch, but he also developed working arrangements with them. In the media, he attacked them as special interests and obstacles to better government, while they attacked him as illiberal and antiworker.[5] In practice, however, Mayor Koch granted city workers substantial pay raises, which recouped the income they lost during the fiscal crisis, and increased the number of city workers, which insured that union treasuries grew. In return, many of these unions endorsed Mayor Koch, gave him campaign contributions, and provided workers for his campaigns. None endorsed his mayoral challengers before 1989, and some stuck with him even in 1989.

Mayor Koch also had a symbiotic relationship with the investment bankers who floated the city's bonds. He appointed them as underwriters, and they provided campaign contributions and advised his administration. This mirrored Mayor Koch's relationships with other private market interests. The mayor strongly supported private investment with deeds as well as words. Particularly important were favorable zoning policies, support for specific development projects, tax incentives, and the lowering of the overall tax burden on business. In return, Koch got generally favorable press, the political benefits that spun off specific projects, huge amounts of campaign contributions, and the legitimacy conveyed by strong support from corporate elites. Despite the mayor's continuing personal lack of ease with the culture of the city's corporate elite, and theirs with his, they knew he was "their man." A great number of officials of the Koch administration benefited personally from this alliance, going on to careers in real estate development, investment banking, and municipal finance after their tours of duty in government.

For much of the 1980s, Mayor Koch's strategies for building a dominant political coalition seemed to have made him invincible. Success made him more arrogant, leading to talk about his being "mayor for life." At the height of his power, however, the negative aspects of his strategy began to become evident. His ties to party regulars haunted him, as did the actions of certain commissioners who used their powers of office for their own ends. The widening scandal damaged his standing across the whole span of his supporters and at least momentarily threw the regular Democratic organizations into disarray. His contributions towards heightening racial and ethnic tensions and his attacks on Jesse Jackson and other black leaders cost him support among blacks, Latinos, and white liberals.

As his position with the electorate weakened, so did his ability to use the tools of governance to keep potential opponents in check. Gradually, they were able to form a challenging alliance behind the candidacy of David Dinkins. Because he would need Dinkins's support if he won the primary, Koch and his supporters did not attack Dinkins vigorously. Upon Dinkins's victory they had no choice but to back him against the Republican-Liberal nominee, Rudolph W. Giuliani. Support from Mayor Koch and other white Democratic elected officials undoubtedly helped Dinkins, himself the product of Democratic clubhouse politics, to keep a significant minority of white Democrats from defecting. Giuliani, for his part, was too much the captive of his social base among conservative white Catholics and his organizational base in the Republican party to appeal sufficiently to such swing constituencies as Latinos, white liberals, and outer-borough Jewish Democrats. (Had Ronald Lauder not backed him into a corner, Giuliani might have been able to project a more liberal, Lindsay-like message.) Even so, Giuliani came extremely close to recreating an even more conservative version of the Koch electoral coalition.

The saga of the Koch coalition in New York City politics poses questions that go to the heart of current debates about urban politics and urban political economy. Why, when black, Latino, or neighborhood-oriented mayors came to power in many other large cities, did Mayor Koch's relatively conservative, white, pro-growth coalition gain power in New York? Did situational constraints and imperatives determine the policies he pursued, or did he enjoy some latitude in how he addressed these constraints? What was the relative importance of economic and political factors in shaping his choices? In what sense was the ascendancy of the Koch coalition related to the postindustrial transformation that was reshaping the city? And what does its demise suggest for the future of urban reform in the era of the city's first African-American mayor, David N. Dinkins?

The Koch Coalition in Comparative Perspective

All big cities felt the long-term force of the postindustrial revolution and the shorter-term impacts of the ghetto revolt and community organization of the 1960s, the recession and fiscal crisis of the 1970s, and the decrease of federal aid to cities during the boom years of the 1980s. In every big city, these trends altered the matrix of constituencies and interests from which political actors built political power and the tensions they faced after gaining it. Most big cities elected their first minority mayors, while others elected white, populist, neighborhood-oriented mayors; in a few cases, these trends were fused. In New York, however, neither of these outcomes occurred. Instead, established political forces kept rising but underrepresented constituencies on the margins of the dominant political coalition.

Of the thirty-four central cities with a population of 300,000 or more and a metropolitan population of one million or more in 1980, thirteen moved from white, relatively conservative dominant coalitions to more liberal biracial coalitions over the last twenty years. In descending size, they are Los Angeles, Chicago, Philadelphia, Detroit, Washington, Atlanta, Baltimore, Newark, Oakland, Cleveland, Miami, New Orleans, and San Antonio. At least seven others—Houston, Boston, Minneapolis, Seattle, Denver, San Francisco, and Portland—elected white, liberal neighborhood-oriented reformers to whom minority votes proved important. (White liberal voters supported Latino and black mayoral candidates in Denver and Seattle.) Other cities, such as Pittsburgh and Cincinnati, might also be put in this column.

Roughly two-thirds of the largest and most important central cities therefore experienced a transition in the makeup and policy orientations of their governing coalitions. While intercity competition for investment, the continuing influence of downtown businessmen, reduced federal aid, and the continuing influence of white regulars constrained what these new mayors and their coalitions could do, most made consequential choices about reallocating resources toward neighborhood development and increasing minority hiring in public agencies.

During the 1980s, New York City stood out as a significant exception to this pattern. Most other large cities that did not move towards a biracial or neighborhood-oriented electoral coalition had small minority populations and strongly nonpartisan, "reformed" political cultures, such as Dallas, San Diego, Phoenix, Kansas City, and San Jose.[6] Only a few old, Eastern cities with large minority populations paralleled New York's path: St. Louis, Cleveland (where a white Republican succeeded an early black mayor and a white populist), and Baltimore (where a black mayor was not elected until 1987). In the mid-1980s, New York not only lacked a liberal, inclusive dominant coalition but seemed to have poor prospects for electing one. What accounted for this difference?

Two kinds of factors might be expected to lead to realignments in dominant political coalitions. External factors include changes in the size or interests of urban constituencies and in the conflicts among and within them. Internal factors include the patterns of political organization and competition and the way in which these patterns affect the dynamics of coalition formation. At first sight, it would seem that external factors, such as the emergence of black population majorities, prompted most of the challenges to dominant political coalitions in large cities.[7] Where blacks or Latinos came to constitute a large majority of a city's population, such as in Washington, D.C., Detroit, Atlanta, or Miami, it might plausibly be argued that demography became political destiny.

On closer examination, however, these "objective circumstances" do not adequately explain the political outcomes. Even cities with large minority populations typically required *biracial* coalitions to supplant more conservative white coalitions. It was generally not sufficient for black or Latino candidates to mobilize only their constituencies. Since the white populations of big cities tend to be older, economically better off, and more engaged in the political system, while black and Latino populations are younger, poorer, more estranged from politics, and less likely to be citizens, white populations are better represented in active electorates than in the population. The success of minority challengers thus depends not only on the number and political organization of blacks or Latinos but on the political ideology and organization of whites. White support was crucial to the election not only of Mayor Bradley in Los Angeles but also of Mayor Washington in Chicago and Mayor Kurt Schmoke in Baltimore.

Browning, Marshall, and Tabb focus on the size of the ideologically liberal white vote willing to join an insurgent coalition as a crucial factor in the formation of a biracial coalition.[8] When this constituency has been excluded from the previous dominant coalition and therefore seeks to organize or join a challenging biracial coalition so as to increase its power, it can become a powerful force, as it was in Los Angeles.[9] Conversely, where white liberals achieved power before blacks or Latinos sought to take control of city hall, as in New York, white liberals had much less incentive to join a biracial insurgent coalition.[10] More generally, Martin Shefter has argued that incumbent elites will mobilize a new partisan force demanding inclusion in the dominant coalition only if "a serious cleavage opens up within the political class."[11]

The postindustrial transformation of large central cities increased the chances for such cleavages by reducing the white, blue-collar and small business constituencies that provided the social base for regular Democratic or "machine" politics while expanding the strata of both white professionals and minority service workers who would provide the social base for either white reform or minority empowerment challenges to the prevailing coalitions. In many large, old central cities, however, regular Democratic party organizations remained a powerful factor shaping local political mobilization and competition. Although weakened in many respects, they still adapted better than has been commonly recognized.[12] Indeed, in some ways they became stronger, particularly by putting campaign activities previously financed by private contributions onto the public payroll.

Strong regular party organizations like those of the Richard Daley years in Chicago (1955–76) or the Donald Schaefer years in Baltimore (1971–87) deterred elite defections to an insurgent coalition and demobilized and coopted potential opposition.[13] The strength of regular party organizations thus appears to be just as important a determinant of the trajectory of political succession as the size and mobilization of the white liberal reform movement. A divided regular organization, as happened in the post-Daley succession crisis in Chicago, makes white defections to a biracial challenge more likely. Strong and unified regular Democratic party organizations work against the formation of an insurgent biracial coalition.

Read superficially, both external and internal factors would seem to make New York a prime candidate for the rise to power of a liberal, biracial coalition. The postindustrial revolution decimated New York's ethnic, blue-collar industrial constituencies more thoroughly and expanded the highly educated, professional, advanced services labor force more rapidly than in virtually any other large city. The destruction of Tammany Hall, the political mobilization of blacks, the rise of reform Democrats, the election of John V. Lindsay, and the liberalism of the city's political culture, particularly its large Jewish population, should have enabled a liberal biracial coalition to become dominant. But they did not.

The previous discussion sought to lay out the reasons why. Non-Latino whites remained a majority of the general electorate even though they became a minority of New York's population in the mid-1980s. The diminishing size of this group increased the potential for a strategy that would dampen the previous divisions between Jewish and white Catholic voters and stress their common interests relative to blacks and Latinos. But this was only one possible tendency. As in New York, liberal whites, blacks, Latinos, and Asians outnumbered other whites in Los Angeles, and none of these groups could attain power on the basis of an appeal to its constituency alone. But instead of whites mobilizing against the rise of minority influence as in New York, Los Angeles gave rise to a biracial coalition that overturned a white, conservative regime in 1973.[14]

From a comparative perspective, five aspects of New York's case appear to have crucial to the rise of a conservative dominant coalition: (1) the split between white liberals, especially the Jewish population, and the black leadership, (2) the incorporation of white liberal reformers into the political establishment and their attendant demobilization before the rise a minority challenge, (3) the renewed influence of the city's regular Democratic organizations during the mid-1980s, fed by the city's economic revival and their alliance with the mayor, (4) the fragmentation of leadership among blacks and Latinos and the history of competition between them, and (5) the ability of the Koch administration to constrain either public employee unions or community organizations from providing the base for an electoral challenge against him.

Jews make up roughly one-third of New York's white population; they have historically been liberal, reform-oriented, and more willing than other white groups to enter alliances with blacks. Yet a decade of events stretching from the 1966 police review board referendum and the 1968 teachers strikes to the 1977 blackout looting and the election of Mayor Koch in 1977 polarized relations between blacks and Jews, especially those residing outside Manhattan.[15] Mayor Koch made this historically liberal constituency the core of his new conservative coalition. Whether he led them or followed them in their move to the right, he certainly reinforced this shift. The mayor's alliance with the regular Democratic party county organizations and their influence in outer-borough Jewish and Italian-American neighborhoods helped cement the core constituencies of his electoral coalition.

The mayor's career as a Manhattan reform Democrat, his rhetorical attacks on "bosses" and "vested interests," and his willingness to employ "responsible" white liberals also served to incorporate many white reformers into his electoral and governing coalition. This attachment gave them little incentive to join blacks and Latinos, many of whom were Democratic regulars, in challenging him. As one observer noted, "The reformers began dabbling in real estate, and their social agenda narrowed to those liberties protecting their own peculiar life-styles and pathways to success."[16]

At the same time, the regular Democratic clubs and county organizations outside Manhattan prospered during the 1980s through their alliance with the mayor. Contrary to the public image of machine politicians as resistant to racial change, the Democratic party organizations promoted loyal black and Latino elected officials and absorbed a number of successful minority insurgents. Some insurgents made inroads, such as the new generation of blacks associated with the Coalition for Community Empowerment in Brooklyn or the election of Floyd Flake as a congressman from Southeast Queens, but regulars held office in most other black and Latino areas. This increased the political leverage of the Democratic county party organizations and created minority supporters for the Koch administration.

In short, the decay of white liberalism as an independent force and its absorption into the political establishment, together with the revival of regular Democratic party organizations, explain as much about New York's political trajectory under Mayor Koch as do such "objective" factors as its racial composition. While economic and demographic trends undoubtedly have a large impact on city politics, they are only the raw ingredients from which actors in the urban political system construct power.

Neither New York's business elite, the institutional constraints of the fiscal crisis, nor any simple calculus of electoral majorities determined how Edward Koch fashioned his electoral coalition or where he led it. Mayor Koch entered office as a Greenwich Village reformer elected by white liberals, blacks, Latinos, as well as outer-borough Jews. He deliberately chose to redefine this coalition over time along more conservative lines, working hard to attract support from white Catholics even at the cost of losing white liberal and black support. He solidified this electoral alignment through his strong support for the middle class, the use of racially polarizing rhetoric, and policies that reduced spending on welfare recipients, increased spending on jails, and promoted private investment.

To a certain extent, Koch's strategy was rational: he felt that white liberals had nowhere to go and that his policies would appeal to black and

Latino middle-class property owners as well as to white ones. The increase in his black and Latino electoral between 1981 and 1985 and the greater support he received in West Indian and South American neighborhoods as opposed to native-born black and Puerto Rican areas, suggested that the class dimension of his appeal might well cross racial boundaries. But Koch allowed the racial dimension of his appeal to carry him far beyond the bounds of electoral rationality.

Mayor Koch did not need to attack black leaders and white liberal activists so persistently that he would alienate constituencies that had given him valuable support. He could have been far more sensitive to the fact that the increasing racial tension and income polarization of the 1980s were causing Latinos to sheer away from his coalition and identify more closely with blacks. Having demolished his opponents in 1985, the mayor's success blinded him to the dangers inherent in his use of racially polarizing rhetoric and his reliance on Democratic regulars to help control his opponents. In 1989, he reaped what he had sown.

If the decay of white liberalism, the splits between constituencies that would make up a challenging coalition, the revival of regular Democratic political organizations, and the political containment of the organizations that might provide the basis for a challenge explain why a conservative dominant coalition held power in New York after 1977, then what changed to make the election of David Dinkins possible in 1989?

Two broad tendencies made the election of David N. Dinkins possible. First, events were freeing potentially challenging but divided constituencies from their attachments to the Koch administration and driving them toward each other. Blacks and Latinos were becoming more numerous in the city's population, while Mayor Koch's white ethnic social base was continuing to decline. The Koch administration's policies were reinforcing the national tendency toward increased social inequality characteristic of the 1980s.[17] Among blacks, greater inequality placed pressure on established leaders to respond to the plight of the black poor by providing a social base for activists willing to engage in media-oriented street protests. Downward mobility drove Latinos to identify more with the situation of blacks, opening the way for appeals that would stress the similarities between the two groups. Finally, the quality of life in the gentrifying professional neighborhoods in which white liberalism persisted came under increasing pressure from development, homelessness, street crime, and racial tension.

These trends would have meant little without a second important trend, however: the construction of a challenging coalition through the Jackson and Dinkins campaigns of 1988 and 1989 and the decay of the Koch coalition in the wake of the municipal scandals. The Jackson and Dinkins campaigns made a conscious effort to bring blacks, Latinos, and liberal whites together using the organizational infrastructure of unions like Local 1199 and District Council 37, the established minority leadership, and white reform clubs. At a critical juncture, the political scandals weakened the organizational base of the Koch coalition, particularly in the Bronx and Queens, loosened its hold on black and Latino elected officials, and damaged its standing with its core constituents.

If the Koch administration had been able to unite its supporters while dividing its opponents during its ascendancy in the late 1970s and early 1980s, this polarity was reversed during the latter 1980s. But just as objective conditions did not determine how Mayor Koch built his coalition, neither did they make the election of David Dinkins and the rise of his alternative coalition inevitable. Credit must be given to the ability of Dinkins and his allies to overcome the factors that weakened and divided them and to forge a new kind of reform coalition.

The Dinkins coalition resembled those that powered racial succession in other cities to the extent that it relied upon an extraordinary mobilization of his core constituency of blacks. But it differed from them in the degree to which it would have to rely on other constituencies as well. It had to include white liberals, Latinos, and indeed a significant number of the outer-borough Jews and white Catholics who had supported Mayor Koch. This black-led, biracial, and multiethnic insurgent coalition constitutes a fundamentally new element in New York's political development, one that has few national counterparts. But before evaluating its recent difficulties and future prospects, let us turn to the issue of what the Koch era tells us about the relationship between urban politics and its economic context.

The Autonomy of Urban Politics

It is not surprising that Paul Peterson devoted a chapter in his seminal book, *City Limits*, to New York City.[18] As a huge city government that places the largest burden on its resident taxpayers and provides the broadest array of local services, including redistributive social services, New York screams out as a counterexample to Peterson's argument that promoting private investment serves all city interests, while engaging in redistribution ultimately serves none. After an ambivalent discussion about whether New York was in fact really different from other cities, Peterson and Weir found that even if it was, the fiscal crisis restored it to the norm: "Even in the city that was once the nation's wealthiest and most powerful, the importance of economic interests became so painfully apparent that the political changes needed to bring about their effective pursuit were finally introduced." Citing Mayor Koch's fiscal conservatism, they conclude that "deviation no longer continues."[19] As Chapter Two suggested, a range of neo-Marxist thinkers have also offered New York as a case of what happens when popular politics seeks to transgress the boundaries imposed by capital. But did economic interests really dictate political outcomes in New York City after the fiscal crisis?

Aspects of the Koch administration's policies would seem to confirm this view. Certainly, it vigorously promoted private investment in office building construction, in some instances probably giving away more in public incentives than it would reap in increased property taxation.[20] The Koch administration's budgetary policies also deemphasized redistributive spending, especially direct payments to welfare recipients, while increasing basic and developmental services and the capital budget. These would seem to conform to the structuralist argument (whether the left or right version) that economic interests drive urban policy outcomes. There are two flaws in this position, however: the Koch administration also pursued policies directly contrary to economic interests, while its efforts to promote private investment were motivated by political rather than economic concerns.

In the final analysis, the Koch administration did not pursue budgetary austerity. After the early 1980s it rapidly expanded all components of city spending: personnel, compensation levels and benefits, contracting for services, and capital projects. By the late 1980s, the budget was rising as fast as it did in the late 1960s under the supposedly profligate Mayor Lindsay, the burden of city spending on value added was growing once more, and numerous social services were rapidly expanding. The Koch administration increased city employment, expenditures, and taxation levels even after its private economy leveled off in 1988 and 1989 and began to decline in 1990. His actions thus ran flatly contrary to what theories of economic determination would have predicted.

While circumstances allowed these budgetary trends to develop, political concerns motivated and shaped them. The rise of social problems, such as AIDS, crack use, and homelessness, undoubtedly accounted for some of the increases in public spending.[21] But in most cases, spending increases followed directly from the political strategies that Mayor Koch was pursuing to consolidate his political position, for example, in expanding the prison system, increasing compensation to city workers, or extending contracts to community-based service organizations. The Koch administration spent a great deal of money on programs designed neither to promote growth nor to provide basic services but to advance its political agenda. In short, for a considerable period of time and across a wide variety of policy areas, politics counted more than economics.

Indeed, it can be argued that Mayor Koch was motivated more by political than economic concerns in promoting private investment. Peterson tends to assume his conclusion when he argues that economic growth benefits all constituencies in a city and is therefore noncontroversial. In fact, the benefits of growth have highly specific distributive characteristics; development also has sharply negative consequences for some groups. The evidence suggests that Koch pursued pro-growth policies because they favored constituencies whose support he sought, despite their negative impacts on constituencies that were marginal to his electoral coalition. In exchange for these policies, Mayor Koch received collective support from the corporate business elite, which deterred strong challengers. He also received campaign contributions from individual developers, bankers, and lawyers with business before the city. The benefits from these specific projects fed out into a web of contractors, unions, and other interests that were interwoven with the political establishment. Finally, his philosophical support for the market resonated with white middle-class constituents.

The Koch administration thus illustrates how political motives drive policies with respect to the economy better than it demonstrates how economics constrains or creates imperatives for politics. In retrospect, the interregnum of the fiscal crisis proved that the crude application of market constraints on politics was difficult, costly to all, and imprecise in its effects. The business elite of New York City could not assume that political leaders would find it in their natural self-interest to efficiently promote economic growth. Instead, like other constituencies, they had to contribute to the process of building a coalition that would promote their ends. In Mayor Koch, they found a political leader willing and able to do so. His genius lay in his ability to contruct a new kind of dominant political coalition that made the pursuit of economic growth a politically rational thing to do.

The New York City example also suggests that conclusions about the theory of urban politics based on cases like Atlanta, where the political apparatus is relatively weak compared to powerful corporate elites, need to be balanced by looking at cases where government and the leverage of political forces are strong. Participants in New York's real estate development industry would be among the first to assert that the development process is highly political, both in the technical sense of negotiating a complex regulatory process and in the broader sense of the need to have good political connections. While there are many reasons why politicians may be predisposed to favor developers, developers still have to work for and pay for this support. The portrait that Stone draws of the Atlanta business elite's ability to dominate city politics, even under an African-American mayor, would be too one-sided to apply to New York.[22]

The Koch administration shows how the dominant political coalition mediates the relationship between trends in the social structure and urban policy outcomes. Large private corporations could not simply assume that their ability to relocate would force New York City's government to adopt policies that would provide a positive environment for capital investment and private profit. Instead, they had to participate in constructing a coalition that would pursue these ends. In so doing, they entered an arena in which the "rules of the game" conferred a strong position on public sector producer interests and electoral constituencies. They also had to rely on a political entrepreneur, Mayor Edward I. Koch, who could come to power only by building alliances with these other interests. Often this required him to undertake actions (such as raising taxes or spending money on these constituencies) that were not strictly favorable to private market interests.

In sum, political outcomes in New York City can best be understood in light of how political entrepreneurs built a dominant coalition based not only on private market interests but also on electoral constituencies and public sector producer interests. Economic interests enjoyed powerful, indeed systemic advantage in shaping the Koch coalition because it relied on their campaign contributions, the divisible political benefits of their development projects, and the legitimacy conveyed by elite opinion. But they were not the only influence on its trajectory. Mayor Koch also had to shape an electoral majority while managing public sector interest groups. He did not fall from power because of a failure to promote private market interests, but because his successful strategies for building power over electoral constituencies and public sector producer interests ultimately produced unmanageable negative consequences. While an explanatory model based on the process of constructing a dominant political coalition builds on the insights of both the structural and pluralist views, it is superior to either by itself.

Postindustrial Politics

The success of the Koch administration would seem to fly in the face of the thesis that the postindustrial revolution is reshaping the nature of urban politics in large central cities. That view would hold that political formations and constituencies associated with the industrial era, such as Democratic party clubs and the white working class, would recede, while new formations and constituencies, such as community organizations, advocacy groups, young white professionals, and minority workers in the service sector, would advance to power. In New York, by contrast, declining constituencies and supposedly moribund party organizations not only held on to power but built it up. The rise and fall of Mayor Koch would also seem to be summed up in the word "race," certainly a social distinction that long predated the postindustrial revolution.

New York City does illustrate that, at least in one city, Democratic party organizations proved supple in response to the challenges posed by the postindustrial revolution. They responded in several ways: they promoted leaders who represented emerging constituencies, they extended their influence over the funding systems that supported networks of community-based service-delivery organizations, and they prospered through the upward mobility enjoyed by constituencies that had been their core since the 1950s, Italian-Americans and Jews. Most importantly, as the importance of clubs and the patronage jobs to which they gave access waned, elected officials became more important as party leaders, campaign activities were professionalized, campaign personnel moved onto the public payroll, and many functions once provided by political clubs shifted to publicly funded nonprofits tied to or dependent on elected officials.[23] In essence, the regular Democratic organizations pursued the same strategy with respect to the postindustrial transformation that liberal reformers did: they put the costs of their political organizing onto the public budget.

The Koch administration took great advantage of the postindustrial transformation of New York City. The economic boom produced a real estate boom; the Koch administration's strategy for building a governing coalition gained greatly from its close relationship with the development industry. On the electoral side, the Koch coalition took great pains to exploit the fissures being created between middle-class and poor blacks, between blacks and Latinos, and between native-born minorities and the new immigrants. The appeal projected by Mayor Koch was as much class based (defending middle-class values against the threat posed to those values by lower-class social disorganization) as it was racially based. Like the Democratic political clubs, he used postindustrial political tools to develop political leverage over potentially challenging constituencies, especially through the extensive web of contracts to community-based organizations. The Koch administration was an important component of how the postindustrial transformation in New York has tended to consolidate a managerial-professional elite based in the major advanced service industries while dividing and disorganizing the constituencies on its periphery.[24] The Koch administration gave political form to these tendencies.

The Koch administration sought to accelerate the postindustrial transformation; to a considerable degree, its defeat flowed from the negative consequences of its success in attaining that goal. While Mayor Koch had a great deal of help from national policies that promoted the financial services, industrial restructuring, and income inequality, there can be little doubt that these trends were particularly acute in New York City during the 1980s and that the Koch administration also fueled them. If the corruption scandal was one major component of the Koch defeat, then dismay at increasing social polarization—from liberal whites as well as blacks and Latinos—was the other. The Koch coalition and the Dinkins coalition thus do not represent industrial versus postindustrial politics, but alternative strategies of postindustrial politics. They are two sides of the same coin.

The Dinkins Coalition: A New Kind of Urban Reform?

The electoral coalition that David Dinkins put together in the fall of 1989 reorganized the historical pattern of reform in New York City as described by Lowi and Shefter. The Lindsay victories of 1965 and 1969 provided an important precursor. Dinkins assembled his coalition out of similar components: liberal, secular, white professionals (especially from nonprofit services), Jews, blacks, and Latinos. Dinkins also relied heavily on nonparty forms of organizational support like black churches and public employee unions.[25] But he also offered several decisively new elements.

For the first time, an African-American, not a white liberal, provided the leading figure for the reform impulse. (However, many of the campaign's leading black supporters did come from the middle-class professional stratum that had provided the social base for white reform in the past.) In his campaign, public employee unions, particularly Local 1199 of the hospital workers, the United Federation of Teachers, Teamsters Local 237 of housing authority workers, and District Council 37 of city workers, emerged as an effective organizational substitute for the Democratic party.

While the Dinkins primary campaign would seem to have been built purely of postindustrial elements, these sources of support were not quite enough to win the general election. Even though white regular Democrats were likely to defect in massive numbers to the Republican candidate, regular Democratic leaders stood to lose a great deal if Giuliani were elected. Rudolph Giuliani would have come into office with no debts to public sector producer interests, whether public employees or the Democratic party organizations. The Democratic party establishment thus closed ranks behind Dinkins, who, despite his reform credentials as Manhattan borough president, was also a product of the Carver Democratic Club.

Assembling a majority of electoral constituencies in the general election was difficult for Dinkins. He had to appeal to black pride in electing the first African-American to the mayor's office. However much he might present this appeal as similar to that which Mayor Koch had made to Jews, it was bound to trigger racial mistrust in the electorate at large. To win, much less to govern, Dinkins would have to fight this tendency. He won over Latino voters, a crucial swing constituency, by convincing them that he understood their position at the bottom of the social structure in New York's most embattled neighborhoods. He won more than half the white liberal vote by convincing them he would address the city's social problems and racial division. But these would not be enough. He also had to win over a substantial minority of the outer-borough Jewish and white Catholic voters by convincing them he would be fair to whites and hard on crime and that he had the support of white regular Democratic politicians.

The coalition that put David N. Dinkins into office was, like its predecessors, a mixture of contradictory elements: it mobilized blacks on a racial basis, mobilized a black-Latino alliance through both public employee unions and Latino Democratic regulars, mobilized a minority-white liberal alliance through reform political clubs, and mobilized an alliance with some Jewish and white Catholic voters through party regulars. While self-styled "progressive" elements constituted the coalition's major component, they alone could not have delivered victory. The Dinkins coalition thus grafted large elements of the Koch coalition onto a truly alternative reform thrust. The conflicts that formerly took place between the Koch coalition and its critics thus moved inside the Dinkins coalition.

The narrowness of Mayor Dinkins's victory and the conflicts embedded in his electoral coalition have hampered his effort to build a governing coalition. The mayor has not been able or willing to resolve the conflict within his coalition, but has tried instead to satisfy all its parts. The result has been a series of highly contradictory policy steps. His administration granted substantial pay increases to the United Federation of Teachers, which was closely associated with his campaign effort, but he was then forced by growing deficits to lay off thousands of city employees and cut social programs that served his core constituencies. While giving symbolic support to policy innovations designed to respond to his social service advocacy and minority neighborhood constituencies (for example, granting funds to rebuild a substantial part of Harlem or emphasizing neighborhood-based services), Mayor Dinkins has placed his highest priority on balancing the city's budget so as to forestall the city's financial community and state officials from taking over the city's finances. The mayor's single largest programmatic innovation has been a billion-dollar effort to expand the number of police and redeploy them. While this fulfilled his commitment to be tough on crime, quieted the media clamor for action on the issue, and favored outer-borough white constituencies, it also depleted his political capital and sucked funds from policy innovations that would favor his other constituencies.

The Dinkins administration has shown the same inconsistency with respect to private sector interests and development issues. Although he appointed African-Americans and advocates of neighborhood participation to the City Planning Commission, the mayor also favored developers of a number of controversial projects. His administration has shied away from setting up programs to require developers to build low rent housing or hire minority workers. Since the recession in the real estate market has not tested the Dinkins administration's resolve, it remains an open question whether his administration would promote development or side with neighborhood opponents of development.

On the present evidence, we must conclude that although the Dinkins administration contains much promise as a new kind of reform coalition, it has not managed to consolidate and propel policy reform in the ways that Edward Koch was able to empower his coalition. Renewed fiscal crisis has contributed to the administration's problems. Even before it has had a chance to qualify as dominant, the Dinkins coalition has revealed some of its limits. Two are worth reflecting upon: its reliance on public employee unions and its inability to revitalize community organizations as an independent political force.

Theodore Lowi worried long ago that by moving inside the Democratic party, reformers would lose the independent organizational base that the Republican party provided when it offered itself as a basis for fusion campaigns.[26] He had good reason for this concern, for white reformers' entry into the Democratic party sped the decay of the reform thrust in New York City politics and encouraged one-party factionalism. With the Jackson and Dinkins campaigns, public employee unions emerged finally as a substitute for the Republican party as a quasi-party base for political challenges to the dominant coalition.

The central problem with this development is that public employee unions have their own strong institutional goals and, unlike political parties, lack accountability to a broader electorate. A coalition that rises to power on this basis must take care to defend the institutional interests of the unions. While these may often coincide with those of the broader popular constituencies the Dinkins administration seeks to represent, there are also bound to be conflicts. Unions favor higher pay over more employees; in a period of austerity, this means greater layoffs and service reductions. Unions favor direct provision of services by city employees over contracts with community-based service providers. Unions also frequently have a stake in work practices that inhibit the reorganization of services so as to have a more positive impact on service recipients.

These tendencies can be countered only by reaching out to and becoming more accountable to the constituencies public employees serve. Some forward-looking unions like Local 1199 have made efforts in this direction, but most have felt little need to forge alliances with community groups or build political support beyond their immediate membership. They have been more likely instead to forge alliances with regular Democratic elected officials. In local school board elections, for example, the United Federation of Teachers and DC 37 of city workers have been far more likely to support those allied with regular clubs than they have been to support insurgents.

The Dinkins administration has not moved decisively to invigorate community-based service delivery organizations as an independent political force comparable to the unions. Only a few efforts have been made to use the city's fiscal crunch to bring groups together and enlist them in the process of reformulating policies in a more effective manner. An effort by Deputy Mayor Bill Lynch and union leaders to forge a slate of insurgent liberal candidates for the newly redistricted city council seats in 1991 was unwilling to draw community organizations and advocacy groups into its deliberations and explicitly rejected making the empowerment of community organizations part of its platform.[27]

If Mayor Dinkins and his closest allies chose to use the policy tools at hand to mobilize their grass-roots base, they might well contribute something significantly new to New York City's political development: an alliance between the city workers and community-based organizations who produce public services and the neighborhood residents who use them. Such a strategy would make the conflicts within the Dinkins coalition more overt in the short run, but it would produce a more cohesive result in the long run.

To date, Mayor Dinkins has shown caution about pursuing such a strategy. It thus seems likely that the disparate components of the Dinkins coalition will remain in their current state of dissatisfaction. If so, the Dinkins coalition may founder, as have many of its reform predecessors, on its internal contradictions, opening the way to efforts to restore the Koch coalition in some new form.

Afterword

ON NOVEMBER 2, 1993, Rudolph W. Giuliani defeated David Dinkins to become New York City's fourth Republican mayor in this century. Although the 1993 election closely paralleled the 1989 race, small differences in whether and how different groups voted produced a large difference in the ultimate outcome. Dinkins became the first breakthrough black mayor of a large city to be put out of office after only one term. Despite the continuing decline of the city's non-Hispanic white population and evidence that the registered electorate had become more black and Latino since 1989, Giuliani built upon a core of white Catholic and Jewish support to produce a narrow but clear electoral majority. Contrary to the old political saw, demography was not destiny.

This reversal of fortune for New York's liberal, biracial coalition and the renewal of the more conservative Koch coalition raises three crucial questions: How, and more importantly why, did this reversal occur? What prospects does Giuliani's victory hold for a renewed conservative alignment in New York City? And what implications does Dinkins's defeat have for the future of multiracial liberal coalitions in big-city politics, coming as it did after Richard Daley, former prosecutor Edward Rendell, and Republican businessman Richard Riordan succeeded black mayors in Chicago, Philadelphia, and Los Angeles?

How Dinkins Lost and Giuliani Won

The mayoral elections of 1989 and 1993 were far more alike than different. About 1.8 million votes were cast in each, the various groups within the electorate split their votes along quite similar lines, and each had a close margin of about 50,000 votes. The correlation between the number of votes cast in each of the city's 5,300 election districts (EDs) in 1989 and 1993 was .915, and the correlation of support for Dinkins was .967.[1] Each election was also preceded by a campaign that lacked debate on issues, but rather stressed each candidate's personal qualities.

There were, of course, differences. Mayor Dinkins had to run on his record in 1993, not just the vision of future possibilities he put forth in 1989. This record included difficulty in coping with intergroup hostilities in the Korean grocery boycott and Crown Heights, struggles to balance the budget without alienating the public-employee unions, a campaign to hire more cops for a community policing initiative, and launching various community-oriented programs. After his 1989 loss, candidate Giuliani spent four years learning more about city government. He crafted his 1993 campaign as a "fusion" effort to reach out to Latinos and other potential Democratic defectors, especially those who had backed the Koch administration, and to demonstrate that he had positive qualities beyond those of a prosecutor.

As the campaign wound down, however, each candidate focussed increasingly on the other's alleged negative qualities: Giuliani was pilloried as a conservative Republican lacking managerial experience, whose position in the Reagan administration raised questions about his stand on the right to an abortion, while Dinkins was said to be soft on crime, unable or unwilling to protect the rights of both sides in racial conflicts, and a poor manager of the city's affairs. This trend was fed by public opinion polls that showed that voters harbored more negative than positive feelings about the candidates, and by the fact that each candidate seemed to feel more at ease pointing out the other's defects than making the case for his own merits.

In the end, the election proved to be a remarkably narrow contest. Having won by about 47,000 votes in 1989, Dinkins lost the 1993 election by about 50,000 votes. In other words, if fewer than 2 percent of the voters had changed their minds in either election, the outcome would have been different. Yet because the two elections were not precisely alike, the shifting margin of 97,000 votes did put a new cast of characters into City Hall. Table A.1 groups the 1993 results according to the 1989 boundaries for the city's 60 assembly districts (ADs) and compares the two elections according to the predominant characteristics of those ADs. It indicates how much each type of AD contributed to the overall shift in margin between the two candidates.

Majority black ADs contributed one-sixth of the total margin primarily because the overall number of votes they cast declined. (The overall shift in margin produced by EDs in which blacks made up a majority of registered voters was 21,500, or just shy of one-quarter of the total.) Dinkins's proportion of the vote eroded only slightly. Although the grand total of votes cast in 1993 declined 0.6 percent from 1989, votes declined 2.4 percent in majority black ADs and 3.9 percent in majority black EDs. The fact that disproportionately fewer blacks voted thus made a major contribution to Dinkins's defeat. In white Catholic ADs, by contrast, voting actually rose 1.2 percent. Although this may reflect some population loss, it is stunning that over half of the shift produced by the decline of black votes occurred in Harlem, the Mayor's home ground.

In Latino and other minority ADs, the Dinkins cause suffered not only because voters turned out in lower numbers, but also because they were somewhat less inclined to vote for Dinkins than they were in 1989. Except for 1985, when three Latino candidates ran for city-wide office, Latino

TABLE A.1
1989 and 1993 General Mayoral Elections by Assembly District Type

AD Type	1989 Vote	% for Dinkins	1993 Vote	% for Dinkins	% Vote Change 1989– 1993	Change in % for Dinkins	Change in Margin
Black	361,169	89.2	352,645	88.7	−2.4	−0.5	15,057
Mixed minority	116,814	76.7	114,434	74.1	−2.0	−2.6	7,024
Latino	115,202	74.3	108,793	73.5	−5.6	−0.8	4,655
White liberal	329,218	50.6	329,044	48.6	−0.1	−2.0	14,380
Outer-borough Jewish	423,093	28.9	423,884	26.8	0.2	−2.1	21,398
White Catholic	435,951	25.9	441,395	22.6	1.2	−3.9	34,642
Total	1,781,447	50.5	1,770,175	47.8	−0.6	−2.7	97,156

Source: New York City Districting Commission (1989) and Associated Press (1993). The 1989 vote has been adjusted to exclude blank and void ballots; the 1993 vote does not include absentee ballots.

turnout has generally been lower than that of any other group. Despite a bid by Herman Badillo, the city's best-known Puerto Rican politician, to become comptroller, Latino turnout was also low in 1993 and below what it had been in 1989. (The vote in EDs where Latinos constituted a majority of the registered voters declined by 3.0 percent, compared to 3.9 percent in majority black EDs.) The vote also shifted slightly, but perceptibly, away from Dinkins. Given the relatively small number of Latino votes compared to the Latino population, we may estimate that Latino voters contributed roughly 7,500 to the shifting margin between Dinkins and Giuliani. Taken together, the city's minority EDs thus accounted for a bit less than one-third of the total vote shift.

The white liberal areas of Manhattan and brownstone Brooklyn also shifted away from Dinkins. The ADs containing these white liberals cast a relatively high number of votes. They were also less likely to shift away from the mayor than other white ADs. Nonetheless, the declining propensity to vote for Dinkins contributed 14,380 votes to the shift in margin between the candidates. (EDs where whites made up a majority of voters and a majority of these whites were estimated to have given their vote to Dinkins in 1989, produced about 7,700 of this shift.)

White liberal support had been critical to Dinkins's 1989 victory, and its decay was keenly felt by the Dinkins camp. Yet white liberal areas contributed far less to the change in margin than other white areas, and indeed less than did black areas. In fact, the margin shift produced in Latino and white liberal areas was significantly less than in black areas. To the extent that Dinkins's weakness among his core constituencies contributed to his defeat, his greatest failure was among his strongest supporters. The outcome of the election, however, was not decided within constituencies that had favored Dinkins in 1989, but among those that had opposed him.

The vote in white Catholic and outer borough Jewish ADs held up far better than in minority ADs, and it shifted more strongly away from Dinkins. The vote actually increased in white Catholic ADs, which also shifted most strongly toward Guiliani, contributing 34,642 votes to the shift, or about as many as black, Latino, and white liberal areas put together. The ballot measure on whether Staten Island should secede from New York City helped to draw enough voters in that borough to produce 20,800 of the margin shift. The total number of votes cast in Staten Island's white EDs rose 13.6 percent and Dinkins ended up with only 8.1 percent of that vote, down from 12.0 in 1989.

Elsewhere in the city, white Catholic areas contributed about 14,000 votes to the changing margin, whereas Jewish neighborhoods in Brooklyn, Queens, and the Bronx contributed another 24,000 toward the overall shift between Dinkins and Giuliani, primarily through a greater preference for Giuliani. Orthodox and Hasidic Jewish areas like Boro Park, the Lubavitcher community in Crown Heights, and the Satmar in Williamsburg contributed a disproportionate amount to this total, perhaps as much as 12,000.

As a result, the 1993 mayoral electorate was slightly more white and less black and Latino than in 1989 and its preferences were also slightly more racially polarized. The higher the percentage of registered voters who were white, the less likely an ED was to experience a vote decline between 1989 and 1993 and the more likely it was to shift toward Rudolph Giuliani.

In short, Dinkins did not lose the election because of his weaker performance in minority and white liberal neighborhoods but because the voters in white ethnic neighborhoods outside Manhattan turned out in large numbers and shifted against the mayor. While the Dinkins campaign failed to maintain its 1989 performance, the Giuliani campaign made small but crucial improvements. In particular, the Giuliani candidacy achieved an at least temporary reversal of the long-term decline in the vote that had been taking place in more conservative white Catholic and Jewish neighborhoods in the city's outer boroughs.

In addition to the Staten Island secession vote and the shift among outer borough white Catholic and Jewish voters, especially the orthodox, the Giuliani campaign clearly benefitted from the reduced willingness of voters to support his Conservative party opponent. In the 1989 general

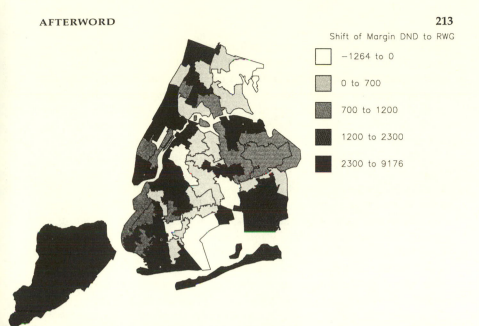

Map A.1. Shift of Margin DND to RWG

election, Conservative party candidate Ronald Lauder, who had spent $13 million attacking Giuliani in the Republican primary, received 2 percent of the vote, even though he did not conduct an active general election campaign. In 1993, Giuliani swallowed his differences with Senator Alphonse D'Amato, who had encouraged Lauder, in order to prevent a Republican primary contest. Though the Conservative party candidate in 1993, George Marlin, was arguably far more able and articulate than Lauder, he lacked Lauder's financing and gained only 0.6 percent of the vote. The difference went directly to Giuliani. In short, the Giuliani campaign won primarily because it was able to build on its strengths, and secondarily because the Dinkins campaign failed to maintain its base. Map A.1 shows how the different ADs contributed to the resulting shift in margin.

Why Blacks and Latinos Were Less Likely to Vote

Although election data tell us a great deal about which groups turn out to vote, whom they choose, and what demographic characteristics are related to these results, they tell us nothing about the voters' motives, values, or perceptions. For this we must turn to public opinion surveys. A May 1993 survey taken by the *New York Times* and CBS News provides us with some information about why potential Dinkins supporters might have stayed home.[2] It indicates that the electorate was not particularly happy with the choice between Dinkins and Giuliani. When the voters were asked whether they liked their choice, 43 percent said they were unsatisfied, while only 47 percent indicated satisfaction.[3] Although black respondents liked their choice better than other groups, 32 percent still said they were unsatisfied and 13 percent were unsure. Even 41 percent of registered white Catholics said they were unsatisfied and 8 percent unsure. During the campaign, antipathy toward Dinkins helped Giuliani overcome skepticism among his potential white supporters, while Dinkins was not able to use concern about Giuliani to maximize his black and Latino support.

Voters had highly ambivalent views about both candidates. Overall, only 35 percent of the registered voters had a favorable reaction to Dinkins, while 41 percent had an unfavorable reaction and 24 percent were undecided. Voters were somewhat more unsure about Giuliani: only 30 percent were favorable and 34 percent unfavorable, while 36 percent were undecided. As might be expected, white Catholics were the most likely to favor Giuliani and disapprove of Dinkins, while blacks had the opposite reaction.

Dinkins's difficulty was clearly related to the fact that many people, even among blacks and others who had supported him in 1989, had concluded that he had performed poorly as mayor. Only among blacks and white liberals did more voters approve of his job performance than disapproved; even so, 39 percent of white liberals and 15 percent of blacks disapproved, while 11 percent of both groups were unsure. More tellingly, a healthy majority of registered voters judged the Dinkins mayoralty to have been a full or partial failure. Even among black registered voters, 31 percent felt this way, as did 56 percent of Latino voters and 52 percent of white liberals.

Registered voters were evenly divided on the related question of whether Dinkins was a strong leader. Three-quarters of blacks felt so, but all other groups had a much more negative evaluation of Dinkins's leadership. By contrast, a clear majority of the voters thought Giuliani was a strong leader, including 44 percent of the black voters.

Those black voters who arrived at this negative judgment of Dinkins's job performance and leadership qualities were faced with a quandary: they had doubts about Dinkins, but very few could ultimately bring themselves to vote for Giuliani instead of Dinkins. Most evidently resolved their dilemma by not voting. This was apparently also true among the relatively large number of Latino and white liberal registered voters who liked the mayor but thought he lacked leadership skills and had performed poorly— although they proved more willing than blacks to vote for Giuliani.

What lay at the root of the negative judgments about Dinkins among black and Latino voters? The 1993 CBS/*New York Times* survey suggests that differences in demographics, views about conditions in the city, and evaluations of specific aspects of the Dinkins mayoralty all contributed to lower support for Dinkins. Among black registered voters, religion and education were associated with modest differences in support for Dinkins, whereas gender, age, parenthood, income, or union membership were not. Protestants and better-educated black registered voters were about 5 percentage points more likely to say they were going to vote for Dinkins, while Catholics and those with a high-school education or less were more unsure. (Republicans and conservatives were also less likely to support Dinkins than Democrats and liberals.) These factors bore a similar and even stronger relationship with whether voters thought Dinkins's mayoralty had been a success, although union members were 11 percentage points less likely to think so than those who were not.

Differences of views about the city and its problems had a stronger impact among black voters than did demographic traits. A quarter of the black registered voters thought the city would become a better place in the decade, and they were 16 percentage points more likely to support Dinkins than the 42 percent of black registered voters who thought the city was likely to become worse. Similarly, those who thought the city had become safer (13 percent of black voters) were 18 percentage points more likely to favor Dinkins than the 51 percent of black voters who thought it had become more dangerous. Remarkably, however, whether or not anyone in one's family had experienced a crime in the last year made no difference in likelihood of supporting Dinkins.

Gaps also appeared concerning feelings about whether one's neighborhood would be better (12 points), whether one's life was improving (11 points), or whether race relations were improving (8 points). Clearly, many black voters translated their perceptions or experiences about economic recession, declining quality of life in their city and neighborhoods, and personal insecurity into a pessimism that "stuck" to the mayor. The many black registered voters who thought their lives were getting worse were 33 percentage points less likely to judge Dinkins a success than those who thought life was improving, while those who saw their neighborhoods worsening were 40 percentage points less likely to deem him a success.

Differences in evaluating specific aspects of Dinkins's mayoralty had the strongest impact on such overall judgments. The issues of how Dinkins was handling race relations, crime, and the economy stand out. A majority of black voters thought Dinkins was helping race relations, a third thought he had made no difference, and 5 percent thought he had harmed them. The second group was 12 percentage points less likely to say they would vote for Dinkins, while the third group was 38 points less likely. There was a 31-point gap on voting for Dinkins between those who thought race relations would improve after his reelection and those who thought they would not.

Similar patterns occurred with respect to crime and the economy. A third of black registered voters did not think Dinkins was making a difference on crime, and they were 21 percentage points less likely to say they would vote for him. Half felt Dinkins had had little impact on the economy, and they were 12 points less likely to say they were voting for Dinkins. In short, even though most black registered voters favored Dinkins, thought he had done a good job, and were ready to vote for his reelection, many were dissatisfied with trends in their lives and how Dinkins was handling race relations, crime, and the economy. These dissatisfactions were associated with less willingness to vote for Dinkins and a greater tendency to judge his administration a failure. For many black registered voters, these feelings must have culminated in a decision not to go to the polls on election day.

The CBS/*New York Times* poll suggests that these forces had a broadly similar and even larger impact on Latino registered voters, with one or two differences. Catholics were again less likely than Protestants to favor Dinkins, but better-educated voters were somewhat more likely to favor Giuliani. Similarly, Republicans were about 10 percentage points more likely to back Giuliani, but ideology did not make much difference. Gender, age, income, family status, and union membership were also not associated with strong differences.

As with blacks, differences in perceptions about whether one's life was improving were strongly associated with different prospective vote choices among Latino registered voters. More than two-thirds thought their life was getting worse, and they were 63 percentage points less likely to support Dinkins and 50 percentage points more likely to support Giuliani than the small number (10 percent) who thought things were getting better. Whether Latinos perceived the city and their neighborhoods as becoming safer or more dangerous had similar, if less pronounced, effects. (Most thought the city was getting worse and were divided about whether their neighborhoods were the same or worse.) Again, perception was far more important than the reality: whether or not anyone in one's family had experienced a crime in the last year did not affect how Latino registered voters said they would vote.

Even more than with blacks, this judgment depended on how Latino registered voters judged Dinkins to be handling race relations and the economy. There was a 28-point difference between those who thought Dinkins was helping race relations and those who thought he was making no difference, and a 55-point difference depending on perceptions of how Dinkins was handling the economy: fewer than a third thought he was helping on race relations and barely one in ten thought he was improving the economy. There was also a 56-point gap on Dinkins's perceived handling of crime, and a majority thought he was not doing a good job.

In short, Latino registered voters often felt that their lives and their environments were deteriorating. They also thought Dinkins was doing a poor job on race relations, crime, and the economy. Among those who had generally favorable views of the mayor, these judgments evidently coalesced into a decreased likelihood of voting. They also caused normally Democratic voters to defect to Giuliani, as happened in all the other non-black voting groups.

Why Democratic Voters Defected

The 1993 exit poll conducted by Voter Research and Surveys provides the best evidence about why these voters defected to Giuliani.[4] Predictably, Table A.2 shows that voters from different backgrounds not only voted different ways, but defected at different rates.[5] The net black defection to Giuliani (defection to Giuliani minus defection to Dinkins) was virtually nonexistent (0.2 percent of the black vote). Net defection to Giuliani among other voters ranged from 13 percent among Latinos to 36 percent of those Jews who said they were not liberals. Net defection among white liberals, the pivotal white group in which loyal Democrats outnumbered loyal Republicans by more than two to one, was 16 percent. Net defection was also 16 percent among white Catholics because, as Table A.2 indicates, most were firmly ensconced in the loyal Giuliani column.

Other demographic characteristics had clear but less strong relationships with the net rate of defection. Older voters, male voters, better edu-

TABLE A.2
Defection by Voter Type, 1993 Election (row percentage)

| | | | | Loyal | Total | |
| | Democrat | Shift to | Loyal | Republican/ | No. of | Column |
Voter Type	Defector	Dinkins	Democrat	Conservative	Respondents	%
Black	3.1	2.9	92.3	1.7	404	27.2
Latino	14.3	1.2	54.7	29.8	177	11.9
Non-Catholic white liberal	19.2	2.3	55.0	23.5	158	10.7
Nonliberal Jewish	40.8	4.4	9.3	45.4	151	10.1
Nonliberal white Protestant/ others	22.6	2.7	14.6	60.1	142	9.5
White Catholic	17.9	1.7	10.6	69.8	428	28.8
Asian	22.2	3.9	30.8	43.2	25	1.7
Total	18.4	2.4	43.4	37.7	1,485	100.0

Source: Voter Research and Surveys, 1993 mayoral election exit poll.

cated voters, higher income voters, employed voters, married voters, heterosexual voters, independents, moderates, and those who decided on the day of the election were all 3 to ten net percentage points more likely to defect to Giuliani than those who had the opposite characteristics. Being in a union household or having children in school made less difference. As in the CBS/*New York Times* attitude poll, however, defection was more strongly associated with perceptions about trends in the city and the quality of the candidates than with these demographic traits.

Overall, the voters ranked crime, race relations, and the quality of life as the most important problems facing the city, with jobs and the economy following. Among those who ranked each of these issues as most important, the net rates of defection were 17 percent, 7 percent, 16 percent, and 8 percent. In other words, those who focussed on crime and the quality of life were most likely to defect toward Giuliani, while those named race relations or the recession were less likely to do so. (The only issue that cut in favor of Dinkins was abortion, but only 1.3 percent of the voters listed this as the most important issue.) The majority of voters who thought the city was less safe were 17 net percentage points more likely to defect than those who thought conditions were stable; they in turn were 5 percentage points more likely to defect than the small group (15 percent of the total) who thought it was safer. (The perception of crime once more made much more difference than the experience of crime, which strikingly had little impact on net defection.)

Similarly, voters identified toughness, experience, and fairness as the leading qualities they liked in their candidates. Toughness cut strongly for Giuliani (a net of 27 percent of those ranking this quality highest defected), while the other two had lesser net impacts (2 percent and 9 percent). On secondary qualities, however, such as ability to unite the city and competence, Dinkins suffered badly (net defections of 22 and 12 percent of these groups). Overall, those who thought Giuliani was anti-black (about a third of the total voters) were only one-third as likely to defect as those who did not; those who thought Dinkins was anti-Jewish (40 percent of the total) were twice as likely to defect.

These broad patterns held across the specific ethnic groups, with some interesting variations. Latinos showed a somewhat greater concern than other groups for the schools, and those who did have this concern were more likely to defect. Substantially more white liberals found the quality of life and race relations to be the city's most pressing problem than did other groups, and a net of 27 percent of the former and 14 percent of the latter defected, or almost twice the rates for the overall population. White Catholics were highly focused on crime as the city's most important issue, and a net of 13 percent defected on that basis. Jews who were not liberals were also highly focused on crime, and a whopping net of 44 percent of those who ranked this issue highest defected to Dinkins, a far higher percentage than for any other white group. (White liberals, for example, were far less likely to see crime as a problem or defect on that basis.) Most Jews thought Dinkins was anti-Jewish, and those who did were 21 percentage points more likely to defect than those who did not. The minority of non-liberal Jewish voters who thought Giuliani was anti-black were actually 6 points *more* likely to defect to him than the majority who did not think so. (These factors did not make much difference for white Catholics.)

Although there was a great deal of stability between how the voting groups chose in 1989 and 1993, there was enough net defection from Dinkins to Giuliani to shift the outcome of the election. Some of this defection took the silent form of not voting, but most was expressed in changed preferences in the voting booth. The overall electorate harbored reservations about both candidates, but black and white voters each had stronger concerns about one of the two. In the end, the perceptions that crime was growing, the city was less safe, the quality of life worsening, and race relations becoming more difficult, together with a desire to see more toughness and competence in the mayor, led many former Dinkins supporters (as well as new entrants to the electorate) to pull the lever for Giuliani.

The issue of race, as always, hovered in the background. Yet Dinkins's race, as such, had little impact on the outcome. (Only about 3.5 percent of the voters said race was the candidates' quality motivating their vote and of these more chose the black candidate than the white one.) Certainly, the perception that Dinkins was anti-Jewish had a heavy impact on the Jewish vote, but perceptions of how the two candidates approached blacks and Jews did not have strong affects on other groups. Race played out instead through issues that moved Latino and white voters to vote for Giuliani, the candidate of their race, even though he came from a party to which few of them belonged and was someone about whom they harbored doubts.[6]

The Future of the Koch Coalition Under Mayor Giuliani

The Giuliani coalition of the 1993 general election closely resembles the Koch coalition of the 1989 Democratic primary election. The former succeeded where the latter failed because Giuliani rallied his forces against a somewhat dispirited opponent, whereas Edward Koch was the battered candidate facing a newcomer. Since Mayor Dinkins had clearly lost ground in some constituencies without making obvious gains in others, and since key backers like the Teachers Union seemed less willing to help staff his campaign, the 1993 election appeared to be Giuliani's to lose.

Giuliani made a poor start by appearing at a police rally against the mayor that nearly became a riot, but thereafter he avoided obvious mistakes and shrewdly moved to bolster his position. By patching up with Senator D'Amato, he fended off a potential challenge from his right. By selecting Puerto Rican and orthodox Jewish Democrats as running mates, he blunted Dinkins's attempt to use partisanship against him. Finally, endorsements from widely admired Democrats such as Koch and the late Bob Wagner and open or covert support from white regular Democratic clubs also aided his cause.

In the end, however, this produced an extremely narrow victory. As mayor, Guiliani faces a mirror image of Dinkins's problem in 1989: how can he substantially broaden his initial electoral coalition to provide a firmer base for his governing coalition? Between 1977 and 1985, Mayor Koch passed this test. Between 1989 and 1993, Mayor Dinkins obviously did not. If anything, Giuliani faces an even more daunting challenge than did Dinkins. Just as Dinkins had to overcome the differences between his black supporters and the Latino, white liberal, and Jewish voters he needed to add to this base, Giuliani must add people who have quite different life situations and outlooks to his core of white ethnic support.

If, as is likely, the Democrats do not nominate a black person for mayor in 1997, then Giuliani will lose the racially motivated defectors he received in 1993. Dinkins entered the 1993 campaign knowing he could count on perhaps 45 percent of the vote. Giuliani may well enter the 1997 election with an even smaller reliable base. (The normal Republican city-wide vote in races for governor or president is, after all, only about 35 percent.) On the other hand, Mayor Giuliani may well benefit from an expanding local economy.

Giuliani's search for broader support must begin with the 1985 Koch coalition, not Koch's 1989 coalition. Although Koch won most Jewish and white Catholic votes in 1985, he also attracted a majority of the Latino and white liberal vote and a substantial minority of the black vote. To do the same, Giuliani needs to understand how and why Koch achieved his strength in the mid-1980s. Though he lacks Koch's ties to either the Manhattan reform Democrats or the regular Democratic clubs outside Manhattan, he can employ some of Koch's strategies and create some new ones of his own.

Giuliani has already been able to attract roughly half of the white liberal vote. Although criticism from white liberal Democrats such as Ruth Messinger and Mark Green may erode this support, white liberal reformers have long sought to improve the efficiency and effectiveness of government. If Giuliani can do a better job of managing the difficult trade-offs between levels of taxation, employee compensation and staffing, and service delivery than Mayor Dinkins, he will go a long way toward retaining the white liberal vote. The city's continued fiscal difficulties may require him to take positions that are unpopular with the many white liberals who are tied to the public sector, but they will also provide him with opportunities for making bureaucratic change.

In 1993, white liberals were highly concerned about crime and the declining quality and safety of public spaces. By "declining quality of life," voters evidently mean graffiti and dirty streets, threatening behavior by panhandlers, the homeless, and "squeegee-men," and the implicit tolerance for criminal behavior that their presence might suggest.[7] Mayor Giuliani has staked his political reputation on reducing crime and these perceived threats to the quality of public spaces. If he has some success, it would clearly consolidate his support not only from white liberals but also from the many non-liberal Jewish voters concerned with these issues.

The inclusion of underrepresented groups has been the second historic theme of urban reform. In addition to being strong proponents of "reinventing" government, two of Mayor Giuliani's Republican predecessors, Fiorello LaGuardia and John V. Lindsay, both stressed bringing new groups into city government and making it more responsive to their needs. To build a strong governing coalition and win reelection by a larger margin, Giuliani must find ways to put this principle to work in the mid-1990s.

Jim Sleeper has argued that reformist white mayors who succeed black mayors who gained office on a platform of black empowerment can build what he calls "Rainbow II."[8] This he defines as "commercial deregulation, better public safety, less onerous taxation and tougher union contracts" combined with "protecting basic rights and mobilizing economic coalitions" rather than "touting racial group rights and policies that are gratuitously destructive of traditional families."[9] He identifies Latinos, Asians, and other new immigrants as a potential new majority (along with the non-Hispanic white minority) that holds values consonant with these positions.

New York City's large and increasingly diverse Latino population is one obvious target for a Giuliani strategy of inclusion. This population is relatively conservative, predominantly Catholic, and reveres traditional family values even though many do not live in traditional families. Many Latino immigrants are building ethnic commercial enclaves, acquiring properties and small businesses, and striving for upward mobility. Moreover, though Latinos are divided along national origin lines and their leadership is fragmented, many share the feeling that blacks are ahead of them in the process of ethnic empowerment and have sometimes blocked their progress. At the same time, Latinos, especially Puerto Ricans and Dominicans, are the poorest New Yorkers. These groups experienced the least group upward mobility during the 1980s, strongly adhere to the Democratic party, and share similar political outlooks with blacks.[10] Latinos are a promising constituency for Giuliani, but he must embrace and promote their cause while avoiding actions that trigger the class, partisan, or minority dimensions of their political identity.

Asian immigrants will be fertile ground for Republicans in the future for many of the reasons already mentioned in connection with Latino immigrants. The small number of Asian voters decisively favored Giuliani in 1993. Unfortunately for him, however, only a small fraction of the new Asian and Latin immigrants are citizens. Mayor Giuliani and the Republican party have a long-term interest in reversing this condition, but these groups are not likely to have an impact on New York City's electoral politics in the near future.

Finally, Giuliani should not mistakenly believe black public opinion to be monolithic just because more than nine out of ten African Americans voted against him. Mayor Koch's ability, for most of his tenure, to draw support from a sizable minority of the black electorate even when he was at odds with black leaders was an important key to his political ascendancy. He won this support by appealing to the more middle-class, property-owning, immigrant, and Catholic parts of the black community who arguably have a greater exposure to crime and the other negative consequences of black poverty than do any whites. He was also careful to attain tacit support from black local elected officials by supporting groups and programs they favored.

It was only when Koch consistently attacked figures with broad support in the black community, particularly Jesse Jackson, that he lost his black support and freed black clubhouse politicians from the webs of political obligation in which he had bound them. If Giuliani avoids the same trap, parts of the black electorate may potentially be available to him.

Can Giuliani fulfill these two dimensions of the reform ideal as practiced by his Republican-Fusion predecessors? However difficult it may be for him to improve public services, it will be a greater challenge to construct a new rainbow coalition. His core white Catholic and Jewish supporters do not constitute an electoral majority and will become less numerous over time. Large gulfs in political outlook separate Republicans from the white liberals, Latinos, and blacks whom Giuliani needs to win over. He must find ideological themes, policy strategies, and personal alliances that bridge these gaps.

Even though Giuliani appears to understand this challenge, he has failed to acknowledge the pain black voters felt over Dinkins's defeat. He has generated ill feelings among black leaders in the aftermath of an altercation between the police and members of a black Muslim mosque, and he has appointed only two blacks and four Latinos among his fifty highest-paid personal staff members. He also ended the price preference given to minority firms in the city's procurement program and proposed budget cuts that will have a major negative impact on social services. Although his repudiation of granting blacks or other groups privileged access to government benefits strikes a responsive chord with some, a consistent failure to take minority group interests into account will generate opposition. If Giuliani threatens the well-being of all the diverse public-sector producer interests housed by the Democratic party and gives them cause to unite, he will be a one-term mayor.

The Failure of the Dinkins Coalition and the Future of Urban Liberalism

Though it will be hard for Giuliani to reconstruct the Koch coalition, those who would reconstruct a new multiracial, multiethnic liberal coalition face no easy task. Such an effort must begin with understanding why the Dinkins administration did not succeed in consolidating and expanding his electoral base.

To some extent, Mayor Dinkins's failure was tactical. Even though the city's violent crime rate declined between 1990 and 1993, and even though the Dinkins administration poured all its political capital into increasing the size of the police force, the electorate neither perceived the crime situation to be improving nor credited Dinkins for his efforts. The mayor also allowed the perception that he was not capable of closely managing the city's affairs to become widespread. Like the media-driven "crime panic," this "competency panic" called for forthright measures from Dinkins to change perceptions both among opinion-shapers and the electorate.[11] This he never managed to do. The mayor also seemed to be relying on an increased black electorate that never materialized. Despite these failings, however, Dinkins did run an extremely close race, given the many forces he could not control, especially the impact of a severe recession.

That Dinkins managed to come so close can only be cold comfort for those who would build a renewed liberal coalition, however. As the president of one of the city's most successful reform Democratic clubs observed,

> the margin of the mayoral election was only as close as it was because a great many white Democrats voted for Dinkins with the most tightly gritted teeth imaginable. . . . You don't have to be Jim Sleeper to recognize that liberalism is clearly not speaking to the white middle class, or the remnants of the white working class, or the burgeoning immigrant class . . . or even many of the Brownstone Bourgeoisie."[12]

What are the sources of this deeper disarray of urban liberalism?

Race, of course, will continue to be a major problem for the construction of a multiracial liberal coalition. On the one hand, blacks have historically been underrepresented in urban politics and they continue to face discrimination in housing and the labor market. The struggle for black empowerment has been, and continues to be, a defining element in the democratization of American urban society. On the other hand, however, blacks in New York City and many other cities now have relatively high rates of registration and turnout, elect representatives in proportion to their population size, and are more likely to have public jobs than other, more rapidly growing minority groups such as Latinos, Asians, and other immigrant groups. In some nontrivial senses, blacks have become part of the political establishment. Other groups sometimes interpret blacks' attempt to consolidate and build on these gains as blocking their own advance.

This is particularly important because urban politics is less and less about "politics in black and white." In cities where blacks became the majority of the electorate during or before the 1980s, the establishment of descriptive representation is no longer the issue. Now, white minorities influence which of several competing black candidates will win office, as in the most recent Detroit mayoral election. Only in a few more cities are blacks likely to become a clear majority of the electorate in the next decade. In most other cities without black majorities, immigration is likely to make the population more diverse even as non-Hispanic whites themselves become minorities.[13] Indeed, native-born blacks and their children may also make up a declining proportion of cities like New York, Los Angeles, or Miami.

In such cities, multiracial liberal coalitions can only succeed by drawing on white liberals and Latinos, as well as African Americans. This cannot be done on a platform of appearing to favor blacks over other coalition partners. It also cannot be done when the electorate is polarized along racial lines, since blacks will come up on the short side. Yet African Americans are the most reliably Democratic of any voting group and the largest single racial/ethnic component of the electorate in New York City. They must be a central building block in a multiracial liberal coalition.

The evolution of black political leadership will have a major impact on whether such a coalition can be fashioned in New York City. Just as Dinkins's election was the greatest achievement of his generation of black leaders, his defeat spells the end of their ability to shape events. Apart from the possible exception of Charles Rangel, none of Dinkins's peers has the standing to win a mayoral election. While many black political leaders of the baby-boom generation have great promise, only Al Sharpton is well known across the city's black neighborhoods and none can claim the allegiance of all local black leaders.[14] Only one, David Paterson, has run for a city-wide office, and his 1993 Democratic primary campaign for the public advocate position won only 19 percent of the vote. It is doubtful that any younger black candidate could win the 40 percent of Democratic primary vote needed to avoid a runoff against other candidates. (Although blacks might make up about a third of the Democratic primary electorate, no likely black candidate could count on winning all of that vote or attracting wide support outside the black community.)

Many black leaders are angry over Dinkins's defeat and are pondering whether to establish a black third party that would punish white defectors. Although this anger may abate, the Afrocentric feeling that feeds it will not. Despite the poor prospects for victory in the 1997 primary, a candidate like Al Sharpton will probably run simply to claim the power inherent in a large but not decisive black vote. What other black leaders do in this case will be extremely important. If they unite behind such a candidacy, then the ultimate Democratic victor would inherit a deeply divided party.

If, however, a sufficient number of black leaders focus on how to construct a progressive alliance that crosses racial and ethnic boundaries, then the prospects for a victory for progressive Democrats will be considerably enhanced. Black voters have shown repeatedly that they will not vote for a black candidate simply because of his or her race. If a significant number of black leaders endorse a nonblack candidate in 1997, black support can be pivotal to that candidate's victory in the general election as well as the primary. But where will that candidate come from?

In descending order of size within the Democratic primary electorate, four constituencies might generate such a candidate: white Catholics, Latinos, white liberals, and Jews who do not identify themselves as liberals. Except for the liberals, who live in areas represented by reform clubs, these constituencies are associated with the regular Democratic party organizations. Each will probably produce one or more candidates for the 1997 primary.

Although it is hard to tell who will prevail, it seems likely that the competition will come down to a Latino candidate and a white liberal. Though white Catholics are the largest group after blacks, with roughly 18 percent of the Democratic primary vote, they already favor Giuliani most heavily. The best-known Democrat from this background, Council Speaker Peter Vallone, is also not likely to risk his current base of power by running for mayor. Jewish voters living outside Manhattan, forming roughly 10 percent of the Democratic electorate, are its waning political establishment. The best-known politician from this background may be Alan Hevesi, recently elected comptroller, who is also not likely to risk this office in a bid for the mayoralty.

A Latino candidate will certainly run. Though Latinos account for roughly 15 percent of the Democratic electorate, they are plagued by low turnout, little awareness of their leadership, and a low regard for them.[15] The most likely Latino candidate, Bronx Borough President Fernando Ferrer, will draw well not only from Latinos but from black, white Catholic, and even Jewish regular Democrats. Whether the regular Democratic party organizations can provide real support for him will be an interesting test of whether their oft-reported demise is a fact.

With about 13 percent of the Democratic electorate, white liberals will provide his main competitors in the likely form of Manhattan Borough President Ruth Messinger and Public Advocate Mark Green, Jewish Manhattanites with firm progressive credentials. If both run, they will undermine each other. If they do not, and if a strong black candidate does not polarize the election along racial lines, the long-standing Catholic/Jewish and regular/reform cleavages may reassert themselves in the Democratic primary. Since the two groups are roughly evenly matched, black voters would then determine the outcome.

Those who would put together a progressive coalition of white liberal, other Jewish, and black voters, together with elements of the Latino and white Catholic population, thus have their work cut out. Unlike the regular Democrats, these disparate groups lack a forum in which to work out their differences, strike bargains, and unite behind a single candidate. The Dinkins mayoralty did not leave behind a way for backers like the public employee unions, the reform political clubs, community-based organizations, and black churches to meet regularly and interact on equal terms. Such bargaining as will occur is likely to be organized by potential candidates, and will thus be partial, secretive, and serial, rather than open and inclusive. The creation of such a forum should be high on the agenda for those who would forge a multiracial liberal coalition.

Proponents of such a coalition must also address the issues that deeply concern all voters, but especially middle-class white voters. Foremost among them is the perception that crime is rampant, the streets unsafe, intergroup relations uncivil, and the quality of life decaying. Dinkins attempted to address these issues without political success. The fate of Rudolph Giuliani's mayoralty will depend to a considerable degree on how he deals with them. Since liberals do not think that Giuliani's approaches, namely more jails and more arrests, will change the situation, it behooves them to develop proposals that actually will have an impact on the fear of crime. They must find ways to divert the young men who commit most crimes into more constructive alternatives, to strengthen the ability of neighborhoods to control threatening behavior in public spaces, and to minimize the risks of those who are now most exposed to criminal behavior. In addition, they must examine the origins of the fear of crime and find ways to change that as well.

Liberals must also acknowledge public dissatisfaction with government performance and the widespread view that public-sector producer interests run government for their own benefit. Liberals find this difficult because public-employee unions and other entities supported by public funds provide much of the funding, campaign workers, and other resources that advance the liberal Democratic cause. Yet if liberals are to restore legitimacy to the notion of positive government, they must find ways to make it more responsive to its customers, perhaps through further decentralization and greater accountability to local communities. As they work on such issues, those seeking to forge a new transracial liberal coalition would do well to balance their reliance on public-employee unions by involving local voluntary organizations, churches, and block clubs as well.

New York and many other large cities are entering a critical period of their political development. They are moving beyond a politics of black and white into an environment in which forming a majority electoral coalition, not to mention a durable governing coalition, will be a far more complicated task. It is a period that desperately needs a new vision, new leaders, and a thorough dialogue among the potential participants in forging a new liberal coalition.

Notes

Chapter One

1. Thierry Noyelle, testimony to the New York City Commission on the Year 2000, p. 3.

2. Clarence Stone, *Regime Politics: Governing Atlanta 1964–1988* (Lawrence: University Press of Kansas, 1989), p. 6.

3. The term "postindustrial" has its critics. Daniel Bell, in *The Coming of Post-Industrial Society* (New York: Basic Books, 1973), comes close to defining postindustrialism as a postcapitalist mode of production in which knowledge displaces capital. Neo-Marxists as well as neo-mercantilists like Stephen S. Cohen and John Zysman, in *Manufacturing Matters: The Myth of the Post-Industrial Economy* (New York: Basic Books, 1987), argue that this claim is vastly overstated. I use this term to underscore the following features of contemporary capitalism: (a) the central role of multilocational corporations in organizing markets, (b) their increasing dependence on specialized producer services that utilize professional expertise, (c) the increasingly global scale of organizational activity and the attendant concentration of high-level activities in key cities while lower-level activities are diffused, (d) the reorganization of the labor process within corporate and other economic units, and (e) the growing importance of nonprofit and public organizations alongside, and intertwined with, private sector service activities. While I argue that postindustrial capitalism differs fundamentally from the industrial version, it remains capitalist, and knowledge-holding professionals clearly remain subordinate. On this point, see Elliot Freidson, "Professional Powers in Work Organizations," *Professional Powers* (Chicago: University of Chicago Press, 1986), chapter 8.

4. Chapter Two further defines the concept of a dominant coalition and argues that it should be central to the analysis of urban political power. My usage is closely related to that of Clarence Stone and Stephen Elkin, who employ the notion of "urban regime." Stone defines such a regime as "the informal arrangements by which public bodies and private interests function together in order to be able to make and carry out governing decisions," managing the tension between "the popular control of the formal mechanisms of government" and "private ownership of business enterprise." See *Regime Politics*, p. 6. See also Stephen Elkin, *City and Regime in the American Republic* (Chicago: University of Chicago Press, 1987). My approach emphasizes the variability among urban governing coalitions that result from the latitude for and creativity required to build them, as well as the need to distinguish between specific coalitions and the more general "rules of the game," while Stone and Elkin emphasize how basic institutional relationships create broad similarities in all such governing coalitions or regimes. These differences should not obscure the basic similarity of our approaches, however.

5. A seminal study of the politics of racial succession is Rufus Browning, Dale Marshall, and David Tabb, *Protest Is Not Enough* (Berkeley: University of California Press, 1984).

6. On the concept of "postreform" administrations, see Clarence Stone, Robert K. Whelan, and William J. Murin, *Urban Policy and Politics in a Bureaucratic Age* (Englewood Cliffs, N.J.: Prentice-Hall, 1979), chapters 8 and 9.

7. John Mollenkopf, "New York, The Great Anomaly," in Rufus Browning, Dale Marshall, and David Tabb, eds., *Racial Politics in American Cities* (New York: Longman, 1990); John Mollenkopf, "The Decay of Liberalism: One Party Politics New York Style," *Dissent* Special Issue, "In Search of New York" (Fall 1987).

8. Low was mayor in 1902–03, Mitchel in 1914–17. For the seminal discussion of fusion mayoralties, in which Republican reformers rally Democratic dissidents, see Theodore J. Lowi, *At the Pleasure of the Mayor* (New York: Free Press, 1964), pp. 183–207. Koch was able to run with Republican endorsement in 1981.

9. Were it not for the racial aspect of Koch's appeal, one might classify Ed Koch as a "new fiscal populist," following Terry Nichols Clark and Lorna Crowley Ferguson, *City Money: Political Processes, Fiscal Strain, and Retrenchment* (New York: Columbia University Press, 1983), p. 4: "Often liberal Democrats in background, they became fiscal conservatives through personal conviction or fiscal constraint. They seek to ease the burden on the average taxpayer while still responding to the disadvantaged. They are fiscally conservative, but liberal on social issues like race." Koch, however, was at best ambivalent on racial issues and was often capable of inflammatory attacks on black leaders; in the long run, his administration was anything but fiscally conservative.

10. See Chapter Six.

11. Thomas Bailey and Roger Waldinger, "The Changing Ethnic/Racial Division of Labor," in John Mollenkopf and Manuel Castells, eds., *Dual City: Restructuring New York* (New York: Russell Sage Foundation, 1991), pp. 43–78.

12. For example, the coming of age of the turn-of-the century immigrants and the Depression triggered the New Deal realignment. Writing about the national level, W. D. Burnham observes that "after a more or less extended period of stability, broadly-based discontent with the existing political order begins to emerge and then to crystallize. At a certain point the intrusion of a proximate tension-producing event, in a context of growing discontent, triggers either the creation of new major-party organizations or the capture of one of the older parties by insurgents against the status quo. This proximate event may be economic, as were the depressions of 1893 and 1929, or political, as were the events leading from the Kansas-Nebraska Act of 1854 to the election of Lincoln; usually it has been a mixture of both elements." W. N. Chambers and W. D. Burnham, eds., *The American Party Systems* (New York: Oxford University Press, 1967), "Party Systems and the Political Process," p. 288. See also W. D. Burnham, *Critical Elections and the Mainsprings of American Politics* (New York: W. W. Norton, 1970); and V. O. Key, Jr., "A Theory of Critical Elections," *Journal of Politics* 17 (February 1955): 3–18. For New York City, see Lowi, *At the Pleasure of the Mayor*, chapter 8: "The Reform Cycle."

13. Browning, Marshall, and Tabb, *Protest Is Not Enough*, chapters 1 and 2. In addition, Michael Preston et al., eds., *The New Black Politics: The Search for Political Power*, 2d ed. (New York: Longman, 1987), and Browning, Marshall, and Tabb, eds., *Racial Politics in American Cities*, offer studies of specific cities and commentary on their broader significance.

14. My analysis builds on the argument presented in the second part of Ira Katznelson's *City Trenches: Urban Politics and the Patterning of Class in the United States* (New York: Pantheon, 1981) rather than on the more famous but also more problematic argument in the first part that the physical separation of work and residence in nineteenth-century cities led to the suppression of the class dimension in urban politics.

15. Paul Peterson asserts in the introduction to *The New Urban Reality* (Washington, D.C.: Brookings Institution, 1985), p. 1, that large cities are an "anachronism" that "must simply accept a less exalted place in American political and social life than they once enjoyed." His *City Limits* (Chicago: University of Chicago Press, 1981) argues that a lack of power constrains the ability of local politics to influence key issues and that all parties in local politics share a "unitary interest" in promoting economic growth.

16. Compare Peterson's arguments with Adolph Reed, "The Black Urban Regime: Structural Origins and Constraints," in Michael P. Smith, ed., *Power, Community, and the City*, Comparative Urban and Community Research, vol. 1 (New Brunswick, N.J.: Transaction Books, 1988), pp. 138–189. The empirical evidence on how much difference black mayors make in the distribution of public benefits is mixed. Browning, Marshall, and Tabb, *Protest Is Not Enough*, as well as Peter Eisinger, "Black Mayors and the Politics of Racial Economic Advancement," in Harlan Hahn and Charles Levine, eds., *Readings in Urban Politics* 2d ed. (New York: Longman, 1984), pp. 249–260, argue that they have a considerable impact, while Kenneth R. Mladenka, "Blacks and Hispanics in Urban Politics," *American Political Science Review* 83:1 (March 1989): 165–191, argues that they have little independent impact on patterns of minority employment in city government.

17. See Peterson, *City Limits*, chapter 10, co-authored by Margaret Weir, as well as Charles Morris, *The Cost of Good Intentions* (New York: W. W. Norton, 1980).

18. See Chapter Six as well as Charles Brecher and Raymond Horton, "The Public Sector," in John Mollenkopf and Manuel Castells, eds., *Dual City: The Restructuring of New York* (New York: Russell Sage Foundation, 1991), and "Political Change in New York City, 1961–1989," paper presented to the 1990 Annual Meeting of the American Political Science Association, San Francisco.

19. In asking this question, this book seeks to complement and extend Martin Shefter's *Political Crisis/Fiscal Crisis: The Collapse and Revival of New York City* (New York: Basic Books, 1985).

20. Lowi, *At the Pleasure of the Mayor*, chapter 8.

21. E. B. White, *Here Is New York* (New York: Harper and Brothers, 1949), p. 22.

22. Therese E. Byrne and David Shulman, "Manhattan Office Market II: Beyond the Bear Market," Salomon Brothers, May 1991, figure 7.

23. Regional Plan Association, "New York in the Global Economy: Studying the Facts and the Issues," paper presented to World Association of Major Metropolises meeting, Mexico City, April 1987.

24. For example, see Bernard Gifford, "New York City and Cosmopolitan Liberalism," *Political Science Quarterly* 93 (1978–79): 559–584.

25. U.S. Congress, Congressional Budget Office, *New York City's Fiscal Problem: Its Origin, Potential Repercussions, and Some Alternative Policy Responses* (Washington, D.C.: U.S. Government Printing Office, 1975), table 7; Sidney Schwartz, "New York City's Fiscal Crisis: How It Developed, Why It Persists," *City Almanac* 15:3 (October 1980): 1–24; Brecher and Horton, "The Public Sector."

26. White, *Here Is New York*, p. 24. White (pp. 42–43) notes that "the collision and intermingling of these millions of foreign-born people representing so many races and creeds make New York a permanent exhibit of the phenomenon of one world. The citizens of New York are tolerant not only from disposition but from necessity. The city has to be tolerant, otherwise it would explode in a radioactive cloud of hate and rancor and bigotry."

27. As Shefter points out, more often through their defeat than their success. Martin Shefter, "Political Incorporation and the Extrusion of the Left: Party Politics and Social Forces in New York City," *Studies in American Political Development* 1 (1986): 50–90.

28. U.S. Congress, Subcommittee on Economic Stabilization, House Committee on Banking, Finance and Urban Affairs, 95th Congress, First Session, "Securities and Exchange Commission Staff Report on Transactions in Securities of the City of New York" (August 1977), gives a detailed chronology of these events. On March 31, 1975, the city government had $14 billion in outstanding debt, of which almost half was short term. For trends in expenses and revenues, see Brecher and Horton, "Political Change in New York City, 1961–1989."

29. Morris, *The Cost of Good Intentions*, provides a good discussion of the fiscal practices leading up to the crisis, while Shefter, *Political Crisis/Fiscal Crisis*, analyzes its political causes and consequences.

30. William K. Tabb, *The Long Default* (New York: Monthly Review Press, 1982). See also Robert W. Bailey, *The Crisis Regime* (Albany: State University of New York Press, 1984).

31. Eric Lichten, *Class, Power, and Austerity: The New York City Fiscal Crisis* (South Hadley, Mass.: Bergin and Garvey, 1986), pp. 159–184; Steven London, "Authoritarian Responses to New York City's Fiscal Crisis" (Ph.D. dissertation, New York University, 1984).

32. Peterson and Weir, *City Limits*, chapter 10.

33. Raymond Horton, "Sayre and Kaufman Revisited: New York City Government in the Post-1965 Period," paper presented to the 1977 Annual Meeting of the American Political Science Association.

34. Chapter Six; Brecher and Horton, "Political Change in New York City, 1961–1989"; and David Grossman, Lester Salamon, and David Altschuler, *The New York Nonprofit Sector in a Time of Government Retrenchment* (Washington, D.C.: Urban Institute Nonprofit Sector Project, 1986).

35. U.S. Department of Commerce, Census Bureau, 1990 Census, Pl94–171 file for New York City.

36. Raphael J. Sonenshein, "Biracial Coalition Politics in Los Angeles," in Rufus Browning, Dale Marshall, and David Tabb, eds., *Racial Politics in American Cities* (New York: Longman, 1990), pp. 33–48; Sonenshein, "The Dynamics of Biracial Coalitions: Crossover Politics in Los Angeles," *Western Political Quarterly* 42:2 (June 1989): 333–353.

37. Richard E. DeLeon, "The Progressive Urban Regime: Ethnic Coalitions in San Francisco," Working Paper No. 7, Public Research Institute, San Francisco State University, December, 1988.

38. Paul Kleppner, *Chicago Divided: The Making of a Black Mayor* (DeKalb, Ill.: Northern Illinois University, 1985), chapter 7.

39. See Howard A. Scarrow, *Parties, Elections, and Representation in the State of New York* (New York: New York University Press, 1983), pp. 87–91.

40. National Council of State Legislatures (NCSL) Reapportionment Task Force, *Reapportionment Law: The 1990s* (Denver, Colo.: National Conference of State Legislatures, 1989), chapter III, "Racial and Ethnic Discrimination—The Voting Rights Act," pp. 41–72; M. David Gelfand and Terry Allbritton, "Voting Rights Aspects of the Structure of the New York City Board of Estimate" (memorandum to the New York City Charter Revision Commission, January 1988).

41. See Arthur Klebanoff, "The Demographics of Politics: Legislative Constituencies and the Borough of Brooklyn, 1950–1965" (Senior honors thesis, Yale University, 1969); Harold X. Connelly, *A Ghetto Grows in Brooklyn: Bedford Stuyvesant* (New York: New York University Press, 1977); and Charles Green and Basil Wilson, *The Struggle for Black Empowerment in New York City: Beyond the Politics of Pigmentation* (New York: Praeger, 1989). For a contrary view, see Jeffrey Gerson, "Building the Brooklyn Machine: Jewish and Black Succession in the Brooklyn Democratic Party Organization, 1919–1964" (Ph.D. dissertation, Political Science Program, CUNY Graduate Center, 1990).

42. For a similar argument at the national level, see Frances Fox Piven and Richard Cloward, *Why Americans Don't Vote* (New York: Pantheon, 1988).

43. J. Phillip Thompson, "The Impact of the Jackson Campaigns on Black Politics in New York, Atlanta, and Oakland" (Ph.D. dissertation, Political Science Program, City University of New York Graduate Center, 1990), chapter 1, gives an excellent overview of black politics in New York City as of 1989.

44. See Chapter Four below and John Mollenkopf, "Political Inequality," in Mollenkopf and Manuel Castells, eds., *Dual City: Restructuring New York* (New York: Russell Sage Foundation, 1991).

45. Edward I. Koch, *Politics* (New York: Simon and Schuster, 1985), p. 225.

46. Alan Ware, *The Breakdown of Democratic Party Organization, 1940–1980* (New York: Oxford University Press, 1985), discusses the reasons for this decline; Norman N. Adler and Blanche Blank, *Political Clubs in New York* (New York: Praeger, 1975), contrast the state of club activity in the early 1970s with that observed by Roy V. Peel, *Political Clubs of New York City* (New York: Putnam, 1935).

47. Jack Newfield and Wayne Barrett, *City for Sale: Ed Koch and the Betrayal of New York* (New York: Harper and Row, 1988), give ample evidence that the regular organizations commanded patronage during the Koch era. See also the hearings on patronage before the New York State Commission on Government Integrity (Feerick Commission), January 9–10 and April 4–5, 1989.

48. See Chapter Three.

49. Roger Waldinger, "Immigration and Urban Change," *Annual Review of Sociology* 15 (1989): 211–232. For overviews of New York City, see Nancy Foner, ed., *New Immigrants in New York* (New York: Columbia University Press, 1987); and Emanuel Tobier, "The 'New' Immigration in the New York Metropolitan Region: Characteristics and Consequences," unpublished paper New York University Graduate School of Public Administration, 1988. Even among Chinese, there are significant differences among Taiwanese, Hong Kong Chinese, and those from the mainland.

50. Mark H. Maier, *City Unions: Managing Discontent in New York City* (New Brunswick, N.J.: Rutgers University Press, 1987).

51. Charles V. Hamilton, "The Patron-Recipient Relationship and Minority Politics in New York City," *Political Science Quarterly* 94:2 (1979): 211–227.

52. Raymond Wolfinger, "Why Political Machines Have Not Withered Away and Other Revisionist Thoughts," *Journal of Politics* 34:2 (May 1972): 365–398, distinguishes between hierarchically organized political machines, few of which now exist, and machine politics, a more generalized political culture that persists in old industrial cities. For a comparative analysis of the strength of this culture, see David Mayhew, *Placing Parties in American Politics* (Princeton: Princeton University Press, 1986).

Chapter Two

1. Anthony Giddens, *A Contemporary Critique of Historical Materialism* (Berkeley: University of California Press, 1981), p. 140.

2. Clarence Stone, "Social Stratification, Nondecision-making, and the Study of Community Power," *American Politics Quarterly* 10:3 (July 1982): 275.

3. An early version of this chapter was published as "Who (Or What) Runs Cities and How?" *Sociological Forum* 4:1 (Spring 1989): 119–137.

4. Edward Banfield, *Political Influence* (Glencoe, Ill.: Free Press, 1961); Robert Dahl, *Who Governs?* (New Haven, Conn.: Yale University Press, 1961); Wallace Sayre and Herbert Kaufman, *Governing New York City: Politics in the Metropolis* (New York: Russell Sage Foundation, 1960). Nelson Polsby, *Community Power and Political Theory: A Further Look at Problems of Evidence and Inference*, 2d, enlarged edition (New Haven, Conn.: Yale University Press, 1980), restates and defends the pluralist position against some of its critics.

5. Robert J. Waste, "Community Power and Pluralist Theory," in Robert J. Waste, ed., *Community Power: Directions for Future Research* (Beverly Hills, Calif.: Sage, 1986), pp. 117–137, gives a valuable overview of the variants of pluralist thinking, including those that emphasized social stratification and the predominant influence of private interests. Examples of these critical pluralists

include Grant McConnell, *Private Power and American Democracy* (New York: Vintage, 1966); and Theodore Lowi, "The Public Philosophy: Interest-Group Liberalism," *American Political Science Review* 61 (March 1967): 5–24. See also Elmer Eric Schattschneider, *The Semisovereign People: A Realist's View of Democracy in America* (New York: Holt, Rinehart and Winston, 1960).

6. Sayre and Kaufman, *Governing New York City: Politics in the Metropolis* (New York: W. W. Norton, 1965) (paperback edition with a new introduction), pp. xxxvi, xl, xli.

7. Sayre and Kaufman, *Governing New York City*, p. 738. Lowi, "The Public Philosophy: Interest-Group Liberalism," explores the negative implications of parceling out public authority to private interests. In *At the Pleasure of the Mayor*, Lowi puts far greater emphasis on the importance of parties and electoral coalitions than did Sayre and Kaufman.

8. Peter Bachrach and Morton Baratz, "Two Faces of Power," *American Political Science Review* 56 (December 1962): 947–952; Clarence Stone, "Systemic Power in Community Decision Making: A Restatement of Stratification Theory," *American Political Science Review* 74 (1980): 978–990; Stone, "Social Stratification, Nondecision-making, and the Study of Community Power," 275–302; John Manley, "Neo-Pluralism: A Class Analysis of Pluralism I and Pluralism II," *American Political Science Review* 77:2 (June 1983): 368–383.

9. See also Peter Bachrach and Morton Baratz, *Power and Poverty* (New York: Oxford University Press, 1970).

10. Stone, "Social Stratification, Nondecision-making, and the Study of Community Power." Stone applies and develops this view in his *Regime Politics*, especially chapters 1 and 11.

11. Manley, "Neo-Pluralism."

12. Charles Tiebout, "A Pure Theory of Local Expenditures," *Journal of Political Economy* 64 (1956): 416–424; Peterson, *City Limits*. For an early critique of Tiebout that is still among the best, see Richard C. Hill, "Separate and Unequal: Governmental Inequality in the Metropolis," *American Political Science Review* 68 (December 1974): 1557–1568.

13. For overviews of this literature, see Michael P. Smith, ed., *Cities in Transition: Class, Capital, and the State* (Beverly Hills, Calif.: Sage, 1984), particularly Smith's introductory essay, Christopher Pickvance's "Structuralist Critique in Urban Studies," and Robert Beauregard's defense of structuralism, "Structure, Agency, and Urban Redevelopment," chapters 1–3. Other interesting discussions include Marc Gottdeiner, *The Decline of Urban Politics: Political Theory and the Crisis of the Local State* (Beverly Hills, Calif.: Sage, 1987), chapters 3–6; Harvey Boulay, "Social Control Theories of Urban Politics," *Social Science Quarterly* 59:4 (March 1979): 605–621, with responses by Katznelson and Gordon pp. 622–631; Charles Jaret, "Recent Neo-Marxist Urban Analysis," *Annual Review of Sociology* (1983): 605–638; Michael P. Smith, *City, State, and Market: The Political Economy of Urban Society* (New York: Basil Blackwell, 1988), chapters 1, 3, and 9; and Susan E. Clarke and Andrew Kirby, "In Search of the Corpse: The Mysterious Case of Local Politics," *Urban Affairs Quarterly* 25:3 (March 1990): 389–412.

14. For a summary of such works, see Robert Alford and Roger Friedland, *Powers of Theory: Capitalism, the State, and Democracy* (New York: Cambridge University Press, 1985), part III.

15. David Harvey, *Social Justice and the City* (Baltimore, Md.: Johns Hopkins University Press, 1973), part II; Harvey, *The Urbanization of Capital* (Baltimore, Md.: Johns Hopkins University Press, 1985), particularly chapter 1, "The Urban Process Under Capitalism," originally published in 1978; Harvey, *Consciousness and the Urban Experience: Studies in the History and Theory of Capitalist Urbanization* (Baltimore, Md.: Johns Hopkins University Press, 1985); David Gordon, "Capitalism and the Roots of Urban Fiscal Crisis," in R. Alcaly and D. Mermelstein, eds., *Fiscal Crisis of American Cities* (New York: Vintage, 1977), pp. 82–112; David Gordon, Rick Edwards, and Michael Reich, *Segmented Work, Divided Workers* (New York: Cambridge University Press, 1982).

16. Gordon and his colleagues have developed the concept of the "social structure of accumulation" to cope with this problem, but this formulation continues to undertheorize the role of the state and politics.

17. Robert Alford and Roger Friedland, "Political Participation and Public Policy," *Annual Review of Sociology* 1 (1975): 429–479.

18. Harvey, *Urbanization of Capital*, "Urban Politics and Uneven Capitalist Development," p. 158.

19. Roger Friedland and Donald Palmer, "Park Place and Main Street: Business and the Urban Power Structure," *Annual Review of Sociology* 9 (1984): 406–407. Frances Fox Piven and Roger Friedland, "Public Choice and Private Power," in A. Kirby et al., eds., *Public Service Provision and Urban Development* (New York: St. Martin's Press, 1984), pp. 390–420, reach a similar conclusion, though they emphasize the importance of a fragmented government structure for promoting interplace competition.

20. Harvey Molotch, "The City as a Growth Machine," *American Sociological Review* 8:2 (1976): 309–330; John Logan and Harvey Molotch, *Urban Fortunes: The Political Economy of Place* (Berkeley: University of California Press, 1987). My *The Contested City* (Princeton: Princeton University Press, 1983) develops a related argument in chapter 6 that private investment, reinforced by conservative national administrations, migrated to Southwestern cities to avoid the political conflict in older Northeastern cities.

21. Tabb, *Long Default*, pp. 15, 20, 132.

22. See Lichten, *Class, Power and Austerity*; and London, "Authoritarian Responses to New York City's Fiscal Crisis."

23. Horton, "Sayre and Kaufman Revisited." Horton is a professor at the Columbia University's Graduate School of Business and president of the Citizens Budget Commission.

24. Ivan Szelenyi is one of the few to apply this analysis to the former "actually existing socialisms," in "Structural Changes and Alternatives to Capitalist Development in the Contemporary Urban and Regional System," *International Journal of Urban and Regional Research* 5:1 (1981): 1–14.

25. Manuel Castells, "Collective Consumption and Urban Contradictions in Advanced Capitalism," in Castells, *City, Class and Power* (New York: St. Martin's Press, 1978). For critiques, see B. Theret, "Collective Means of Consump-

tion, Capital Accumulation and the Urban Question," *International Journal of Urban and Regional Research* 6:3 (1982): 345–371; and Gottdeiner, *Decline of Urban Politics*, p. 95.

26. Frances Fox Piven and Richard Cloward, *Regulating the Poor* (New York: Pantheon, 1971) and *Poor People's Movements* (New York: Pantheon, 1979).

27. Ira Katznelson, *Black Men, White Cities* (New York: Oxford University Press, 1973); "The Crisis of the Capitalist City: Urban Politics and Social Control," in W. Hawley et al., *Theoretical Perspectives on Urban Politics* (Englewood Cliffs, N.J.: Prentice-Hall, 1976); *City Trenches*.

28. Katznelson comments on his differences with Castells and Piven and Cloward in *City Trenches*, pp. 210–215. Castells comments on Katznelson, Piven, and Cloward in *City and the Grassroots* (Berkeley: University of California Press, 1983), pp. 298–301.

29. Theret, "Collective Means of Consumption"; Enzo Mingione, *Social Conflict and the City* (New York: St. Martin's Press, 1981); Gottdeiner, *Decline of Urban Politics*, pp. 95–107; Paolo Ceccarelli, "Politics, Parties, and Urban Movements: Western Europe," in Susan and Norman Fainstein, eds., *Urban Policy Under Capitalism* (Beverly Hills, Calif.: Sage, 1982).

30. *Poor People's Movements*, p. 3.

31. Ibid., p. 29.

32. Ibid., p. 32.

33. Katznelson, *City Trenches*, pp. 203–204. See also John Mollenkopf, "Community and Accumulation," in Michael Dear and Alan Scott, eds., *Urbanization and Urban Planning in Capitalist Societies* (New York: Methuen, 1981), pp. 319–338.

34. James O'Connor, *The Fiscal Crisis of the State* (New York: St. Martin's Press, 1973); Claus Offe, *Contradictions of the Welfare State*, ed. John Keane (London: Hutchinson, 1984).

35. Roger Friedland, *Power and Crisis in the City* (London: Macmillan Press, 1982).

36. Roger Friedland, Frances Piven, and Robert Alford, "Political Conflict, Urban Structure, and the Fiscal Crisis," *International Journal of Urban and Regional Research* 1:3 (1977): 447–461.

37. Piven and Friedland, "Public Choice and Private Power," p. 390. See also Frances Piven, "Federal Policy and Urban Fiscal Strain," *Yale Law and Policy Review* 2:2 (Spring 1984): 291–320; and Stephen David and Paul Kantor, "Urban Policy in the Federal System: A Reconceptualization of Federalism," *Polity* 16 (Winter 1983): 283–304.

38. Shefter, *Political Crisis/Fiscal Crisis*.

39. Tiebout, "Pure Theory of Public Expenditures."

40. Jay Forrester, *Urban Dynamics* (Cambridge, Mass.: MIT Press, 1969).

41. Peterson, *City Limits*, p. 12.

42. Ibid., p. 20.

43. Ibid., p. 6.

44. Peterson, ed., *New Urban Reality*, p. 1.

45. Peterson, *City Limits*, pp. 187, 197, 199. This view is countered not only by Shefter but by Morris, *Cost of Good Intentions*, and by Charles Brecher and

Raymond D. Horton, "Community Power and Municipal Budgets," in Irene Lurie, ed., *New Directions in Budget Theory* (Albany: State University of New York Press, 1988), who argue that the changing balance of political influence did shape budgetary outcomes over time.

46. Peterson, *City Limits*, p. 209. As Chapter Six will show, however, New York City's budget expanded as rapidly during the 1983–89 period as it did in the late 1960s.

47. See, for example, Manuel Castells, *The Informational City* (London: Basil Blackwell, 1989); Castells and J. Henderson, "Techno-economic Restructuring, Socio-political Processes, and Spatial Transformation," in J. Henderson and M. Castells, eds., *Global Restructuring and Territorial Development* (London: Sage, 1987); Robert Beauregard, ed., *Economic Restructuring and Political Response* (Newbury Park, Calif.: Sage, 1989); David W. Harvey and Alan Scott, "The Practice of Human Geography: Theory and Empirical Specificity and the Transition from Fordism to Flexible Accumulation," in W. MacMillan, ed., *Remodeling Geography* (Oxford: Basil Blackwell, 1989); Alan Scott, "Flexible Production Systems and Regional Development: The Rise of New Industrial Spaces in North America and Western Europe," *International Journal of Urban and Regional Research* 12:2 (1988): 171–186; Scott and Michael Storper, eds., *Production, Work, Territory: The Geographical Anatomy of Industrial Capitalism* (Boston: Allen & Unwin, 1986).

48. Piven and Friedland, "Public Choice and Private Power," p. 414.

49. On this point see Ray Pahl, "Stratification and the Relations between the States and Urban and Regional Development," *International Journal of Urban and Regional Research* 1:1 (1977): 6–19.

50. Beauregard, "Structure, Agency, and Urban Redevelopment," tries valiantly but unsuccessfully to rebut this criticism.

51. Harvey, *Urbanization of Capital*, pp. 146, 148.

52. Joseph Schumpeter, "The Crisis of the Tax State," *International Economic Papers* 4:5 (1954): 7. Frances Piven brought this citation to my attention.

53. Mollenkopf, *Contested City*; Clarence Stone and Heywood T. Sanders, eds., *The Politics of Urban Development* (Lawrence: University of Kansas Press, 1987); Gregory D. Squires, ed., *Unequal Partnerships: The Political Economy of Urban Development in Postwar America* (New Brunswick, N.J.: Rutgers University Press, 1989).

54. For discussions of state-centered analysis, see Stephen Krasner, "Approaches to the State: Alternative Conceptions and Historical Dynamics," *Comparative Politics* 17 (January 1984): 223–248; Theda Skocpol, "Bringing the State Back In," in P. Evans, Dietrich Ruschemeyer, and Theda Skocpol, eds., *Bringing the State Back In* (New York: Cambridge University Press, 1985), pp. 3–37; and my introduction to *Power, Culture, and Place* (New York: Russell Sage Foundation, 1988). Note the use of "augment" rather than "replace."

55. Fred Block, "Beyond Relative Autonomy: State Managers as Historical Subjects," *Socialist Register 1980*, 228.

56. Castells, *City and the Grassroots*, p. 299, remarks that "the concept of social movement is strictly unthinkable in Marxist theory."

57. For an earlier effort along these lines, see Mollenkopf, "Community and Accumulation."

58. Clarence Stone, *Economic Growth and Neighborhood Discontent* (Chapel Hill: University of North Carolina Press, 1976); Stone, "Preemptive Power: Floyd Hunter's *Community Power Structure*," *American Journal of Political Science* 32 (February 1988): 82–104; Stone, *Regime Politics*; Martin Shefter, "New York City's Fiscal Crisis: The Politics of Inflation and Retrenchment," *The Public Interest* 48 (Summer 1977): 98–127; Shefter, *Political Crisis/Fiscal Crisis*; John Mollenkopf, "The Postwar Politics of Urban Development," *Politics and Society* 5:3 (Winter 1975): 247–295; Mollenkopf, *Contested City*.

59. Stone, "Systemic Power"; Stone, "Social Stratification, Nondecision-Making, and the Study of Community Power"; Stone, "Power and Social Complexity," in R. Waste, ed., *Community Power*; and Stone, "Preemptive Power." The themes of these essays receive their fullest development in Stone, *Regime Politics*.

60. Stone, "Preemptive Power," pp. 31–38. See also Reed, "Black Urban Regime," pp. 138–189.

61. Shefter, *Political Crisis/Fiscal Crisis*, pp. 44–81, 139–148, 151–162, 166–173, 184–188.

62. Ted Robert Gurr and Desmond King, *The State and the City* (Chicago: University of Chicago Press, 1987), chapters 1–3.

63. Steffens offered a still-useful schematic analysis of the urban boss as a pivotal point between a hierarchy of business interests (including organized crime) and a pyramid of electoral organization. See Lincoln Steffens, *Autobiography* (New York: Harcourt Brace, 1931), p. 596.

64. Even David Harvey concedes that "class alliances" are based on a complex joining of sections of different classes, but like many other structuralists he leaves this insight untheorized. Harvey, "The Place of Urban Politics," *Urbanization of Capital*, pp. 148–149.

65. For evidence that neighborhood organizations continue to be important relative to other forces in urban politics, see Paul Schumaker, Allan Cigler, and Howard Faye, "Bureaucratic Perceptions of the Municipal Group Universe: 1975 and 1986," in Harold Baldersheim et al., *New Leaders, Parties, and Groups in Local Politics* (forthcoming).

66. Browning, Marshall, and Tabb, *Protest is Not Enough*, chapters 4–6; see also John Mollenkopf, "On the Causes and Consequences of Neighborhood Political Mobilization," paper presented to the 1973 Annual Meeting of the American Political Science Association, New Orleans.

67. Albert Karnig and Susan Welch, *Black Representation and Urban Policy* (Chicago: University of Chicago Press, 1980); and Eisinger, "Black Mayors and the Politics of Racial Economic Advancement," pp. 249–260. Mladenka, "Blacks and Hispanics in Urban Politics," pp. 165–191, argues that African-American and Latino mayors do not have much independent impact on policy outcomes, but that minority council majorities do have some impact.

68. Mollenkopf, *Contested City*. See also Todd Swanstrom, "Urban Populism, Uneven Development, and the Space for Reform" in Scott Cummins, ed., *Corporate Elites and Urban Development* (Albany: State University of New York Press, 1987).

69. Michael Aiken and Guido Martinotti, "Left Politics, the Urban System, and Public Policy," in K. Newton, ed., *Urban Political Economy* (London: Pinter,

1980), pp. 85–116; Edmond Preteceille, "Crise hégémonique et restructuration territoriale de l'état. La gauche et la decentralisation en France," *Revue Internationale d'Action Communautaire* 15:53 (Spring 1985): 49–59.

70. Castells, *City and the Grassroots*, p. 318.

71. David Truman, *The Governmental Process* (New York: Knopf, 1951).

72. Martin Shefter, "Political Parties, Political Mobilization, and Political Demobilization," in Thomas Ferguson and Joel Rogers, eds., *The Political Economy* (Armonk, N.Y.: M. E. Sharpe, 1984), pp. 140–148; Shefter, "Political Incorporation and the Extrusion of the Left," pp. 50–90.

73. Ware, *Breakdown of Democratic Party Organization, 1940–1980*, provides a useful overview of the literature though his case study of how New York City overestimates party decline.

74. Browning, Marshall, and Tabb, eds., *Racial Politics in American Cities*.

75. Preston et al., eds., *New Black Politics*, part III.

76. Raphael J. Sonenshein, "Biracial Coalitions in Big Cities: Why They Succeed, Why They Fail," in Rufus Browning, Dale Marshall, and David Tabb, eds., *Racial Politics in American Cities* (New York: Longman, 1990); Richard Keiser, "Amicability or Polarization? Patterns of Political Competition and Leadership Formation in Cities with Black Mayors" (Institute of Governmental Studies, University of California at Berkeley, 1988); Swanstrom, "Urban Populism, Uneven Development, and the Space for Reform"; Bryan Jones and Lynn Bachelor with Carter Wilson, *The Sustaining Hand: Community Leadership and Corporate Power* (Lawrence: University of Kansas Press, 1986).

77. Stone and Sanders, *Politics of Urban Development*; Squires, ed., *Unequal Partnerships*.

Chapter Three

1. White, *Here Is New York*, p. 22.

2. Kenneth Phillips, Office of the Chairman, Citicorp, "Testimony before the New York City Commission on the Year 2000," May 9, 1987, Municipal Archives, City of New York, p. 4.

3. Walter Stafford, *Closed Labor Markets: Underrepresentation of Blacks, Hispanics, and Women in New York City's Core Industries* (New York: Community Service Society, 1985), p. 1.

4. Two different but equally emphatic statements of this viewpoint are Cohen and Zysman, *Manufacturing Matters*; and Donald A. Hicks, *Advanced Industrial Development* (Boston: Oelgeschlager, Gunn, and Hain, 1985). See also note 4 to Chapter 1.

5. U.S. Department of Commerce, Bureau of the Census, *City and County Data Book 1988* (Washington, D.C.: U.S. GPO, 1988), table C.

6. Saskia Sassen, *The Mobility of Labor and Capital* (New York: Cambridge University Press, 1988) and *The Global City* (Princeton, N.J.: Princeton University Press, 1991).

7. Regional Plan Association, "New York in the Global Economy." More generally, see Norman Glickman, "International Trade, Capital Mobility, and Economic Growth: Some Implications for American Cities and Regions in the

1980s," in Donald Hicks and Norman Glickman, eds., *Transition to the 21st Century* (Greenwich, Conn.: JAI Press, 1983), 205–240; Thierry Noyelle and Tom Stanback, *The Economic Transformation of American Cities* (Totowa, N.J.: Rowman and Allanheld, 1983); and David Vogel, "New York, London, and Tokyo: The Future of New York as a Global and National Financial Center," in Martin Shefter, ed., *Capital of the American Century?* (forthcoming).

8. John Mollenkopf and Manuel Castells, eds., *Dual City: Restructuring New York* (New York: Russell Sage Foundation, 1991). See also Roger Waldinger, "Changing Ladders and Musical Chairs: Ethnicity and Opportunity in Post-industrial New York," *Politics and Society* 15:4 (1986–87): 369–402; Bailey and Waldinger, "Changing Ethnic Division of Labor"; and Andres Torres, "Human Capital, Labor Segmentation, and Interminority Relative Status: Black and Puerto Rican Labor in New York City, 1960–1980" (Ph.D. dissertation, New School for Social Research, 1988).

9. For example, William DiFazio chronicles the decline of the longshoremen in "Hiring Hall Community on the Brooklyn Waterfront," in Vernon Boggs, Gerald Handel, and Sylvia Fava, eds., *The Apple Sliced* (South Hadley, Mass.: Bergin and Garvey, 1984), pp. 50–67.

10. City of New York, Human Resources Administration, Office of Policy and Program Development, *Dependency*, volume 5 (October 1989), table 3. See also Emanuel Tobier, *The Changing Face of Poverty: Trends in New York City's Population in Poverty 1960–1990* (New York: Community Service Society, 1984).

11. City of New York, Human Resources Administration, Office of Policy and Program Development, *Dependency* (June 1988); U.S. Department of Labor, Bureau of Labor Statistics, New York Regional Office, "The Current Population Survey as an Economic Indicator for New York City," table 6.

12. See Stafford, *Closed Labor Markets*.

13. For a discussion of these trends, see John Mollenkopf, "The Postindustrial Transformation of the Political Order in New York City," in John Mollenkopf, ed., *Power, Culture, and Place* (New York: Russell Sage Foundation, 1988), pp. 223–258.

14. My title is borrowed from Klaus Brake, *Phönix in der Asche–New York verändert seine Stadtstruktur* (Oldenburg: Bibliotheks- und Informationssystem der Universität Oldenburg, 1988).

15. William Kornblum and James Beshers, "White Ethnicity" in John Mollenkopf, ed., *Power, Culture, and Place*, discuss this process in Queens.

16. Shefter, *Political Crisis/Fiscal Crisis*.

17. This term originated with Matthew Drennan et al., *The Corporate Headquarters Complex in New York City* (New York: Conservation of Human Resources Project, 1977); see also Drennan, "Economy," in Charles Brecher and Raymond Horton, eds., *Setting Municipal Priorities 1982* (New York: Russell Sage Foundation, 1981), pp. 55–88; and Drennan, "Local Economy and Local Revenues," in Brecher and Horton, eds., *Setting Municipal Priorities 1984* (New York: New York University Press, 1983), pp. 15–45.

18. Regional Plan Association (RPA), "New York in the Global Economy," p. 1.

19. Ibid., p. 4. The classic statement remains Robert G. Albion, *The Rise of New York Port [1815–1860]* (New York: Scribner, 1939). See also Diane Lindstrom, "Economic Structure in Antebellum New York," in John Mollenkopf, ed., *Power, Culture, and Place* (New York: Russell Sage Foundation, 1988), pp. 3–23.

20. Matthew Drennan, "Local Economy and Local Revenues," in Charles Brecher and Raymond Horton, *Setting Municipal Priorities, 1988* (New York: New York University Press, 1987), pp. 20–35.

21. Thierry Noyelle and Penny Peace, "The Information Industries: New York's New Export Base," paper prepared for conference on "Future Shocks to New York," Citizens Budget Commission, New York, January 24, 1989, p. 28.

22. Drennan, "Local Economy and Local Revenues," *SMP 1988*, p. 25.

23. John Mollenkopf, "The Corporate Legal Services Industry," *New York Affairs* 9:2 (1985): 34–49.

24. Drennan, "Local Economy and Local Revenues" *SMP 1988*, p. 27.

25. Ibid., p. 28.

26. Thierry Noyelle, "The Future of New York as a Financial Center," paper prepared for conference on "Future Shocks to New York," Citizens Budget Commission, January 24, 1989, table 6.

27. Ibid., table 5.

28. Ibid., table 1.

29. Mollenkopf, "Corporate Legal Services Industry," p. 40.

30. Drennan, "Local Economy and Local Revenues," *SMP 1988*, pp. 33–34. See also Thierry Noyelle and Anna Dutka, *International Trade in Business Services: Accounting, Advertising, Law and Management Consulting* (Cambridge, Mass.: Ballinger, 1988).

31. Matthew Drennan, "Information Intensive Industries," *Environment and Planning A* 21 (1989): 1611, 1612, tables 6 and 7.

32. Phillips, "Testimony before the Commission on the Year 2000," pp. 2–3.

33. Cited in Laurie Wilson and Ibraham Al-Muhanna, "The Political Economy of Information: Transborder Data Flows," *Journal of Peace Research* 22:4 (1985): 293.

34. Gerald Lowe, "Telecommunications Impact of Financial Industry Relocations," Walsh-Lowe & Associates, paper presented to conference on Financial Services in New York State, New York University Urban Research Center, June 8, 1988.

35. Noyelle, "Future of New York," p. 18.

36. Mitchell Moss, "The Telecommunications Infrastructure in the City of New York," Policy Analysis Division, Office of Economic Development, City of New York, September 1985.

37. Regina Armstrong, "The Nonprofit Sector of the Region's Economy" *Regional Plan News* (September 1982), p. 9.

38. Vera Zolberg, "New York Cultural Institutions: Ascendant or Subsidant?" in Martin Shefter, ed., *Capital of the American Century* (forthcoming).

39. Thomas Bailey, *Immigrants and Natives: Contrasts and Competition* (Boulder, Colo.: Westview Press, 1988), analyzes immigrants in New

York's fast-growing restaurant industry for which young professionals are a prime clientele.

40. F. W. Dodge/DRI Construction Information as presented in Regional Economic Analysis Group, Office of Business Development, Port Authority of New York and New Jersey, *The Regional Economy: Review 1988, Outlook 1989*, March 1989, p. 21.

41. Cushman and Wakefield, Inc., *Directory of Manhattan Development* (New York: Cushman and Wakefield, December 1988), p. iv.

42. Byrne and Shulman, "Manhattan Office Market II," p. 21.

43. See also New York State Department of Labor, "A Quarter Century of Changes in Employment Levels and Industrial Mix" (Bureau of Labor Market Information, 1984), p. 38.

44. Rosalyn Silverman, "Trends in New York City Employment—A Different Perspective," *The Regional Economist* 4:2 (Spring 1986): 1–4.

45. Emanuel Tobier, "Manhattan's Business District in the Industrial Age" in John Mollenkopf, ed., *Power, Culture, and Place* (New York: Russell Sage Foundation, 1988).

46. Roger Waldinger, *Through the Eye of the Needle* (New York: New York University Press, 1988). Even in the diamond-cutting industry, however, much production has moved offshore.

47. For an analysis of the performance of the New York City economy relative to the suburbs and the United States during the four recessions and expansions before the current recession, see Matthew Drennan, "The Local Economy," in Charles Brecher and Raymond D. Horton, *Setting Municipal Priorities 1990* (New York: New York University Press, 1989), pp. 27–49.

48. Foner, ed., *New Immigrants in New York*; Leif Jensen, *The New Immigration* (New York: Greenwood Press, 1989).

49. For the earlier migrations, see Ira Rosenwaike, *A Population History of New York* (Syracuse, N.Y.: Syracuse University Press, 1972), who provides historical statistics. Major studies include Robert Ernst, *Immigrant Life in New York City, 1825–1863* (New York: Columbia University Press, 1949); Moses Rischin, *The Promised City: New York's Jews, 1870–1914* (Cambridge: Harvard University Press, 1962); Thomas Kessner, *The Golden Door: Italian and Jewish Mobility in New York City, 1880–1915* (New York: Oxford University Press, 1976); Nathan Glazer and Daniel Patrick Moynihan, *Beyond the Melting Pot* (Cambridge, Mass.: MIT Press, 1963).

50. Waldinger, "Changing Ladders and Musical Chairs."

51. Regina Armstrong, "New York and the New Immigration," paper presented to the conference on "Future Shocks to New York," Citizens Budget Commission, January 24, 1989; Roger Waldinger, "Comments on Armstrong."

52. Ralph Smith, ed., *The Subtle Revolution: Women at Work* (Washington, D.C.: Urban Institute, 1979); Kathleen Gerson, *Hard Choices: How Women Decide about Work, Career, and Motherhood* (Berkeley: University of California Press, 1985).

53. Mollenkopf, "Post-industrial Transformation."

54. These conclusions are drawn from using the ancestry question in the 1980 Census public-use microdata sample. Those of a given ancestry may include for-

eign born as well as any generation of descent. The largest Jewish ancestry is Russian. Spatially, this ancestry is strongly correlated with Polish, Hungarian, and Romanian, but approximately 15 percent of those of Polish ancestry are Catholic. Many Jews did not give an ancestry in the 1980 Census. Thus Russian ancestry can only be used as a rough proxy for Jewish heritage.

55. Mollenkopf, "Post-industrial Transformation," tables A.1–A.4.

56. On the initial specializations, see David Ward, *Cities and Immigrants* (New York: Oxford University Press, 1971); and Ward, *Poverty, Ethnicity, and the American City, 1840–1925* (New York: Cambridge University Press, 1989).

57. Thomas Bailey, "Black Employment Opportunities," in Charles Brecher and Raymond D. Horton, eds., *Setting Municipal Priorities, 1990* (New York: New York University Press, 1989), pp. 80–109. See also Torres, "Human Capital"; Stafford, *Closed Labor Markets*; and Walter Stafford with Edwin Dei, *Employment Segmentation in New York City Municipal Agencies* (New York: Community Service Society, 1989).

58. Bailey, "Black Employment Opportunities," p. 91.

59. Philip Weitzman, *Worlds Apart: Housing, Race/Ethnicity and Income in New York City, 1978–1987* (New York: Community Service Society, 1989); income figures from City of New York, Human Resources Administration, Office of Policy and Program Development, *Dependency* (June 1988), table 2, p. 8.

60. See Frank DeGiovanni and Lorraine Minnite, "Housing and Neighborhood Change," in John Mollenkopf and Manuel Castells, eds., *Dual City: Restructuring New York*(New York: Russell Sage Foundation, 1991).

61. Erol Ricketts and Ronald Mincy, "Growth of the Underclass 1970–1980" (unpublished paper, Urban Institute, February 1988), find that with less than 3 percent of the national population, New York City had 17 percent of its underclass census tracts.

62. Brecher and Horton, "Public Sector," has framed this discussion. Except where noted, references to budgetary numbers are drawn from this source, especially tables 1 and 3. For more extended discussion, see Chapter Six.

63. For accounts of this period, see Morris, *Cost of Good Intentions*, and U.S. House of Representatives, Subcommittee on Economic Stabilization, Committee on Banking, Finance and Urban Affairs, 95th Congress, First Session, "Securities and Exchange Commission Staff Report on Transactions in Securities of the City of New York" (August 1977). Specific figures below are drawn from Charles Brecher and Raymond Horton, "Political Change in New York City 1961–1989," paper presented to the 1990 Annual Meeting of the American Political Science Association, San Francisco, tables 1 and 3.

64. Federal aid figures from City of New York, *Comprehensive Annual Report of the Comptroller* for the relevant fiscal years, Statistical Section, Part III, "General Fund Revenues and Other Financing Sources—Ten Year Trend."

65. 1989 figures are extrapolated from Brecher and Horton, "Public Sector," based on Citizens Budget Commission, "Five-Year Pocket Summary of New York City Finances, Fiscal Year 1989–90" (September 1989).

66. For one of the few studies of professionals in New York, see Steven Brint, "Upper Professionals: A High Command," in John Mollenkopf and Manuel Cas-

tells, eds., *Dual City: Restructuring New York* (New York: Russell Sage Foundation, 1991), pp. 155–176.

67. Ibid., pp. 172–173.

68. New York State Department of Labor, *NYC Labor Area Summary* (December 1988), p. 2. This figure includes roughly 200,000 employees, so-called "nonmayoral" agencies not under direct control by New York City government, particularly the Board of Education, the Transit Authority, and the Housing Authority, and the Health and Hospitals Corporation, so it does not correspond with figures given in municipal reports.

69. Grossman, Salamon, and Altschuler, *New York Nonprofit Sector*, pp. xxii, xxiv.

70. Roger Waldinger, "Race and Ethnicity," in Charles Brecher and Raymond D. Horton, eds., *Setting Municipal Priorities, 1990* (New York: New York University Press, 1989) pp. 51–79.

Chapter Four

1. Lowi, *At the Pleasure of the Mayor*, p. 197.

2. Interview, August 18, 1987.

3. Jim Chapin, "Who Rules New York Today?" *Dissent* Special Issue, "In Search of New York" (Fall 1987): 472.

4. For other conceptualizations of political interests in New York City, see Charles Brecher and Raymond D. Horton, "Political Change in New York City, 1961–1989," paper presented to the 1990 Annual Meeting of the American Political Science Association, San Francisco, Calif.; and Jewel Bellush, "Clusters of Power: Interest Groups," in Jewel Bellush and Dick Netzer, eds., *Urban Politics New York Style* (Armonk, N.Y.: M. E. Sharpe, 1990), pp. 296–338.

5. According to the 1988 *City and County Data Book*, U.S. Department of Commerce, Bureau of the Census, table 3, only Washington, D.C., had more city government employees per 10,000 population in 1985, while only Washington and Columbus, Ohio, had higher property taxes per capita. The *New York Times*, May 10, 1991, p. 1, confirmed this pattern for 1989. New York spent more than twice the amount per capita from its own revenues on public services than did either Los Angeles/Los Angeles County or Chicago/Cook County.

6. In 1983, the state assumed the New York City rent regulation system. See Emanuel Tobier and Barbara Espejo, "Housing," in Gerald Benjamin and Charles Brecher, eds., *The Two New Yorks: State-City Relations in the Changing Federal System* (New York: Russell Sage Foundation, 1988), pp. 445–478, for a discussion of city intervention into the housing market.

7. Modern city government in New York City dates from the establishment of "Greater New York" in 1898 out of the formerly independent counties of New York (Manhattan), the Bronx, Kings (Brooklyn), Queens, and Richmond (Staten Island). A 1902 charter reform created the Board of Estimate, including the five borough presidents, as a counterweight to the mayor. See David Hammack, *Power and Society: Greater New York at the Turn of the Century* (New York: Russell Sage Foundation, 1982), chapters 7–9. Subsequent charter reforms, how-

ever, steadily enhanced the mayor's power relative to the boroughs, whose presidents came to be associated with the regular Democratic party county organizations. For a discussion, see Joseph P. Viteritti, "The Tradition of Municipal Reform: Charter Revision in Historical Perspective," in Frank J. Mauro and Gerald Benjamin, eds., "Restructuring the New York City Government: The Reemergence of Municipal Reform," *Proceedings of the Academy of Political Science* 37:3 (1989): 16–30. The 1975 charter reform sought to decentralize government by giving charter status and expanded influence to the city's fifty-nine community boards, but it also enhanced the mayor's power.

8. New York City has been a paragon of administrative reform. See Martin J. Scheisl, *The Politics of Efficiency: Municipal Administration and Reform in America 1880–1920* (Berkeley: University of California Press, 1977).

9. Sayre and Kaufman, *Governing New York City*, pp. 39, 73.

10. See State Charter Revision Commission for New York City, "The Structure, Powers, and Functions of New York City's Board of Estimate" (New York, September 1973) for a history of the board and an analysis of its votes, which found that only 5.2 percent of the matters before it were decided by a split vote in the early 1970s.

11. This pattern persisted for many decades; see Sayre and Kaufman, *Governing New York City*, chapter 17.

12. Ibid., p. 196.

13. Except that then-Manhattan Councilman Robert Dryfoos defected to a Bronx-Queens-Staten Island coalition to enable Queens Councilman Peter Vallone to defeat a candidate put forward by Brooklyn regular organization and the Manhattan reformers in January 1986. For a discussion of the council's history, see Lenore Chester, *Borough Representation* (New York: Citizens Union Foundation, 1989), pp. 29–38, 44–74.

14. Newfield and Barrett, *City for Sale*, p. 381.

15. Maier, *City Unions*.

16. Raymond D. Horton, "Fiscal Stress and Labor Power," paper presented to the Industrial Relations Research Association Annual Meeting, New York, December 28–30, 1985.

17. "City Contracts and the City Charter," *The Charter Review* 1:4 (Spring 1988): 1. See also Dick Netzer, "Privatization," in Charles Brecher and Raymond D. Horton, eds., *Setting Municipal Priorities, 1984* (New York: New York University Press, 1983).

18. Grossman, Salamon, and Altschuler, *New York Nonprofit Sector*, pp. xxii, xxiv.

19. The Republicans have clubs in some ADs and county organizations in all five boroughs, but are far weaker and rest on a much narrower organizational base than do the Democrats. The other parties generally lack organization at the AD level.

20. In Manhattan and Queens, larger ADs are divided into several parts, each with its own leaders and clubs.

21. The following table shows the mean percentage on the relevant variables drawn from the 1980 census across the types of ADs. The white, black, Latino, and Asian categories have been calculated to be mutually exclusive. (In the census,

	N	White	Jewish	Italian	Irish	Black	Latino	Asian
Black	13	12.1	2.2	2.7	1.1	68.2	17.3	1.4
Mixed	5	15.3	2.4	4.2	1.4	32.5	43.8	7.3
Latino	5	16.5	2.6	3.2	2.3	25.5	55.4	1.3
White Liberal	9	71.3	15.7	7.4	5.8	7.1	16.7	3.8
White Catholic	15	75.1	9.4	23.4	6.7	5.9	14.1	4.0
Outer-borough Jewish	13	79.1	19.2	13.8	6.6	8.4	8.4	3.4

Latinos may be of any race; in all the calculations in this book they have been separated out to form a mutually exclusive group. Jewish, Italian, and Irish are answers to the census long-form question on ancestry; Jewish uses Russian and Polish ancestries as an imperfect proxy, and they underestimate the numbers of Jews far more than the Italian or Irish ancestry questions do for their respective populations. Mixed minority ADs are those in which blacks and Latinos outnumber whites but neither is a majority.

22. V. O. Key, Jr., *Southern Politics in State and Nation* (New York: Vintage, 1949), chapter 14. See also Julian Baim, "Southern Politics: New York Style," paper presented to the 1983 Annual Meeting of the New York State Political Science Association, New York City.

23. In addition to the sources noted in the previous chapter, see Richard C. Wade, "The Withering Away of the Party System," in Jewel Bellush and Dick Netzer, eds., *Urban Politics New York Style* (Armonk, N.Y.: M. E. Sharpe, 1990), pp. 271–295.

24. Compare Adler and Blank, *Political Clubs in New York*, with Roy V. Peel, *Political Clubs of New York*. When Peel wrote in the early 1930s, the great Tammany Sachem Charles Murphy had died only a few years earlier, and Edward Flynn and John McCooey were charting strong political careers in the Bronx and Brooklyn; Queens leader Maurice Connely had just been jailed. Despite fragmentation, the Seabury Commission's hearings on corruption, and Fiorello LaGuardia's election in 1933, Peel found approximately 1,000 assembly district-level clubs that he called "centers of community action." By 1972, Adler and Blank's attempt to replicate Peel's study found only 262 clubs and concluded that they occupied a much lesser place in the city's political system. Ware, *Breakdown of Democratic Party Organization, 1940–1980*, echoes this finding.

25. Lowi, *At the Pleasure of the Mayor*, chapter 8.

26. Sayre and Kaufman, *Governing New York City*, p. 185: "A split occurs when a faction within a party decides not to support the party's candidate for a particular office, and to back the faction's own selection for that office in opposition to the party's choice, entering the faction's candidate under the label of either a party or an independent body already in existence or of an independent body especially created for this purpose."

27. Martin Shefter, "Party, Bureaucracy, and Political Change in the United States," in Louis Maisel and Joseph Cooper, eds., *The Development of Political Parties: Patterns of Evolution and Decay*, Sage Electoral Studies Yearbook, vol. 4 (Beverly Hills, Calif.: Sage, 1979). See also Mayhew, *Placing Parties in American Politics*.

28. Wolfinger, "Why Political Machines Have Not Withered Away," pp. 365–398.

29. Some wags define a reformer as a regular who has not yet won office and gotten a political job. Brooklyn and Queens county leaders Meade Esposito and Donald Manes, later the center of political scandals, both started out as reformers.

30. Lowi, *At the Pleasure of the Mayor*; Shefter, "New York City's Fiscal Crisis," pp. 98–127.

31. The sources for the data in table 4.1 are the following: Board of Elections computer printout of district leaders by contested status of election (July 1987); consensus of estimates of club strength provided in the summer of 1977 by Norman Adler (former political director for DC 37, AFSCME, and the Assembly speaker), Audrey Bynoe (former staff director of the Coalition for Community Empowerment), Prof. Dan Kramer (College of Staten Island), Prof. Edward Rogowsky (Brooklyn College and former director of Community Board Affairs, Brooklyn borough president's office), Prof. Kenneth Sherrill (Hunter College and former district leader, 67th AD), and the late Mark Schwartzberger (former aide to Assemblyman Alan Hevesi, Queens). The 52nd AD (white) was adjusted from split control to reform to reflect the victory of reformers subsequent to 1987. A number of Manhattan and Queens ADs are divided into two to four parts, each with two district leaders.

32. White and black reform district leaders in Brooklyn did not have sufficient numbers nor a sufficiently close alliance to challenge the white regulars for the county leadership during the 1980s, even though the regulars were split into two factions. When charter reform forced Borough President Howard Golden to give up the county party leadership in October 1990, however, an alliance of black regulars and reformers and white reformers, with tacit support from Golden, elected a black assemblyman, Clarence Norman Jr., to the county leadership. Norman had been associated with Al Vann's Coalition for Community Empowerment but also developed good relations with the county organization. *New York Newsday*, October 30, 1990, p. 27.

33. Sayre and Kaufman, *Governing New York City*, p. 149.

34. For a comment on this skill by a consummate practitioner, see John C. Walter, *The Harlem Fox: J. Raymond Jones and Tammany, 1920–1970* (Albany: State University of New York Press, 1989), pp. 130–131. See also Aaron D. Maslow, "New York's Election Law: Whose Fault Is It? What Changes Are Necessary?" *Talking Turkey* 3 (June–July 1984): 28–30.

35. *New York Times*, August 25, 1985, p. A38.

36. In the fall of 1987, two state senators and an aide were indicted on charges of using of state employees to run political campaigns. The *New York Times* reported that "legislative campaign committees, which barely existed 15 years ago, have displaced political parties in many campaign financing and other operations. The legislative campaign committees use squads of legislative aides who are

skilled in public relations, fund raising, mailings and other campaign techniques. These committees have at least as many resources as money-starved political parties, the politicians said." *New York Times*, September 17, 1987, p. B6.

37. This insight was brought home to me by Jeffrey Gerson's work on Brooklyn regular Democratic politics.

38. Hamilton, "Patron-Recipient Relationship," pp. 211–227, analyzes this development. He concludes that the patron-recipient relationship demobilizes the recipients in electoral politics, but my view is that it channels and tends to control it.

39. The major attempt to explain this fact remains Ira Katznelson, *City Trenches*. See also Michael Wallace, "Changing Concepts of Party in the United States: New York, 1815–1828," *American Historical Review* 74 (December 1968); Amy Bridges, *A City in the Republic: Antebellum New York and the Origins of Machine Politics* (New York: Cambridge University Press, 1985); Martin Shefter, "The Emergence of the Political Machine: An Alternative View," in Willis Hawley et al., *Theoretical Perspectives on Urban Politics* (Englewood Cliffs, N.J.: Prentice-Hall, 1976); Shefter, "The Electoral Foundations of the Political Machine: New York City, 1884–1897," in Joel Silbey et al., eds., *American Electoral History: Quantitative Studies in Popular Voting Behavior* (Princeton: Princeton University Press, 1978); and Shefter, "Political Incorporation and the Extrusion of the Left," pp. 50–90.

40. General elections for state and city offices draw fewer voters: about 1.7 million voted in gubernatorial elections, while only about 1.3 million voted for mayor.

41. This electorate is also crucial to who wins the governorship, since New York City voters make up 60 percent of the statewide Democratic primary vote, and Democratic candidates have won the gubernatorial election since Nelson Rockefeller left office in 1973.

42. If no candidate wins a plurality of at least 40 percent in the September Democratic primary, the two highest vote-getters hold a runoff one month later. The Democratic nominee faces those of other parties in November. Only when large numbers of Democrats defect to an independent or fusion candidacy, as in the cases of Fiorello LaGuardia and John Lindsay, do Democrats not prevail. Democratic political campaigns thus target their efforts on the so-called prime voters who regularly participate in Democratic primaries.

43. For a more extended argument on this point, from which this section is drawn, see Mollenkopf, "Political Inequality."

44. Demographic changes since 1980 might affect these results, but the available evidence points toward a *decline* of the native-born black voting-age population during the 1980s, and a stabilization of the Puerto Rican and white voting-age populations. Thus the conclusion probably remains valid. See Michael A. Stegman, *Housing and Vacancy Report, New York City, 1987* (New York: Department of Housing Preservation and Development, City of New York, April 1988), table 2.1.

45. Waldinger, "Race and Ethnicity," p. 75.

46. A recent study by the Commonwealth of Puerto Rico in New York City estimated that 26 percent of voting age Latinos were not citizens. Nydia Ve-

lazquez et al., "Puerto Rican Voter Registration in New York City: A Comparison of Attitudes between Registered and Non-Registered Puerto Ricans" (New York City: Commonwealth of Puerto Rico, Department of Labor and Human Resources, Migration Division, January 1988), p. 2. Evelyn Mann, head of the Population unit at the Department of City Planning, estimates that 200,000 foreign-born people falsely claimed to be citizens in the 1980 Census. Of course, some of these people may also be registered to vote.

47. Calculated from League of Women Voters of the City of New York Education Fund, *They Represent You 1987–1988* (New York: League of Women Voters, 1989).

48. Theodore Lowi wrote of the cyclical nature of reform that it illustrates "many of the most important aspects of political behavior: the political generation, the alternating patterns of exhilaration and apathy and of issue orientation versus party orientation, the effects of charisma and habit, and so on." Lowi, *At the Pleasure of the Mayor,* p. 179.

49. On how the direct election of district leaders brought reformers into the Democratic party, see John Davenport, "Skinning the Tiger: Carmine DeSapio and the End of the Tammany Era," *New York Affairs* 3:1 (1975): 72–93.

50. The phrase is, of course, from Katznelson, *City Trenches,* chapter 6.

51. Ibid., 177.

52. Edward T. Rogowsky, Louis H. Gold, and David W. Abbott, "Police: The Civilian Review Board Controversy," in Jewel Bellush and Stephen M. David, eds., *Race and Politics in New York City: Five Studies in Policy-Making* (New York: Praeger, 1971), pp. 59–97. On black-Jewish relations in this period and the shift of outer-borough Jews away from their liberal alignment, see Louis Harris and Bert Swanson, *Black-Jewish Relations in New York City* (New York: Praeger, 1970).

53. This anguished period generated substantial commentary; see Maurice R. Berube and Marilyn Gittell, eds., *Confrontation at Ocean Hill-Brownsville: The New York School Strike of 1968* (New York: Praeger, 1969); Barbara Carter, *Pickets, Parents, and Power: The Story behind the New York City Teachers Strike* (New York: Citation Press, 1971); Diane Ravitch, *The Great School Wars, New York City 1805–1973* (New York: Basic Books, 1974); Maier, *City Unions,* chapter 8.

54. Jonathan Rieder, *Canarsie: The Jews and Italians of Brooklyn against Liberalism* (Cambridge: Harvard University Press, 1985).

55. Penn Kimball, *The Disconnected* (New York: Columbia University Press, 1972), p. 170.

56. The following paragraphs draw on John Mollenkopf, "The Politics of Racial Advancement and the Failure of Urban Reform: The Case of New York City," paper prepared for a colloquium on "The Changing Situations of Black Americans and Women: Roots and Reverberations in U.S. Social Politics since the 1960s," held April 25–27, 1985, Center for the Study of Industrial Societies, University of Chicago.

57. Walter, *The Harlem Fox,* pp. 124–130, 150–161; Kenneth Clark, *Dark Ghetto* (New York: Harper and Row, 1965), pp. 159–162; Thompson, "Impact of the Jackson Campaigns," chapter 1.

58. See Green and Wilson, *Struggle for Black Empowerment in New York City*, pp. 104, 107–108; Thompson, "Impact of the Jackson Campaigns," chapter 1.

59. The poverty program spawned a new, more independent black electoral political stratum nationally as well as citywide. Peter K. Eisinger, "The Community Action Program and the Development of Black Political Leadership," in Dale Marshall, ed., *Urban Policy Making* (Beverly Hills, Calif.: Sage, 1979), finds that the first wave of black elected officials who went into state legislatures often had CAP backgrounds. Regarding New York City, Stephen David concluded that "by staffing these community-action groups with people from the community and by permitting them to engage in political activities, the Mayor [Lindsay] increased the possibilities that these organizations would become centers of support for him against the candidate of the regular Democratic organization." Stephen David, "The Community Action Controversy," in Jewell Bellush and Stephen David, eds., *Race and Politics in New York City: Five Studies in Policy-Making* (New York: Praeger, 1971), p. 50.

60. In 1991, Assemblyman Clarence Norman was able to put together such a coalition, which brought minority district leaders together with white reformers and one faction of the white regulars.

61. As Martin Shefter notes, "Although factionalism saps the political strength of New York's racial minorities, it is more a symptom than the ultimate cause of their weakness. Such factionalism characterizes politics under conditions of low electoral mobilization: politicians who do not undertake to outmobilize their opponents seek to prevail by outmaneuvering them." Shefter, *Political Crisis/Fiscal Crisis*, p. xv.

62. Angelo Falcon, "Black and Latino Politics in New York City: Race and Ethnicity in a Changing Urban Context," *New Community* 14:3 (Spring 1988): 370–384.

63. Velazquez et al., "Puerto Rican Voter Registration," p. 11.

64. Motives for this action apparently included a desire to forestall a threatened symbolic candidacy by a black woman, Laura Blackburne, anger at Badillo because he had not bowed out of the 1977 mayoral primary in favor of Percy Sutton, and a desire not to draw support away from David Dinkins, who was attempting for the second time to win the Manhattan borough presidency. Black women legislators felt excluded from this process, suggesting that black leaders are divided by gender as well as by borough and political orientation.

65. Susan S. Fainstein and Norman I. Fainstein, "The Changing Character of Community Politics in New York City: 1968–1988," in John Mollenkopf and Manuel Castells, eds., *Dual City: Restructuring New York* (New York: Russell Sage Foundation, 1991), pp. 315–332.

66. Marilyn Gittell, *Limits to Citizen Participation: The Decline of Community Organizations* (Newbury Park, Calif.: Sage, 1980). In the wake of the activism of the 1960s in northern Manhattan, Katznelson found a "familiar pattern of territorial, ethnic, and personal loyalties" produced the "sharply over-represent[tation of] one segment of the community" in school board politics while the poverty program lapsed into "ethnic politics of a traditional kind." Katznelson, *City Trenches*, pp. 176–177.

67. One example is provided by the collapse of a citywide coalition of seeking to influence city government's spending priorities for the community development block grant (CDBG) program. See Edward Rogowsky and Elizabeth Strom, *Improving CDBG Services through University Involvement: Report of a Study on the Community Development Process in New York City* (New York: Robert F. Wagner, Sr. Institute of Urban Public Policy, City University of New York Graduate Center, August 1989), pp. 29–31.

68. Thanks to Ron Hayduk for compiling figures from the New York City Board of Elections candidate expense filings.

69. *New York Times*, August 11, 1985, p. B2.

70. These figures come from an unpublished study undertaken by Linda Gibb and Jennifer Kaplan for the New York City Charter Revision Commission, March 1988.

71. Fritz Schwartz, chairperson of the Charter Revision Commission, called the city a "land town where land is extraordinarily valuable and scarce," Charter Revision Clearinghouse Project, "Notes on the Meetings of the 1989 Charter Revision Commission," (Citizens Union Foundation, nd), p. 1; Sidney M. Robbins and Nestor E. Terleckj, *Money Metropolis* (Cambridge: Harvard University Press, 1960).

72. "For Some the 'Who' Is the Same: The Currency Which Perpetuates the Permanent Government," *Talking Turkey* 3 (June–July 1984): 26. For a description of the political connections of many of these firms, see Jack Newfield and Paul DuBrul, *The Permanent Government: Who Really Runs New York?* (New York: Pilgrim Press, 1981).

73. Gibb and Kaplan, unpublished study for the Charter Commission.

74. Sayre and Kaufman, *Governing New York City*, p. 171.

75. "Campaign Contributions to Members of the Board of Estimate and the Democratic County Committees, 1981–86" (report by State Senator Franz Leichter, December 22, 1986). Earlier reports documented the timing of large contributions and specific Board of Estimate actions: "Examples of Close Correlations between Campaign Contributions and Board of Estimate Votes" (November 1985).

76. *New York Times*, November 27, 1985, p. B6.

77. The article (ibid.) reported that "the Mayor and several other board members said that contributions did not influence their votes but that they gave contributors access—the right to have a phone call returned or to present their case."

78. Shefter, *Political Crisis/Fiscal Crisis*, pp. 158–174, grants these monitors, as well as the "reform vanguard" of policy thinkers, more influence than in retrospect they actually exerted.

79. Sometimes the amenities have not even been directly related to the project. See Special Committee on the Role of Amenities in the Land Use Process, *The Record of the Association of the Bar of the City of New York* 43:6 (October 1988): 653–697.

Chapter Five

1. Chapin, "Who Rules New York Today?" p. 478.

2. Shefter, *Political Crisis*, p. 176.

3. Accounts of Edward I. Koch's political career may be found in Ken Auletta, "The Mayor," a two-part profile in *The New Yorker* (September 10 and 17, 1979); Arthur Browne, Dan Collins, and Michael Goodwin, *I, Koch: A Decidedly Unauthorized Biography of the Mayor of New York City, Edward I. Koch* (New York: Dodd, Meade, 1985); and Newfield and Barrett, *City for Sale*, chapter 4; as well as Koch's own books, *Mayor* (New York: Simon and Schuster, 1984) and *Politics*.

4. Auletta writes, "Koch stunned his liberal constituents by opposing the introduction of a low income high rise housing development in the middle income white community by addressing a group led by Jerry Birbach, a local loudmouth who became to many a symbol of northern racism." Auletta, "Mayor," p. 41.

5. U.S. House of Representatives, Subcommittee on Economic Stabilization, Committee on Banking, Finance, and Urban Affairs, 95th Congress, First Session, "Securities and Exchange Commission Staff Report on Transactions in Securities of the City of New York" (August 1977), chapter 3, pp. 34–42.

6. Roman Hedges and Jeffrey Getis, "A Standard for Constructing Minority Legislative Districts: The Issue of Effective Voting Equality," Working Paper No. 6, Rockefeller Institute of Government, State University of New York Albany, 1983, table 1.

7. *New York Times*, September 9, 1977, p. 13. The survey "indicated that the Cuomo and Koch constituencies were almost identical in their concern for issues and in the fact that better than a third decided within the last two weeks." Reformers leaned to Koch, while regulars leaned to Cuomo; both appealed more to moderates than to liberals (who preferred Abzug) or conservatives (who favored Beame). Koch scored well in the last week on the issue of crime for his favoring of the death penalty. But the *Times* noted that "the campaign was noteworthy for a lack of issues despite numerous debates among the seven Democratic candidates." The effort of candidates seeking to unseat the mayor to distinguish themselves from each other "became a matter of style, slogans, and imagery."

8. Auletta, "Mayor"; Newfield and Barrett, *City for Sale*, chapter 4.

9. This account draws on Newfield and Barrett, *City for Sale*, chapter 4, and Koch's account in *Mayor*.

10. Newfield and Barrett, *City for Sale*, p. 134. Newfield and Barrett write that Koch promised to appoint people suggested by Esposito, but Koch claims he only promised to take Esposito's phone calls and consider his requests.

11. Ibid., p. 137.

12. When the percentage of Koch votes by AD in the runoff is regressed against the percentages received by the other candidates in the initial primary, the following partial correlations (beta weights) are achieved: .903 for Abzug, .758 for Sutton, .887 for Beame, and .635 for Badillo; the equation had an adjusted R squared of .598; all terms were significant at the .001 level. For a discussion of ecological regression, see Laura Irwin Langbein and Allan J. Lichtman, *Ecological Inference* (Beverly Hills, Calif.: Sage, 1978). Langbein and Lichtman show that if individual data are grouped into aggregates according to an independent variable, aggregation bias is minimized and the resulting inferences do not run afoul of the ecological fallacy. Since ADs were initially drawn to group different ethnic groups, initial candidate preference was a proxy for ethnicity, and the primary was so highly ethnically polarized, this equation should be a good approximation

of the underlying individual relationships. It might be improved, of course, if the 5,300 election districts rather than the 65 assembly districts could be used as a unit of analysis, but this was not possible.

13. Regressing the fall in the number of votes between the primary and runoff by AD on the votes cast for other candidates produces partial correlations (beta weights) of the following magnitudes: .591 for Sutton, .789 for Abzug, .199 for Badillo, and −.473 for Koch. (The partial for Beame, −.135, was not significant at the .001 level.) The adjusted R squared for this equation was .746. As before, all terms were significant at .001.

14. *New York Times*, September 23, 1977, p. B9.

15. Douglas Schoen and Mark Penn, the mayor-elect's pollsters, noted that "New York City voters now have a deep suspicion of candidates supported by the political Establishment, and by Election Day Mr. Koch found himself surrounded by a disparate group of political, labor, and business leaders who were united in just one thing: they sensed a Koch victory. . . . By Election Day he appeared to the electorate like a man allied with the same forces that were behind Abraham Beame four years earlier." *New York Times*, November 11, 1977, p. A25.

16. Partial correlations (beta weights) for the relationship between the Koch percentage in the general election by AD and the other primary candidacies were .989 for Sutton, .779 for Abzug, .823 for Badillo, and .753 for Beame, with an adjusted R squared of .822; partial correlations for the relationship with the growth in the vote between the runoff and the general elections were −.505 for Badillo, −.331 for Sutton, and .282 for Abzug; the partial correlation for Beame was not significant; the adjusted R squared was .517.

17. Martin Shefter, *Political Crisis/Fiscal Crisis: The Collapse and Revival of New York City* (New York: Basic Books, 1987), introduction to the paperback edition, pp. xiii, 176–177.

18. According to Ken Auletta, however, the main thing Koch seems to have taken away from the experience of going South to offer his services as a civil rights lawyer was anger at the double standard of white liberals who were interested only in assaults on black civil rights workers, not white civil rights workers. Auletta, "Mayor," p. 37.

19. On the relationship between blacks and Democratic regulars, see Thompson, "Impact of the Jackson Campaigns on Black Political Mobilization in New York, Oakland, and Atlanta," chapter 1. J. Raymond Jones as told to John C. Walter, *The Harlem Fox* (Albany: State University of New York Press, 1989), describes J. Raymond Jones' role in enlarging black influence within the Tammany organization. Gerson, "Building the Brooklyn Machine," describes how the regular organization absorbed and prospered from black electoral challenges in Brooklyn. Adler and Blank's study of political clubs, *Political Clubs in New York*, found that only 5 percent of black club members belonged to reform clubs.

20. Newfield and Barrett, *City for Sale*, pp. 118–123, 136; Auletta, "Mayor," p. 46. "It was soon apparent," Auletta writes, "that Koch was as uncomfortable with the black establishment as with the white establishment. Tensions rose again when he moved boldly to reorganize the poverty program so as to eliminate the jobs of many middlemen who controlled poverty funds. Since the middlemen were recommended by or close to black elected officials, Koch was stepping on toes."

21. Shefter, *Fiscal Crisis/Political Crisis.*

22. Ibid., p. 177.

23. Ibid., p. 179.

24. Interview with John LoCicero, May 24, 1982.

25. Regressing the gain in Koch's share of the vote in 1981 over his share in the 1977 runoff against the initial 1977 preferences produced the following partial correlations: .754 for Cuomo, .179 for Beame, −.151 for Abzug, −.160 for Sutton, and −.159 for Badillo (all terms significant at .001 except for Sutton at .03 and Badillo at .09). The adjusted R squared was .919.

26. Vote demobilization compared to the previous runoff primary had partial correlations of .361 for Cuomo, .488 for Beame, −.197 for Abzug, −.229 for Sutton; the Badillo coefficient was not significant. The adjusted R squared was .661.

27. *New York Times*, July 8, 1983, p. B1. This marked the establishment of the Coalition for a Just New York, "a group of political, religious and community leaders whose chief goal is a dramatic increase in the registration of minority voters." Led by Brooklyn Assemblyman Al Vann, the group had initially been a looser formation to push the candidacy of Dr. Thomas Minter as chancellor of the Board of Education. Initially included were Basil Paterson, Congressmen Charles Rangel, Major Owens, and Ed Towns, Bronx Community College President Roscoe Brown, Rev. Herbert Daughtry, and Rev. Calvin Butts. Vann also mounted a "Strive for '85" registration campaign in Brooklyn, looking toward both his run for the Borough Presidency and a citywide challenge to Koch.

28. For a description of this classification of ADs, see chapter four. Black ADs had a black population majority in 1980, Latino ADs had a Latino majority, and in mixed minority ADs, these two groups outnumbered non-Latino whites. The majority non-Hispanic white ADs were then sorted by ethnicity, using the ancestry data from the 1980 Census Standard Tape File 4 to determine where white Catholics or Jews predominated. Chapter Four, note 21, gives the ethnic breakdown. "White liberal" ADs are Manhattan and Brooklyn ADs where a large proportion of the white population had professional occupations.

29. Attention was drawn to the substantial underregistration of Puerto Ricans by Ronald Calitri, Angelo Falcon, and Harry Rodriguez-Reyes, Juan Moreno, and José Sanchez, "Latino Voter Registration in N.Y.C.: Statistics for Action" (New York: Institute for Puerto Rican Policy, August 1982).

30. Thompson, "Impact of the Jackson Campaigns on Black Politics in New York, Atlanta, and Oakland," chapter 2, gives the most complete discussion of these events. See also Mollenkopf, "Politics of Racial Advancement"; and Green and Wilson, *Struggle for Black Empowerment in New York City*, pp. 105–107.

31. *New York Times*, August 27, 1985, p. A1.

32. *New York Times*, August 29, 1985, p. B3.

33. Interview with Jerry Skurnick, a senior official of the 1985 campaign and deputy to John LoCicero, the mayor's special assistant for political matters, July 9, 1990.

34. *New York Times*, August 10, 1985, p. B1.

35. *NBC News Poll Results New York City Democratic Primary*, September 10, 1985; WABC-TV/*Daily News* Exit Poll "Profile of the Answers."

36. Regressing the percentage of the Koch vote onto the 1980 Census-derived ethnic makeup of the 60 ADs drawn in 1982, partial correlations (beta weights)

of the following magnitudes were calculated: .555 with Russian ancestry (a rough proxy for the Jewish population), .615 with those of Italian ancestry, .865 with those of Irish ancestry, −.211 with blacks, and .162 with the Latino population (all statistically significant at the .05 level or better). The adjusted r squared of the model was .787.

37. WABC-TV/*Daily News* Exit Poll, "Profile of the Answers," item 8.

38. Regressing the Koch percentage on characteristics of the white population across ADs, partial correlations (beta weights) of .182 with white mean income and −.056 with the percentage of whites working in the professions were calculated after controlling for the white percentage of the population, both significant at the .01 level.

39. Jones to Walter, *The Harlem Fox.*

40. *NBC News Poll Results, New York City Democratic Primary,* September 10, 1985.

41. In a 1987 *New York Newsday* poll of Brooklyn residents, 62 percent of blacks rated Vann favorably, while 38 percent rated him unfavorably. Mayor Koch, by contrast, was rated favorably by 64 percent and unfavorably by 36 percent. *New York Newsday,* November 5, 1987, p. 26.

42. In Queens, Donald Manes served as both borough president and county leader until his suicide in early 1986; subsequently, former deputy borough president Claire Shulman served as borough president, while Congressman Tom Manton, another organization stalwart, served as county leader. In Brooklyn, Howard Golden held both offices from 1984 until 1991. County leader Nicholas LaPorte, Sr., served as a councilman and then deputy borough president in Staten Island until a Republican was elected in 1989. In the Bronx, county leader Stanley Friedman was responsible for the election of Borough President Stanley Simon; after the indictment and subsequent conviction of Stanley Friedman and Simon in 1986, former city council member Fernando Ferrer served as borough president and Assemblyman George Friedman as county leader. The Bronx and Brooklyn have both faced conflict over racial succession. In the former, almost all minority elected officials are part of the county organization and Borough President Ferrer has crafted a new balance among black, Puerto Rican, and white politicians. He thus resolved some of the tensions that Stanley Friedman had suppressed but that erupted after his fall. In Brooklyn, Al Vann and the Coalition for Community Empowerment challenged the county organization in the years before 1984, when Meade Esposito retired as county leader. After 1984, when black insurgents and black regulars could not agree on a minority successor to Esposito, Howard Golden became county leader as well as borough president. He was challenged, however, by another regular faction led by Assemblyman Anthony Genovesi, who had been chief staff person for Assembly Speaker Stanley E. Fink. Mayor Koch forged strong links with Friedman, Manes, Staten Island Borough President Ralph Lamberti, and the Genovesi faction of the Brooklyn organization. By the end of the 1980s, after much skirmishing, the Golden faction had developed a modus vivendi with the Genovesi faction that gave the former the upper hand. The Golden-led county organization also succeeded in coopting some CCE members while seeking to punish Vann and some others. When Golden had to give up the county leadership in 1991 as a result of a new state law forbidding it, black

Assemblyman Clarence Norman was elected county leader with support from black regulars and insurgents, white liberal reformers, and tacit support from Golden.

43. Only in the final years of the Koch administration did his grip on the Board of Estimate begin to break down.

44. On these matters, see Newfield and Barrett, *City for Sale*.

45. See testimony given to state Commission on Government Integrity, chaired by John D. Feerick, held on January 9 and 10 by the Talent Bank's former director as well as senior personnel officials in the Department of Environmental Protection about how DeVincenzo's appointment control system worked. See also testimony given on April 4 and 5, 1989, by DeVincenzo and LoCicero.

46. For an agency perspective on how DeVincenzo applied pressure to select politically endorsed candidates at all levels, see the testimony of Ms. Sherri Roth, personnel planning unit, DEP, and Mr. Roger Martin, former DEP director of personnel, January 9, 1989, before the Commission on Government Integrity.

47. See New York State Commission on Government Integrity (Leerick Commission), "The Role of the Mayor's Talent Bank in Placing Job Candidates: A Case Study of Park Department Placements," exhibit 72.

48. *New York Newsday*, January 29, 1989, p. 19.

49. Office of State Senator Franz Leichter, "Campaign Contributions to Members of the Board of Estimate and the Democratic County Committees, 1981–1986," (December 22, 1986). The disparate industry representatives tended to make large contributions exclusively to Mayor Koch or, in two cases, to Koch and Stein. Real estate developers and their lawyers contributed more widely. Securities firms seeking to participate in city bond offerings tended to contribute primarily to Koch and Goldin, the two officials responsible for choosing such participants. See also Leichter, "The Top 75 Contributors to the Campaigns of Members of the NYC Board of Estimate and to the Five County Party Committees (Republican and Democratic), 1981–1988" (February 25, 1988).

50. Office of State Senator Franz Leichter, "Examples of Close Correlations between Campaign Contributions and Board of Estimate Votes (Chronological Order)" (November 1985).

51. Not all of those favored by contracts from the Koch administration were aligned with the county organizations. In Queens, for example, Koch supported the housing and social service activities of Reverend Floyd Flake long before he ran successfully against a black regular opponent to win the congressional seat vacated by Joseph Addabbo's death. Flake in return provided consistent support for Koch until the 1989 mayoral race.

52. See also Jim Sleeper, *The Closest of Strangers: Liberalism and the Politics of Race in New York* (New York: W. W. Norton, 1990).

53. Falcon, "Black and Latino Politics in New York City," pp. 370–384.

Chapter Six

1. Shefter, *Political Crisis/Fiscal Crisis*, p. 199.

2. Jim Sleeper, "Boom and Bust with Ed Koch," *Dissent* Special Issue, "In Search of New York" (Fall 1987): 449.

3. Charles Brecher and Raymond D. Horton, "Retrenchment and Recovery: American Cities and the New York Experience," *Public Administration Review* 45 (March/April 1985): 267–274.

4. Charles Brecher and Raymond D. Horton, "Political Change in New York City 1961–1989," paper presented to the 1990 Annual Meeting of the American Political Science Association, San Francesco. All references to years in the following discussion are to the end of relevant fiscal years of the city of New York, which end on June 30th.

5. Brecher and Horton, "Public Sector," table 4.1.

6. The following discussion has been influenced heavily by the work of Charles Brecher and Raymond Horton. The tables follow the general design and methodology set forth by Brecher and Horton, but the specific figures are my own calculations from the *Comprehensive Annual Financial Report of the Comptroller* for the relevant fiscal years. Adjustments for real dollar amounts are based on U.S. Department of Labor, Bureau of Labor Statistics, *Consumer Price Index for All Urban Consumers (CPI-U), New York, NY and Northeastern NJ*, series for 1976 to the present, 1982–1984 = 100, to which the tables refer as "1983 dollars."

7. Brecher and Horton draw on and modify Peterson's distinctions between redistributive, developmental, and allocational functions; Peterson in turn drew on Theodore Lowi and James Q. Wilson. See Peterson, *City Limits*, chapter 3; Theodore Lowi, "Four Systems of Policy, Politics, and Administration," *Public Administration Review* 32:4 (July/August 1972): 298–310.

8. This table follows the method used in Brecher and Horton, "Public Sector," table 4.2; the base years and calculations are my own. This table excludes pension payments, which Brecher and Horton included under "other allocative" in their table.

9. For figures on poverty, see City of New York, Human Resources Administration, Office of Policy and Program Development, *Dependency: Economic and Social Data for New York City, June 1988*, vol. 5 (1989). For the rent burden, see DeGiovanni and Minnite, "Housing and Neighborhood Change."

10. Raymond D. Horton, "Expenditures, Services, and Public Management," *Public Administration Review* (September/October 1987): 378–384.

11. Unfortunately, such an analysis is beyond the scope of this book.

12. This table follows table 7.2 in Brecher and Horton, "Community Power and Municipal Budgets." See also Brecher and Horton, "Political Change in New York City, 1961–1989."

13. Figures on the 1970 and 1983 labor cost and the share of compensation in labor-cost increases are from Horton, "Fiscal Stress and Labor Power," table 1; FY 1990 figure from Citizens Budget Commission, "Five-Year Pocket Summary of New York City Finances," September 1989.

14. The 1990 census reported that 14,000 people lived on Rikers Island. The whole city jail system holds about 24,000 prisoners. The state prison system also expanded greatly. For one account of life on Rikers, see Pierre Raphaël and Henri Tincq, *Dans L'enfer de Rikers Island: Aumônier de prison à New-York* (Paris: Centurion, 1988).

15. For critiques of this process from contrasting perspectives, see Katherine Kennedy and Mitchell S. Bernard, "New York City Zoning: The Need for Re-

form" (New York: Natural Resources Defense Council and the Women's City Club, June 1989); and Daniel Sandy Bayer, "From Schools to Skyscrapers: Building an Effective Development Process for New York City" (New York: Economic Development Committee, New York City Partnership, April 1990).

16. For an analysis of New York's economic development policies during the first part of the Koch era, see John Mollenkopf, "Economic Development," in Charles Brecher and Raymond Horton, eds., *Setting Municipal Priorities, 1984* (New York: New York University Press, 1983); for city planning, see Mollenkopf, "City Planning," in Charles Brecher and Raymond D. Horton, eds., *Setting Municipal Priorities, 1990* (New York: New York University Press, 1989). Valuable overviews include Norman I. and Susan S. Fainstein, "Economic Restructuring and the Politics of Land Use Planning in New York City," *Journal of the American Planning Association* 53:2 (Spring 1987): 237–248; Douglas Muzzio and Robert W. Bailey, "Economic Development, Housing, and Zoning: A Tale of Two Cities," *Journal of Urban Affairs* (Winter 1986): 1–18; and Hank V. Savitch, *Post-Industrial Cities: Politics and Planning in New York, Paris, and London* (Princeton: Princeton University Press, 1988), chapters 2 and 3. See also Brake, *Phönix in der Asche.*

17. Such activities prompted the president of the Real Estate Board to worry in 1988 that "demonstrations, articles, and anti-development propaganda . . . were making us wonder whether it was becoming impossible to develop in New York." *New York Times,* February 7, 1988, p. 58.

18. Robert F. Pecorella, "Coping with Crises: The Politics of Urban Retrenchment," *Polity* 17 (Winter 1984): 298–316, argues that this role was granted in return for community acceptance of retrenchment. The ambiguous role of community boards in planning is discussed in Peter Marcuse, "Neighborhood Policy and the Distribution of Power: New York City's Community Boards," *Policy Studies Journal* 16 (Winter 1987–88): 277–89.

19. Paul Goldberger, remarks to Manhattan Institute conference on *New York Unbound,* December 5, 1988. Former deputy mayor and Planning Commission Chairman John Zucotti added that the complexity of the regulatory system "has robbed the city of its capacity to think through its own future." See also Brendan Gill, "The Skyline: On the Brink," *New Yorker* (November 11, 1987): 113–126; Ada Louise Huxtable, "Stumbling toward Tomorrow: The Decline and Fall of a New York Vision," *Dissent* (Fall 1987): 453–462; and The Architectural League of New York, *Building New York: Death of a Vision* (New York: Architectural League, 1988).

20. For discussions of the loft-conversion issue before the Koch administration's major regulatory initiative, see James R. Hudson, *The Unanticipated City: Loft Conversions in Lower Manhattan* (Amherst: University of Massachusetts Press, 1985); and Sharon Zukin, *Loft Living: Culture and Capital in Urban Change* (Baltimore, Md.: Johns Hopkins University Press, 1982). For a description and rationale for this initiative, see City of New York, Department of City Planning, *Lofts: Balancing the Equities,* February 1981.

21. For a range of views on the Times Square project, see the special issue on "The Redevelopment of 42nd Street," *City Almanac* 18:4, ed. Susan S. Fainstein (Summer 1985).

22. As an example of the extent to which these efforts went, Mayor Koch

decided not to reappoint Martin Gallant, longtime vice chairman of the Planning Commission, because he persisted in questioning some of the projects favored by the mayor and the chairman.

23. *The Park Slope Paper*, October 5–11, 1985, p. 17.

24. In this sense, Mayor Koch did not try to develop what Steven Elkin called "the commercial republic" in *City and Regime in the American Republic*, pp. 120–121. For a description of how one city did try to make private investment work for public purposes, see Richard E. DeLeon and Sandra S. Powell, "Growth Control and Electoral Politics in San Francisco: The Triumph of Urban Populism," *Western Political Quarterly* 42 (1989): 307–331; and Richard E. DeLeon, "The Triumph of Urban Populism in San Francisco?" paper presented to the 1990 Annual Meeting of the American Political Science Association, San Francisco.

25. John Mollenkopf, "The 42nd Street Development Project and the Public Interest," *City Almanac* 18:4, pp. 12–16.

26. The project was stymied for more than five years by lawsuits, criticism of project design and scale, and difficulties in raising financing and securing tenants. However, in the spring of 1989, the last lawsuits were dismissed, and Prudential Insurance issued a $150 million letter of credit that enabled the UDC to begin condemnation proceedings. *New York Times*, April 26, 1989, p. B3. In 1991, however, Prudential backed out and the project appeared to be in jeopardy once more.

27. *New York Times*, May 18, 1989, p. B1. The *Times*' Paul Goldberger found the project a "conspicuous case of gigantism," a failure to "stem the tide of overbuilding in Manhattan and divert it more evenly across the entire city." Goldberger, "Shaping the Face of New York," in Peter D. Salins, ed., *New York Unbound: The City and the Politics of the Future* (New York: Basil Blackwell, 1988), pp. 135, 137.

28. City of New York, Department of City Planning, *Midtown Development* (June 1981).

29. City of New York, Department of City Planning, *Midtown Development Review* (July 1987).

30. In at least one instance, the Macklowe Hotel on West 44th Street, the desire to meet this deadline led to illegal demolition of a single-room occupancy (SRO) facility.

31. Kennedy and Bernard, "New York City Zoning," p. 33.

32. New York State Office of the Deputy State Comptroller for the City of New York, "New York City Planning Commission Granting Special Permits for Bonus Floor Area," Report A-23–88 (September 15, 1988).

33. In some cases, promised amenities had not been delivered five years after the completion of the building. In others, such as the building at 1991 Broadway, a bonus was granted for what amounts to a ground-floor restaurant. See Kennedy and Bernard, "New York City Zoning," p. 9.

34. Tobier, "Manhattan's Business District in the Industrial Age," pp. 77–103, gives a detailed analysis of the rise of loft space in Manhattan and the collapse of industrial demand beginning in the 1950s.

35. See Roger Waldinger, "Displacement Pressures on Manhattan Manufacturing Industries and Job Retention Strategies," Office of Economic Develop-

ment, Policy Analysis Division (November 1982). Waldinger concluded that, while it is impossible to estimate exactly what impact local versus industrywide influences had on manufacturing in Manhattan, the intense real estate development of the secondary commercial market in the "valley" between midtown and downtown doomed all but the most firmly rooted agglomerations.

36. For a thorough analysis of housing and neighborhood development trends during the 1980s based on the Housing and Vacancy Survey, see DeGiovanni and Minnite, "Patterns of Neighborhood Change."

37. To ensure that new buildings do not rise above the established roof line, contextual zones do not permit certain previously allowed bonuses. New buildings must also meet landscaping, building security, and design guidelines. At the same time, however, greater lot coverage is allowed, so that the resulting construction is not necessarily less dense.

38. The author served as the designee of the chairman of the City Planning Commission on the ICIB in 1980 and 1981.

39. Mollenkopf, "Economic Development," p. 147.

40. Josh Rubin, "It's Still Christmas Every Day: The NYC Industrial and Commercial Incentive Program," report from the Office of State Senator Franz S. Leichter, June 1990.

41. City of New York, Office of the Comptroller, *Comprehensive Annual Financial Report of the Comptroller*, Fiscal Year 1989, p. 244. This includes abatements given for housing rehabilitation as well as commercial construction.

42. Matthew Drennan has calculated that the average job generates $2,000 per year in personal and business tax payments to the city. Thus, the city's real estate tax exemptions would be cost effective only if they created more than 100,000 jobs, or about one-third of the employment gain since 1977, a possibility Drennan discounts. Matthew Drennan, "What It Costs to Save a Job," *New York Newsday*, March 15, 1989, p. 61. Stanley Grayson, deputy mayor for economic development, countered Drennan by saying that Chase would still pay $230 million in taxes over 25 years on its new Brooklyn facility. But unless Chase moved all 5,000 jobs out of the city, it would have paid some of these taxes anyway. And even if the city "bought" 5,000 jobs with a $235 million abatement, it "paid" more than gained.

43. See Dennis Keating, "Linking Downtown Development to Broader Community Goals: An Analysis of Linkage Policies in Three Cities," *Journal of the American Planning Association* (Spring 1986): 134–142; and M. E. Brooks, *A Survey of Housing Trust Funds* (Center for Community Change: Washington, D.C., April 1988). Kennedy and Bernard, "New York City Zoning," reports Boston's $6-a-square-foot fee goes to a housing trust fund and a neighborhood job-training program, while San Francisco charges $5.86 a square foot for affordable housing, $2 for future downtown parks, $5 for transit improvements, and $1 for affordable child care.

44. Special Committee on the Role of Amenities in the Land Use Process, *The Record of the Association of the Bar of the City of New York* 43:6 (October 1988): 653–697. See also Elizabeth A. Deakin, "The Politics of Exactions," *New York Affairs* (Winter 1988): 96–112.

45. For an assessment of the original program that finds that it would fall far short of housing needs, see Michael Stegman, "Housing," in Charles Brecher and Raymond Horton, eds., *Setting Municipal Priorities, 1988* (New York: New York University Press, 1987), pp. 207–211. For a spirited attack on the program in action, see Bonnie Brower, "Missing the Mark: Subsidized Housing for the Privileged, Displacing the Poor, An Analysis of the City's 10-Year Plan" (New York: Association for Neighborhood Housing and Development, Inc., and the Housing Justice Campaign, August 1989).

46. For an analysis of this period in Chicago, see Arnold R. Hirsch, *Making the Second Ghetto: Race and Housing in Chicago 1940–1960* (New York: Cambridge University Press, 1983). Camilo Vergara has made this argument with respect to New York City's current housing program in his 1991 exhibit at the Municipal Art Society, "Building the New American Ghetto."

47. Stegman, "Housing," and DeGiovanni and Minnite, "Patterns of Neighborhood Change."

48. New York City instead established a target for hiring locally owned, small businesses as subcontractors on city-supported projects and procurement.

49. Like all large cities, New York does operate a manpower training program through its Department of Employment and the local Private Industry Council, spending about $170 million in FY 1986. However, the elements of this program were not coordinated with each other, much less the economic development policy arena. For an evaluation of these programs, see Thomas Bailey, "Employment and Training Programs," in Charles Brecher and Raymond D. Horton, eds., *Setting Municipal Priorities, 1988* (New York: New York University Press, 1987), pp. 163–196.

50. Byrne and Shulman, "Manhattan Office Market II," figure 7, p. 11.

51. *New York Newsday*, November 2, 1987, p. 30.

52. For example, see Waldinger, *Through the Eye of the Needle.*

53. In instances where firms in declining industries owned their premises, they often found that their loft buildings were worth more than their businesses. The owners of these firms profited from the process of displacement.

54. Planning Center, *Land Use Leaders* (New York: Municipal Arts Society, 1990) lists eighty community-based organizations across the city that have actively opposed development or supported downzoning of their neighborhoods.

55. *New York Times*, November 29, 1987, p. 1; *New York Times*, May 14, 1989, Section 10, p. 1.

56. Real compensation includes salaries (72.8 percent of the total in FY 1989), pensions (13.6 percent), and fringe benefits (13.6 percent).

57. Related but somewhat different tables are offered in Horton, "Fiscal Stress and Labor Power"; Brecher and Horton, "Community Power and Municipal Budgets"; and Brecher and Horton, "Political Change in New York City, 1961–1989," appendix table 7. Looking at a somewhat broader span of the fiscal crisis between 1975 and 1983, Brecher and Horton found that rising pension benefits actually drove real compensation rates up, as the unions attempted to protect their retirees from the high inflation of the period. City employment therefore had to be reduced an extra amount during the fiscal crisis to offset this increase, with some added negative impact on the level of services.

58. Mollenkopf, "The Post-Industrial Transformation"; Waldinger, "Changing Ladders and Musical Chairs," pp. 369–402; Bailey and Waldinger, "Changing Ethnic Division of Labor"; and chapter three above.

59. Stafford with Dei, *Employment Segmentation in New York City Municipal Agencies*. Their appendix tables on employees by race/ethnicity and sex by agency were based on data supplied by the New York City Commission on Human Rights.

60. The Board of Education is not included in the City of New York's EEO-4 reports and refused to make its own report available.

61. For elaboration of these points, see Stafford with Dei, *Employment Segmentation in New York City Municipal Agencies*.

62. See ibid., pp. 12–18.

63. The largely Jewish UFT had fought hard when the community-control movement sought control over hiring and firing of teachers and principals. Under Albert Shanker's leadership, it had a generally conservative political orientation, supporting Mayor Koch in his first two reelection campaigns. Its growth was thus politically positive from the mayor's point of view. Like the city as a whole, the UFT experienced some racial succession during the 1980s and became somewhat more progressive after Shanker relinquished the presidency to Sandra Feldman in 1986.

64. The total OTPS figure in table 6.7 differs from the total figure in table 6.2 because table 6.7 excludes lump-sum payments to other agencies, like the Housing Authority or the library system, that are considered OTPS in the overall budget but do not actually represent contracting to outside entities.

65. For an overview of the growth of these functions, see Donna W. Kirchheimer, "Public Entrepreneurship and Subnational Government," *Polity* 22:1 (Fall 1989). Her "Sheltering the Homeless in New York City: Expansion in an Era of Government Contraction," *Political Science Quarterly* 104 (Winter 1989–90), analyzes the political factors that influenced the growth of the emergency shelter system.

66. See Alan J. Abramson and Lester M. Salamon, *Government Spending and the Nonprofit Sector in New York City* (Washington, D.C.: Urban Institute, 1986); and Grossman, Salamon, and Altschuler, *New York Nonprofit Sector*.

67. The city makes direct payments to private hospitals for the Medicaid-eligible patients and also supports the Health and Hospital Corporation, which uses funds from the city and other sources to pay for affiliations contracts under which the private teaching hospitals staff HHC facilities and receive overhead support.

68. The Integrated Comprehensive Contract Information System was adopted in 1986 and scheduled to go into operation in 1989, but it has not yet done so by 1992; *New York Times*, April 4, 1988, p. B1; *New York Times*, August 2, 1990, p. B4. The charter reform established the Procurement Policy Board appointed by the mayor and the comptroller to issue uniform rules for granting contracts. Previously, contracts over $10,000 not awarded by competitive sealed bid required approval by the Board of Estimate. The new system allows agencies to grant noncompetitive contracts up to $100,000; over that amount, they must hold hearings on the award, and over $2 million they must have approval of the mayor. The

awards are not subject to city council review, giving the mayor considerably increased power.

69. Katznelson, *City Trenches*; J. David Greenstone and Paul Peterson, *Race and Authority in Urban Politics* (New York: Russell Sage Foundation, 1973).

70. Testimony of Major Owens, "Public Hearing on Restructuring and Reorganizing the New York City Community Action Program," November 16, 1978, p. 77, Municipal Archives. Velez ran poverty programs in the South Bronx and Wright in Brownsville, Brooklyn. Both were closely associated with the regular Democratic party organizations. See Jack Newfield and Paul Du Brul, *The Abuse of Power: The Permanent Government and the Fall of New York* (New York: Viking Press, 1977), pp. 221–230.

71. City of New York, Community Development Agency, "Community Action for the 1980's: A Report on the Reorganization of the N.Y.C. Community Action Program," September 1981, p. 7.

72. Owens testimony, p. 76. The Ford Foundation reference was to then-deputy mayor Haskell Ward, formerly of the Ford Foundation.

73. Annette Fuentes, "What's Poverty Got to Do with It? Is the CDA Fighting Poverty or Funding Patronage?" *City Limits* (November 1984): 13, 18.

74. The argument that the receipt of public funds politically demobilized black and Latino communities is made in Hamilton, "Patron-Recipient Relationship," pp. 211–227.

75. For overviews of this sort of conflict in other cities, see Mollenkopf, *Contested City*; Stone and Sanders, *Politics of Urban Development*.

76. Peterson, *City Limits*, p. 209, concluded: "If New York once deviated from the pattern followed by most cities, the city's business elites, politicians, and voters have all ensured that such deviation no longer continues." Yet in the space of less than a decade, the political forces that drove this deviation had reasserted themselves.

77. See Leon Fink and Brian Greenberg, *Upheaval in the Quiet Zone: A History of Hospital Workers' Union Local 1199* (Urbana: University of Illinois Press, 1989), chapters 9 and 10.

78. Flake, who was elected to Congress as an insurgent black candidate in Southeastern Queens, built his following with the help of a substantial number of city housing development and social service contracts.

79. Some experts warned even in the early 1980s that the basic causes of fiscal crisis had not been removed and that they would reappear with any significant downturn in the economy. Schwartz, "New York City's Fiscal Crisis," pp. 1–24.

Chapter Seven

1. Edward Koch oral history given in 1975, Columbia University, as quoted in Auletta, "Mayor."

2. Chapin, "Who Rules New York Today?" p. 472. Chapin (p. 477) notes, "The left in New York had major influence in the past because it could attract allies (with rather different goals) from the top of the society. Right now these allies are missing: there is no serious upper-class opposition, no serious party opposition, and no serious press criticism."

3. As cited in Jim Sleeper, "Boodling, Bigotry, and Cosmopolitanism: The Transformation of a Civic Culture," *Dissent* Special Issue, "In Search of New York" (Fall 1987): 413.

4. Mollenkopf, "Politics of Racial Advancement and the Failure of Urban Reform"; Mollenkopf, "Decay of Liberalism," pp. 492–495.

5. For details of the scandal, see Newfield and Barrett, *City for Sale*.

6. *New York Times*, January 9, 1987, p. B2.

7. For a discussion of the ethnological background to such assaults, see Kornblum and Beshers, "White Ethnicity."

8. For a discussion of the impact of these events, see Sleeper, *Closest of Strangers*, chapter 7.

9. This was akin to the media-driven "crime waves" that periodically crop up; see Mark Fishman, "Crime Waves as Ideology," *Social Problems* 25:5 (June 1978): 531–555.

10. See Thompson, "The Impact of the Jackson Campaigns on Black Politics in New York, Atlanta, and Oakland," chapter 1.

11. *New York Times*, April 10, 1988, p. B1, reported that those awaiting Jackson's appearance "poured out of their homes. They leaned from windows, lined streets, ran down sidewalks exclaiming: 'Jesse's here!' trying to glimpse him, snap his picture, or touch him. . . . 'This one I'm not going to wash,' said Sonia Findley in the Bedford-Stuyvesant section of Brooklyn, gazing at the hand that had just brushed against the candidate. . . . At the Pilgrim Cathedral Baptist Church in Bedford-Stuyvesant, 2,000 people waited for seven hours on Saturday, unaware that an overscheduled campaign had canceled the stop, until Jesse Jackson Jr. came and told them his father could not make it."

12. *Amsterdam News*, April 8, 1988, p. 1.

13. See Asher Arian, Arthur Goldberg, John Mollenkopf, and Edward Rogowsky, *Changing New York City Politics* (New York: Routledge, 1991), chapter 3.

14. *New York Times*, April 21, 1988, p. D25.

15. *New York Newsday*, February 23, 1989, p. 4.

16. *Daily News*, January 31, 1989, p. 16.

17. *New York Times*, March 28, 1989, p. B3. The *Times* headlined its article "Non-Hispanic Catholics and Koch: After Three Terms, a Crisis in Faith."

18. *New York Times*, June 22, 1989, p. B4. When asked what they liked most about the mayor, respondents referred more often to his personality and outspokenness than to his handling of specific issues, but these traits were also given most frequently as what people liked least about him.

19. Giuliani entered the campaign with great fanfare, but after waffling on the abortion question and having it reported that his law firm had represented a Panamanian bank tied to General Manuel Noriega, his support plummeted 14 points between May and July, according to a *New York Newsday* poll published July 31, 1989, p. 4. Still, the poll found Giuliani leading Lauder by a margin of 62 points to 22.

20. For additional discussion, see Arian, Goldberg, Mollenkopf, and Rogowsky, *Changing New York City Politics*, chapter 4.

21. On the day of the primary election, Dinkins deployed some 7,000 volunteers, many union members, at about half of the city's 1,573 polling sites.

22. *New York Newsday*, July 27, 1989, p. 25.

23. *New York Times*, August 2, 1989, p. B1.

24. *New York Post*, July 31, 1989, p. 4.

25. *New York Newsday*, May 1, 1989, p. 3, reported that Giuliani attacked Koch for using "code words as a way of dividing people and gaining political support" and for "dividing one religious group from a racial group or an ethnic group from another ethnic group" on WABC's "Eyewitness News Conference."

26. See Michael Stone, "What Really Happened in Central Park: The Night of the Jogger—and the Crisis of New York," *New York Magazine* (August 14, 1989): 30–43.

27. References to exit-poll data are from the CBS/*New York Times* poll on September 12, 1989, graciously provided by Dr. Kathleen Frankovic of CBS News. This poll was based on a random sample voters questioned at 39 polling sites throughout the city. Pollsters interviewed 2,014 Democratic primary voters and 513 Republican primary voters as the voters left the polling places. The error due to sampling was plus or minus 3 percentage points for Democratic voters and 5 percentage points for Republican voters.

28. Calculated by the author from the CBS/*New York Times* exit-poll data.

29. Arian, Goldberg, Mollenkopf, and Rogowsky, *Changing New York City Politics*, chapter 7.

30. For a development of the concept of racially based mistrust, see ibid., chapters 6 and 7.

31. The estimates of the Dinkins vote in these two paragraphs are based on ecological regression analysis of the voting results and racial make-up of the city's 4,368 voter tabulation districts.

32. This reverses the contrast drawn three decades ago in James Q. Wilson, "Two Negro Politicians: An Interpretation," *Midwest Journal of Political Science* 4 (November 1960): 346–369.

33. See Sleeper, *Closest of Strangers*.

34. Further discussion may be found in Arian, Goldberg, Mollenkopf, and Rogowsky, *Changing New York City Politics*, chapter 6.

35. See ibid., for an elaboration of these points.

Chapter Eight

1. Lowi, *At the Pleasure of the Mayor*, pp. 183, 210.

2. Sleeper, "Boodling, Bigotry, and Cosmopolitanism," p. 413.

3. Shefter, *Political Crisis/Fiscal Crisis*, p. 235.

4. The final state of the Koch electoral coalition can be modeled by regressing the percentage of the Koch vote by AD onto the percentage of the AD that is made up by blacks, Latinos, Italians, and those of Jewish ancestries as well as an index of regular Democratic club strength. This equation has an r^2 of .87; the constant is 50 percentage points and the beta weights (partial correlations) are −.710 for percent black, −.233 for percent Latino, .199 with district club strength (all significant at .01 or better), .114 with Jewish ancestry (significant at .26) and .042 with Italian ancestry (significant at .61). Since club strength covaries with the Jewish and Italian population, these later beta weights are to some extent interchange-

able. It is noteworthy that club strength exerts a strong positive influence on the vote for Koch after controlling for blacks and Latino percentage, however.

5. One of Mayor Koch's closest friends and advisers on labor issues, David Margolis, owner of Colt Industries, went through a long and bitter dispute with its unionized employees during the mid-1980s.

6. Studies of "reformed" political cultures show unresponsiveness to blue-collar constituencies. See Robert Alford and Eugene Lee, "Voting and Turnout in American Cities," *American Political Science Review* 62 (September 1968): 796–813; Robert Lineberry and Edmund Fowler, "Reformism and Public Policies in American Cities," *American Political Science Review* 61 (September 1967): 701–716; and Albert Karnig and Oliver Walter, "Municipal Voter Participation: Trends and Correlates," in Dennis Judd, ed., *Public Policy Across States and Communities* (Greenwich, Conn.: JAI Press, 1985), pp. 169–178. In large Southwestern cities like San Diego, Phoenix, or Dallas, nonpartisan, at-large elections and city managers have reinforced the depoliticized, business-dominated nature of urban political competition. See Mollenkopf, *Contested City*, chapter 6.

7. Browning, Marshall, and Tabb do not exaggerate when they say that "the civil rights movement and its local manifestations and successors became a critical test of the openness of the American political system and of the ability of the American political process to respond to the demands of hitherto excluded groups for equal treatment before the law and for equal access to government." Browning, Marshall, and Tabb, *Protest Is Not Enough*, pp. 2–3. But the achievement of these demands was, as they point out, a complex process.

8. Browning, Marshall, and Tabb, *Protest Is Not Enough*, pp. 18, 36–47, passim.

9. Sonenschein, "Biracial Coalition Politics in Los Angeles," pp. 33–49.

10. Sonenschein, "Biracial Coalitions in Big Cities," pp. 193–211.

11. Shefter, "Political Parties, Political Mobilization, and Political Demobilization," in Thomas Ferguson and Joel Rogers, eds., *The Political Economy* (Armonk, N.Y.: M. E. Sharpe, 1984), pp. 140–148.

12. This point has been made by Wolfinger, "Why Political Machines Have Not Withered Away," pp. 365–398; and Mayhew, *Placing Parties in American Politics*.

13. Kevin O'Keeffe, *Baltimore Politics 1971–1986: The Schaefer Years and the Struggle for Succession* (Washington, D.C.: Georgetown University Monograph in American Studies No. 3, 1986). William Grimshaw, "The Daley Legacy: A Declining Politics of Party, Race, and Public Unions," in Samuel Gove and Louis Masotti, eds., *After Daley: Chicago Politics in Transition* (Urbana: University of Illinois Press, 1982), pp. 57–87.

14. Harlan Hahn, David Klingman, and Harry Pachon, "Cleavage, Coalitions, and the Black Candidate: The Los Angeles Mayoralty Elections of 1969 and 1973," *Western Political Quarterly* 19:1 (December 1976): 507–520, argued that white support for Bradley's initial victory was more blue collar than middle class, but Robert Halley, Alan Acock, and Thomas Greene, "Ethnicity and Social Class: Voting Patterns in the 1973 Los Angeles Municipal Elections," *Western Political Quarterly* 19:1 (December 1976): 521–530, counter this position. Both

agree that Jews were among the most supportive white constituencies. For the long view of Bradley's coalition, see Sonenschein, "Biracial Coalition Politics in Los Angeles," and Raphael J. Sonenschein, "The Prospects of Multiracial Coalitions in Post-Incorporation Los Angeles," paper presented to the 1990 Annual Meeting of the American Political Science Association, San Francisco.

15. Harris and Swanson, *Black-Jewish Relations in New York City*, observed that "there is little doubt that the events of 1967 and 1968 which culminated in three teacher strikes marked a decisive turning point" in the polarization of Jewish-black attitudes, p. 131. See also Arian, Goldberg, Mollenkopf, and Rogowsky, *Changing New York City Politics*, chapter 6.

16. Sleeper, *Closest of Strangers*, p. 111.

17. For discussions of national trends, see Bennett Harrison and Barry Bluestone, *The Great U-Turn: Corporate Restructuring and the Polarizing of America* (New York: Basic Books, 1988); and Frank Levy, *Dollars and Dreams: The Changing American Income Distribution* (New York: Russell Sage Foundation, 1987).

18. Peterson, *City Limits*, chapter 10, co-authored with Margaret Weir.

19. Ibid., p. 209.

20. Chapter Six and Mollenkopf, "Economic Development."

21. Kirchheimer, "Sheltering the Homeless in New York City."

22. Stone, *Regime Politics*.

23. For this insight, I am indebted to Jeffrey Gerson, "Building the Brooklyn Machine."

24. Manuel Castells and John Mollenkopf, "Conclusion: Is New York a Dual City?" in John Mollenkopf and Manuel Castells, eds., *Dual City: Restructuring New York* (New York: Russell Sage Foundation, 1991), pp. 399–418.

25. Theodore Lowi, "Machine Politics—Old and New," *The Public Interest* (Fall 1967): 83–92.

26. Lowi observed that "the democratization of the rules of the dominant party in Manhattan might in the long run destroy the reform cycle by removing its most important condition," *At the Pleasure of the Mayor*, p. 185.

27. This is my conclusion from conversations with key organizers of this effort.

Afterword

1. These calculations draw on a data set initially constructed by the New York City Districting Commission, which computerized results for the 1989 election. Associated Press provided the 1993 results, which do not include absentee, void, or blank ballots; blank and void ballots were excluded from the 1989 results to provide comparable data. The 1993 results were reallocated to 1989 precinct boundaries according to the number of voters registered in each block and split block at the time of redrawing precinct boundaries in 1992. I am deeply indebted to David Olson, Cui Jiuxu, and Cheng Zeming for their assistance in creating this data set, as well as to the Districting Commission's executive director, Alan Gartner.

2. Thanks go to Kathleen Frankovic, Chris Von der Haar, and their staff at the CBS News Polling Unit for providing this survey as well as their 1989 general

exit poll. The survey was undertaken May 10–14, 1993, with 1,273 adults at randomly chosen telephone numbers; individual respondents were weighted so as to reflect the overall population breakdown by race, gender, and age.

3. The subsequent analysis is based upon respondents who said that they were registered to vote, who made up two-thirds of the total. Those who were not registered were more undecided about the candidates, less favorable toward Dinkins, and far less attentive to politics than the registered voters.

4. My thanks go to Murray Edelman and Cynthia Talcov of Voter Research and Surveys for giving me access to the 1993 exit poll, which interviewed 1,788 voters as they exited from polling sites selected to represent the entire electorate; the results are further weighted to ensure comparability on gender, race, age, and so on.

5. This survey allows us to measure defection in at least two ways. The 1993 vote can be compared to the recollection of the 1989 vote. This has the virtue of tracking how a person's choices changed over time. It appears, however, that about 20 percent of the 1993 electorate did not vote in the 1989 election; among those who recall voting in 1989, two-thirds reported favoring Dinkins even though the election was virtually a dead heat. A second way is to compare the 1993 vote for mayor to the 1993 vote for public advocate. This measure of defection allows us to include all 1993 voters who had preferences in those races and focuses on those who voted for Giuliani for mayor but chose the Democrat for public advocate. It does not tell us, however, how these voters might have voted in 1989. Since the two measures have quite similar associations with other factors, this analysis uses the second, more inclusive definition.

6. For further discussion of these issues, see Asher Arian, Arthur Goldberg, John Mollenkopf, and Edward Rogowsky, *Changing New York City Politics* (New York: Routledge, 1991), preface and chapter 9.

7. *The Quality of Urban Life: An Exploration* (New York: Citizens Union Foundation of the City of New York, 1993), p. 1.

8. Jim Sleeper, "The End of the Rainbow," *New Republic* (November 1, 1993): 20–25.

9. Ibid., p. 22.

10. Carolyn E. Setlow and Renae Cohen, *1992 New York City Intergroup Relations Survey* (New York: American Jewish Committee, 1993); Douglas Muzzio and Luis A. Miranda, Jr., *Hispanic New Yorkers on Nueva York* (New York: Hispanic Federation of New York City, May 18, 1993).

11. On the media's role in reinforcing public fear of crime, see Steven M. Gorelick, "Cosmology of Fear," *Media Studies Journal* 6:1 (Winter 1992): 17–29.

12. Curtis Chase, "The Republican Challenge," *The Citizen* (newsletter of the Central Brooklyn Independent Democrats; New York: January 1994).

13. On shifts in the demographic composition of U.S. cities, see William H. Frey and Reynolds Farley, "Latino, Asian, and Black Segregation in Multi-Ethnic Metro Areas: Findings from the 1990 Census" (Research Report 03–278, Population Studies Center, University of Michigan; Ann Arbor, April 1993).

14. Jonathan P. Hicks, "For Black Politicians, a Debate of Strategy and Leadership," *New York Times*, February 2, 1994, p. 81.

15. Muzzio and Miranda, "Hispanic New Yorkers."

References

Abramson, Alan J., and Lester M. Salamon, *Government Spending and the Non-profit Sector in New York City* (Washington, D.C.: Urban Institute, 1986).

Adler, Norman N., and Blanche Blank, *Political Clubs in New York* (New York: Praeger, 1975).

Aiken, Michael, and Guido Martinotti, "Left Politics, the Urban System, and Public Policy," in Kenneth Newton, ed., *Urban Political Economy* (London: Pinter, 1980), pp. 85–116.

Albion, Robert G., *The Rise of New York Port [1815–1860]* (New York: Scribner, 1939).

Alford, Robert, and Eugene Lee, "Voting and Turnout in American Cities," *American Political Science Review* 62 (September 1968): 796–813.

Alford, Robert, and Roger Friedland, "Political Participation and Public Policy," *Annual Review of Sociology* 1 (1975): 429–479.

———, *Powers of Theory: Capitalism, the State, and Democracy* (New York: Cambridge University Press, 1985).

Architectural League of New York, *Building New York: Death of a Vision* (New York: Architectural League, 1988).

Arian, Asher, Arthur Goldberg, John Mollenkopf, and Edward Rogowsky, *Changing New York City Politics* (New York: Routledge, 1991).

Armstrong, Regina, "The Nonprofit Sector of the Region's Economy," *Regional Plan News* (September 1982) pp. 1–6.

———, "New York and the New Immigration," paper prepared for conference on "Future Shocks to New York," Citizens Budget Commission, New York, January 24, 1989.

Auletta, Ken, "The Mayor," *The New Yorker* (September 10 and 17, 1979).

Bachrach, Peter, and Morton Baratz, "Two Faces of Power," *American Political Science Review* 56 (December 1962): 947–952.

———, *Power and Poverty* (New York: Oxford University Press, 1970).

Bailey, Robert W., *The Crisis Regime* (Albany: State University of New York Press, 1984).

Bailey, Thomas, "Employment and Training Programs," in Charles Brecher and Raymond D. Horton, eds., *Setting Municipal Priorities, 1988* (New York: New York University Press, 1987), pp. 163–196.

———, *Immigrants and Natives: Contrasts and Competition* (Boulder, Colo.: Westview Press, 1988).

———, "Black Employment Opportunities," in Charles Brecher and Raymond D. Horton, eds., *Setting Municipal Priorities, 1990* (New York: New York University Press, 1989), pp. 80–109.

Bailey, Thomas, and Roger Waldinger, "The Changing Ethnic/Racial Division of Labor," in John Mollenkopf and Manuel Castells, eds., *Dual City: Restructuring New York* (New York: Russell Sage Foundation, 1991), pp. 43–78.

Baim, Julian, "Southern Politics: New York Style," paper presented to the 1983 Annual Meeting of the New York State Political Science Association, New York City.

Banfield, Edward, *Political Influence* (Glencoe, Ill.: Free Press, 1961).

Bayer, Daniel Sandy, "From Schools to Skyscrapers: Building an Effective Development Process for New York City," (New York: Economic Development Committee, New York City Partnership, April 1990).

Beauregard, Robert, "Structure, Agency, and Urban Redevelopment," in Michael P. Smith, ed., *Cities in Transition: Class, Capital, and the State* (Beverly Hills, Calif.: Sage, 1984), pp. 51–72.

————, ed., *Economic Restructuring and Political Response* (Newbury Park, Calif.: Sage, 1989).

Bell, Daniel, *The Coming of Post-Industrial Society* (New York: Basic Books, 1973).

Bellush, Jewel, "Clusters of Power: Interest Groups," in Jewel Bellush and Dick Netzer, eds., *Urban Politics New York Style* (Armonk, N.Y.: M. E. Sharpe, 1990), pp. 296–338.

Berube, Maurice R., and Marilyn Gittell, eds., *Confrontation at Ocean Hill-Brownsville: The New York School Strike of 1968* (New York: Praeger, 1969).

Block, Fred, "Beyond Relative Autonomy: State Managers as Historical Subjects," *Socialist Register 1980*, pp. 219–234.

Boulay, Harvey, "Social Control Theories of Urban Politics," *Social Science Quarterly* 59:4 (March 1979): 605–621.

Brake, Klaus, *Phönix in der Asche—New York verändert seine Stadtstruktur* (Oldenburg: Bibliotheks- und Informationssystem der Universität Oldenburg, 1988).

Brecher, Charles, and Raymond D. Horton, "Retrenchment and Recovery: American Cities and the New York Experience," *Public Administration Review* 45 (March/April 1985): 267–274.

————, "Community Power and Municipal Budgets," in Irene Lurie, ed., *New Directions in Budget Theory* (Albany, N.Y.: State University of New York Press, 1988).

————, "Political Change in New York City, 1961–1989," paper presented to the 1990 Annual Meeting of the American Political Science Association, San Francisco.

————, "The Public Sector," in John Mollenkopf and Manuel Castells, eds., *Dual City: The Restructuring of New York* (New York: Russell Sage Foundation, 1991), pp. 103–128.

Bridges, Amy, *A City in the Republic: Antebellum New York and the Origins of Machine Politics* (New York: Cambridge University Press, 1985).

Brint, Steven, "Upper Professionals: A High Command," in John Mollenkopf and Manuel Castells, eds., *Dual City: Restructuring New York* (New York: Russell Sage Foundation, 1991), pp. 155–176.

Brooks, M. E., *A Survey of Housing Trust Funds* (Center for Community Change: Washington, D.C., April 1988).

Brower, Bonnie, "Missing the Mark: Subsidized Housing for the Privileged, Displacing the Poor, An Analysis of the City's 10-Year Plan" (New York: Association for Neighborhood Housing and Development, Inc., and the Housing Justice Campaign, August 1989).

Browne, Arthur, Dan Collins, and Michael Goodwin, *I, Koch: A Decidedly Unauthorized Biography of the Mayor of New York City, Edward I. Koch* (New York: Dodd, Meade, 1985).

Browning, Rufus, Dale Marshall, and David Tabb, *Protest Is Not Enough* (Berkeley: University of California Press, 1984).

————, eds., *Racial Politics in American Cities* (New York: Longman, 1990).

Burnham, Walter Dean, *Critical Elections and the Mainsprings of American Politics* (New York: W. W. Norton, 1970).

Calitri, Ronald, Angelo Falcon, and Harry Rodriguez-Reyes, Juan Moreno, and José Sanchez, "Latino Voter Registration in N.Y.C.: Statistics for Action" (New York: Institute for Puerto Rican Policy, August 1982).

Carter, Barbara, *Pickets, Parents, and Power: The Story behind the New York City Teachers Strike* (New York: Citation Press, 1971).

Castells, Manuel, *City, Class and Power* (New York: St. Martin's Press, 1978).

————, *City and the Grassroots* (Berkeley: University of California Press, 1983).

————, *The Informational City* (London: Basil Blackwell, 1989).

Castells, Manuel, and J. Henderson, "Techno-economic Restructuring, Socio-political Processes, and Spatial Transformation," in J. Henderson and M. Castells, eds., *Global Restructuring and Territorial Development* (London: Sage, 1987), pp. 251–287.

Castells, Manuel, and John Mollenkopf, "Conclusion: Is New York a Dual City?" in John Mollenkopf and Manuel Castells, eds., *Dual City: Restructuring New York* (New York: Russell Sage Foundation, 1991), pp. 399–418.

Ceccarelli, Paolo, "Politics, Parties, and Urban Movements: Western Europe," in Susan and Norman Fainstein, eds., *Urban Policy Under Capitalism* (Beverly Hills, Calif.: Sage, 1982).

Chambers, W. N., and W. D. Burnham, eds., *The American Party Systems* (New York: Oxford University Press, 1967).

Chapin, Jim, "Who Rules New York Today?" *Dissent* Special Issue, "In Search of New York" (Fall 1987): 472–478.

Chester, Lenore, *Borough Representation* (New York: Citizens Union Foundation, 1989).

City of New York, Community Development Agency, "Community Action for the 1980's: A Report on the Reorganization of the N.Y.C. Community Action Program" (September 1981).

————, Department of City Planning, *Lofts: Balancing the Equities* (February 1981).

————, Department of City Planning, *Midtown Development* (June 1981).

————, Department of City Planning, *Midtown Development Review* (July 1987).

————, Human Resources Administration, Office of Policy and Program Development, *Dependency: Economic and Social Data for New York City, June 1987*, vol. 4 (June 1988).

————, Human Resources Administration, Office of Policy and Program Development, *Dependency: Economic and Social Data for New York City, June 1988*, vol. 5 (October 1989).

————, Office of the Comptroller, *Comprehensive Annual Report of the Comptroller* (various years).

Clark, Kenneth, *Dark Ghetto* (New York: Harper and Row, 1965).

Clark, Terry Nichols, and Lorna Crowley Ferguson, *City Money: Political Processes, Fiscal Strain, and Retrenchment* (New York: Columbia University Press, 1983).

Clarke, Susan E., and Andrew Kirby, "In Search of the Corpse: The Mysterious Case of Local Politics," *Urban Affairs Quarterly* 25:3 (March 1990): 389–412.

Cohen, Stephen S., and John Zysman, *Manufacturing Matters: The Myth of the Post-Industrial Economy* (New York: Basic Books, 1987).

Connelly, Harold X., *A Ghetto Grows in Brooklyn: Bedford Stuyvesant* (New York: New York University Press, 1977).

Dahl, Robert, *Who Governs?* (New Haven, Conn.: Yale University Press, 1961).

David, Stephen, "The Community Action Controversy," in Jewell Bellush and Stephen David, eds., *Race and Politics in New York City: Five Studies in Policy-Making* (New York: Praeger, 1971), pp. 25–58.

David, Stephen, and Paul Kantor, "Urban Policy in the Federal System: A Reconceptualization of Federalism," *Polity* 16 (Winter 1983): 283–304.

Davenport, John, "Skinning the Tiger: Carmine DeSapio and the End of the Tammany Era," *New York Affairs* 3:1 (1975): 72–93.

Deakin, Elizabeth A., "The Politics of Exactions," *New York Affairs* (Winter 1988): 96–112.

DeGiovanni, Frank, and Lorraine Minnite, "Patterns of Neighborhood Change," in John Mollenkopf and Manuel Castells, eds., *Dual City: Restructuring New York* (New York: Russell Sage Foundation, 1991), pp. 267–312.

DeLeon, Richard E., "The Progressive Urban Regime: Ethnic Coalitions in San Francisco," Working Paper No. 7, Public Research Institute, San Francisco State University, December 1988.

————, "The Triumph of Urban Populism in San Francisco?" paper presented to the 1990 Annual Meeting of the American Political Science Association, San Francisco.

DeLeon, Richard E., and Sandra S. Powell, "Growth Control and Electoral Politics in San Francisco: The Triumph of Urban Populism," *Western Political Quarterly* 42 (1989): 307–331.

DiFazio, William, "Hiring Hall Community on the Brooklyn Waterfront," Vernon Boggs, Gerald Handel, and Sylvia Fava, eds., *The Apple Sliced* (South Hadley, Mass.: Bergin and Garvey, 1984), pp. 50–67.

Drennan, Matthew, "The Economy," in Charles Brecher and Raymond Horton, eds., *Setting Municipal Priorities 1982* (New York: Russell Sage Foundation, 1981), pp. 55–88.

————, "Local Economy and Local Revenues," in Brecher and Horton, eds., *Setting Municipal Priorities 1984* (New York: New York University Press, 1983), pp. 15–45.

———, "Local Economy and Local Revenues," in Charles Brecher and Raymond Horton, *Setting Municipal Priorities, 1988* (New York: New York University Press, 1987), pp. 20–35.

———, "The Local Economy," in Charles Brecher and Raymond D. Horton, *Setting Municipal Priorities 1990* (New York: New York University Press, 1989), pp. 27–49.

———, "Information Intensive Industries," *Environment and Planning A* 21 (1989): 1603–1618.

Drennan, Matthew, et al., *The Corporate Headquarters Complex in New York City* (New York: Conservation of Human Resources Project, 1977).

Eisinger, Peter K., "The Community Action Program and the Development of Black Political Leadership," in Dale Marshall, ed., *Urban Policy Making* (Beverly Hills, Calif.: Sage, 1979), pp. 127–144.

———, "Black Mayors and the Politics of Racial Economic Advancement," in Harlan Hahn and Charles Levine, eds., *Readings in Urban Politics* 2d ed. (New York: Longman, 1984), pp. 249–260.

Elkin, Stephen, *City and Regime in the American Republic* (Chicago: University of Chicago Press, 1987).

Ernst, Robert, *Immigrant Life in New York City, 1825–1863* (New York: Columbia University Press, 1949).

Fainstein, Norman I., and Susan S. Fainstein, "Economic Restructuring and the Politics of Land Use Planning in New York City," *Journal of the American Planning Association* 53:2 (Spring 1987): 237–248.

Fainstein, Susan S., ed., *City Almanac* 18:4, Special Issue on "The Redevelopment of 42nd Street" (Summer 1985).

Fainstein, Susan S., and Norman I. Fainstein, "The Changing Character of Community Politics in New York City: 1968–1988," in John Mollenkopf and Manuel Castells, eds., *Dual City: Restructuring New York* (New York: Russell Sage Foundation, 1991), pp. 315–332.

Falcon, Angelo, "Black and Latino Politics in New York City: Race and Ethnicity in a Changing Urban Context," *New Community* 14:3 (Spring 1988): 370–384.

Fink, Leon, and Brian Greenberg, *Upheaval in the Quiet Zone: A History of Hospital Workers' Union Local 1199* (Urbana, Ill.: University of Illinois Press, 1989).

Fishman, Mark, "Crime Waves as Ideology," *Social Problems* 25:5 (June 1978): 531–555.

Foner, Nancy, ed., *New Immigrants in New York* (New York: Columbia University Press, 1987).

Forrester, Jay, *Urban Dynamics* (Cambridge, Mass.: MIT Press, 1969).

Freidson, Elliot, *Professional Powers* (Chicago: University of Chicago Press, 1986).

Friedland, Roger, *Power and Crisis in the City* (London: Macmillan Press, 1982).

Friedland, Roger, Frances Fox Piven, and Robert Alford, "Political Conflict, Urban Structure, and the Fiscal Crisis," *International Journal of Urban and Regional Research* 1:3 (1977): 447–461.

Friedland, Roger, and Donald Palmer, "Park Place and Main Street: Business and the Urban Power Structure," *Annual Review of Sociology* 9 (1984): 406–407.

Fuentes, Annette, "What's Poverty Got to Do With It? Is the CDA Fighting Poverty or Funding Patronage?" *City Limits* (November 1984): 13, 18.

Gelfand, M. David, and Terry Allbritton, "Voting Rights Aspects of the Structure of the New York City Board of Estimate" (memorandum to the New York City Charter Revision Commission, January 1988).

Gerson, Jeffrey, "Building the Brooklyn Machine: Jewish and Black Succession in the Brooklyn Democratic Party Organization, 1919–1964" (Ph.D. dissertation, Political Science Program, City University of New York Graduate Center, 1990).

Gerson, Kathleen, *Hard Choices: How Women Decide about Work, Career, and Motherhood* (Berkeley: University of California Press, 1985).

Giddens, Anthony, *A Contemporary Critique of Historical Materialism* (Berkeley: University of California Press, 1981).

Gifford, Bernard, "New York City and Cosmopolitan Liberalism," *Political Science Quarterly* 93 (1978–79): 559–584.

Gill, Brendan, "The Skyline: On the Brink," *New Yorker* (November 11, 1987): 113–126.

Gittell, Marilyn, *Limits to Citizen Participation* (Beverly Hills, Calif.: Sage, 1980).

Glazer, Nathan, and Daniel Patrick Moynihan, *Beyond the Melting Pot* (Cambridge, Mass.: MIT Press, 1963).

Glickman, Norman, "International Trade, Capital Mobility, and Economic Growth: Some Implications for American Cities and Regions in the 1980s," in Donald Hicks and Norman Glickman, eds., *Transition to the 21st Century* (Greenwich, Conn.: JAI Press, 1983), pp. 205–240.

Goldberger, Paul, "Shaping the Face of New York," in Peter D. Salins, ed., *New York Unbound: The City and the Politics of the Future* (New York: Basil Blackwell, 1988), pp. 127–140.

Gordon, David, "Capitalism and the Roots of Urban Fiscal Crisis," in R. Alcaly and D. Mermelstein, eds., *Fiscal Crisis of American Cities* (New York: Vintage, 1977), pp. 82–112.

Gordon, David, Rick Edwards, and Michael Reich, *Segmented Work, Divided Workers* (New York: Cambridge University Press, 1982).

Gottdeiner, Marc, *The Decline of Urban Politics: Political Theory and the Crisis of the Local State* (Beverly Hills, Calif.: Sage, 1987).

Green, Charles, and Basil Wilson, *The Struggle for Black Empowerment in New York City: Beyond the Politics of Pigmentation* (New York: Praeger, 1989).

Greenstone, J. David, and Paul Peterson, *Race and Authority in Urban Politics* (New York: Russell Sage Foundation, 1973).

Grimshaw, William, "The Daley Legacy: A Declining Politics of Party, Race, and Public Unions," in Samuel Gove and Louis Masotti, eds., *After Daley: Chicago Politics in Transition* (Urbana, Ill.: University of Illinois Press, 1982), pp. 57–87.

Grossman, David, Lester Salamon, and David Altschuler, *The New York Nonprofit Sector in a Time of Government Retrenchment* (Washington, D.C.: Urban Institute Nonprofit Sector Project, 1986).

Gurr, Ted Robert, and Desmond King, *The State and the City* (Chicago: University of Chicago Press, 1987).

Hahn, Harlan, David Klingman, and Harry Pachon, "Cleavage, Coalitions, and the Black Candidate: The Los Angeles Mayoralty Elections of 1969 and 1973," *Western Political Quarterly* 19:1 (December 1976): 507–520.

Halley, Robert, Alan Acock, and Thomas Greene, "Ethnicity and Social Class: Voting Patterns in the 1973 Los Angeles Municipal Elections, *Western Political Quarterly* 19:1 (December 1976): 521–530.

Hamilton, Charles V., "The Patron-Recipient Relationship and Minority Politics in New York City," *Political Science Quarterly* 94:2 (Summer 1979): 211–227.

Hammack, David, *Power and Society: Greater New York at the Turn of the Century* (New York: Russell Sage Foundation, 1982).

Harris, Louis, and Bert Swanson, *Black-Jewish Relations in New York City* (New York: Praeger, 1970).

Harrison, Bennett, and Barry Bluestone, *The Great U-Turn: Corporate Restructuring and the Polarizing of America* (New York: Basic Books, 1988)

Harvey, David, *Social Justice and the City* (Baltimore, Md.: Johns Hopkins University Press, 1973).

———, *The Urbanization of Capital* (Baltimore, Md.: Johns Hopkins University Press, 1985).

———, *Consciousness and the Urban Experience: Studies in the History and Theory of Capitalist Urbanization* (Baltimore, Md.: Johns Hopkins University Press, 1985).

Harvey, David, and Alan Scott, "The Practice of Human Geography: Theory and Empirical Specificity and the Transition from Fordism to Flexible Accumulation," in W. MacMillan, ed., *Remodeling Geography* (Oxford: Basil Blackwell, 1989).

Hedges, Roman, and Jeffrey Getis, "A Standard for Constructing Minority Legislative Districts: The Issue of Effective Voting Equality" (Working Paper No. 6, Rockefeller Institute of Government, State University of New York Albany, 1983).

Hicks, Donald A., *Advanced Industrial Development* (Boston: Oelgeschlager, Gunn, and Hain, 1985).

Hill, Richard C., "Separate and Unequal: Governmental Inequality in the Metropolis," *American Political Science Review* 68 (December 1974): 1557–1568.

Hirsch, Arnold R., *Making the Second Ghetto: Race and Housing in Chicago 1940–1960* (New York: Cambridge University Press, 1983).

Hirschhorn, Larry, *Beyond Mechanization* (Cambridge, Mass.: MIT Press, 1984).

Horton, Raymond D., "Sayre and Kaufman Revisited: New York City Government in the Post-1965 Period," paper presented to the 1977 Annual Meeting of the American Political Science Association, Washington, D.C.

———, "Fiscal Stress and Labor Power," paper presented to the Industrial Relations Research Association Annual Meeting, New York, December 28–30, 1985.

————, "Expenditures, Services, and Public Management," *Public Administration Review* (September/October 1987): 378–384.

Hudson, James R., *The Unanticipated City: Loft Conversions in Lower Manhattan* (Amherst, Mass.: University of Massachusetts Press, 1985).

Huxtable, Ada Louise, "Stumbling toward Tomorrow: The Decline and Fall of a New York Vision," *Dissent* Special Issue, "In Search of New York," (Fall 1987): 453–462.

Jaret, Charles, "Recent Neo-Marxist Urban Analysis," *Annual Review of Sociology* (1983): 605–638.

Jensen, Leif, *The New Immigration* (New York: Greenwood Press, 1989).

Jones, Bryan, and Lynn Bachelor, with Carter Wilson, *The Sustaining Hand: Community Leadership and Corporate Power* (Lawrence: University of Kansas Press, 1986).

Karnig, Albert, and Susan Welch, *Black Representation and Urban Policy* (Chicago: University of Chicago Press, 1980).

Karnig, Albert, and Oliver Walter, "Municipal Voter Participation: Trends and Correlates," in Dennis Judd, ed., *Public Policy Across States and Communities* (Greenwich, Conn.: JAI Press, 1985), pp. 169–178.

Katznelson, Ira, *Black Men, White Cities* (New York: Oxford University Press, 1973).

————, "The Crisis of the Capitalist City: Urban Politics and Social Control," in W. Hawley et al., *Theoretical Perspectives on Urban Politics* (Englewood Cliffs, N.J.: Prentice-Hall, 1976), pp. 214–229.

————, *City Trenches: Urban Politics and the Patterning of Class in the United States* (New York: Pantheon, 1981).

Keating, Dennis, "Linking Downtown Development to Broader Community Goals: An Analysis of Linkage Policies in Three Cities," *Journal of the American Planning Association* (Spring 1986): 134–142.

Keiser, Richard, "Amicability or Polarization? Patterns of Political Competition and Leadership Formation in Cities with Black Mayors" (Institute of Governmental Studies, University of California at Berkeley, 1988).

Kennedy, Katherine, and Mitchell S. Bernard, *New York City Zoning: The Need for Reform* (New York: Natural Resources Defense Council and the Women's City Club, June 1989).

Kessner, Thomas, *The Golden Door: Italian and Jewish Mobility in New York City, 1880–1915* (New York: Oxford University Press, 1976).

Key, V. O., Jr., *Southern Politics in State and Nation* (New York: Vintage, 1949).

————, "A Theory of Critical Elections," *Journal of Politics* 17 (February 1955), pp. 3–18.

Kimball, Penn, *The Disconnected* (New York: Columbia University Press, 1972).

Kirchheimer, Donna W., "Public Entrepreneurship and Subnational Government," *Polity* 22:1 (Fall 1989): 119–142.

————, "Sheltering the Homeless in New York City: Expansion in an Era of Government Contraction," *Political Science Quarterly* 104 (Winter 1989–90): 607–623.

Klebanoff, Arthur, "The Demographics of Politics: Legislative Constituencies and the Borough of Brooklyn, 1950–1965" (Senior honors thesis, Yale University, 1969).

Kleppner, Paul, *Chicago Divided: The Making of a Black Mayor* (DeKalb, Ill.: Northern Illinois University, 1985).

Koch, Edward I., *Mayor* (New York: Simon and Schuster, 1984).

———, *Politics* (New York: Simon and Schuster, 1985).

Kornblum, William, and James Beshers, "White Ethnicity" in John Mollenkopf, ed., *Power, Culture, and Place* (New York: Russell Sage Foundation, 1988), pp. 201–222.

Krasner, Stephen, "Approaches to the State: Alternative Conceptions and Historical Dynamics," *Comparative Politics* 17 (January 1984): 223–248.

Langbein, Laura Irwin, and Allan J. Lichtman, *Ecological Inference* (Beverly Hills, Calif.: Sage, 1978).

League of Women Voters of the City of New York Education Fund, *They Represent You 1987–1988* (New York: League of Women Voters, 1989).

Leichter, Office of State Senator Franz, "Examples of Close Correlations between Campaign Contributions and Board of Estimate Votes (Chronological Order)" (November 1985).

———, "Campaign Contributions to Members of the Board of Estimate and the Democratic County Committees, 1981–86" (December 22, 1986).

———, "The Top 75 Contributors to the Campaigns of Members of the NYC Board of Estimate and to the Five County Party Committees (Republican and Democratic), 1981–1988" (February 25, 1988).

Levy, Frank, *Dollars and Dreams: The Changing American Income Distribution* (New York: Russell Sage Foundation, 1987).

Lichten, Eric, *Class, Power, and Austerity: The New York City Fiscal Crisis* (South Hadley, Mass.: Bergin and Garvey, 1986).

Lindstrom, Diane, "Economic Structure in Antebellum New York," in John Mollenkopf, ed., *Power, Culture, and Place* (New York: Russell Sage Foundation, 1988), pp. 3–23.

Lineberry, Robert, and Edmund Fowler, "Reformism and Public Policies in American Cities," *American Political Science Review* 61 (September 1967): 701–716.

Logan, John, and Harvey Molotch, *Urban Fortunes: The Political Economy of Place* (Berkeley: University of California Press, 1987).

London, Steven, "Authoritarian Responses to New York City's Fiscal Crisis" Ph.D. dissertation, New York University, 1984).

Lowe, Gerald, "Telecommunications Impact of Financial Industry Relocations," Walsh-Lowe & Associates, paper presented to conference on Financial Services in New York State, New York University Urban Research Center, June 8, 1988.

Lowi, Theodore J., *At the Pleasure of the Mayor: Patronage and Power in New York City 1898–1958* (New York: Free Press, 1964).

———, "The Public Philosophy: Interest-Group Liberalism," *American Political Science Review* 61 (March 1967): 5–24.

———, "Machine Politics—Old and New," *The Public Interest* (Fall 1967): 83–92.

———, "Four Systems of Policy, Politics, and Administration," *Public Administration Review* 32:4 (July/August 1972): 298–310.

Maier, Mark H., *City Unions: Managing Discontent in New York City* (New Brunswick, N.J.: Rutgers University Press, 1987).

Manley, John, "Neo-Pluralism: A Class Analysis of Pluralism I and Pluralism II," *American Political Science Review* 77:2 (June 1983): 368–383.

Marcuse, Peter, "Neighborhood Policy and the Distribution of Power: New York City's Community Boards," *Policy Studies Journal* 16 (Winter 1987–88): 277–289.

Mayhew, David. *Placing Parties in American Politics* (Princeton, N.J.: Princeton University Press, 1986).

McConnell, Grant, *Private Power and American Democracy* (New York: Vintage, 1966).

Mingione, Enzo, *Social Conflict and the City* (New York: St. Martin's Press, 1981).

Mladenka, Kenneth R., "Blacks and Hispanics in Urban Politics," *American Political Science Review* 83:1 (March 1989): 165–191.

Mollenkopf, John, "On the Causes and Consequences of Neighborhood Political Mobilization," paper presented to the 1973 Annual Meeting of the American Political Science Association, New Orleans.

———, "The Postwar Politics of Urban Development," *Politics and Society* 5:3 (Winter 1975): 247–295.

———, "Community and Accumulation," in Michael Dear and Alan Scott, eds., *Urbanization and Urban Planning in Capitalist Societies* (New York: Methuen, 1981), pp. 319–338.

———, *The Contested City* (Princeton, N.J.: Princeton University Press, 1983).

———, "Economic Development," in Charles Brecher and Raymond D. Horton, eds., *Setting Municipal Priorities, 1984* (New York: New York University Press, 1983), pp. 131–157.

———, "The Corporate Legal Services Industry," *New York Affairs* 9:2 (1985): 34–49.

———, "The Politics of Racial Advancement and the Failure of Urban Reform: The Case of New York City," paper prepared for a colloquium on "The Changing Situations of Black Americans and Women: Roots and Reverberations in U.S. Social Politics since the 1960s," April 25–27, 1985, Center for the Study of Industrial Societies, University of Chicago.

———, "The 42nd Street Development Project and the Public Interest," *City Almanac* 18:4, Special Issue on the Redevelopment of 42nd Street (Summer 1985), pp. 12–16.

———, "The Decay of Liberalism: One Party Politics New York Style," *Dissent* Special Issue, "In Search of New York" (Fall 1987): 492–495.

———, "The Postindustrial Transformation of the Political Order in New York City," in John Mollenkopf, ed., *Power, Culture, and Place* (New York: Russell Sage Foundation, 1988), pp. 223–258.

———, "Who (Or What) Runs Cities and How?" *Sociological Forum* 4:1 (Spring 1989): 119–137.

————, "City Planning," in Charles Brecher and Raymond D. Horton, eds., *Setting Municipal Priorities, 1990* (New York: New York University Press, 1989), pp. 141–172.

————, "New York, The Great Anomaly," in Rufus Browning, Dale Marshall, and David Tabb, eds., *Racial Politics in American Cities* (New York: Longman, 1990), pp. 75–87.

————, "Political Inequality," in John Mollenkopf and Manuel Castells, eds., *Dual City: Restructuring New York* (New York: Russell Sage Foundation, 1991), pp. 333–358.

————, ed., *Power, Culture, and Place* (New York: Russell Sage Foundation, 1988).

Mollenkopf, John, and Manuel Castells, eds., *Dual City: Restructuring New York* (New York: Russell Sage Foundation, 1991).

Molotch, Harvey, "The City as a Growth Machine," *American Sociological Review* 8:2 (1976): 309–330.

Morris, Charles, *The Cost of Good Intentions* (New York: W. W. Norton, 1980).

Moss, Mitchell, "The Telecommunications Infrastructure in the City of New York," Policy Analysis Division, Office of Economic Development, City of New York, September 1985.

Muzzio, Douglas, and Robert W. Bailey, "Economic Development, Housing, and Zoning: A Tale of Two Cities," *Journal of Urban Affairs* (Winter 1986): 1–18.

National Council of State Legislatures Reapportionment Task Force, *Reapportionment Law: The 1990s* (Denver, Colo.: National Conference of State Legislatures, 1989).

Netzer, Dick, "Privatization," in Charles Brecher and Raymond Horton, eds., *Setting Municipal Priorities, 1984* (New York: New York University Press, 1983), pp. 158–187.

New York State Commission on Government Integrity (Feerick Commission), Hearings, January 9–10 and April 4–5, 1989.

————, "The Role of the Mayor's Talent Bank in Placing Job Candidates: A Case Study of the Parks Department" (unpublished staff report), no date.

New York State Department of Labor, *NYC Labor Area Summary* (December 1988).

————, "A Quarter Century of Changes in Employment Levels and Industrial Mix" (Bureau of Labor Market Information, 1984).

New York State Office of the Deputy State Comptroller for the City of New York, "New York City Planning Commission Granting Special Permits for Bonus Floor Area," Report A-23-88 (September 15, 1988).

Newfield, Jack, and Wayne Barrett, *City for Sale: Ed Koch and the Betrayal of New York* (New York: Harper and Row, 1988).

Newfield, Jack, and Paul Du Brul, *The Abuse of Power: The Permanent Government and the Fall of New York* (New York: Viking Press, 1977).

————, *The Permanent Government: Who Really Runs New York?* (New York: Pilgrim Press, 1981).

Noyelle, Thierry, Testimony to the New York City Commission on the Year 2000, May 9, 1987, Municipal Archives, City of New York.

———, "The Future of New York as a Financial Center," paper prepared for conference on "Future Shocks to New York," Citizens Budget Commission, January 24, 1989.

Noyelle, Thierry, and Anna Dutka, *International Trade in Business Services: Accounting, Advertising, Law and Management Consulting* (Cambridge, Mass.: Ballinger, 1988).

Noyelle, Thierry, and Penny Peace, "The Information Industries: New York's New Export Base," paper prepared for conference on "Future Shocks to New York," Citizen's Budget Commission, New York, January 24, 1989.

Noyelle, Thierry, and Tom Stanback, *The Economic Transformation of American Cities* (Totowa, N.J.: Rowman and Allanheld, 1983).

O'Connor, James, *The Fiscal Crisis of the State* (New York: St. Martin's Press, 1973).

Offe, Claus, *Contradictions of the Welfare State*, ed. John Keane (London: Hutchinson, 1984).

O'Keeffe, Kevin, *Baltimore Politics 1971–1986: The Schaefer Years and the Struggle for Succession* (Washington, D.C.: Georgetown University Monograph in American Studies No. 3, 1986).

Pahl, Ray, "Stratification and the Relations between the States and Urban and Regional Development," *International Journal of Urban and Regional Research* 1:1 (1977): 6–19.

Pecorella, Robert F., "Coping with Crises: The Politics of Urban Retrenchment," *Polity* 17 (Winter 1984): 298–316.

Peel, Roy V., *Political Clubs of New York City* (New York: Putnam, 1935).

Perlmutter, Ted, "The Theoretical Practice of Urban Protest: A Neo-Gramscian Critique of Recent Marxian Theories" (Harvard Center for European Studies, 1986).

Peterson, Paul, *City Limits* (Chicago: University of Chicago Press, 1981).

———, ed., *The New Urban Reality* (Washington, D.C.: Brookings Institution, 1985).

Phillips, Kenneth, Office of the Chairman, Citicorp, "Testimony before the New York City Commission on the Year 2000," May 9, 1987, Municipal Archives, City of New York.

Piven, Frances Fox, "Federal Policy and Urban Fiscal Strain," *Yale Law and Policy Review* 2:2 (Spring 1984): 291–320.

Piven, Frances Fox, and Richard Cloward, *Regulating the Poor* (New York: Pantheon, 1971).

———, *Poor People's Movements* (New York: Pantheon, 1979).

———, *Why Americans Don't Vote* (New York: Pantheon, 1988).

Piven, Frances Fox, and Roger Friedland, "Public Choice and Private Power," in A. Kirby et al., eds., *Public Service Provision and Urban Development* (New York: St. Martin's Press, 1984), pp. 390–420.

Planning Center, *Land Use Leaders* (New York: Municipal Arts Society, 1990).

Polsby, Nelson, *Community Power and Political Theory: A Further Look at Problems of Evidence and Inference*, 2d, enlarged ed. (New Haven, Conn.: Yale University Press, 1980).

Port Authority of New York and New Jersey, Office of Business Development, Regional Analysis Group, *The Regional Economy: Review 1988, Outlook 1989* (March 1989).

Preston Michael, et al., eds., *The New Black Politics: The Search for Political Power*, 2d ed. (New York: Longman, 1987).

Preteceille, Edmond, "Crise hégémonique et restructuration territoriale de l'état. La gauche et la decentralisation en France," *Revue Internationale d'Action Communautaire* 15:53 (Spring 1985): 49–59.

Raphaël, Pierre, and Henri Tincq, *Dans l'enfer de Rikers Island: Ammônier de prison à New-York* (Paris: Centurion, 1988).

Ravitch, Diane, *The Great School Wars, New York City 1805–1973* (New York: Basic Books, 1974).

Reapportionment Task Force, *Reapportionment Law: The 1990s* (Denver, Colo.: National Conference of State Legislatures, 1989).

Reed, Adolph, "The Black Urban Regime: Structural Origins and Constraints," in Michael P. Smith, ed., *Power, Community, and the City*, Comparative Urban and Community Research, vol. 1 (New Brunswick, N.J.: Transaction Books, 1988), pp. 138–189.

———, "New York in the Global Economy: Studying the Facts and the Issues," paper presented to World Association of Major Metropolises meeting, Mexico City, April 1987.

Ricketts, Erol, and Ronald Mincy, "Growth of the Underclass 1970–1980," *Journal of Human Resources* 25:1 (Winter 1990): 137–145.

Rieder, Jonathan, *Canarsie: The Jews and Italians of Brooklyn against Liberalism* (Cambridge: Harvard University Press, 1985).

Rischin, Moses, *The Promised City: New York's Jews, 1870–1914* (Cambridge: Harvard University Press, 1962).

Robbins, Sidney M., and Nestor E. Terleckj, *Money Metropolis* (Cambridge: Harvard University Press, 1960).

Rogowsky, Edward T., Louis H. Gold, and David W. Abbott, "Police: The Civilian Review Board Controversy," in Jewel Bellush and Stephen M. David, eds., *Race and Politics in New York City: Five Studies in Policy-Making* (New York: Praeger Publishers, 1971), pp. 59–97.

Rogowsky, Edward T., and Elizabeth Strom, *Improving CDBG Services through University Involvement: Report of a Study on the Community Development Process in New York City* (New York: Robert F. Wagner, Sr. Institute of Urban Public Policy, City University of New York Graduate Center, August 1989).

Rosenwaike, Ira, *A Population History of New York* (Syracuse, N.Y.: Syracuse University Press, 1972).

Rubin, Josh, "It's Still Christmas Every Day: The NYC Industrial and Commercial Incentive Program" (A report from the Office of State Senator Franz Leichter, June 1990).

Sassen, Saskia, *The Mobility of Labor and Capital* (New York: Cambridge University Press, 1988).

———, *The Global City* (Princeton, N.J.: Princeton University Press, 1991).

Savitch, Hank V., *Post-Industrial Cities: Politics and Planning in New York, Paris, and London* (Princeton, N.J.: Princeton University Press, 1988).

Sayre, Wallace, and Herbert Kaufman, *Governing New York City: Politics in the Metropolis* (New York: W. W. Norton, 1965).

Scarrow, Howard A., *Parties, Elections, and Representation in the State of New York* (New York: New York University Press, 1983).

Schattschneider, Elmer Eric, *The Semisovereign People: A Realist's View of Democracy in America* (New York: Holt, Rinehart and Winston, 1960).

Scheisl, Martin J., *The Politics of Efficiency: Municipal Administration and Reform in America 1880–1920* (Berkeley: University of California Press, 1977).

Schumaker, Paul, Allan Cigler, and Howard Faye, "Bureaucratic Perceptions of the Municipal Group Universe: 1975 and 1986," in Harold Baldersheim et al., *New Leaders, Parties, and Groups in Local Politics* (forthcoming).

Schumpeter, Joseph, "The Crisis of the Tax State," *International Economic Papers* 4:5 (1954): 8–17.

Schwartz, Sidney, "New York City's Fiscal Crisis: How It Developed, Why It Persists," *City Almanac* 15:3 (October 1980): 1–24.

Scott, Alan, "Flexible Production Systems and Regional Development: The Rise of New Industrial Spaces in North America and Western Europe," *International Journal of Urban and Regional Research* 12:2 (1988): 171–186.

Scott, Alan, and Michael Storper, eds., *Production, Work, Territory: The Geographical Anatomy of Industrial Capitalism* (Boston: Allen & Unwin, 1986).

Shefter, Martin, "The Emergence of the Political Machine: An Alternative View," in Willis Hawley et al., *Theoretical Perspectives on Urban Politics* (Englewood Cliffs, N.J.: Prentice-Hall, 1976).

———, "New York City's Fiscal Crisis: The Politics of Inflation and Retrenchment," *The Public Interest* 48 (Summer 1977): 98–127.

———, "The Electoral Foundations of the Political Machine: New York City, 1884–1897," in Joel Silbey et al., eds., *American Electoral History: Quantitative Studies in Popular Voting Behavior* (Princeton, N.J.: Princeton University Press, 1978).

———, "Party, Bureaucracy, and Political Change in the United States," in Louis Maisel and Joseph Cooper, eds., *The Development of Political Parties: Patterns of Evolution and Decay*, Sage Electoral Studies Yearbook, vol. 4 (Beverly Hills, Calif.: Sage, 1979), pp. 211–265.

———, "Political Parties, Political Mobilization, and Political Demobilization," in Thomas Ferguson and Joel Rogers, eds., *The Political Economy* (Armonk, N.Y.: M. E. Sharpe, 1984), pp. 140–148.

———, *Political Crisis/Fiscal Crisis: The Collapse and Revival of New York City* (New York: Basic Books, 1985).

———, "Political Incorporation and the Extrusion of the Left: Party Politics and Social Forces in New York City," *Studies in American Political Development* 1 (1986): 50–90.

———, ed., *Capital of the American Century?* (forthcoming).

Silverman, Rosalyn, "Trends in New York City Employment—A Different Perspective," *The Regional Economist* 4:2 (Spring 1986): 1–4.

Skocpol, Theda, "Bringing the State Back In," in P. Evans, Dietrich Ruschemeyer, and Theda Skocpol, eds., *Bringing the State Back In* (New York: Cambridge University Press, 1985), pp. 3–37.

Sleeper, Jim, "Boodling, Bigotry, and Cosmopolitanism: The Transformation of a Civic Culture," *Dissent* Special Issue, "In Search of New York" (Fall 1987): 413–419.

———, "Boom and Bust with Ed Koch," *Dissent* Special Issue "In Search of New York" (Fall 1987): 437–452.

———, *The Closest of Strangers: Liberalism and the Politics of Race in New York* (New York: W. W. Norton, 1990).

Smith, Michael P., *City, State, and Market: The Political Economy of Urban Society* (New York: Basil Blackwell, 1988).

———, ed., *Cities in Transition: Class, Capital, and the State* (Beverly Hills, Calif.: Sage, 1984).

Smith, Ralph, ed., *The Subtle Revolution: Women at Work* (Washington, D.C.: Urban Institute, 1979).

Sonenshein, Raphael J., "The Dynamics of Biracial Coalitions: Crossover Politics in Los Angeles," *Western Political Quarterly* 42:2 (June 1989): 333–353.

———, "Biracial Coalition Politics in Los Angeles," in Rufus Browning, Dale Marshall, and David Tabb, eds., *Racial Politics in American Cities* (New York: Longman, 1990), pp. 33–48.

———, "Biracial Coalitions in Big Cities: Why They Succeed, Why They Fail," in Rufus Browning, Dale Marshall, and David Tabb, eds., *Racial Politics in American Cities* (New York: Longman, 1990), pp. 193–211.

———, "The Prospects of Multiracial Coalitions in Post-Incorporation Los Angeles," paper presented to the 1990 Annual Meeting of the American Political Science Association, San Francisco.

Special Committee on the Role of Amenities in the Land Use Process, *The Record of the Association of the Bar of the City of New York* 43:6 (October 1988): 653–697.

Squires, Gregory D., ed., *Unequal Partnerships: The Political Economy of Urban Development in Postwar America* (New Brunswick, N.J.: Rutgers University Press, 1989).

Stafford, Walter, *Closed Labor Markets: Underrepresentation of Blacks, Hispanics, and Women in New York City's Core Industries* (New York: Community Service Society, 1985).

Stafford, Walter, with Edwin Dei, *Employment Segmentation in New York City Municipal Agencies* (New York: Community Service Society, 1989).

Steffens, Lincoln, *Autobiography* (New York: Harcourt Brace, 1931).

Stegman, Michael A., "Housing," in Charles Brecher and Raymond D. Horton, eds., *Setting Municipal Priorities, 1988* (New York: New York University Press, 1987), pp. 207–211.

———, *Housing and Vacancy Report, New York City, 1987* (New York: Department of Housing Preservation and Development, City of New York, April 1988).

Stone, Clarence, *Economic Growth and Neighborhood Discontent* (Chapel Hill, N.C.: University of North Carolina Press, 1976).

————, "Systemic Power in Community Decision Making: A Restatement of Stratification Theory," *American Political Science Review* 74 (1980): 978–990.

————, "Social Stratification, Nondecision-making, and the Study of Community Power," *American Politics Quarterly* 10:3 (July 1982): 275–302.

————, "Power and Social Complexity" in Robert J. Waste, ed., *Community Power: Directions for Research* (Beverly Hills, Calif.: Sage, 1986), pp. 77–113.

————, "Preemptive Power: Floyd Hunter's *Community Power Structure* Reconsidered," *American Journal of Political Science* 32 (February 1988): 82–104.

————, *Regime Politics: Governing Atlanta 1964–1988* (Lawrence, Kan.: University Press of Kansas, 1989).

Stone, Clarence, and Heywood T. Sanders, eds., *The Politics of Urban Development* (Lawrence, Kan.: University of Kansas Press, 1987).

Stone, Clarence, Robert K. Whelan, and William J. Murin, *Urban Policy and Politics in a Bureaucratic Age* (Englewood Cliffs, N.J.: Prentice-Hall, 1979).

Stone, Michael, "What Really Happened in Central Park: The Night of the Jogger and the Crisis of New York," *New York Magazine* (August 14, 1989): 30–43.

Swanstrom, Todd, "Urban Populism, Uneven Development, and the Space for Reform," in Scott Cummins, ed., *Corporate Elites and Urban Development* (Albany, N.Y.: State University of New York Press, 1987).

Szelenyi, Ivan, "Structural Changes and Alternatives to Capitalist Development in the Contemporary Urban and Regional System," *International Journal of Urban and Regional Research* 5:1 (1981): 1–14.

Tabb, William K., *The Long Default* (New York: Monthly Review Press, 1982).

Theret, B., "Collective Means of Consumption, Capital Accumulation and the Urban Question," *International Journal of Urban and Regional Research* 6:3 (1982): 345–371.

Thompson, J. Phillip, "The Impact of the Jackson Campaigns on Black Politics in New York, Atlanta, and Oakland" (Ph.D. dissertation, Political Science Program, City University of New York Graduate Center, 1990).

Tiebout, Charles, "A Pure Theory of Local Expenditures," *Journal of Political Economy* 64 (1956): 416–424.

Tobier, Emanuel, *The Changing Face of Poverty: Trends in New York City's Population in Poverty 1960–1990* (New York: Community Service Society, 1984).

————, "The 'New' Immigration in the New York Metropolitan Region: Characteristics and Consequences," unpublished paper, New York University Graduate School of Public Administration, 1988.

————, "Manhattan's Business District in the Industrial Age," in John Mollenkopf, ed., *Power, Culture, and Place* (New York: Russell Sage Foundation, 1988), pp. 77–103.

Tobier, Emanuel, and Barbara Espejo, "Housing," in Gerald Benjamin and Charles Brecher, eds., *The Two New Yorks: State-City Relations in the Changing Federal System* (New York: Russell Sage Foundation, 1988), pp. 445–478.

Torres, Andres, "Human Capital, Labor Segmentation, and Inter-minority Relative Status: Black and Puerto Rican Labor in New York City, 1960–1980" (Ph.D. dissertation, New School for Social Research, New York, 1988).

Truman, David, *The Governmental Process* (New York: Knopf, 1951).

U.S. Congress, Congressional Budget Office, *New York City's Fiscal Problem: Its Origin, Potential Repercussions, and Some Alternative Policy Responses* (Washington, D.C.: U.S. Government Printing Office, 1975).

U.S. Department of Commerce, Bureau of the Census, *City and County Data Book 1988* (Washington, D.C.: U.S. Government Printing Office, 1988).

————, Bureau of the Census, 1990 Census, Pl94–171 file for New York City.

U.S. Department of Labor, Bureau of Labor Statistics, New York Regional Office, "The Current Population Survey as an Economic Indicator for New York City."

U.S. House of Representatives, Subcommittee on Economic Stabilization, Committee on Banking, Finance and Urban Affairs, 95th Congress, First Session, "Securities and Exchange Commission Staff Report on Transactions in Securities of the City of New York" (August 1977).

Velazquez, Nydia, et al., "Puerto Rican Voter Registration in New York City: A Comparison of Attitudes between Registered and Non-Registered Puerto Ricans," (New York City: Commonwealth of Puerto Rico, Department of Labor and Human Resources, Migration Division, January 1988).

Viteritti, Joseph P., "The Tradition of Municipal Reform: Charter Revision in Historical Perspective," in Frank J. Mauro and Gerald Benjamin, eds., "Restructuring the New York City Government: The Reemergence of Municipal Reform," *Proceedings of the Academy of Political Science* 37:3 (1989): 16–30.

Vogel, David, "New York, London, and Tokyo: The Future of New York as a Global and National Financial Center," in Martin Shefter, ed., *Capital of the American Century?* (forthcoming).

Wade, Richard C., "The Withering Away of the Party System," in Jewel Bellush and Dick Netzer, eds., *Urban Politics New York Style* (Armonk, N.Y.: M. E. Sharpe, 1990), pp. 271–295.

Waldinger, Roger, "Displacement Pressures on Manhattan Manufacturing Industries and Job Retention Strategies," City of New York, Office of Economic Development, Policy Analysis Division (November 1982).

————, "Changing Ladders and Musical Chairs: Ethnicity and Opportunity in Post-industrial New York," *Politics and Society* 15:4 (1986–87): 369–402.

————, *Through the Eye of the Needle* (New York: New York University Press, 1988).

————, "Immigration and Urban Change," *Annual Review of Sociology* 15 (1989): 211–232.

————, "Race and Ethnicity," in Charles Brecher and Raymond D. Horton, eds., *Setting Municipal Priorities, 1990* (New York: New York University Press, 1989), pp. 51–79.

Wallace, Michael, "Changing Concepts of Party in the United States: New York, 1815–1828," *American Historical Review* 74 (December 1968).

Walter, John C., *The Harlem Fox: J. Raymond Jones and Tammany, 1920–1970* (Albany: State University of New York Press, 1989).

Ward, David, *Cities and Immigrants* (New York: Oxford University Press, 1971).

————, *Poverty, Ethnicity, and the American City, 1840–1925* (New York: Cambridge University Press, 1989).

Ware, Alan, *The Breakdown of Democratic Party Organization, 1940–1980* (New York: Oxford University Press, 1985).

Waste, Robert J., "Community Power and Pluralist Theory," in Robert J. Waste, ed., *Community Power: Directions for Future Research* (Beverly Hills, Calif.: Sage, 1986), pp. 117–137.

Weitzman, Philip, *Worlds Apart: Housing, Race/Ethnicity and Income in New York City, 1978–1987* (New York: Community Service Society, 1989).

White, E. B., *Here Is New York* (New York: Harper and Brothers, 1949).

Wilson, James Q., "Two Negro Politicians: An Interpretation," *Midwest Journal of Political Science* 4 (November 1960): 346–369.

Wilson, Laurie, and Ibraham Al-Muhanna, "The Political Economy of Information: Transborder Data Flows," *Journal of Peace Research* 22:4 (1985): 281–301.

Wolfinger, Raymond, "Why Political Machines Have Not Withered Away and Other Revisionist Thoughts," *Journal of Politics* 34:2 (May 1972): 365–398.

Zolberg, Vera, "New York Cultural Institutions: Ascendant or Subsidant?" in Martin Shefter, ed., *Capital of the American Century* (forthcoming).

Zukin, Sharon, *Loft Living: Culture and Capital in Urban Change* (Baltimore, Md.: Johns Hopkins University Press, 1982).

Index